Prehistoric Lowland Maya Environment and Subsistence Economy

Papers of the Peabody Museum
of Archaeology and Ethnology
Harvard University

Volume 77

Prehistoric Lowland Maya Environment and Subsistence Economy

Edited by Mary Pohl

with contributions by Paul R. Bloom, Helen Sorayya Carr, Edward S. Deevey, Jr., Nancy L. Hamblin, S. E. Garrett-Jones, Charles H. Miksicek, Hattula Moholy-Nagy, Mary Pohl, Amadeo M. Rea, Don S. Rice, Prudence M. Rice, Julie Stein, B. L. Turner II, Hague H. Vaughan, Richard R. Wilk, Frederick Matthew Wiseman

Peabody Museum of Archaeology and Ethnology
Harvard University, Cambridge, Massachusetts
1985

Distributed by Harvard University Press

Second Printing 1987
ISBN 0-87365-203-7
Library of Congress Catalog Card Number 84-62626
Printed in the United States of America

In memory of my parents, who encouraged me in my profession and supported the publication of this volume

Contents

Figures

Tables

Preface

A dearth of data has frustrated attempts to reconstruct prehistoric Maya environment and subsistence. Summing up Harrison and Turner's volume, *Pre-Hispanic Maya Agriculture*, Harris (1978: 318) observed "in trying to assess the scale, relative importance, and interrelationships of Classic Maya cultivation systems . . . we encounter a paralyzing lack of information." Harris (1978: 308, 323) cited limited information on past environmental changes and nonagricultural sources of food, particularly fauna, as other problem areas. In the same volume, Willey (1978: 334) predicted that "working the sequence out by securing the right kinds of evidence is going to be very difficult and something that will be with us for a long time."

The objective of this collection is to provide data that research specialists associated with interdisciplinary projects have produced over the past 15 years. We present selected studies that are available at this time.

This book is not a synthesis of ancient Maya subsistence economy and environment. Indeed certain authors openly disagree with one another. Some of these disputes may be based on differences in research technique; others are a matter of differences in interpretation. Such controversy is instructive. By analyzing the methods and theoretical principles by which specialists work, we can gain insight into archaeological procedures. The contributions in this volume demonstrate that we must have more data of the kind represented here before we can begin to explain the rise and fall of Maya civilization in processual terms.

References

Harris, D. R.
1978   "The Agricultural Foundation of Lowland Maya Civilization: A Critique," in *Pre-Hispanic Maya Agriculture*, edited by P. D. Harrison and B. L. Turner II, University of New Mexico Press, Albuquerque, pp. 301–323.

Willey, G. R.
1978   "Pre-Hispanic Maya Agriculture: A Contemporary Summation." In *Pre-Hispanic Maya Agriculture*, edited by P. D. Harrison and B. L. Turner II, University of New Mexico Press, Albuquerque, pp. 325–335.

Introduction

Chapter 1

Interdisciplinary Research in Lowland Maya Archaeology

Mary Pohl

Exploration and Early Data Collection

Data on ancient Maya environment and subsistence depend on effective interdisciplinary research. Cooperation began early in the Maya area. Biologists and archaeologists made their way through Belize into the forests of Petén, Guatemala, when the region became accessible in the 1920s and 1930s. O. F. Cook of the U.S. Department of Agriculture made the first botanical collecting trip to the area in 1922.

Beginning in 1930, the Carnegie Institution of Washington and the Museum of Zoology of the University of Michigan jointly sponsored biological research. A. V. Kidder, chairman of the Division of Historical Research at the Carnegie Institution, was instrumental in funding this work because he was motivated by a keen interest in environmental as well as subsistence problems of the Maya area. Under the auspices of the joint Michigan-Carnegie project, Bartlett (1935) and Lundell (1937) studied vegetation, Murie (1935) mammals, van Tyne (1935) birds, Stuart (1935) herpetofauna, Hubbs (1935) fish, and Goodrich and van der Schalie (1937) molluscs. The Carnegie archaeologists lent equipment, cleared red tape with government officials, and shared their camp. One can sense the exuberance of discovery behind the scientific classifications that resulted from this biological research.

Some of the work did have direct relevance for reconstructing ancient Maya subsistence economy. Goodrich and van der Schalie (1937: 44) suggested that the Maya had introduced specimens of *Pachychilus corvinus indifferens*, found in a subfossil state out of their natural habitat on the shores of Lake Petén and Lake Eckibix. We believe that Indians ate *Pachychilus* in prehistoric times. At sites like Barton Ramie (Willey et al. 1965) and Lubaantun (Hammond 1975: 384), archaeologists have found the shells with the tips of their spires systematically removed. Present-day mollusc eaters in the area prepare this shellfish by removing the tips, but predation by crabs produces the same effect (Covich, personal communication, 1982). Since the shells occurred in

archaeological refuse, their use as human food is the likely explanation. In recent times, residents of the village of San Andres, located on Lake Petén, have tried to introduce *Pachychilus*, again without success.

Lundell (1933, 1937, 1938) speculated on the plants the Maya exploited and suggested that the present-day distribution of ramón trees (*Brosimum alicastrum*), which bear edible "nuts" or seeds, was due to human manipulation of the forest in prehistoric times. He pointed out that ramón ripens from March to May, the time when corn supplies are lowest in the system of wet season swidden agriculture on uplands.

One of the archaeological issues that arose was the relationship of the tropical forest environment to swidden agriculture, an extensive cultivation technique that the descendants of the ancient Maya were practicing. Morley (1920) suggested that the Maya had abandoned the ceremonial centers of Petén because the *milpa* system caused soil exhaustion and crop failure. O. F. Cook (1921) also believed that swidden agriculture had limited the Maya, and he hypothesized that grass had eventually invaded overworked land, causing the downfall of civilization.

Lundell (1933), along with others (Ower 1927; Schufeldt 1950: 225–226; Thompson 1931: 228–229), noted the presence of ruined terraces in northern Petén, southern Campeche, and southwestern Belize and proposed that the Maya had employed a more "advanced" system than swidden agriculture, that is, intensive cultivation.

In 1931 the Carnegie group at Uaxactun invited C. W. Cooke (1931) of the U.S. Geological Survey to visit the site. Cooke theorized that the swamps or *bajos* near Uaxactun had once been lakes, and he suggested that the amount of corn the Maya needed to support themselves had led them to clear extensive tracts of land, causing severe erosion and the eventual infilling of the lakes. The stratigraphy observed in a pit dug by Ledyard Smith in the Bajo de Joventud in 1932 appeared to support this theory.

The high population density indicated by the mounds located at Uaxactun as well as the evidence for terraces and erosion impressed Oliver Ricketson (Ricketson and Ricketson 1937: 12–13). He argued that the ancient Maya must have employed intensive agriculture. Actually Ricketson underestimated settle-

Mary Pohl is associate professor, Department of Anthropology, Florida State University, Tallahassee.

ment density; although the mounds around Uaxactun had not been tested for contemporaneity, Ricketson did not think that more than one in four were occupied at any one time (Ashmore and Willey 1981: 15).

During the 1930s the Carnegie Institution archaeologists working at Chichen Itza in northern Yucatán were conducting their own research on subsistence, concentrating on the swidden system, which the Maya were practicing in the area. They initiated a series of studies of the productive capacity of corn farming with a view toward estimating prehistoric population (Emerson n.d.; Kempton 1935; Emerson and Kempton 1935; Steggerda 1941; Hester 1951, 1952, 1953, 1954). These researchers debated the effects of successive cropping and the relative importance of weed competition and the loss of soil fertility on decline in yield. Between 1933 and 1938 Steggerda, a physical anthropologist, conducted tests of cropping intensity on experimental milpa plots. He and Benedict, the Carnegie nutritionist, analyzed the food of contemporary Yucatec Maya (Benedict and Steggerda 1936).

The heyday of the Carnegie era was a time of basic data collection and classification. Though they devoted most of their efforts to constructing a cultural and chronological framework for Maya archaeology, the Carnegie researchers did attempt to address ecological and economic questions, and they enlisted a variety of specialists to help them. Nevertheless, Maya research and particularly the contributions of the Carnegie Institution came to be criticized for being too descriptive and for lacking a theoretical orientation (Kluckhohn 1940).

Cultural Process, Cultural Ecology, and Settlement Studies

The push for addressing cultural process was strong when archaeological activity resumed after World War II, and Steward argued for the study of settlement patterns as the key to cultural adaptations, including subsistence. Under Steward's influence, Willey conducted his settlement pattern studies, first in the Viru Valley of Peru and then in the Maya area around Barton Ramie in the Belize Valley from 1953 to 1956 (Ashmore and Willey 1981: 10). Willey reasoned, "Until we have more real knowledge of Maya settlement, the archaeologist will be in no position to attack the problems of demography or of prehistoric agricultural techniques and productiveness. Arguments of milpas versus intensive farming . . . will remain insoluble until we can pin down the facts of habitation" (Willey 1956:113–114).

Though he oriented his research toward prehistoric economics, Willey advocated continuing the slow but essential task of basic data collection that was the hallmark of the Carnegie era. He eschewed the glamour of major ceremonial centers and investigated plebian life in the Belize Valley, employing Ledyard Smith as his field director and dedicating the final report to the Carnegie archaeologists. Later in the 1960s he turned his attention to a regional study of the Pasión Valley, Guatemala, excavating the centers of Altar de Sacrificios and Seibal and attempting to trace lesser occupation in the difficult swamps and forests along the river.

Following Willey's lead, Maya archaeologists focused on settlement pattern, and many workers contributed information (see Ashmore 1981). The large-scale projects at Tikal in Petén, Guatemala, and at Dzibilchaltun in northeast Yucatán attempted to define the "sustaining area" around the sites (Haviland 1963; Puleston 1973; Kurjack 1974). Studies of the environment continued. For example, at Tikal, Stuart (1958) observed herpetofauna, Smithe and Paynter (1963) reported on birds, Rick (1968) investigated mammals, and Olson (1959) was brought in to analyze soils.

In addition to his direct influence on Willey, Steward acted as a general catalyst for the cultural ecological approach to the development of Maya civilization. After Steward encouraged archaeologists to apply Wittfogel's theory of the role of intensive, hydraulic agriculture in culture change, Palerm and Wolf (1957: 28) speculated on the potential of canals in the Motagua Valley for irrigation. In the early 1950s, Sanders conducted settlement pattern survey and excavation in the Chontalpa region of Tabasco and later in northeastern and coastal Quintana Roo for the Carnegie Insitution. Sanders focused on the question of how Maya society evolved in its ecological setting by synthesizing data on settlement patterns, population densities, ethnohistory, ethnography, and environmental resources (Sanders 1962–63).

Just after World War II, the modern political states that now divide the Maya Lowlands were setting their sights on agricultural development. Among other projects, land use surveys with an emphasis on soil mapping were conducted (Simmons, Tarano, and Pinto 1959; Wright et al. 1959). Synthesizers like Sanders have made effective use of the data, though by and large the information does not provide the detail that archaeologists need to reconstruct local prehistoric economic patterns. Working in Belize, Wright again drew attention to the presence of terraces and suggested that further analysis be done on their soils.

During this period, Deevey and Cowgill produced pioneering interdisciplinary studies. Deevey, a limnologist, had a long-standing research interest in Mexico and Central America. Although his scope was much broader than the relatively recent Maya occupation, Deevey and palynologist Tsukada (Tsukada and

Deevey 1967) speculated on harmonics in swidden practices on the basis of evidence recovered from cores in four lakes in El Salvador and Guatemala, including Lake Izabal in the Maya Lowlands. Under Deevey's direction, Covich (1970) investigated paleoecology of lakes in the Yucatán Peninsula, including effects of prehistoric disturbances.

Ursula Cowgill, while in Petén in 1960 with her husband, George Cowgill, an archaeologist, re-evaluated the Carnegie studies, as well as other theories about Maya agriculture. Cowgill (1960, 1961, 1962; Cowgill and Hutchinson 1963 a and b; Cowgill et al. 1966) took soil samples from modern agricultural plots around Flores and teamed up with limnologist Hutchinson and palynologist Tsukada for the analysis of a pit she dug in the Bajo de Santa Fe at Tikal and two cores she took from Lake Petén. Cowgill concluded that milpa agriculture was productive enough to have sustained Maya civilization and questioned the idea that the bajos were silted-in lakes. Cowgill challenged Meggers's (1954, 1957) hypothesis that tropical forest environments by their nature offered limited subsistence potential.

By the mid-1960s the settlement pattern studies had led to heated debate about the subsistence base of the Maya. The dispersed settlement pattern that characterized the Maya Lowlands was thought to represent an adaptation to extensive agriculture (Sanders and Price 1968: 197). Enough data had been accumulated on settlement to demonstrate that population was very much higher than archaeologists had previously imagined. Thus the question of how civilization developed in the tropical forest based on swidden technology crystallized into a major issue.

Some University of Pennsylvania students associated with the Tikal Project suggested subsistence alternatives. Using ethnohistoric, ethnographic, and botanical data, Bronson (1966) proposed that agriculture was based on the cultivation of root crops, which would have provided a higher caloric return relative to labor input and had a higher potential for both surplus production and storageability. Puleston (1968) developed Lundell's idea that the prehistoric Maya practiced arboriculture centering on the ramón tree, whose seeds were abundant and high in protein, a dietary component nutritionists considered of paramount importance in the 1960s.

Recent Interdisciplinary Research

The subsistence question stimulated a new cycle of interdisciplinary research. The first development in 1968 was Siemens's (Siemens and Puleston 1972) chance discovery, through aerial reconnaissance, of drained fields and canals along the Candelaria River in southern Campeche, Mexico. Siemens, a geographer,

collaborated with archaeologist Puleston in the excavation and mapping of these features, first on the Candelaria and then beginning in 1973 along the Río Hondo in northern Belize (Siemens 1977). Ethnozoologist Pohl and soil scientist Bloom were among the collaborators on the Río Hondo Project; they have been carrying on the work since Puleston's untimely death and have been joined by geomorphologist Stein.

Deevey formed the Central Petén Historical Ecology Project in 1972 with archaeologists Don and Prudence Rice, as well as with palynologists Vaughan and Wiseman. In 1973 as a member of R. E. W. Adams's Río Bec Ecological Project, Turner investigated terraces around Becan, Campeche. Turner subsequently formed his own interdisciplinary team — first to work with Willey and Baudez at Copan, Honduras, beginning in 1977 and later with Peter Harrison on drained fields at Pulltrouser Swamp, northern Belize, in 1979 and 1981.

Archaeologists have made advances in the recovery of ecological and subsistence data at many archaeological sites. In 1973 Pohl worked with the Instituto de Antropología e Historia de Guatemala's excavations at Tikal, water-screening samples of Terminal Late Classic midden from abandoned rooms in Group G. She recovered botanical specimens, including the tuber *Xanthosoma*, as well as many small bones. Norman Hammond introduced an approach to excavation and recovery honed on small, local sites in Europe. Wing has been analyzing the faunal remains, and in 1978 Miksicek joined Hammond's Cuello Project to manage a full-scale flotation operation. In the course of their study of Postclassic occupation on Cozumel Island, Sabloff and Rathje sampled middens that provided Hamblin's data on fish and birds. Carr has undertaken the analysis of faunal remains screened from Freidel's excavation of Cerros. The analysis of these remains from habitation contexts will greatly enhance our knowledge of prehistoric economic activity. Since past studies have dwelt on agriculture, the increased interest in animal resources will provide a more balanced view of ancient subsistence.

Researchers have made progress in their investigation of prehistoric ecology and diet, but the work has led to some controversy. Bloom, Pohl, and Stein have views about the construction of wetland fields that are different from Turner's and Harrison's. Wiseman, on the one hand, and Vaughan and Deevey, on the other, dispute the effects of early Postclassic depopulation in Petén on the vegetation. Wilk questions Turner's assumptions about links between population pressure and agricultural intensification.

Now that faunal samples from a number of sites are available, we can begin to synthesize information on procurement of meat and the exploitation of animals for status paraphernalia. The data reveal an unexpected variability and challenge some of our assumptions, the role of fish in the diet, for example. Fauna are providing an appreciation of the ritual contexts of Maya economic life and the importance of animal symbolism in agricultural rites.

Some subjects remain to be studied. One of the most significant is the impact of predators and diseases on crops, and basic research on plant pests has yet to be done in the Maya Lowlands. We have hints of the importance of such information. In her study of Petén milpas, Cowgill (1960, 1962) found that weed competition and decline in soil fertility could not completely explain the milpero's abandonment of a plot after two years; she did note that corn borers and leaf-cutting ants were prevalent in second year plots (Cowgill 1962: 382). The preservation in wetland environments like those around San Antonio Río Hondo is so good, we may even recover the remains of prehistoric insects with which to assess agricultural problems.

References

Ashmore, W., editor
1981   *Lowland Maya Settlement Patterns.* University of New Mexico Press, Albuquerque.

Ashmore, W., and G. R. Willey
1981   "A Historical Introduction to the Study of Lowland Maya Settlement Patterns." In *Lowland Maya Settlement Patterns*, edited by W. Ashmore. University of New Mexico Press, Albuquerque, pp. 3–18.

Bartlett, H. H.
1935   *A Method of Procedure for Field Work in Tropical American Phytogeography Based upon a Botanical Reconnaissance in Parts of British Honduras and the Petén Forest of Guatemala.* Botany of the Maya Area, Miscellaneous Paper 1. Carnegie Institution of Washington, Washington, D.C.

Benedict, F. G., and M. Steggerda
1936   "Food of the Present-Day Maya Indians of Yucatán," *Carnegie Institution of Washington, Contributions to American Archaeology* 465:155–188.

Bronson, B.
1966   "Roots and the Subsistence of the Ancient Maya," *Southwestern Journal of Anthropology* 22:251–279.

Cook, O. F.
1921   "Milpa Agriculture: A Primitive Tropical System," *Annual Report of the Smithsonian Institution, 1919*, Washington, D.C.

Cooke, C. W.
1931   "Why the Mayan Cities of the Petén District, Guatemala, Were Abandoned," *Journal of the Washington Academy of Science* 21.

Covich, A. P.
1970   "Stability of Molluscan Communities: A Paleolimnologic Study of Environmental Disturbance in the Yucatán Peninsula." Ph.D. dissertation, Yale University.

Cowgill, U. M.
1960   "Soil Fertility, Population, and the Ancient Maya," *Proceedings of the National Academy of Sciences* 46:1009–11.
1961   "Soil Fertility and the Ancient Maya," *Transactions of the Connecticut Academy of Arts and Sciences* 42:1–56.
1962   "An Agricultural Study of the Southern Maya Lowlands," *American Anthropologist* 64:273–286.

Cowgill, U. M., and G. E. Hutchinson
1963a "Ecological and Geochemical Archaeology in the Northern Maya Lowlands," *Southwestern Journal of Anthropology* 19:267–285.
1963b *El Bajo de Santa Fe.* Transactions of the American Philosophical Society 53, Philadelphia.

Cowgill, U. M., G. E. Hutchinson, A. A. Racek, C. E. Goulden, R. Patrick, and M. Tsukada
1966 *The History of Laguna de Petenxil, a Small Lake in Northern Guatemala.* Memoirs of the Connecticut Academy of Arts and Sciences 17, New Haven.

Emerson, R. A.
n.d. "A Preliminary Study of the Milpa System of Maize Culture as Practiced by the Maya Indians of the Northern Part of the Yucatán Peninsula." Manuscript, Tozzer Library, Harvard University.

Emerson, R. A., and J. H. Kempton
1935 "Agronomic Investigations in Yucatán," *Carnegie Institution of Washington Yearbook* 39:138–142.

Goodrich, C., and H. van der Schalie
1937 *Mollusca of Petén and North Alta Vera Paz, Guatemala.* University of Michigan, Museum of Zoology, Miscellaneous Publications 34.

Hammond, N.
1975 *Lubaantun: A Classic Maya Realm.* Peabody Museum Monographs, no. 2, Harvard University.

Haviland, W. A.
1963 "Excavation of Small Structures in the Northeast Quadrant of Tikal, Guatemala." Ph.D. dissertation, Department of Anthropology, University of Pennsylvania.

Hester, J. A., Jr.
1951 "Agriculture, Economy and Population Density of the Maya," *Carnegie Institution of Washington Yearbook* 51:266–271.
1952 "Agriculture, Economy and Population Density of the Maya," *Carnegie Institution of Washington Yearbook* 52:288–292.
1953 "Maya Agriculture," *Carnegie Institution of Washington Yearbook* 53:297–298.
1954 "Natural and Cultural Bases of Ancient Maya Subsistence Economy." Ph.D. dissertation, University of California at Los Angeles.

Hubbs, C. L.
1935 *Fresh-Water Fishes Collected in British Honduras and Guatemala.* University of Michigan, Museum of Zoology, Miscellaneous Publication 28.

Kempton, J. H.
1935 *Report on Agricultural Survey.* Carnegie Institution of Washington. Report to the Government of Mexico on the 12th year of Chichen Itza Project and Allied Investigations.

Kluckhohn, C.
1940 "The Conceptual Structure in Middle American Studies." In *The Maya and Their Neighbors*, edited by C. L. Hay, R. L. Linton, S. K. Lothrop, H. L. Shapiro, and G. C. Vaillant. Appleton-Century, New York.

Kurjack, E. B.
1974 *Prehistoric Lowland Maya Community and Social Organization.* Tulane University, Middle American Research Institute Publication 38.

Lundell, C. L.
1933 "The Agriculture of the Maya," *Southwest Review* 19:65–77.
1937 *The Vegetation of Petén.* Carnegie Institution of Washington, Publication 478.
1938 "Plants Probably Utilized by the Old Empire Maya of Petén and Adjacent Lowlands," *Michigan Academy of Science, Arts, and Letters* 24:37–56.

Meggers, B. J.
1954 "Environmental Limitation on the Development of Culture," *American Anthropologist* 56:801–823.
1957 "Environmental Limitation on Maya Culture: A Reply to Coe," *American Anthropologist* 59:888–890.

Morley, S. G.
1920 *The Inscriptions at Copan.* Carnegie Institution of Washington, Publication 219.

Murie, A. M.
1935 *Mammals from Guatemala and British Honduras.* University of Michigan, Museum of Zoology, Miscellaneous Publication 26.

Olson, G. W.
1969 "Description and Data on Soils of Tikal, El Petén, Guatemala, Central America." Cornell University, Department of Agronomy, Mimeo 69-2.

Ower, L. H.
1927 "Features of British Honduras," *Geographical Journal* 70:373–86.

Palerm, A., and E. R. Wolf
  1957 "Ecological Potential and Cultural Develop-
         ment in Mesoamerica." In *Studies in
         Human Ecology*. Anthropological Society
         of Washington and Pan American Union
         Social Science, Monograph 3.

Puleston, D. E.
  1968 "*Brosimum alicastrum* as a Subsistence
         Alternative for the Classic Maya of the
         Central Southern Lowlands." M.A. thesis,
         University of Pennsylvania. University
         Microfilms, Ann Arbor.
  1973 "Ancient Maya Settlement Patterns and En-
         vironment at Tikal, Guatemala: Implica-
         tions for Subsistence Models." Ph.D.
         dissertation, University of Pennsylvania.
         University Microfilms, Ann Arbor.

Rick, A. M.
  1968 "Mammals from Tikal, Guatemala." M.S.
         thesis, Department of Biology, Carleton
         University, Ottawa, Canada.

Ricketson, O. G., Jr., and E. B. Ricketson
  1937 *Uaxactun, Guatemala, Group E, 1926–31*.
         Carnegie Institution of Washington, Publi-
         cation 477.

Sanders, W. T.
  1962 "Cultural Ecology of the Maya Lowlands,
         Part I." *Estudios de Cultura Maya* 2:79–
         121.
  1963 "Cultural Ecology of the Maya Lowlands,
         Part II." *Estudios de Cultura Maya* 3:203–
         241.

Sanders, W. T., and B. Price
  1968 *Mesoamerica: The Evolution of a Civiliza-
         tion*. Random House, New York.

Schufeldt, P. W.
  1950 "Reminiscences of a Chiclero." In
         Morleyana. School of American Research
         and Museum of New Mexico, Santa Fe.

Siemens, A. H., editor
  1977 *The Río Hondo Project: An Investigation
         of the Maya of Northern Belize*. Journal of
         Belizean Affairs 5.

Siemens, A. H., and D. E. Puleston
  1972 "Ridged Fields and Associated Features in
         Southern Campeche: New Perspectives on
         the Lowland Maya," *American Antiquity*
         37:228–239.

Simmons, C., S. Tarano, and J. Pinto
  1959 *Clasificación de reconocimiento de los
         suelos de la republica de Guatemala*.
         Ministerio de Agricultura, Instituto Agro-
         Pecuaria, Guatemala.

Smithe, F. B., and R. A. Paynter
  1963 *Birds of Tikal, Guatemala*. Bulletin of
         Museum of Comparative Zoology 128. 5.

Steggerda, M.
  1941 *Maya Indians of Yucatán*. Carnegie Institu-
         tion of Washington, Publication 531.

Stuart, L. C.
  1935 *A Contribution to a Knowledge of the
         Herpetology of a Portion of the Savanna
         Region of Central Petén, Guatemala*. Uni-
         versity of Michigan Museum of Zoology,
         Miscellaneous Publication 29.
  1958 *A Study of the Herpetofauna of the Uaxac-
         tun-Tikal Area of Northern El Petén,
         Guatemala*. University of Michigan, Con-
         tribution of the Laboratory of Vertebrate
         Biology 75.

Thompson, J. E. S.
  1931 *Archaeological Investigations in the South-
         ern Cayo District, British Honduras*. Field
         Museum of Natural History, Publication
         301, Anthropological Series 17. 3.

Tsudaka, M., and E. S. Deevey
  1967 "Pollen Analyses from Four Lakes in the
         Southern Maya Area of Guatemala and El
         Salvador." In *Quarternary Paleoecology*,
         edited by E. J. Cushing and H. E. Wright,
         Jr. Yale University Press, New Haven.

van Tyne, J.
  1935 *The Birds of Northern Petén, Guatemala*.
         University of Michigan, Museum of
         Zoology, Miscellaneous Publication 27.

Willey, G. R.
  1956 "Problems Concerning Prehistoric Settle-
         ment Patterns in the Maya Lowlands." In
         *Prehistoric Settlement Patterns in the New
         World*, edited by G. R. Willey, Viking
         Fund Publications in Anthropology, 23,
         pp. 107–114. Wenner-Gren Foundation for
         Anthropological Research, New York.

Willey, G. R., W. R. Bullard, Jr., J. B. Glass, and
J. C. Gifford
  1965 *Prehistoric Maya Settlements in the Belize
         Valley*. Peabody Museum Papers, vol. 54,
         Harvard University.

Wright, A. C. S., D. H. Romney, R. H. Arbuckle,
and V. E. Vial
  1959 *Land in British Honduras: Report of the
         British Honduras Land Use Survey Team*.
         Colonial Research Publication 24. Her Maj-
         esty's Stationery Office, London.

Part I
The Development and Impact of Ancient Maya Agriculture

Section A: Cultivation Techniques and Crops

Mary Pohl and Charles H. Miksicek

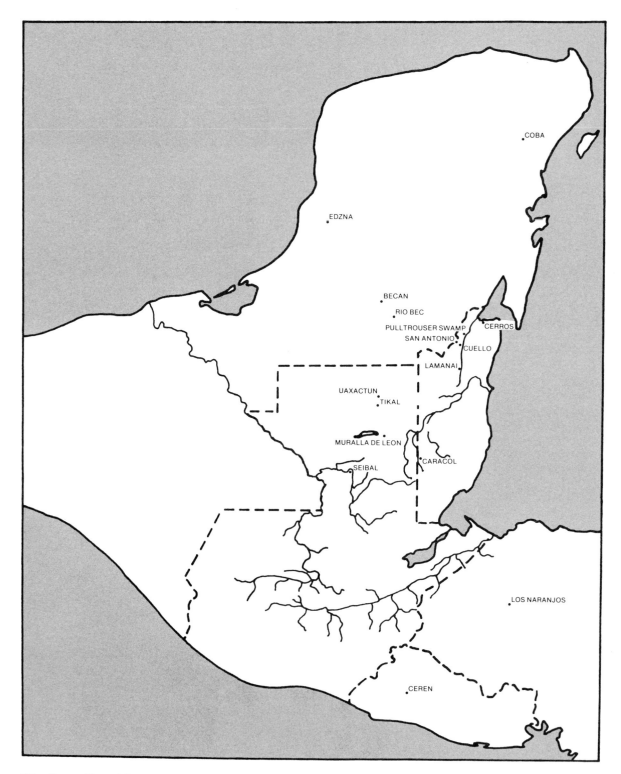

Sites discussed in part I.

Terraces

The interdisciplinary research conducted over the past 15 years has begun to clarify the ideas that early researchers put forward. More information is becoming available on the terraces. Construction has now been reported from eastern and central Petén, Guatemala, south-central Belize, western Honduras, and southern Campeche and Quintana Roo, Mexico (Turner 1974b, 1979, 1983a; Harrison and Turner 1978; Turner and Johnson 1979; Healy, van Waarden, and Anderson 1980; Healy 1982; Healy et al. 1983; D. S. Rice 1982), and the full extent of terracing is still unknown. Turner (1974a) estimated that relic terraces covered more than 10,000 km² in the Río Bec zone of southern Mexico. The density of terracing varies throughout southern Campeche and Quintana Roo (Turner 1974: 119), and terraces appear to have a discontinous distribution in the upper Belize river region or Vaca plateau. In the latter area, structures cluster on the western slopes of the Maya mountains where the hilly region joins the plateau (Healy 1982). Such an irregular pattern makes estimates of distribution difficult.

The idea that structures in Río Bec are terraces at all has been challenged; Sanders (1979:495–496) and Hammond (1982:489) suggest that they are field boundary walls. Hammond points out that some slopes are too shallow to warrant modification, and Sanders wants to group the structures in the same category as walls on flat terrain identified on Cozumel Island (Sabloff and Rathje 1975) and on the adjacent mainland of the Yucatán Peninsula (Fletcher 1978; Tony Andrews, personal communication, 1971).

Most terraces (Healy 1982; Turner 1974b) are of the linear sloping dry field variety though more check dam features of the type recorded earlier by Ruppert and Dennison (1943) were also found in hillside ravines in the Río Bec area. Río Bec terraces occurred on slopes of 4° to 47°. As one would expect, distance between terraces was directly related to degree of slope.

Chronology is beginning to be defined, although, as with most agricultural architecture, dating of structures is difficult. Turner relied primarily on the dating of surrounding settlement in assigning terraces in the Río Bec zone to the Late Classic period (Turner 1974b; Harrison and Turner 1978:343). In Belize, poorly preserved ceramics and a radiocarbon date of 790 A.D. ±110 from a terrace near the site of Caracol also point to a general Late Classic date (Healy 1982).

On the other hand, terraces from Mountain Cow and Zayden Creek, Belize, have a substantial Early Classic ceramic component, and construction might have begun earlier at these sites (Healy, van Waarden, and Anderson 1980).

Construction techniques vary. Terraces at Hatzcap Ceel, Belize (Healy 1982), resemble a spider's web, giving the appearance of an irregular growth pattern, and a relatively high number of house mounds occur among the terraces: about one house per 0.5 hectare, a figure close to that for Río Bec (Turner 1974b). At Zayden Creek terrace layout is more orderly with house structures located well above the terrace slopes and even outside the terraced zone. With the exception of Caracol Hill A, the Belize terraces lack the interconnecting "walkways" characteristic of the Río Bec region (Turner 1974b). As Healy (1982) points out, we need further insight into the social implications of these differences in terrace layout.

There are indications that terrace construction was labor intensive. The presence at Caracol of molluscs, such as *Pachychilus*, a genus that lives in flowing water, and the characteristics of soils both in Río Bec and in Belize suggest that earth was brought in from other locations and physically transported up hillsides (Turner 1979; Healy 1982).

The function of terraces is open to debate. Turner (1979) believes that Río Bec terraces trapped soil and controlled erosion. Healy (1982) suggests that the structures provide even distribution of hill-slope rainwater over the terraced zone. In his analysis of terracing throughout the New World, Donkin (1979) proposes that one of the most significant roles of terraces is to conserve moisture. D. S. Rice (1982) believes that terraces in central Petén had a dual function. When the torrential wet season rains come, terraces may slow down runoff; later, when the *canicula*, or little dry season, hits, they serve as reservoirs of moisture. Turner (1982) cautions against broad generalizations, suggesting that terraces may be adapted to specific local conditions. We need more information on those local conditions.

Unfortunately, we have virtually no evidence of agricultural techniques or crops. Preservation in terrace soils is poor, and archaeologists have not yet recovered pollen or phytoliths. Nevertheless, pollen and radiocarbon dates from the large southern reservoir at Caracol indicate that corn (*Zea mays*) was cultivated in the area during the Classic period, and since terraces ring the site, Healy (1982) makes the reasonable suggestion that this crop was growing on the terraces (though maize pollen might have blown in from upland swiddening). Turner (1979) assumes that terraces would have been more or less continuously cropped, since fallowing would have produced vegetation that would have destroyed terrace structures.

Charles H. Miksicek is a doctoral candidate, Office of Arid Lands Studies, University of Arizona, Tucscon. See chapter 1 for Mary Pohl's affiliation.

Water Management

Most of the controversy about Maya cultivation centers on the exploitation of wetlands as illustrated in this book. In the literature this farming technique has been called ridged, raised, riverbank, and drained field agriculture. Wetland agriculture is a universal term used here.

Everyone acknowledges that ditching wetlands was a labor-intensive proposition. Turner and Harrison (1983) have modified their views about the work involved in constructing platforms at Pulltrouser Swamp (see Turner and Harrison 1981). They now believe that the Maya accomplished most raising by mounding up the soil taken directly from the canals, although they still believe that some material was brought in from uplands and mixed in with the swamp muck to create the planting platforms (Turner, personal communication, 1983). One of the key pieces of evidence for extraneous matter is the presence of a limited number of upland plant macrofossils in the "fill." One alternative explanation for these materials is that the Maya brought them in as mulch. Bloom and Crum's analysis of soils in northern Belize has revealed that phosphorus may have been low enough to cause cultivators to fertilize the soils. Some extraneous materials might also have washed in from adjacent uplands.

Apart from the work involved in constructing the fields, there is the question of how much labor was needed to cultivate them. We would like to know whether wetland fields were used for cultivating many crops requiring considerable hand care and even transplanting like present-day *chinampas* of Central Mexico. Excavations at San Antonio Río Hondo and Pulltrouser Swamp have so far yielded pollen and botanical evidence for a narrow range of crops, notably maize and possibly cotton; cultivation appears to have been fairly specialized. Nevertheless, the Río Hondo evidence suggests that the Maya expended some effort in composting to increase soil fertility (chap. 2).

The frequency of cropping and the productivity of wetland fields is a matter of debate. Using molluscan evidence, Bloom, Pohl, and Stein infer that the Maya cropped riverbank wetlands in the dry season, and Siemens (1980, 1983) argues that wetlands in Veracruz were suitable for seasonal cultivation as well. Turner (personal communication, 1983) believes that fields in swamps like Pulltrouser must have been cultivated more intensively, perhaps double-cropped. His reasoning is based primarily on his perception of fields as labor intensive investments, not worth the effort for limited use.

One model for the origin of ancient Maya wetland cultivation appears to be seasonal riverbank and *bajo* farming practiced today in many areas of the tropical

Lowlands, including Petén, Guatemala (Cowgill 1961), and southern Belize (Wilk 1981 and chap. 4). These data must be adjusted to take prehistoric local conditions into account. The question of productivity provides one example. At San Antonio Río Hondo, soil analysis indicates that Preclassic fields were very fertile, though yields would probably have been reduced if the Maya returned to crop there after an episode of ponding, which left deposits of less desirable soil (chap. 2).

Although Puleston's (1977) claim that wetland agriculture dates back to about 1000 B.C. is now supported by another date from San Antonio Río Hondo (chap. 2), we still do not know how early the practice originated. D. S. Rice's (1978) hypothesis that agricultural activity initially focused on uplands in Petén, Guatemala, was based primarily on his observation that settlement was located in these areas. Ceramics have not yet been found in Preclassic fields at San Antonio Río Hondo, however, and wetland cultivation cannot be related to habitation found so far in the immediate vicinity.

It has been argued that upland cultivation would have required less labor than wetland agriculture and that the Maya between the New and Hondo rivers would logically have taken up the latter after they experienced land pressure due to population increases (Turner and Harrison 1981:404; Turner 1983b). On the other hand, one might suggest that riverine cultivation would have appeared advantageous because the fertility of the enriched peats would have obviated the exceedingly laborious task of continual forest clearance associated with shifting cultivation on uplands. Wilk (chap. 4) thinks that the scarcity of tree-cutting implements in Early and Middle Preclassic levels at Cuello supports this line of reasoning.

The presence of remains of upland trees in early deposits at Cuello does not rule out the possibility that the Maya practiced riverine cultivation. One would expect that the residents of Cuello exploited or tended fruiting trees in the upland forest where the center itself is situated. There is other evidence that the inhabitants foraged beyond the environs of the site. They brought back pine (*Pinus caribea*), probably from savannas located 6 km away (Hammond and Miksicek 1981). Fish remains and razor grass seeds (*Scleria* sp. and *Cladium* sp.; Hammond and Miksicek 1981) indicate that they frequented swampy and aquatic environments too.

Wilk (personal communication, 1981) suggests that the Akwē-Shavante of Brazil (Maybury-Lewis 1967:35–52) may provide a model for earliest Maya cultivation practices. The Akwē-Shavante make their living primarily by hunting deer and gathering nuts, roots, and fruits. Aboriginally they planted beans, pumpkins, and especially maize for ceremonial exchanges. They spent only a month or less clearing (by repeated burning before the introduction of metal tools), planting, and harvesting along riverbanks.

Not only is the date of earliest wetland agriculture in doubt, the extent of cultivation at any one point in time is also unknown. Using the Jet Propulsion Laboratory's synthetic aperture, side-looking airborne radar, combined with ground checks at five spot localities in Belize and Petén, Adams and his colleagues (Adams 1980, 1982; Adams, Brown, and Culbert 1981) think that they have identified extensive linear patterning in the Maya Lowlands. Between 1,250 and 2,500 km² may be involved. They believe that 20 percent of these linear features have a characteristic lattice configuration that they assume represents prehistoric canal networks, and they point out that this estimate of canal frequency may well be conservative because the resolution of the radar is sufficient to pick up only the larger ditches. The observation that major Classic centers, rank ordered by an assessment of volume and extent of large-scale architecture, are located near swamps bolsters their hypothesis that the Maya must have modified these wetlands to support the large population that archaeologists have estimated. The assumption that drained field zones were in maximum use at the time of peak densities in the Late Classic period is based on Boserup's (1965) theory that, within limits, cultivation systems respond in intensity to population growth and pressures. Despite Adams's arguments, Siemens (1980) hesitates to accept the fact that so many of these features are artificial, agricultural, prehistoric, or contemporaneous until thorough investigation has been conducted in more areas. We are cautious about the relationship between architectural features and population density.

The question of the relationship between ditched fields and social organization has been raised. The arrangement of some canals in regular grids may imply planning (Hammond, personal communication, 1982). Hammond (1982:489) believes that the circumstantial evidence of massive public architecture at sites like Lamanai demonstrates that Late Preclassic Maya society was organized such that field construction could have been collective and centrally directed. On the other hand, Siemens (1980) emphasizes variations in patterning and points out that the occurrence, in clusters, of fields investigated so far on Albion Island suggests that the system was built by fairly small communities, perhaps by kin groups.

Canals in wetlands may have served for drainage and for dipper or pot irrigation. Ethnographic examples of this dual function can be found in the *tablones* that Mathewson (1984) studied at Aguacatan, Highland Guatemala, and in the ditched swamps of the eastern Llanos of Venezuela (Denevan and Bergman 1975). At Late Preclassic Cerros, Scarborough (1983) hypothesizes that reservoirs and trun-

cated feeder canals in the vicinity of the main wetland canal and field complex may have been used to impound water for drier months. Siemens (1980) stresses that this would not have been true irrigation.

Water management at Late Preclassic Edzna, located in the drier zone of Yucatán, was a monumental feat (Matheny 1976, 1978, 1982). Twenty-one canals and 25 reservoirs had an estimated storage capacity of more than 2 million m³ of water. One canal involved the removal of about 900,000 m³ of soil. Fish's (1978) pollen evidence for *Isoetes* suggests the Maya may have begun by enlarging naturally wet places. The magnitude to which the system grew leads Matheny to postulate that the water was used for pot irrigation, as well as for culinary and possibly defensive requirements.

The Maya may have built dams for irrigation. Turner and Johnson (1979) argue that stonework of a dam located at the headwaters of a tributary of the Copan River looks ancient and possibly dates to the Late Classic period when prehistoric population was at its peak. (As with many agricultural features, chronological control is a problem.) The structure once impounded a spring, perhaps to create a head high enough to channel water to a large area of level terrain lying at an elevation slightly higher than the spring. Since the Copan Valley lies in a rain shadow, water is particularly crucial there.

Swidden Systems

In the effort to investigate possible technological alternatives, especially intensive agriculture, swidden cultivation has received little attention recently. Sanders (1979) still maintains that upland swidden agriculture was the predominant mode, and the pollen evidence (chaps. 5, 6, 7) indicates that the Maya carried out very extensive forest clearance in the lowlands, even though the precise dating is a matter of debate. Unfortunately, we have very little excavation data for upland fields. At Cerén, El Salvador, Sheets (1982) uncovered Classic period maize fields preserved by volcanic eruption, indicating that corn was planted on top of ridges spaced about 40 cm apart. Sheets believes that the ridges conserved moisture, and the depressions aided rain runoff. Sheets further suggests that the milpa needed little fallowing, like similar fields today in the Highlands. Since Sheets argues that Cerén is ecologically like the Maya Lowlands, his unique find is relevant to the issue at hand.

The real beauty of the Maya suite of agrotechnologies and crops is its diversity. Over much of the lowlands, swidden agriculture probably never went out of fashion. The Maya repertory of crops and cropping techniques could be adapted to each specific locality to maximize productivity and also to produce regional specialization, which could promote trade and exchange.

Tree Cropping

The use of tree crops is well documented for the early historic period, and we can assume that the Spaniards' eyewitness descriptions apply to the Late Postclassic period as well. The Maya planted fruit trees around their residences for shade and for food, especially in times of shortage, and they also encouraged economically useful trees on *milpa* land (Marcus 1982:249). They planted orchards of commercial cacao for elite use and perhaps also fruit trees such as nance (*Byrsonima crassifolia*). Jones (1982:288) cautions that the degree to which orchard crops other than cacao were grown on a significant scale remains unclear. The question is what is significant. Although a few trees around each house might not seem significant, that pattern extended over the lowlands as a whole adds up to a lot of produce.

Ramón is consistently mentioned as a starvation food in the ethnohistoric literature (Marcus 1982:250). A systematic examination of the occurrence of ramón (*Brosimum alicastrum*) and other economically important species at the archaeological sites of Tikal, Coba, and Lamanai, as well as natural limestone outcrops, has indicated that we can more realistically attribute the present distribution of these trees to colonization after Maya abandonment rather than to the presence of orchards in Classic times (Lambert and Arnason 1978, 1982; Miksicek 1979). An inventory of vegetation quadrants and soil analyses from site and nonsite contexts around Lamanai demonstrated that ruins with ramón trees growing on them had more nitrogen, higher organic matter, higher water holding capacity, more magnesium, and lower sodium content.

The pollen and faunal evidence is consistent with the idea that the present-day characteristics of the forest reflect natural processes of species competition and selection at a late date. In pollen diagrams from central Petén, Guatemala, and northern Belize, the highest percentages of *Brosimum* type pollen vary inversely with disturbance indicators (Hansen, in press). In Terminal Late Classic fauna from Seibal and Tikal (Instituto de Antropología e Historia de Guatemala excavations), animals that depend heavily on ramón, such as spider and howler monkeys and fruit-eating bats, are poorly represented.

One of the indirect lines of evidence Puleston (1971) used to build up his ramón hypothesis was his observation that the seeds did not spoil in *chultun* experiments he conducted at Tikal. Miksicek recently repeated this experiment in a Late Preclassic *chultun* excavated at Cuello (Miksicek et al. 1981b). He found

that after five months tubers like *Xanthosoma, Dioscoria,* and *Manihot,* not included in Puleston's original study, as well as shelled maize stored in an open vessel were in good condition. Ramón with pericarp had decomposed; the sample of ramón seeds without pericarp had germinated but was still edible. Most smoked maize had some fungal growth, and some unsmoked maize had germinated.

At least four sixteenth-century sources indicate that maize was stored in underground pits: Landa (Tozzer 1941:195) and the Motul dictionary (Marcus 1982:247) for Yucatán; Viana, Gallego, and Cadena (1955) for Alta Verapaz, Guatemala; and Cortés (MacNutt 1908) for the Usumacinta River region. Landa says corn was stored as insurance against years when crops failed, and in Alta Verapaz smoked maize was said to have been kept underground for an entire year (Viana, Gallego, and Cadena, 1955:21–22; Reina and Hill 1980:77). The evidence strongly suggests that the Maya stored maize underground, but the experimental results arouse skepticism about the length of time the corn would have remained edible, and one might also question whether the chultuns would have been sufficient to provision large centers for any length of time.

The primary prehistoric function of chultuns may have been for relatively short-term storage and redistribution in settlement centers. In Cortés's account,

> We reached the said village of Tepetitan, which we also found burned and deserted, thus causing us double hardship. We found some fruits of the country inside and some fields of maize in the neighborhood, unripe . . . we also discovered under the burnt houses, some granaries which contained small quantities of maize; this was of great help in the extreme necessity to which we were reduced.
>
> (MacNutt 1908:241)

At the time of the conquest, the Maya were conducting frequent raids for slaves and sacrificial victims (Roys 1943). Since Cortés was the first to cross this area, we can assume that flight before approaching adversaries was a native practice. Subterranean storage may have been one strategy to ensure that some food remained when the population repossessed the settlement.

Several pieces of information support this hypothesis. Chultuns occur in the Río Bec region and especially in northeast Petén, areas where ancient fortifications have been discovered. Fortified sites at Muralla de Leon (Macanche), Petén, Becan and Edzna, Campeche, and Los Naranjos, northern Honduras (Matheny 1976; Rice and Rice 1981; Webster 1974; Baudez and Becquelin 1973) date to the Late Preclassic and Protoclassic periods, the same time that chultuns appear. Gotthilf (personal communication, 1982) collected present-day folk tradition in Yucatán describing chultuns as emergency storage facilities.

The prehistoric Maya may have stored their maize in chultuns as well as in granaries located in the countryside as they did in early historic times (Hellmuth 1977). In the Río Bec region, where chultuns are less abundant than at Tikal (Thomas 1974:143), grain may also have been kept in small, above-ground auxiliary buildings associated with house sites similar to granaries in modern Maya farmsteads (Eaton 1975:68).

Although Puleston's ramón hypothesis has not been substantiated, an expanding list of carbonized botanical remains demonstrates the use of a variety of tree crops in prehistoric times. From Classic period settlements around Pulltrouser Swamp, we have evidence for avocado (*Persea americana*, charcoal), nance (*Byrsonima crassifolia*, charcoal), hogplum (*Spodias* spp., charcoal), guava (*Psidium guajava*, charcoal), cacao (*Theobroma* sp., charcoal), siricote (*Cordia dodecandra*, charcoal), mamey zapote (*Calocarpum mammosum*, charcoal), calabash tree (*Crescentia* sp., charcoal), and sapodilla (*Manilkara zapota*, charcoal). Uncarbonized seeds from a wild-sized papaya (*Carica papaya*) and allspice (*Pimenta dioca*) were also recovered, but these may be recent intrusions (Miksicek 1983; Turner and Miksicek 1984). Classic period flotation samples from Copan (Turner and Miksicek 1984) have yielded avocado (carbonized seed fragments), nance (charcoal), cacao (charcoal), guava (charcoal), and copal (*Protium copal*, charcoal). Archaeobotanical remains from a Classic period midden at Tikal, analyzed by C. Earle Smith (personal communication, cited in Turner and Miksicek 1984) included avocado (charred seeds), hogplum (charred seeds), coyal palm (*Acrocomia* spp., charred seeds), sapodilla (charred seeds), and nance (uncarbonized seeds). An impressive list of carbonized seeds has recently been reported by Nancy Stenholm (1984) from an Early Classic house from the Mirador Plaza at Kaminaljuyu. These include hogplum, avocado, and mamey.

In Preclassic contexts at Cuello, we have avocado (charcoal), jauacte palm (*Bactris* sp., charred seeds), mamey (charred seeds and charcoal), nance (charred seeds and charcoal), hogplum (charcoal), guava (charcoal), sapodilla (charcoal), star apple (*Chrysophyllum* sp., charred seeds and charcoal), and cacao (charcoal) (Hammond and Miksicek 1981; Turner and Miksicek 1984). Preclassic horizons at San Antonio Río Hondo on Albion Island have yielded calabash tree (charcoal and uncarbonized gourd rind), hogplum (charred seed), avocado (charcoal), copal (charcoal), and nance (charcoal). An additional species, hackberry (*Celtis* spp.), has been recovered from several sites. Although the fruits are edible, the seeds are always uncarbonized (because they are preserved by the high calcium carbonate content of the bony endocarp), and they often occur in clusters suggestive of rodent caches. As this species is a common early successional species in recently cleared areas and because the possibility exists for nonhuman introduction into archaeological contexts, the question of Maya use of hackberry as food is still unresolved.

Although there is abundant evidence for the use of fruit trees by the Lowland Maya, the hypothesis for tree cropping is more problematic. The recovery of wood charcoal from these species is only indirect evidence for their use as food plants. All these species are underrepresented or missing from the pollen record, but then most of these species are insect-pollinated and do not produce copious amounts of pollen. Wiseman (personal communication, 1981) sampled the soil of a modern cacao plantation in central Belize and found no evidence for cacao pollen even beneath actively flowering trees. It is not surprising that pollen samples from Edzna (Fish 1978) yielded only sporadic evidence for hackberry and no other tree crops.

Avocado, hogplum, mamey, and nance have been recovered from the earliest Preclassic Maya contexts. It is tempting to assume that even during Early Preclassic times, fruit trees were planted in dooryard orchard-gardens. Wiseman (personal communication, 1982) has suggested that the dispersed pattern of Maya settlement may be partially explained if fruit trees were planted in the intervening spaces between the housemounds. The relationship between orchards and Maya residence patterns was also suggested by the settlement survey at Coba (Folan, Fletcher, and Kintz 1979).

Root Crops

The role of root crops in the ancient Maya diet is still difficult to define. In the ethnohistorical literature of the sixteenth and seventeenth centuries, roots are famine foods (Marcus 1982:253). Tubers may be underrepresented in the archaeological record because they are usually prepared by boiling or leaching and are therefore unlikely to be preserved (Hammond and Miksicek 1981:265). A Terminal Late Classic carbonized *Xanthosoma* root occurred in refuse protected in an abandoned room in Group G at Tikal (Pohl 1980). An unidentified, charred root fragment from Late Preclassic Cuello hints at earlier use of tubers (Hammond and Miksicek 1981:267). We have no information on whether these roots were wild or cultivated, however.

Archaeologists have suggested that tubers may have been grown on wetland fields. Wild yam (*Discorea* cf. *mexicana*) has been recovered from Preclassic wetland fields at San Antonio Río Hondo, but the woody tissue of this root, together with its high oxalate and steroid content, make it an unlikely source of food (Miksicek 1982).

Cultigens

Flotation has produced a great deal of evidence on crops, but we must be aware of possible biases in the data (Hammond and Miksicek 1981:265). Patterns of preparation and disposal have a great deal to do with whether remains are preserved. Maize kernels and cacao seeds that are roasted or parched can get accidentally burned, but beans and squash, which are usually boiled, are only rarely preserved. A chance case was the pot of beans in the little house at Cerén preserved because of a volcanic eruption (Sheets 1979). Tree crops, whose fruit is eaten raw, would normally only show up if the wood is used for fuel or if seeds are discarded into a fire. Small fragments of wood are more likely to end up in archaeological deposits than large pieces, which are usually carried away. It is best to combine macrofossil evidence with that obtained from pollen and artifacts.

Both pollen and botanical data demonstrate that maize was the principal crop of the Maya beginning as early as Early Preclassic times (Miksicek 1980; Miksicek et al. 1981a). The Cuello evidence consists only of cob and kernel fragments, so we lack information on ear length, plant form, and most important, productivity. Nevertheless, we have some data on a variety of types of Preclassic maize.

The Swasey maize varieties from Cuello are essentially identical to the earliest types of maize recovered from South America. They were part of a distinct lineage that spread throughout tropical Central America and coastal South America during Early Preclassic times. Middle and Late Preclassic maize types from Cuello show a much stronger relationship to highland Mexican varieties and more teosinte introgression. These data suggest a thorough understanding of plant manipulation by early Maya farmers, with a willingness to improve established lines by selection and to adopt new varieties of crops (Miksicek et al. 1981a).

Cucurbits (squash and gourds) were a significant element in the early diet. Carbonized rind fragments (*Cucurbita* cf. *moschata*) were recovered throughout the Cuello sequence in frequencies second only to maize (Hammond and Miksicek 1981). *Cucurbita moschata* seeds were identified from the midden at Tikal by Smith (in Turner and Miksicek 1984). Both squash and bottle gourd (*Lagenaria siceraria*) are reported by Stenholm (1984) from the Early Classic house at Kaminaljuyu. Puleston recovered an uncarbonized squash peduncle from Albion Island, but this context also contained some glass and historic trash so the squash stem could be historic. Fish (1978) identified squash pollen from Late Preclassic floors at Edzna.

We tend to think of beans (*Phaseolus vulgaris* and other species) as a staple in the native Central American diet, and yet they are severely under-represented in the Maya archaeobotanical record. Small, charred bean cotyledons have been recovered from both Cuello and settlements around Pulltrouser Swamp (Hammond and Miksicek 1981; Miksicek 1983). Initially these were thought to represent a wild species of *Phaseolus*, but they also could be a small cultivated form similar to varieties still grown in southern Mexico and Central America. Stenholm (1984) recovered charred beans from Kaminaljuyu. A charred kidney bean was recovered from deposits that may date to the Late Preclassic or Early Classic periods at San Antonio Río Hondo (Miksicek, personal communication to Pohl 1981). Charred beans were also recovered from Terminal Late Classic refuse in Group G at Tikal (Orrego, personal communication, 1973). The scarcity of beans is probably more a matter of preservation and recovery than of absence from the prehistoric diet. Beans are usually prepared by soaking and boiling and are not likely to become carbonized. When they are charred, the cotyledons are very fragile and do not preserve well (Hammond and Miksicek 1981:268).

Chile may have been another Lowland Maya crop. Several small carbonized chile seeds have been recovered from Middle Swasey and Early Mamom (Bladen) contexts at Cuello (Turner and Miksicek 1984). Although these are in the size range of wild and feral chiles (*Capsicum annuum* var. *aviculare*), this form called "bird chile," tepine, or chile mash is a commonly cultivated condiment found in gardens throughout Mexico and Central America. Stenholm (1984) also recovered chile seeds from Kaminaljuyu.

Cotton pollen from wetland fields (Wiseman 1981, 1982, 1983) and from the site of Edzna (Fish 1978), charred cotton seeds from Cuello (*Gossypium* cf. *hirsutum*; Hammond and Miksicek 1981:267), and the actual remains of cloth from Cerros (Freidel and Scarborough 1979) seem to document the importance of this fiber crop to the ancient Maya. Maize and cotton are emerging as the two crops most strongly associated with the wetland agricultural systems of the Maya Lowlands. While bulk grains such as corn would be difficult to ship (other than by canoe), and other foodstuffs would be too perishable to transport long distances, cotton fiber and finished textiles may have been significant items for trade and tribute in the larger Maya economic system.

In the past 15 years the groundwork for the "new ecological orthodoxy" has been laid in the Maya Lowlands. We have progressed from armchair speculation to arguments based on archaeological and paleoecological data. We have recovered an impressive list of crops including maize, beans, squash, cotton, chiles, and a variety of fruit trees. A great diversity of agricultural techniques have been postulated such as wetland fields, terraces, upland swiddens, and dooryard gardens. And yet, there are many questions still to be answered. How exactly did these cropping systems operate? How did the intensive agrotechnologies fit into the larger Classic Maya socio-economic system? What led to agricultural intensification and diversification? What plant products, foodstuffs, raw products, and finished goods moved through the Maya exchange system? How ecologically stable were these extensive agricultural systems? Did an inherent instability of intensive agriculture in the tropics contribute to the collapse of Maya civilization? Perhaps in the next 15 years we can answer some of these questions fundamental to our understanding of the growth and demise of Classic Maya society.

References

Adams, R. E. W.
1980   "Swamps, Canals, and Locations of Ancient Maya Cities," *Antiquity* 54:206–214.
1982   "Ancient Maya Canals: Grids and Lattices in the Maya Jungle," *Archaeology* 35:28–35.

Adams, R. E. W., W. E. Brown, Jr., and T. P. Culbert
1981   "Radar Mapping, Archaeology and Ancient Maya Land Use," *Science* 213:1457–63.

Baudez, C. F., and P. Becquelin
1973   *Archéologie de Los Naranjos, Honduras.* Mission Archéologique Française au Mexique, Mexico City.

Boserup, E.
1965   *The Conditions of Agricultural Growth: The Economics of Agrarian Change Under Population Pressure.* Aldine, Chicago.

Cowgill, U. M.
1961   "Soil Fertility and the Ancient Maya," *Transactions of the Connecticut Academy of Arts and Sciences* 42:1–56.

Denevan, W. M., and R. W. Bergman
1975   "Karinya Indian Swamp Cultivation in the Venezuelan Llanos." *Yearbook of the Association of Pacific Coast Geographers* 37:23–37.

Donkin, R. A.
1979   *Agricultural Terracing in the Aboriginal New World.* Viking Fund Publications in Anthropology 56.

Eaton, J. D.
1975   "Ancient Agricultural Farmsteads in the Río Bec Region of Yucatán." In *Contribution of the University of California Archaeological Research Facility* 27. Berkeley and Los Angeles.

Fish, S. K.
1978   "Palynology of Edzna: Environment and Economy." Paper presented at the 43rd annual meeting of the Society for American Archaeology, Tucson.

Fletcher, L. A.
1978   "Linear Features at Coba, Quintana Roo, Mexico." Ph.D. dissertation, State University of New York at Stony Brook.

Folan, W. J., L. A. Fletcher, and E. R. Kintz
1979   "Fruit, Fiber, Bark, and Resin: Social Organization of a Maya Urban Center." *Science* 204:697–701.

Freidel, D. A., and V. L. Scarborough
1979   "Subsistence, Trade and the Development of the Coastal Maya." Paper presented at

the History and Development of Maya Subsistence, a conference in memory of Dennis E. Puleston, St. Paul.

Hammond, N.
1982   "The Exploration of the Maya World," *American Scientist* 20:482–495.

Hammond, N., and C. H. Miksicek
1981   "Ecology and Economy of a Formative Maya Site at Cuello, Belize," *Journal of Field Archaeology* 8:259–269.

Hansen, B. S.
In prep.   "Pollen Stratigraphy of Laguna de Cocos." In *Ancient Maya Wetland Cultivation on Albion Island, Northern Belize*, edited by Mary Pohl. University of Minnesota, Publications in Anthropology 2.

Harrison, P. D., and B. L. Turner II, editors
1978   *Pre-Hispanic Maya Agriculture*. University of New Mexico Press, Albuquerque.

Healy, P.
1982   "Ancient Maya Terraces at Caracol, Belize." Paper presented at the conference Lowland Maya Environment and Agriculture, Minneapolis.

Healy, P. F., C. van Waarden, and T. J. Anderson
1980   "Nueva evidencia de antiguas terrazas mayas en Belice." In *La agricultura intensiva prehispanica*, edited by W. M. Denevan. América Indígena 40, pp. 773–796.

Healy, Paul F., J. D. H. Lambert, J. T. Arnason, and R. J. Hebda
1984   "Caracol, Belize: Evidence of Ancient Maya Agricultural Terraces," *Journal of Field Archaeology* 10:397–410.

Hellmuth, N.
1977   "Cholti-Lacandon (Chiapas) and Peten-Ytza Agriculture, Settlement Pattern, and Population." In *Social Process in Maya Prehistory*, edited by Norman Hammond. Academic Press, New York, pp. 421–448.

Jones, G. D.
1982   "Agriculture and Trade in the Colonial Period: Southern Maya Lowlands." In *Maya Subsistence*, edited by K. V. Flannery. Academic Press, New York, pp. 275–293.

Lambert, J. D. H., and J. T. Arnason
1978   "Distribution of Vegetation on Maya Ruins and Its Relationship to Ancient Land Use," *Turrialba* 28:33–41.

1982   "Ramón and Maya Ruins: An Ecological, Not an Economic Relation," *Science* 216:298–299.

MacNutt, F. A.
1908   *Letters of Cortés*. Letter 5, vol. 2. G. P. Putnam's Sons, New York.

Marcus, J.
1982   "The Plant World of the Sixteenth- and Seventeenth-century Lowland Maya." In *Maya Subsistence*, edited by K. V. Flannery. Academic Press, New York, pp. 239–273.

1983   "Lowland Maya Archaeology at the Crossroads," *American Antiquity* 48. 3: 454–488.

Matheny, R. T.
1976   "Maya Lowland Hydraulic Systems," *Science* 193:639–646.

1978   "Northern Maya Lowland Water-Control Systems." In *Pre-Hispanic Maya Agriculture*, edited by P. D. Harrison and B. L. Turner II. University of New Mexico Press, Albuquerque, pp. 185–210.

1982   "Ancient Lowland and Highland Maya Water and Soil Conservation Strategies." In *Maya Subsistence*, edited by K. V. Flannery. Academic Press, New York, pp. 157–178.

Mathewson, K.
1984   *Irrigation Horticulture in Highland Guatemala: The Tablón System of Panajachel*. Westview Press, Boulder.

Maybury-Lewis, D.
1967   *Akwẽ-Shavante Society*. Clarendon Press, Oxford.

Miksicek, C.
1979   "The Mayan Dooryard Garden." Manuscript in the possession of the author.

1983   "Macrofloral Remains of the Pulltrouser Area: Settlements and Fields." In *Pulltrouser Swamp: Ancient Maya Habitat, Agriculture, and Settlement*, edited by B. L. Turner and P. D. Harrison. University of Texas Press, Austin, pp. 94–104.

Miksicek, C. H., R. McK. Bird, B. Pickersgill, S. Donaghey, J. Cartwright, and N. Hammond
1981a   "Preclassic Lowland Maize from Cuello, Belize," *Nature* 289:56–59.

Miksicek, C. H., K. J. Elsesser, I. A. Wuebber, K. O. Bruhns, and N. Hammond
1981b   "Rethinking Ramón: A Comment on Reina and Hill's Lowland Maya Subsistence," *American Antiquity* 46:916–919.

Pohl, M.
1980   "The Terminal Late Classic Period Economy at Tikal." Paper presented at the 45th annual meeting of the Society for American Archaeology, Philadelphia.

Puleston, D. E.
1971 "An Experimental Approach to the Function of Classic Maya Chultuns," *American Antiquity* 36:322–326.
1977 "The Art and Archaeology of Hydraulic Agriculture in the Maya Lowlands." In *Social Process in Maya Prehistory*, edited by N. Hammond. Academic Press, London, pp. 449–467.

Reina, R. E., and R. M. Hill II
1980 "Lowland Maya Subsistence: Notes from Ethnohistory and Ethnography," *American Antiquity* 45:74–79.

Rice, D. S.
1978 "Population Growth and Subsistence Alternatives in a Tropical Lacustrine Environment." In *Pre-Hispanic Maya Agriculture*, edited by P. D. Harrison and B. L. Turner II. University of New Mexico Press, Albuquerque, pp. 35–61.
1982 "The Central Petén Grasslands: Genesis, Dynamics and Land Use." Paper presented at the conference Lowland Maya Environment and Agriculture, Minneapolis.

Rice, D. S., and P. M. Rice
1981 "Muralla de Leon: A Lowland Maya Fortification," *Journal of Field Archaeology* 8:271–288.

Roys, R. L.
1943 *The Indian Background of Colonial Yucatán.* Carnegie Institution of Washington, Publication 548.

Ruppert, K., and J. H. Dennison
1943 *Archaeological Reconnaissance in Campeche, Quintana Roo and Petén.* Carnegie Institution of Washington, Publication 543.

Sabloff, J. A., and W. L. Rathje
1975 *Changing Pre-Columbian Commercial Systems.* Peabody Museum Monographs, no. 3, Harvard University.

Sanders, W. T.
1979 "The Jolly Green Giant in Tenth Century Yucatán, or Fact and Fancy in Classic Maya Agriculture," *Reviews in Anthropology* 6:493–506.

Scarborough, V. L.
1983 "A Preclassic Maya Water System," *American Antiquity* 43:720–744.

Sheets, P. D.
1979 "Maya Recovery from Volcanic Disaster: Ilopongo and Cerén," *Archaeology* 32:32–42.
1982 "Prehistoric Agricultural Systems in El Salvador." In *Maya Subsistence*, edited by K. V. Flannery. Academic Press, New York, pp. 99–118.

Siemens, A. H.
1980 "Reconsidering the Raised Fields of Tropical Lowland Mexico and Central America." Manuscript in the possession of the editor.
1982 "Prehispanic Agricultural Use of the Wetlands of Northern Belize." In *Maya Subsistence*, edited by K. V. Flannery. Academic Press, New York, pp. 205–225.
1983 "Oriented Raised Fields in Central Veracruz," *American Antiquity* 48:85–102.

Stenholm, Nancy A.
1984 "Views from the Floor: Botanical Remains from an Early Classic House at Kaminaljuyu, Guatemala." Paper presented at the 7th Annual Ethnobiology Conference, Seattle, Wash.

Thomas, P. M., Jr.
1974 "Prehistoric Settlement at Becan: A Preliminary Report." In *Preliminary Reports on Archaeological Investigations: The Río Bec Area, Campeche, Mexico.* Tulane University Middle American Research Institute, Publication 31.

Tozzer, A. M.
1941 *Landa's Relación de las cosas de Yucatán.* Peabody Museum Papers, no. 18, Harvard University.

Turner, B. L., II
1974a "Prehistoric Intensive Agriculture in the Mayan Lowlands," *Science* 185:118–124.
1974b "Prehistoric Intensive Agriculture in the Mayan Lowlands: New Evidence from the Río Bec Region." Ph.D. dissertation, Department of Geography, University of Wisconsin, Madison. University Microfilms, Ann Arbor.
1979 "Prehistoric Terracing in the Central Maya Lowlands: Problems of Agricultural Intensification." In *Maya Archaeology and Ethnohistory*, edited by N. Hammond and G. R. Willey. University of Texas Press, Austin, pp. 103–115.
1982 "Review of *Maya Subsistence*, edited by K. V. Flannery," *Science* 217:345–346.
1983a *Once Beneath the Forest: Prehistoric Terracing in the Río Bec Region of the Maya Lowlands.* Dellplain Latin American Series no. 13. Westview Press, Boulder.
1983 "Constructional Inputs for Major Agrosystems of the Ancient Maya." In *Drained Field Agriculture in Central and South America*, edited by J. P. Darch. British Archaeological Reports, International Series 189, Oxford.

Turner, B. L., II, and W. M. Denevan
In   "Prehistoric Manipulation of Wetlands in
press   the Americas: A Raised-Field Perspective."
          In *Prehistoric Intensive Agriculture in the
          Tropics*, edited by I. Farrington. British Ar-
          chaeological Reports, International Series,
          Oxford.

Turner, B. L., II, and P. D. Harrison
1981   "Prehistoric Raised-Field Agriculture in the
          Maya Lowlands," *Science* 213:399-405.

Turner, B. L., II, and P. D. Harrison, editors
1983   *Pulltrouser Swamp: Ancient Maya Habitat,
          Agriculture, and Settlement in Northern
          Belize*. University of Texas Press, Austin.

Turner, B. L., II, and W. C. Johnson
1979   "A Maya Dam in the Copan Valley, Hon-
          duras," *American Antiquity* 44:299-305.

Turner, B. L., II, and Charles H. Miksicek
1984   "Economic Plant Species Associated with
          Prehistoric Agriculture in the Maya
          Lowlands," *Economic Botany* 38. 2:179-193.

Vaughan, H. H.
1979   "Prehistoric Disturbance of Vegetation in
          the Area of Lake Yaxha, Petén,
          Guatemala." Ph.D. dissertation, University
          of Florida. University Microfilms, Ann Ar-
          bor.

Viana, F. P. de, L. Gallego, and G. Cadena
1955   "Relación de la Provincia de la Verapaz
          hecha por los religiosos de Santo Domingo
          de Coban. 2 de diciembre de 1954." *Anales
          de la Sociedad de Geographía e Historia de
          Guatemala* 28:18-31.

Webster, D. L.
1974   *The Fortification of Becan, Campeche,
          Mexico*. Tulane University, Middle
          American Research Institute 31.

Wilk, R. R.
1981   "Agriculture, Ecology and Domestic
          Organization among the Kekchi Maya."
          Ph.D. dissertation, University of Arizona.
          University Microfilms, Ann Arbor.

Wiseman, F. M.
1981   *San Antonio: A Late Holocene Record of
          Agricultural Activity in the Maya
          Lowlands*. Louisiana State University,
          Quarternary Paleoecology Laboratory 9.
1982   "Palynology in Northern Belize." Paper
          presented at the conference Lowland Maya
          Environment and Agriculture, Minneapolis.
1983   "Subsistence and Complex Societies: The
          Case of the Maya." In *Advances in Ar-
          chaeological Method and Theory*, vol. 6,
          edited by Michael B. Schiffer. Academic
          Press, New York, pp. 143-189.

Chapter 2

Analysis of Sedimentation and Agriculture along the Río Hondo, Northern Belize

Paul R. Bloom, Mary Pohl, and Julie Stein

The late Dennis Puleston's (1977, 1978) excavations at San Antonio Río Hondo, northern Belize, contributed to the hypothesis that wetland cultivation allowed the Lowland Maya to support large populations in the tropical forest environment during the Preclassic and particularly during the Classic periods. We have re-examined Puleston's evidence and have concluded that the subject of wetland cultivation is more complex than previously thought.

We believe that fields at San Antonio were probably cultivated during the Preclassic period, though cultivation in swampy terrain may have continued elsewhere. At San Antonio the Maya first practiced river flood-plain cultivation during the dry season, and later they ditched their fields possibly in response to rising water levels associated with a marine transgression. These Late Preclassic fields at San Antonio are therefore ditched fields rather than raised fields. The practice of ditching may have a long history among the Maya extending from Preclassic through early historic times (chap. 3), but this technique of wetland exploitation may result in soil salt accumulation sufficient to hinder cultivation of some crops.

Study Area

The study site is located in the flood plain of a secondary channel of the Río Hondo near the village of San Antonio, northern Belize (18°10′ N, 88°40′ W; fig.

A brief summary of this work appeared in *Nature* 301 (1983).

Paul R. Bloom is associate professor, Department of Soil Science, University of Minnesota, St. Paul. Julie Stein is assistant professor, Department of Anthropology and Quarternary Research Center, University of Washington, Seattle. See chapter 1 for Mary Pohl's affiliation.

The authors wish to thank H. E. Wright, Jr., for comments, particularly on the question of Holocene sea level rise and analogies to salt accumulation in irrigation projects in Iraq. Liz Bjorkman typed and provided editorial help. Funding for this research was provided by the International Agriculture Programs of the College of Agriculture, University of Minnesota, Florida State University, and the Wenner-Gren Foundation for Anthropological Research. The chapter was written while Pohl was a Tinker Foundation postdoctoral fellow.

2.1). The climate is tropical wet-dry in Koeppen's classification. The mean annual rainfall measured at nearby Orange Walk Town is 1,500 mm and varies from 35 mm in March and April to 280 mm in September. The mean annual temperature exceeds 24° C (Wright et al. 1959). The natural vegetation of the flood plain is high marsh forest; deciduous-seasonal forest characterizes the uplands (Wright et al. 1959).

The Río Hondo, which splits in two channels to form Albion Island, flows through a relatively flat, low-lying, karstic landscape. The highest point in the area is the center of Albion Island, which rises to 47 m above sea level.

Folding in the bedrock (McDonald 1979) provides structural control for the river floodplain, which varies in width from 0.5 to 1 km. The river at San Antonio is 65 m wide and up to 7 m deep. Height is 2 m above sea level, and from San Antonio the river flows 75 km into the Caribbean Sea. The gradient of the river is low; there is little visible surface flow except during and after storms.

River gauge data for 1975–77 show that the normal high stage during the wet season is 1 m above the dry season low. A hurricane flood in 1976 overtopped the recorder. Since the Río Hondo Project was initiated in 1973, hurricane floods have occurred in 1976, 1979, and 1980. Local informants report that hurricane floods can exceed normal wet season water levels by more than 2 m.

Antoine, Skarie, and Bloom (1982) reported that the river gauge data suggest tidal variations in river level. We re-examined the data and came to the conclusion that, since the diurnal variations coincided with sunrise and sunset, they were probably the result of solar heating of the recorder.

The soil parent material in the flood plain is calcareous alluvial clay. In the uplands the parent materials are limestone and poorly indurated limestone and chalk, locally called *sascab*, which contains finely divided quartz and gypsum (Wright et al. 1959). On Albion Island well-indurated limestone overlies poorly indurated limestone (Olson 1975).

The upland soils on Albion Island have been classified as Mollisols (Olson 1975) according to the U.S. Department of Agriculture Soil Taxonomy. The

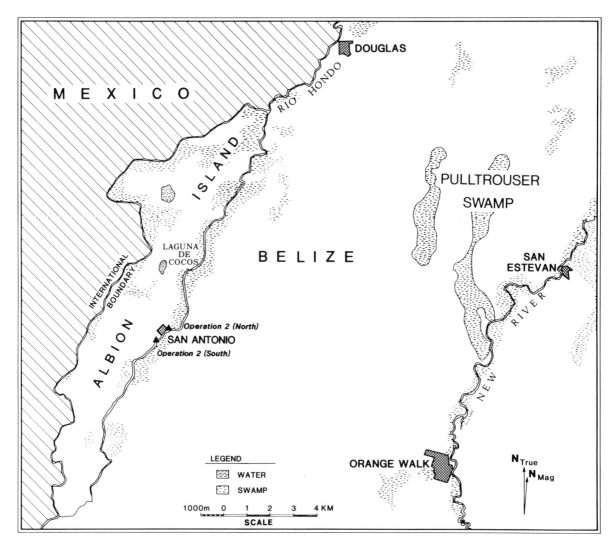

Figure 2.1. Map of San Antonio
region of northern Belize indicating
location of Operations 2 (North) and
2 (South).

most common soils of the region are Rendols (Aubert
and Tavernier 1972). The soils in the study site are
Tropaquents.

Excavation in San Antonio's Wetland Fields

Puleston's excavations conducted in 1973 and 1974
focused on two areas southwest and northeast of the
village of San Antonio (fig. 2.1). Most of the pits and
trenches were at Operation (Op.) 2 (North), including
2B, 2J, and 2W (fig. 2.2). Here the distance from the
edge of the river to the edge of the flood plain is only
80 m. The microrelief in this narrow flood plain sug-

gests irregular convex platforms with shallow concave
ditches. The platforms rise 0.5 m above the bottom of
the ditches. At the height of the rainy season most of
the ditches fill with water, but water does not cover
the platforms. The site has a herbaceous vegetative
cover because grazing livestock and clearance for mos-
quito control have prevented invasion by the native
high marsh forest.

Puleston (1978) postulated two stages of field use.
He believed that the fields were "initially built up out
of flood plain sediments and . . . at a later date were
converted to laboriously constructed limestone marl
platforms." The primary evidence for Stage 1 was the
banded appearance of dark sediments in Trench 2W
(Puleston 1978, fig. 12.4; fig. 2.3 in this chapter).
Puleston thought that the Maya repeatedly placed
muck from canals dug around the fields on top of the
platform surfaces in order to renew fertility. He proposed a second phase of field building on the basis of
the characteristics of the upper sediments of Trenches

2B (fig. 2.4) and 2J, which he called marl, together with the presence of a small number of poorly preserved ceramics, which he thought demonstrated the presence of cultivators.

In 1977 soil scientists Antoine, Skarie, and Bloom (1982) investigated soils at Op. 2 (South) and concluded that although the Maya may have ditched and farmed in the flood plain of the Rio Hondo, there was no compelling evidence for laborious construction of Stage 2 platforms. Soil characteristics at Op. 2 (South)

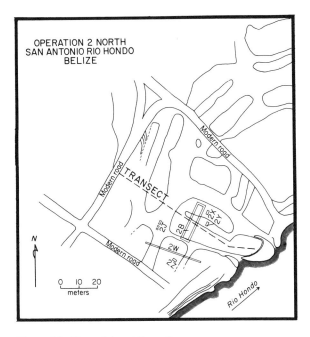

Figure 2.2. *Map of site at Operation 2 (North), San Antonio, Belize. Pits 2B, 2J, and 2W excavated by Puleston in 1973 and 1974. Pits 2X, 2Y, 2Z, and transect by Bloom, Pohl, and Buttleman in 1980.*

Figure 2.3. *Soil stratigraphy in Trench 2W, opened by Puleston in 1973. Horizon designations correspond to those in 2B (fig. 2.4). Numerical designations do not imply chronological sequence of events.*

could not be correlated with Op. 2 (North) on the basis of Puleston's excavation notes. Therefore, soil chemist Bloom and archaeologist Pohl, accompanied by field pedologist Buttleman, returned to San Antonio in 1980 to gather soil samples at Op. 2 (North). Geomorphologist Stein returned with Pohl in 1982 to survey the Río Hondo.

In 1980 we obtained pollen, botanical, mollusc, and soil samples from three 1 by 2 m pits (2X, 2Y, 2Z) by excavating to a depth of 2 m and using a bucket auger to obtain deeper samples. We traced the lateral extent of deposits with a 75 m transect running from river's edge to bedrock outcrop (figs. 2.2 and 2.5). Soils were probed to a depth of 2 m at 8 m intervals along the transect. We also took samples of surface soil and water at selected locations in the region. This chapter presents the results of our analyses since 1980.

We differentiated soil stratigraphic units by color, morphology, organic carbon content, and calcium carbonate content (table 2.1; figs. 2.6, 2.7, 2.8, and 2.9). All the soil samples analyzed contained calcite, quartz, montmorillonite, and kaolinite, and some samples also contained gypsum. Calcite, the only carbonate mineral identified, was found in quantities ranging from 2 to 78 percent (figs. 2.6 and 2.9). Because of the calcite, soil pH values were high, ranging from 6.8 to 7.5. Calcite was probably deposited biogenically and by direct precipitation from solution. Gypsum was probably deposited from solution.

Since we were interested in the conditions of deposition of the silicate minerals (quartz, montmorillonite, and kaolinite), we removed the calcite and gypsum before we did mechanical analysis for particle size determination. We found that unless we removed the gypsum, we got variable data, specifically elevated values for sand and silt.[1] In the field, Buttleman classified the samples as clay loams or silty clays. On the basis of laboratory data, we classified all the

———————

1. Clays were separated by sedimentation and determined by x-ray diffraction of oriented films on glass slides after treatment with K^+ or Mg^{2+} plus glycerol. Calcite was removed by treatment with pH 4 ammonium acetate, and gypsum was removed by dialysis against $(NaPO_3)_6$. Without careful removal of the gypsum, the soils did not disperse well.

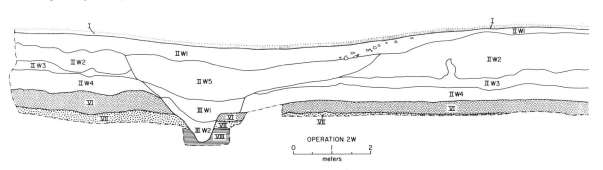

OPERATION 2W

0   1   2
meters

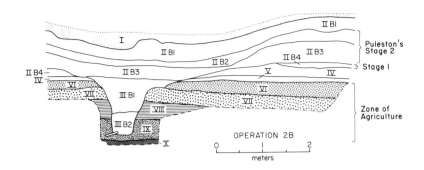

Figure 2.4. Soil stratigraphy in Trench 2B, opened by Puleston in 1973. Horizon designations based on Puleston's field notes and field and laboratory data of Bloom, Pohl, and Buttleman for Pits 2X, 2Y, and 2Z.

Table 2.1. Description and color of soil units, as pictured in figures 2.3 and 2.4.

Designation	Description	Color[a]
I	Clay[b] topsoil, 4–8% o.c.[c]	Brownish black (10YR 3/1)
II	Clay, o.c. <2% over the ancient fields, o.c. 4–10% in the ditches	Light gray (2.5Y 7/1) Brownish gray (10YR 5/1) Yellowish gray (2.5YR 4/1)
III	Shelly clay canal fill, o.c. $\simeq 4\%$	Brownish gray (10YR 4/1)
IV	Shelly marl, o.c. <1.5%	Light gray (2.5Y 7/1)
V	Shelly marl, o.c. $\simeq 6\%$	Yellowish gray (2.5Y 5/1)
VI	High organic carbon clay, o.c. $\simeq 8\%$, many shells	Yellowish gray (2.5Y 4/1) with brownish black (2.5Y 3/1) charcoal fragments
VII	Clay with peaty bands, o.c. $\simeq 8\%$, few shells	Yellowish gray (2.5Y 6/1) and (2.5Y 4/1) with black (2.5Y 2/1) fragments in the bands
VIII	Banded peat, o.c. $\simeq 16\%$	Yellowish gray (2.5Y 6/1) and (2.5Y 4/1) with black (2.5Y 2/1) fragments in the bands
IX	Sapric peat, o.c. $\simeq 20\%$	Black (10YR 2/1)
X	Gleyed clay	Gray (N 5/0)

a. Munsell colors.

b. Laboratory classification after removal of calcium carbonate and gypsum.

c. o.c. = organic carbon.

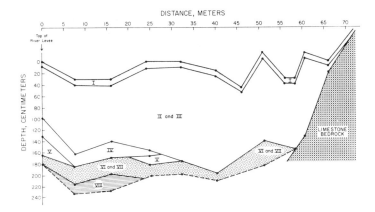

samples as clays. Quartz was the only mineral in the sand fraction. The clay fraction consisted of mont-morillonite with small quantities of kaolinite and quartz.

Sea Level Rise and Regional Stratigraphy

The stratigraphic units record three principal events: deposition of a noncultural substrate of clay (Unit X); a period of agricultural activity and peat accumulation interrupted by sporadic natural sedimentation (Units VI–IX); and finally burial of the field surface under 1.5 m of organic-poor clay (Units I–V). These depositional events were also recorded in the stratigraphy of Op. 2 (South) (Antoine, Skarie, and Bloom 1982). We believe that this sequence can be related in part to a marine transgression.

In his study of the coastal sediments of northern Belize, High (1975) discovered evidence of a rise in sea level. The evidence consisted of 44 subsurface cores taken along the northern coast of Belize. The transgressive sequence resulted in the deposition of three stratigraphic units: (1) a basal gleyed clay interpreted "to have been deposited on a low, grass-covered inland meadow"; (2) a fibrous peat produced by debris from mangroves, whose growth is restricted to a zone from shore to a few feet below sea level. The presence of the mangrove peat indicates that "as the sea rose, . . . the narrow zone suitable for abundant mangrove growth rapidly shifted westward over the land surface." (3) calcareous mud interpreted as resulting from sedimentation occurring in mud-flats and lagoons. "From the initial mangrove swamp at sea level, continued sedimentation raised the surface until mangroves no longer flourished." (High 1975:85–87)

This sequence is similar to the stratigraphic record preserved in the San Antonio fields (fig. 2.4, table 2.1). Unit X is a basal clay corresponding to High's

Unit 1 basal gleyed clays. Units IX and VIII are peats; Units VII and VI are clays high in organic matter. The San Antonio peats are not mangrove peats (like High's Unit 2), but San Antonio is 75 km upstream from the coast, and the plant community would have been different. The other units observed at San Antonio (Units V–II) are all part of a sequence equivalent to High's Unit 3, calcareous muds. Units V–II probably resulted from continued sedimentation below the water table. Because so much sedimentation has occurred, the fields are today only under water during exceedingly high floods, such as those produced by hurricanes. We believe that the rise in river base level, caused by the sea level rise, contributed to a fairly rapid accumulation of peat and calcareous clay. Only in relatively recent times has the river achieved a more or less steady state with its new base level.

Past Agricultural Activity

Stratigraphic and Economic Evidence

The peat units (VIII and IX) and the organic-rich clay units (VI–VII) represent agricultural activity at Op. 2 (North). Sediments contain 0.75 to 2 percent maize pollen (Wiseman, in press) and abundant fragments of carbonized maize stem (Miksicek 1982).

Gossypium pollen also occurred in the peat units, though generally in smaller quantities (0.25 to 1 percent) than corn pollen (Wiseman, in press). The *Gossypium* may well be cultivated cotton. The relative importance of corn and cotton is difficult to evaluate. Since *Gossypium* is insect-pollinated, pollen would only be deposited in the soil where a flower had fallen on the ground. Corn pollen can be blown in from distances of a mile or more. The predominance of corn stem fragments in the macrobotanical sample suggests that corn production was more prevalent in wetland fields.

The data suggest that the Maya cropped wetlands only during the dry season. On the one hand, the units contain 16–20 percent organic carbon, 29–36 percent organic matter, indicating waterlogged conditions. Organic-poor, light colored bands found within the peat of Units VII and VIII demonstrate that sediment was accumulating, most likely during high water stages of the wet season. The variation in particle size distribution of silicate minerals might suggest that changes occurred in depositional environments (fig. 2.7). The calcium plus magnesium concentration in the Río Hondo water is, however, in excess of 10 meq/l, which is sufficient to cause clay flocculation (van Olphen 1963). Thus, any clay particles in the river water would be present as aggregates of larger than clay size, and it is difficult to infer much about the conditions of deposition.

The presence of fresh water molluscs also suggests that during this period, the habitat was wet or flooded much of the time. Covich (personal communication, 1981) has identified the dominant species as *Cochliopina, Pyrgophorus,* and *Pomacea* in relative order of abundance. *Pomacea* is common where water rises and falls seasonally. *Pyrgophorus* indicates continuous moisture. The environment may have been typical of a lake with occasionally fluctuating water depths or of a river margin with relatively stable and frequent invasion from the river habitat. The shells of dead snails can float, and flood waters may have deposited some shells. Nevertheless, the idea that soil was moist at least much of the year is supported by the high organic matter content of the soil in Units VIII and IX, discussed above.

The fields were relatively dry at some point, presumably during the dry season, since cultivation of an upland crop like maize requires that the water table be below the rooting zone. Therefore, we infer that the Maya must have practiced seasonal cultivation, taking advantage of the period of lowest water table.

The clarity of the banding in Units VII and VIII is not what one would expect if the Maya had employed soil tillage. Nevertheless, high organic carbon content, abundant *Zea* pollen, and numerous corn macrofossils (see Pohl, in press) have convinced us that agriculture was involved. Perhaps the farmers planted with dibble sticks and cut the weeds.

The analyses for potassium, phosphorus, and nitrogen show that Units VI–IX are fertile (fig. 2.8). The high analysis for potassium (120 ppm) is difficult to extrapolate to ancient conditions because potassium is mobile. Phosphorus and nitrogen, are not very mobile, however. Total phosphorus is moderate in Units VI–VIII but high in IX.

Wiseman's (in press) pollen analysis reveals surprisingly low percentages of arboreal pollen. *Terminalia*-type, *Quercus,* and *Moraceae* each constitute less than 5 percent of the total pollen. These figures are the lowest yet recorded for northern Belize. The evidence suggests that the Maya had cleared a substantial amount of the forest vegetation in the vicinity of the wetland fields at San Antonio. We believe that they were practicing dry season cultivation on river banks in conjunction with agriculture on uplands during the wet season.

Dating Maya Agriculturalists

Maya cultivators were active on the Río Hondo flood plain well before the florescence of Maya culture. A sample of maize charcoal from Unit IX in Puleston's Op. 2J yielded an uncorrected date of 2620 ± 190 radiocarbon years (DIC 2120). If the carbon isotope fractionation in maize is considered, the reported date may be too young by some 200 years.

Our maize date is close to one Puleston obtained earlier. A hewn post also found in Op. 2J dated at 3060 ± 230 radiocarbon years (uncorrected) (Puleston 1977). One end of the 120 cm post was in the basal clay, and the post lay at a 45° angle from the vertical transecting Units IX, VIII, and VII. Its top penetrated the bottom of a ditch. We are uncertain which unit is to be associated with the deposition of the post, but the artifact may well be contemporary with the charred maize stems, which yielded a similar radiocarbon date. These dates suggest that the Maya practiced wetland agriculture at least by the transition between the Early and Middle Preclassic period.

Ditching

The San Antonio excavations reveal that the Maya later began ditching their riverbank fields. We suspect that the Maya found they had to drain their fields because the water table was rising in response to rising sea level. The ancient ditches at our site were spaced 12 to 20 m apart and varied in depth (as measured from the top of Unit VI, the ancient surface) from 0.5 to 1.0 m. The bottom of one of the ditches was dug into Unit IX and almost to Unit X (fig. 2.4). The bottom of another ditch was in Unit VIII (fig. 2.3), while the bottom of the third ditch was in Unit VII. With the accretion of clayey sediment, the Maya probably had to dig more ditches to provide adequate drainage. The narrow ditch dug into the field exposed in Trench 2B (our Pits 2X and 2Y) was probably put in at a later time than the adjacent ditches. Eventually high water resulted in the termination of agriculture.

High (1975) dates the proposed sea level rise that led to rising water at San Antonio by comparing his sequence to the one reported by Scholl (1964; Scholl, Craighead, and Stuiver 1969) in southern Florida. The Florida sea level curve, which is based on 72 radiocarbon measurements taken on fibrous peats, calcitic mud, and shells, indicates that sea level has risen continuously, though at a generally decreasing rate, dur-

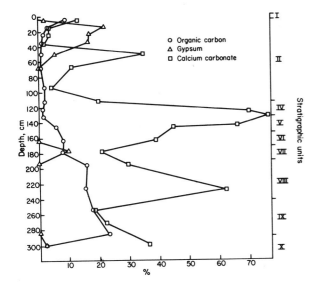

Figure 2.6. Organic carbon, gypsum, and calcium carbonate in Pit 2X.

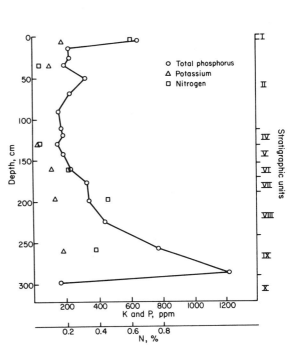

Figure 2.8. Total nitrogen, exchangeable potassium, and total phosphorus in Pit 2X.

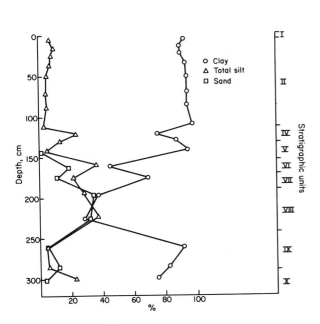

Figure 2.7. Silicate mineral particle size distribution in Pit 2X.

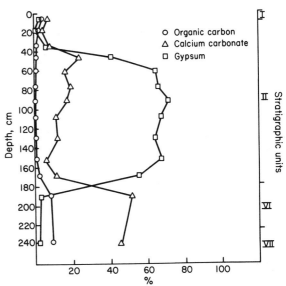

Figure 2.9. Organic carbon, gypsum, and calcium carbonate in Pit 2Z.

ing the last 5,000 years. Land has been submerged at a rate averaging close to 3.5 cm/100 years during the last 4,000 years.

Archaeological evidence points to a date for the submergence of river bank fields at San Antonio. In more recent 1982, 1983 excavations, a Terminal Preclassic sherd turned up near the top of the dark unit (probably equivalent to IX), and a Late Classic sherd lot was recovered from the top of ditched fields signaling abandonment (Ball, personal communication, 1983).

Modern Agriculturalists

Today peasants practice wetland cultivation in many areas of Mexico and Belize (Nigh 1981; Wilk 1981; Orozco-Segovia and Gliessman 1979; Coe and Diehl 1980; Siemens 1980). Most descriptions of wetland agriculture have focused on river bank cultivation, but farmers around Lake Petén and Tikal in central and northern Petén, Guatemala, regularly plant dry season crops in *bajos* (Cowgill 1961; Wiseman, personal communication, 1981; Pohl 1973–74).

Productivity varies. In wetland fields of southern Belize (Wilk, chap. 4), yields per unit of land and labor are slightly less than for upland swidden. On the Coatzacoalcos River, near the Olmec site of San Lorenzo, river bank soils are 55 percent more productive than upland soils even though farmers can only plant in wetlands during the dry season (Coe and Diehl 1980:69). We have already noted that soil fertility was high in ancient wetland fields at San Antonio. The presence of abundant fish bones, primarily Cichlidae (Wing, personal communication, 1981), suggests that the Preclassic Maya worked to make the soil more productive.

Most modern wetland cultivators do not use fire. Siemens (1980) is the only investigator to report the practice of burning in connection with wetland cultivation in Central America. Nevertheless, burning may have been the most effective way of keeping vegetation down before the introduction of metal tools. Carbonized botanical fragments at San Antonio indicate that Preclassic Maya fired the land, probably to clear wet season herbaceous cover. Burning just after harvest may also have helped control crop pests by destroying some of the weed seeds as well as maize pathogens.

The spacing of the San Antonio ditches is appropriate for peat drainage using shallow ditches. Modern cultivators in Malaysia drain peat lands using 1 m deep ditches dug at 20–40 m intervals (Coulter 1950). The narrower spacing is used for clayey peats. Some of these cultivators practice burning that sometimes includes destruction of the surface layer of the peat to release potassium, phosphorus, and micronutrients.

Unlike the prehistoric and early historic Maya, the present-day lowland agriculturalists of Mesoamerica apparently do not ditch their wetland fields. In the Guatemalan Highlands at Aguacatan, Mathewson (1984) described *tablones*, planting beds that are ditched to provide both removal of floodwaters and dry season irrigation. Irrigation at the height of the dry season, as well as drainage, might have been an important function of Preclassic ditches in the Lowlands too.

Post-agricultural Deposition

The termination of agriculture at San Antonio is marked by the deposition of Units IV and V (fig. 2.4), which are composed of a shelly marl that is more than 70 percent calcium carbonate (fig. 2.6). The distribution and relative densities of molluscan species (*Cochliopina* > *Pyrgophorus* > *Biomphalaria* > *Pomacea* > *Stenophysa* > *Gundlachia*) suggest permanent shallow water (littoral zone) over a period of several hundred years with possible fluctuations in water level resulting from river flooding (Covich, personal communication, 1981). The shells are probably natural accumulations rather than midden refuse. *Pomacea* is the only possible economic species, and most individuals are too small to have been a food source. Units IV and V were the only ones with adult individuals. The surface of most of the shells was in excellent and unbroken condition, contrary to what one would expect if the animals had been cooked. Unit III, a shelly clay canal fill, would have been contemporary with Units IV and V.

The soils exhibited variability. Units IV and V, the shelly marl, do not occur in the ditches, nor do they cover all the ancient fields (figs. 2.3, 2.4, and 2.5). Difference in water depth is most likely a significant factor in accounting for the discontinuous nature of these units. The shelly marl was deposited under conditions of relatively shallow water. Water in the ditches (Unit III) would have been deep much of the year. This would have been a different depositional environment, and a different assemblage of molluscs would have lived there. Units IV and V were not found in the trench at 2W (fig. 2.3). In this trench the top of Unit VI was 40 cm above the top of Unit VI at 2B (fig. 2.4), and the water was probably not deep enough to accumulate a shelly marl.

Unit II is a complex unit of fine-grained yellowish to brownish gray clay. In Pit 2Z the soil is not uniform but has streaks of light gray. The silicate mineral fraction is over 90 percent clay and contains no sand. The organic matter content is relatively low; organic carbon is less than 2 percent. The density of snails is low throughout most of the unit, and the species composition is similar to that of Units VIII and IX. A small number of poorly preserved ceramic fragments occurred in Unit II. The ceramic types range from Terminal Preclassic and Protoclassic to Terminal Late Classic (Ball, in press) with some vertical mixing. In addition, we found limestone fragments weighing as much as 450 g, along with sandstone and a worked fragment of chert.

The mixing of the ceramics and the existence of the stones would seem to provide evidence that Unit II was deposited while the Maya were cultivating. This was Puleston's reasoning. Nevertheless, botanical, pollen, and soil evidence suggests that little if any agriculture can be associated with Unit II and that natural deposition is the most reasonable explanation for the accumulation of this unit. The concentration of botanical remains of economic species is lacking. The only pollen of an economic genus is *Zea*, which is 0.75 percent of the total pollen. *Zea* pollen could have blown in from nearby *milpas*. The nitrogen, phosphorus, and potassium contents of samples from Unit II are low (fig. 2.8), indicating that the soil was low in fertility. The calcium carbonate peak at the 60 cm depth (fig. 2.6) corresponds to a zone of mollusc deposition in 2X (fig. 2.4), with a relative abundance of molluscan species similar to that found in Units IV and V. The finding suggests that this zone of Unit II was also deposited under permanent shallow water.

We believe that the accumulation of rock fragments and the vertical mixing of the ceramic debris probably resulted from the close proximity of the study location to a good habitation site on high ground. At San Antonio the distance from the river's edge to firm dry land unaffected by floods is only 80 m. The location of a habitation site near a river was undoubtedly important for a society whose chief mode of transportation was by water. Secondary deposition of soil containing cultural debris and rocks by mass wasting is possible (Stein, in press). This suggestion is corroborated by the fact that at Op. 2 (South), which is farther from high ground and the present-day village, no ceramics were found.

The surface soil, Unit I has the same particle size distribution of minerals as Unit II. The organic matter content, however, is much higher for Unit I; organic carbon is 4–8 percent. The nitrogen, phosphorus, and potassium contents are also higher. The Unit I surface is stable compared to the surfaces formed during the accretion of Unit II, and organic matter has accumulated.

High levels of gypsum occurred in some of the samples of Unit II (figs. 2.6 and 2.9). This is surprising, since gypsum is a relatively soluble mineral and usually accumulates only in soils in arid and semiarid climates (van Alphen and de los Rios Romero 1971). In addition to gypsum accumulation, fine-grained calcite was probably also deposited (figs. 2.6 and 2.9).

Chemical analysis of Río Hondo water showed that it was only slightly undersaturated with respect to gypsum. In the dry season when evapotranspiration greatly exceeds rainfall, the net movement of water is upward. As the soil water is transported upward, it becomes more concentrated with respect to calcium, sulfate, and bicarbonate ions. With sufficient evapotranspiration, the less soluble calcite is deposited followed by deposition of gypsum. At the peak of the wet season, precipitation would be sufficient to cause leaching losses of gypsum and calcite. Nevertheless, because of high water table, the clayey nature of the soil and the convex shape of the surface, most of the precipitation would run off. The greater accumulation of gypsum observed in Pit 2Z (fig. 2.9) compared to Pit 2X (fig. 2.6) probably resulted from greater drying of the surface at 2Z because it is at a higher elevation than at 2X. Seasonal movement of water with solution redistribution of gypsum probably accounts for the nonuniform coloration of Unit II in Pit 2Z (fig. 2.9) (van Alphen and de los Rios Romero 1971; Rust, personal communication, 1980).

Unit VII in Pit 2X contains 10 percent gypsum. This gypsum is probably a residue from the time when Unit VI was the exposed surface. The gypsum content may have been greater at one time, and losses may have occurred either by capillary rise or by percolation of water through the soil. The surface soil in the ditches also contains about 10 percent gypsum deposited by surface evaporation. Calcium carbonate and gypsum are not uniformly deposited in the soil but form light colored mottles.

Turner (chap. 13) challenges our suggestion that relatively little mounding occurred at San Antonio by asking why mounds remain today as surface features. The answer may lie partly in the fact that gypsum and calcium carbonate are soluble; thus, ditches have not filled with sediment to the extent one might expect. In addition, the ancient ditches have continued to provide the path of least resistance for water draining off the floodplain. This water has kept them flushed out.

Along with the gypsum and calcium carbonate, more soluble salts may have been deposited, especially salts of sodium and magnesium. The soil solution electrical conductivity values in Units I and II are moderate to high. (1:2 soil solution; E.C. = 1.6 to 5.0 mmho/cm). The higher value is sufficient to severely limit the production of beans (*Phaseolus vulgaris*) and to cause a reduction in maize yields. Cotton, however, is not affected at these levels of salinity. The salinity data may explain the failure of maize and the success of cotton in Puleston's experimental plots located at Op. 2 (South). This finding also suggests that wetland agriculture may result in problems for the cultivator. The soluble salt question is one of crucial importance in assessing the productivity of ditched fields, and this issue needs further research.

Regional Implications

Surface microrelief similar to that at San Antonio is common in the flood plain of the Río Hondo and in the flood plain of the New River, which is 25 km to the south (fig. 2.1). Agricultural practices similar to those at San Antonio may have been used at other sites, and some of these locations may also have been affected by sea level changes.

Lambert and Arnason (1979) studied a river flood-plain ditched field complex at Barber Creek along the New River, near Lamanai. In a trench across part of one field, they encountered neither a shelly marl deposit nor a buried peat. Their site is further upriver than San Antonio, however, and the effects of a marine transgression may not have registered there. It is also possible that their 2 m trench did not reach such deposits. They did identify a subsurface horizon below about 40 cm that is high in gypsum. Salinity of the surface soils is apparently not great enough to inhibit maize production, because they obtained good maize yields on their experimental plots. Unfortunately, the Barber Creek fields could not be dated.

Fields in depressions (*bajos*) have been excavated at Pulltrouser Swamp, Belize (fig. 2.1), and near Nicolás Bravo, Quintana Roo, Mexico (Turner and Harrison 1981, 1983; Gliessman et al. 1983). Ditches associated with fields in bajos are much wider than those at San Antonio. At Nicolás Bravo the ditches occupy 40 percent of the site. At Pulltrouser Swamp the ditches are 4–7 m wide. When the Maya placed the material excavated from the ditches on the fields, their surfaces were raised to a significantly greater degree than those at San Antonio.

In order to compare fields at San Antonio with those at Pulltrouser Swamp, we used a bucket auger to take samples to a depth of about 1.5 m in both a raised and a channelized field at Pulltrouser Swamp. Using a sampling interval of about 15 cm, we (Bloom and Pohl 1981) found that the soils from 30–130 cm in the Pulltrouser raised field sample contained an average of 62 percent calcium carbonate and gypsum. In some parts of the soil profile, gypsum plus calcium carbonate was 80 percent. This mineral composition is comparable to Pit 2Z at San Antonio. The Pulltrouser raised field contrasts with the channelized field, which contained calcium carbonate but less than 3 percent gypsum. Our results have led us to question whether planting platforms were artificially raised with the addition of upland soils at Pulltrouser Swamp.

Turner and Harrison (1983) argued that the existence of light-colored mottles is one of the lines of evidence for the mixing of soil materials during the building of raised field platforms. Examination of Pulltrouser mottles with an electron microprobe revealed that they are composed of gypsum. After construction of drainage canals, gypsum could have been deposited on raised fields, as well as on the edges of some channelized fields, by upward movement of gypsiferous ground waters and deposition in the soil profile during the dry season as at San Antonio.

Alternatively, the gypsum may be an evaporite deposit from a former shallow lake. Aquatic molluscan species, including *Biomphalaria* and *Pyrgophorus*, indicate that the water in the depression was permanent (Covich 1983). The remains of aquatic flora such as water lilies (*Nymphaea*) (Wiseman 1983) might suggest that the depression was at one point a shallow lake where precipitation of gypsum and calcium carbonate may have contributed to infilling. Seasonal movement of water, which would have increased once the Maya began ditching, would have led to solution redistribution of gypsum producing the mottled appearance (van Alphen and de los Rios Romero 1971; Rust, personal communication, 1980).[2]

Turner (chap. 13) uses variability in particle size as another argument for the artificial character of his raised fields. Based on our experience with soils at San Antonio, we are suspicious about the results of particle size analysis without calcite and gypsum removal.

As at San Antonio, soil solution conductivity measurements at Pulltrouser Swamp indicate that at the present time the soluble salt level is sufficient to limit cultivation of corn and beans. The problem is most acute on the raised fields.

Turner and Harrison (1981, 1983) suggest that the Maya may have begun constructing channelized fields as early as the Late Preclassic period at Pulltrouser Swamp; they think most fields are Late Classic period in date.

Wetland fields have been investigated within the precinct of Cerros, the Late Preclassic ceremonial center near the mouth of the New River (Scarborough 1981, 1983; Freidel and Scarborough 1982). The fields are located in a small depression associated with a major canal system surrounding the site. The ditches are only 1 m wide, and it is not clear whether the Maya used additional earth, perhaps from borrow pits found at the site, to construct raised platforms or whether these are ditched fields like those at San Antonio and Lamanai. Although no gypsum data are available, we do know that the soils have a high salinity, which Scarborough attributes both to evapotranspiration during the dry season and to sea water invasion. Scarborough thinks that the latter is due to hurricanes, though High's (1975) data indicate that the marine transgression could also have played a role.

---

2. Gypsum may be characteristic of hydromorphic environments in the Maya Lowlands. Cowgill and Huchinson (1963) noted gypsum crystals along with unworn flint nodules in sediments of the Bajo de Santa Fe, northern Petén, Guatemala.

Effects of Ditching

Research demonstrates that in the bajos and river flood plains of northern Belize, ditching and the construction of fields in wetlands will lead to gypsum and secondary carbonate accumulation in the subsoil and possibly to the build-up of soluble salts in the rooting zone of agricultural crops. When the native high bush forest of palmetto swamp vegetation is removed and the area is ditched, the ground water is lowered relative to the surface, notably during the dry season. The increased drying of the surface and transpiration of water from a relatively shallow rooting zone of a field crop would result in the upward transport of calcium, magnesium, and sodium sulfate and of bicarbonates by capillary rise. The soluble salts would accumulate nearer the surface. This phenomenon is analogous to the process that leads to salt build-up in irrigation schemes; a historically documented case occurred in the Diyala River region of Iraq (Jacobsen and Adams 1958).

With the rise in water table during the wet season, the surface soil is close to saturation with respect to water content. Since the soil is wet and clayey, rain water will not readily infiltrate and percolate through the profile. Whether soluble salts can accumulate sufficiently to prevent maize production given the 1,500 mm annual rainfall is still an open question. The success of maize on the old ditched fields near Lamanai does not prove that there is no potential for soluble salt accumulation, since this site was forested at the beginning of the experimental cropping and the forest litter layer would promote infiltration of rain water.

Conclusions

The fields at San Antonio are the earliest Maya wetland fields yet found. We conclude that Maya agriculturalists were active at San Antonio by 3000 B.P. or possibly even earlier. The fields at Cerros, Nicolás Bravo, and Pulltrouser Swamp are all thought to have been initiated in the Late Preclassic era or later, that is, after 400 B.C. We think that ditching was a method for the manipulation of poorly drained land. At San Antonio the Maya undertook ditching in response to changes in water table, probably resulting from a marine transgression. The question of Holocene rise in sea level is a controversial subject, and the dating is problematic. Nevertheless, our hypothesis of flooding on the lower reaches of the Río Hondo at the end of the Preclassic period is the one we feel best fits the archaeological and geological evidence available for northern Belize. Ditching wetland fields results in gypsum and secondary carbonate accumulation. Furthermore, ditching may have caused problems with soluble salt accumulation, and research into the salt issue is essential to an assessment of the long-term viability of this ancient agricultural technique.

References

Antoine, P. P., R. L. Skarie, and P. R. Bloom
1982   "The Origin of Raised Fields near San Antonio, Belize: An Alternative Hypothesis." In *Maya Subsistence*, edited by K. V. Flannery. Academic Press, New York, pp. 227–236.

Ashmore, W., editor
1981   *Lowland Maya Settlement Patterns.* School of American Research and University of New Mexico Press, Albuquerque.

Aubert, G., and R. Tavernier
1972   "Soil Survey." In *Soils of the Humid Tropics*, edited by Committee on Tropical Soils, Agricultural Board, National Research Council, National Academy of Sciences, Washington, D.C.

Ball, J. W.
In   "The Ceramics of Albion Island." In *Ancient Maya Wetland Cultivation on Albion Island, Northern Belize*, edited by Mary Pohl. University of Minnesota, Papers in Anthropology.
press

Bloom, P. R., and M. Pohl
1981   "Ancient Exploitation of Wetlands in Northern Belize." Manuscript.

Coe, M. D., and R. A. Diehl
1980   *In the Land of the Olmec.* 2 vols. University of Texas Press, Austin.

Coulter, J. R.
1950   "Peat Formations in Malaya," *Malaya Agriculture Journal* 33:63–81.

Covich, A. P.
1983   "Mollusca: A Contrast in Species Diversity from Aquatic and Terrestrial Habitats." In *Pulltrouser Swamp: Ancient Maya Habitat, Agriculture, and Settlement in Northern Belize*, edited by B. L. Turner and P. D. Harrison. University of Texas Press, Austin, pp. 120–139.

Cowgill, U. M.
1961   "Soil Fertility and the Ancient Maya," *Transactions of the Connecticut Academy of Arts and Sciences* 42:1–56.

Cowgill, U. M., and G. E. Hutchinson
1963   "El Bajo de Santa Fe," *Transactions of the American Philosophical Society* 53:1–51.

Freidel, D. A.
1978   "Maritime Adaptation and the Rise of Maya Civilization: The View from Cerros, Belize." In *Prehistoric Coastal Adaptations*, edited by B. Stark and B. Voorhies. Academic Press, New York, pp. 239–265.

Freidel, D. A. and V. Scarborough
1982   "Subsistence, Trade and Development of the Coastal Maya." In *Maya Subsistence*, edited by K. V. Flannery. Academic Press, New York, pp. 131–155.

Gliessman, S. R., B. L. Turner II, F. J. Rosado May, and M. F. Amador
1983   "Raised Field Agriculture in the Maya Lowlands of Southeastern Mexico." In *Drained Field Agriculture in Central and South America,* edited by J. P. Darch. British Archaeological Reports, International Series 189, pp. 91–110.

Hammond, N.
1981   "Settlement Patterns in Belize." In *Lowland Maya Settlement Patterns*, edited by Wendy Ashmore. School of American Research and University of New Mexico Press, Albuquerque, pp. 157–186.

High, L. R., Jr.
1975   "Geomorphology and Sedimentology of Holocene Coastal Deposits, Belize." In *Belize Shelf: Carbonate Sediments, Clastic Sediments, and Ecology*, edited by K. W. Wantland and W. C. Pusey III. American Association of Petroleum Geologists, Tulsa, pp. 53–96.

Jacobsen, T., and R. McC. Adams
1958   "Salt and Silt in Ancient Mesopotamian Agriculture," *Science* 128:1251–58.

Lambert, J. D. H. and J. T. Arnason
1979   "Raised Field Agriculture Adjacent to the New River Lagoon, Lamanai, Belize." Paper presented at the 43rd International Congress of Americanists, Vancouver.

Mathewson, K.
1984   *Irrigation Horticulture in Highland Guatemala: The Tablón System of Panajachel.* Westview Press, Boulder.

McDonald, R. C.
1979   "Preliminary Report on the Physical Geography of Northern Belize." In *Cuello Project 1978: Interim Report*, edited by Norman Hammond. Archaeological Program, Douglass College, Rutgers University, pp. 79–87.

Miksicek, C. H.
1982   "Plant Macrofossils from Northern Belize: A 3000 Year Record of Maya Agriculture and Its Impact on the Local Environment." Paper presented at the University of Minnesota Conference on Lowland Maya Environment and Agriculture, Minneapolis.

Nigh, R. B.
1981   "Review of Pre-Hispanic Maya Agriculture
        by P. D. Harrison and B. L. Turner II,"
        American Antiquity 46:707–709.

Olson, G. W.
1975   "Study of Soils in the Sustaining Area
        around San Antonio in Northern Belize."
        Cornell University, Agronomy mimeo 75-1.

Orozco-Segovia, A. D. L., and S. Gliessman
1979   "The Marceño in Flood Prone Regions of
        Tabasco, Mexico." Paper presented at the
        43rd International Congress of
        Americanists, Vancouver.

Pohl, M.
1973–   "Field Notes." Material in possession of the
74   author.

Pohl, M., editor
In   *Ancient Maya Wetland Cultivation on Al-*
press   *bion Island, Northern Belize.* University of
        Minnesota, Papers in Anthropology 2.

Puleston, D. E.
1977   "The Art and Archaeology of Hydraulic
        Agriculture in the Maya Lowlands." In
        *Social Process in Maya Prehistory: Studies
        in Memory of Sir Eric Thompson*, edited
        by Norman Hammond. Academic Press,
        London, pp. 449–469.
1978   "Terracing, Raised Fields, and Tree
        Cropping in the Maya Lowlands: A New
        Perspective on the Geography of Power."
        In *Pre-Hispanic Maya agriculture*, edited by
        P. D. Harrison and B. L. Turner II.
        University of New Mexico Press, Albuquer-
        que, pp. 225–246.

Scarborough, V. L.
1980   "The Settlement System in a Late Preclassic
        Maya Community: Cerros, Northern Belize."
        Ph.D. dissertation, Department of
        Anthropology, Southern Methodist
        University.
1983   "A Preclassic Maya Water System,"
        American Antiquity 48:720–744.

Scholl, D. W.
1964   "Recent Sedimentary Record in Mangrove
        Swamps and Rise in Sea Level over the
        Southwestern Coast of Florida, Part 1,"
        Marine Geology 1:334–366.

Scholl, D. W., F. C. Craighead, and M. Stuiver
1969   "Florida Submergence Curve Revised: Its
        Relation to Coastal Sedimentation Rates,"
        Science 163:562–564.

Siemens, A. H.
1980   "Reconsidering the Raised Fields of
        Tropical Lowland Mexico and Central
        America." Manuscript.

Stein, J.
In   "Sedimentation and Maya Agriculture
press   Along Río Hondo, Belize." In *Ancient
        Maya Wetland Cultivation on Albion
        Island, Northern Belize*, edited by Mary
        Pohl. University of Minnesota, Papers in
        Anthropology 2.

Turner, B. L., II, and P. D. Harrison
1981   "Prehistoric Raised Field Agriculture in the
        Maya Lowlands," *Science* 213:399–405.

Turner, B. L., and P. D. Harrison, editors
1983   *Pulltrouser Swamp. Ancient Maya Habitat,
        Agriculture, and Settlement in Northern
        Belize.* University of Texas Press, Austin.

van Alphen, J. G., and F. de los Rios Romero
1971   *Gypsiferous Soils: Notes on Their
        Characteristics and Management.* Interna-
        tional Institute for Land Reclamation and
        Improvement. Wageningen, the Netherlands.

van Olphen, H.
1963   *An Introduction to Clay Colloid Chemistry
        for Clay Technologists, Geologists and Soil
        Scientists.* Interscience Publishers, New York.

Wilk, R. R.
1981   "Agriculture, Ecology, and Domestic
        Organization among the Kekchi Maya."
        Ph.D. dissertation, Department of An-
        thropology, University of Arizona. Univer-
        sity Microfilms, Ann Arbor.

Wiseman, F. M.
1983   "Analysis of Pollen from the Fields at
        Pulltrouser Swamp." In *Pulltrouser Swamp:
        Ancient Maya Habitat, Agriculture, and
        Settlement in Northern Belize*, edited by B.
        L. Turner, II and P. D. Harrison. Universi-
        ty of Texas Press, Austin, pp. 105–119.
In   "San Antonio: A Late Holocene Record of
press   Agricultural Activity in the Maya
        Lowlands." In *Ancient Maya Wetland
        Cultivation on Albion Island, Northern
        Belize.* University of Minnesota, Publica-
        tion in Anthropology 2.

Wright, A. C. S., D. H. Romney, R. H. Arbuckle,
and V. E. Vial
1959   *Land in British Honduras.* Colonial Re-
        search Publication 24. Her Majesty's Sta-
        tionery Office, London.

Chapter 3

An Ethnohistorical Perspective on Ancient Maya Wetland Fields and Other Cultivation Systems in the Lowlands

Mary Pohl

The Spaniards have left us observations on Maya agricultural practices scattered among their accounts of the New World. One can cull these sources for early observations to compare with the archaeological record. This chapter focuses on evidence for wetland field and canal systems and water management in general.

Researchers have concentrated on ancient Maya fields. The Maya economic system must be viewed as a complex of traits that included cultivation, preservation, storage, and transportation.

Ethnohistoric Literature

The eyewitness accounts of the first Europeans to enter the Maya domain are our primary sources. After Cortés crossed the lowlands in 1525, he sent a letter to Charles V, providing details of the settlements he encountered because he was anxious to impress the emperor with his efforts at converting the natives (MacNutt 1908). Bernal Díaz, who accompanied Cortés on his historic march, had an observant eye and a keen memory: he did not compose his *True History of the Conquest of Mexico* until the 1560s, when he had retired to a modest land grant in Guatemala. Though an invaluable source, the passage of time may have caused Díaz to confuse some details. Díaz's rival was López de Gómara, a secular priest who in 1552 began a biography of Cortés based on the conqueror's own account. Contemporaries thought Cortés related it to show himself in the best light. Díaz grumbled, "Whoever reads his [López de Gómara's] *History* will believe that what he says is true, such is the eloquence of his narrative, although it is very contrary to what happened." (Simpson 1964: *xvi, xxi*). In spite of bias, López de Gómara's work reveals many details of Maya life.

More systematic efforts at dealing with the natives followed the conquistadors' initial forays. Many of the

documents are descriptive in nature. As the Spaniards tried to assess the wealth of the lands they had conquered, they assembled data on tribute paid (Paso y Troncoso 1939). Ciudad Real accompanied Fray Alonso Ponce, commissary general of the Franciscan order in New Spain, through Yucatán in 1580 (Noyes 1932) and observed the subsistence practices of the Indians, among other traits. Ciudad Real was a gifted linguist, who is said to have assembled the Motul dictionary (1929), another rich source (Lizana ca. 1630 in Noyes 1932).

Other accounts reflect the Spaniards' attempts to bring the Maya under spiritual and physical control. Using earlier sources such as López de Gómara's *History* and information about Maya customs contributed by his informants Juan (Nachi) Cocom and Gaspar Chi, Bishop Landa composed his *Relación* in 1556 (Tozzer 1941). Justification of his harsh treatment of Indians during the Inquisition of Mani in 1562 may have been the ulterior motive behind Landa's work (Scholes and Roys 1968). In a more straightforward vein, Spanish field commanders sent back to headquarters reports of Indian crops uprooted: ". . . said rocky island is presently totally destroyed and burned under orders of the Lord Captain." (Archivo General de Centro América in Hellmuth 1977:424) Later historians began to compile data on the conquest drawing on documents now buried in archives and in some cases lost. Villagutierre's 1701 history contains errors and omits much anthropological data (Hellmuth 1977:425), but Villagutierre is nevertheless our only source on many points.

We must treat the ethnohistoric documents with caution. Spaniards gathered and presented information for specific purposes; they were not concerned to act as anthropologists. Their reports often contain mistakes and misconceptions. In consulting the data, archaeologists are tempted to project descriptions of life in the early historic period far back into the past, thus compounding the problems involved. Used judiciously, however, the historical record can provide hypotheses about aboriginal Maya life to be compared with data from other sources.

See chapter 1 for Mary Pohl's affiliation. Don Strong provided guidance on insect predators, and Hank Dobyns advised on ethnohistory.

Aboriginal Wetland Agriculture

Ethnohistoric data suggest that wetland field and canal complexes existed at the time of conquest. During his march across the Maya Lowlands, Cortés encountered Indian resistance at Pontonchan, a flourishing commercial center at the mouth of the Usumacinta and Grijalva rivers in Tabasco. A battle took place at Cintla, located amid maize fields to the southwest of Pontonchan and apparently part of the support area for the trade port (Scholes and Roys 1968:37). Cortés's biographer, López de Gómara, describes the fight:

> The meeting place of the two armies was cultivated land, cut up by many ditches and deep streams, difficult to cross, among which our men became confused and disorganized, so Hernan Cortés took his cavalry to find a better ground to the left and to seek cover among the trees . . . The foot went to the right, crossing ditches at every step . . . Our men did some mischief among the Indians . . . but even so could not force them to retreat, because the enemy took cover behind trees and fences.
> (López de Gómara in Simpson 1964:45–46)

These fields may have been ditched fields of the type known archaeologically (Freidel and Scarborough 1979). Other accounts support this hypothesis.

In 1559 conquistadors marched on the Cholti-Lacandon stronghold situated in Lake Miramar, Chiapas. A young attendant entered lakeside fields cut by ditches in order to gather green maize. Several Indians seized the boy, cut out his heart, and offered it as a sacrifice to the sun. The Spanish cavalry was helpless to save him because the horses refused to cross the canals (Villagutierre 1701:61). From the description, these fields also resemble ditched fields.

Another incident that took place during Cortés's march through the interior is more ambiguous. When Cortés reached Ciuatecpan on the Usumacinta River, he found that the Indians had burned the town and fled.

> I sent some of my people, in certain small canoes which were found there, to explore the river on the other side. They soon met a great number of Indians, and saw many cultivated fields, and, proceeding on their way, they reached a large lake where all the people of the town, partly in canoes and partly on small islands had collected.
> (MacNutt 1908:250; see also López de Gómara in Simpson 1964:350)

The Spaniards caught up with the Indians in a lagoon adjacent to the river, terrain where Siemens has demonstrated that ditched fields are often found. The small islands mentioned by Cortés evoke aerial photographs of such complexes (see Siemens 1978).

Since Cortés crossed the Maya Lowlands in the dry season and since archaeological data indicate that flood plain fields were primarily cultivated at that time (chap. 2), the fact that the small islands were beyond the cultivated fields suggests that the islands may have been former fields that had been abandoned.

Sixteenth-century friars in Alta Verapaz reported the practice of wetland cultivation, apparently without ditching (Viana et al. 1955, quoted from Reina and Hill 1980:77). Although the primary crop was wet season swidden, the Indians conducted a second planting in November in low spots and along riverbanks. The harvest took place in May. Productivity of such lands was much greater in the lowlands, and farmers would travel two or three days to find more suitable cropping locations in *tierra caliente*. This account shows that upland and wetland cultivation were parts of an overall subsistence strategy (see chap. 4).

The ethnohistoric accounts support archaeological data pointing to wetland exploitation during the dry season. In addition to the Alta Verapaz account, we know that the battle of Cintla occurred on Lady Day, March 25 (Díaz del Castillo 1956:57). Since the area was described as cultivated land at the time, dry season cropping can be inferred for the contact period.

Crops Grown on Wetland Fields

Corn

The reports of the conquerors suggest that maize was grown on wetland fields. Corn is specifically mentioned at Lake Miramar, and Cintla, the location of Cortés's battle, is the Nahuatl word for corn (Freidel and Scarborough 1979). The Indians of riverine Tabasco were producing a great deal of maize at the time of conquest (table 3.1). Tribute records for the years A.D. 1549–51 show that Chontal and Zoque towns contributed hundreds of bushels of grain. The Chontal community of Tamul, for example, paid 200 *fanegas* (bushels) in tribute while the center of Champoton, Campeche, located on the drier Yucatán Peninsula, paid 6 (Paso y Troncoso 1939).[1]

Corn pollen (Bradbury and Puleston 1974; Wiseman 1983) together with carbonized maize stems (Miksicek 1983) taken from abandoned fields at San Antonio Río Hondo and Pulltrouser Swamp in northern Belize indicate that maize was grown in these fields in prehistoric times. Less is known about varieties of corn and frequency of cropping. The Motul dictionary lists several kinds of maize, including a small variety that ripened in 40 days (Marcus 1982:247). Quick-ripening varieties might have been used for a more limited dry season crop.

Table 3.1. Tribute records from selected towns, A.D. 1549–1551.

Town	Population (tributaries)	Maize (F)	Wax (AR)	Honey (AR)	Mantas	Chickens, turkeys	Salt (F)	Fish (AR)	Beans (F)	Cacao (X)	Chile (F)
TABASCO											
Tabasco	25					24				20	
Tacotalpa	120	200				72				60	
Tecomaxagua	180	200				80				100	
Ucelutlan	170	200			10[a]	100			6	70	2
Tapixulapa	175	200			8	100			6	70	2
Tamul	120	200		2(CAN)		100				80	2(CA)
Teapa	100	100				100			8	50	2
Zaguatan	135	200				100			6	80	2(CA)
CAMPECHE											
Champoton	420	6			420	300		80	5		
Campeche	630	10	6	3	630	400	50	100[b]	1		
Becal	100	1.5	4	0.5	100	60			1		
Tenabo	330	4.5	15	0.5	130	280	6		0.5		
Tacul	480	6	20	3	480	320	10		1		
Teçenote and Mopila	240	3	8	1	240	160	6		0.5		
Maxcanu	260	3.5	11	1	260	180			0.5		
YUCATAN											
Çiho	410	6	16	2	410	300			1		
Popala	430	6	16	2	430	300			1		
Tachay	620	11	40	4	620	450			2		
Papacal	680	10	40	4	680	450			2		
Texan	320	4	12	2	320	250			1		
Mani	970	14	45	4	970	800			1.5		
Mama	440	6	17	2	440	300			1		
QUINTANA ROO											
Cozumel	220	3	8	1	220	160	6	6	1.5		
Enpole	17	0.5			17	20	1	2	1.5		
Mape	28	0.5	2	3(AZ)	28	20	2	2	2(CE)		

Source: L. Feldman from Paso y Troncoso 1939.

Note: The tribute records reveal that some regional differences in production existed, but within any given region, each community contributed the same products. The Maya pattern contrasts with that of central Mexico, where goods were more diverse.

F = fanegas (bushels), AR = arrobas, CAN = cantaros, AZ = azumbres, CE = celemines, X = xiquipiles, CA = cargas.

a. Pieces of clothing.
b. Dried fish.

Beans

Viana et al. (1955, quoted in Reina and Hill 1980:77) report that beans and tuberous plants (*frijoles y batatas*) were planted in wetlands of Alta Verapaz in the sixteenth century. Puleston recovered a carbonized bean fragment at San Antonio (Miksicek, personal communication, 1981), possibly dating to the end of the Preclassic or Early Classic period (chap. 2).

Root Crops

On his march through the western Maya Lowlands, Cortés reported finding abundant tubers (manioc), along with chiles, at Usumacinta settlements such as Ciuatecpan and Iztapan (MacNutt 1908:243, 249). These foods provided sustenance to the army because the maize was too immature to eat in many places. In 1586 Spanish field commanders reported destroying root crops in Cholti-Lacandon fields in the same area (Archivo General de Centro América 1937, quoted in Hellmuth 1977:424). The latter tubers were evidently growing in milpas located in upland terrain.

Thompson (1981) has demonstrated that pictures of roots occur in prehistoric Maya art. No evidence for edible root crops has yet been recovered from excavations in fields, however. Tuber pollen may be difficult to find because of characteristics of distribution or preservation. Opal phytoliths should not be subject to such problems, but the search for this kind of evidence proved fruitless at San Antonio and Pulltrouser Swamp (Wiseman, personal communication, 1980).

The Maya no doubt ate tubers (Bronson 1966), but roots have industrial uses as well; for example, the starch can be employed as a sizing for cloth. Today cassava is used as a starch in the vicinity of Lake Petén (Reina 1967:8).

Cotton

Sixteenth-century tribute records (table 3.1) demonstrate that textiles were the specialty of the Yucatec Maya living on the Yucatán Peninsula (Paso y Troncoso 1939). Cotton was also produced by the Chontal Indians of Acalan (MacNutt 1908:264) and by the Itza of Petén, Guatemala (Jones 1982). Fragments of cotton textile uncovered at Cerros (Freidel and Scarborough 1979; Scarborough, personal communication, 1980) provide evidence for cloth manufacture by the early part of the Late Preclassic period.

Gossypium type pollen is rare at the Late Preclassic site of Edzna (Fish 1978) and in wetland fields of northern Belize (Bradbury and Puleston 1974; Wiseman 1980, 1983). The scarcity is due at least in part to the fact that plants of this family are insect-pollinated. The pollen type also presents basic problems of identification. Cultivated cotton cannot be distinguished from wild cotton, and *Gossypium* type pollen may even come from Malvaceae other than cotton (Wiseman 1980). Detailed research on pollen morphology with the aid of a scanning electron microscope must be conducted before definitive information about the *Gossypium* type pollen associated with archaeological features is available.

Cacao

The European explorers remarked that cacao (*Theobroma*) was grown along the rivers draining the western Maya region, and their observations are supported by the sixteenth-century tribute records (table 3.1). Dahlin (1979) has suggested that wetland fields were used for cacao production. Like cotton and root crops, cacao has proven difficult to trace. At Pulltrouser Swamp, cacao remains were rare in occupation refuse, and no evidence for the tree was found in the fields (Miksicek 1983). The role of cacao in Maya society prior to the Postclassic period and the technology of its production remain an enigma.

Amaranth

Chenopodiaceae are characteristic of pollen profiles obtained by palynologists working in the Lowland Maya area (Tsukada 1966; Wiseman 1978, 1980, 1983; Vaughan 1979; Bradbury and Puleston 1974; Fish 1978). Unfortunately, identification to the genus or species level can once again be achieved only with the help of a scanning electron microscope. Some archaeologists have speculated that this pollen refers to edible chenopods and amaranths, including cultivated grain amaranth.

Describing Yucatán in 1588, Ciudad Real listed plants and animals used by the Maya, and he noted the garden vegetables that had been introduced by the Spaniards. In addition, "There are wormwood, the basil of the same country and cresses, purslane and amaranth, all of which greatly resemble those of Spain, of which there are ruta, fennel and plaintain (genus *Plantago*), and certain other plants." (Noyes 1932:310). In the Mediterranean, amaranth had long been a domesticated plant (Dobyns 1979). The context of Ciudad Real's remarks suggests that he observed amaranth either being cultivated or exploited for economic purposes.

Like tubers, amaranth may have been associated with textiles and with food. Seventeenth-century ethnohistoric sources report that amaranth made a superior dye because the thread was strengthened as well as colored. The Maya also used ash obtained from amaranth as a soap (*Yerbas y Hechicherias del Yucatán* quoted in Roys 1931:385).

Early colonial references to amaranth in Maya languages (Yucatec, Cakchiquel, and Pokom) are rare. *Tez* is the Yucatec word for the plant. The Motul dictionary defines *Tezcuntah* as "to salute, it is an ancient word with which they saluted the great lords. *Texcuntec ix ahau*" (Roys 1931:285) No tribute payments are recorded, however. The Maya dictionaries and tribute lists stand in contrast to the Nahua, Tarascan, Otomi, Mixtec, and Zapotec records, which indicate that amaranth held a special place among these groups. The Yucatec Maya were familiar with amaranth and treated it with reverence, but the plant was apparently of marginal significance in the sixteenth century (Feldman, personal communication, 1979).

All ethnohistoric references to amaranth come from Yucatán. The drier environment in that area may have made amaranth more suitable for cultivation (Miksicek, personal communication, 1980).

Maya Cropping Strategies

Wetland fields and canals were designed to manipulate water. Present-day Maya farmers consider crop pests the most significant ecological factor after water. The subject of predation on crops has not received the attention it deserves. Research on various kinds of vegetation, ranging from British trees to tropical crops like sugar cane and cacao, has shown that only a few hundred years are required for a full suite of predators to develop (Strong 1979). In the Maya area, palynological evidence for maize cultivation dates to about 2000 B.C. (Tsukada 1966; Vaughan 1979). A herbivore asymptote would certainly have been reached by 1100 B.C., the date suggested for river margin cultivation at San Antonio Río Hondo. Plant pests were no doubt plentiful by the second millennium B.C., though the amount of herbivory is more difficult to reconstruct.

Entomological studies in Costa Rica (Janzen 1973a) have revealed a striking migration of insects to riparian forest and other moist refugia in areas with pronounced dry seasons. These insects appear to be in reproductive diapause. Many species do not need the specialized diets of their reproductive phase, and they may feed on a wider range of plants in the dry season. By visiting many kinds of plants, dry season insects may spread plant diseases more effectively.

Much of the Lowland Maya region is characterized by a seasonal environment today. One might postulate that wetland fields were vulnerable to herbivory and crop diseases in the past. The Spaniards do not describe the strategies the Maya employed to deal with crop pests, but some hypotheses may be presented on the basis of ethnohistoric and ethnographic observation together with entomological research.

The ancient Maya could have counteracted the effects of insect herbivory in several ways. They may have manipulated plant defense guilds, groups of plants that act together to repel insects (Atsatt and O'Dowd 1976). Recent experiments have begun to provide information on just how such defense organizations work. In New York state, for example, when collards were interplanted with tomato and tobacco, the flea beetle was inhibited from colonizing the collards and laying eggs (Tahvanainen and Root 1972). The odors from the tomato and tobacco plants interfere with the ability of the flea beetle to orient itself and to exploit the collards.

Present-day Maya agriculturalists practice intercropping, and the ethnohistoric data suggest that this practice was more elaborate in the past. In the seventeenth century, Father Gabriel de Artiga reported that maize, calabazas, beans, chile, pineapples, tobacco, sweet cane, platanos, batatas, chayotes, grava (*cochinilla*), and cotton were all grown in Petén milpas (Archivo General de Indias, quoted in Hellmuth 1977:436). Anthropologists have long recognized that mixtures of plants enhance soil fertility, but the effects of intercropping may be more complex. Further information about the mechanics of plant guilds among Maya crops is needed. Such data may be most helpful for understanding upland or swidden agriculture, however. So far the pollen and plant macrofossils taken from wetland fields, together with ethnohistoric descriptions, suggest that this form of agriculture was reserved for a few species of plants.

The role of weeds in Maya agriculture has been hotly debated (Steggerda 1941; Cowgill 1961; Urrutia 1967). In experimental cultivation, Urrutia found that weeding was beneficial to soil fertility and corn production in swidden plots at Uaxactun, Guatemala. Present-day Lowland Maya farmers weed their milpas and sow squash plants, which cover the ground to keep competing vegetation in abeyance.

Pollen taken from wetland fields and canal sediment in northern Belize indicates that large numbers of weeds were growing on cultivated land (Bradbury and Puleston 1974; Wiseman 1983). Wiseman has suggested that the abundant weed pollen may indicate grass fallowing of the fields. Fallowing might not account for all weed pollen, however.

Perhaps archaeologists have been uncritical in their attitude toward these plants. Weeds may help the farmer in his battle with predatory insect populations. In controlled experiments conducted in temperate zones, fewer herbivorous insects and more stable populations were found on collards grown in a weedy field than in a field maintained as a collard monoculture. Similarly, two species of aphid were more attracted to clean-cultivated plots of brussels sprouts than to weedy ones. In another test, the cabbage butterfly laid the same number of eggs in cultivated and uncultivated plots, but the mortality rate of the larvae was higher in the weedy environment (Pimentel, Smith, Dempster, quoted in Cromartie 1975). These studies suggest that agriculturalists might benefit from the presence of a certain number of weeds. Weeds are a mixed blessing, however. They would have to be kept in densities that do not compete with crops and in species combinations that provide protection against herbivores.

Another strategy might have been one involving complex crop rotation or fallowing systems. Such systems might have been imposed on a group of agriculturalists by a centralized authority.

Today a Maya milpero's success is dependent in large part on the activities of his neighbors. At San Antonio Río Hondo, for example, increasing numbers of farmers have taken up cane production since 1964. As a result, those insects that prey on traditional subsistence crops are concentrated on the remaining fields. One harassed milpero declared, "Let them eat cane" and turned his field over to the cash crop. Insects devastated the milpa next to his.

At the present time the cultivation of a crop such as cotton in tropical and subtropical regions is dependent upon the use of chemicals. Before these aids were introduced, farmers had to time their activities to outwit crop predators. In the absence of pesticides, one of the most effective strategies might be to take large areas out of cotton production for a period of time (Janzen 1973b:1214). Ethnohistoric data indicate that the Inca employed such a tactic; their compulsory, seven-year rotation of potatoes was effective in combating potato cyst nematodes in the Peruvian Andes (Glass and Thurston 1978). Perhaps the necessities of agrarian policy contributed to the character of Maya society. The Maya stela cult and associated glyphs demonstrate that prehistoric lowlanders were obsessed with the formation of political and territorial alliances (Marcus 1976).

The mature tropical forest itself may provide a barrier to insects. In Costa Rica, less than 1 percent overlap was found between species of insects in primary forest understory and adjacent disturbed vegetation, even in areas where the dry season is mild enough to permit luxuriant vegetation all year. In contrast, as much as 15 percent overlap was found in a comparable situation in Kansas (Janzen 1973a).

The protective effect of high forest might explain reports of unusually long periods of productivity for Maya "milpas" in the historic era. For example, Fray Gabriel de Artiga testified that "When they clear a new field they make a little hut in it and the milpa produces fruit for more than 20 years giving, without rest, two harvests each year" (Archivo General de Indias, quoted in Hellmuth 1977:436). Although the

priest had not been around long enough to witness such a milpa, his statement about productivity may be regarded as generally accurate (Hellmuth 1977:436). Some ethnohistoric accounts suggest that high forest was present in the historic era; many Indians are said to have fled into the forests to escape the conquistadors. The López de Gómara and Díaz accounts of the Battle of Cintla indicate that trees were growing in the vicinity of the putative wetland fields. "The . . . fields were crowded with Indians running to take refuge in the thick woods near by." (Díaz del Castillo 1956:59)

The Function of Canals

Fishing

Thompson (1974) suggested that canals were exploited for fish. He based this theory on the Putun *cacique* Pablo Paxbolon's account of his entrada up the Candelária River in 1566 (Scholes and Roys 1968:188–189). Paxbolon was on an expedition to round up idolatrous Indians near Itzamkanac, the former Chontal capital. His men fished in the "lagoons" there in order to replenish their food supply, but Paxbolon's narrative does not indicate whether fishing was a regular pursuit in the area. The apostate Indians were located in their fields.

The evidence for fishing in the archaeological record is difficult to interpret. Fish bones are scarce during the Classic period at many inland sites, including Seibal on the Pasión River (chap. 9). Perhaps the data are subject to recovery basis. Nevertheless, at Tikal only a single, small catfish spine was found in Terminal Late Classic midden that was water-sieved through window screen, and no freshwater fish occurred in settlement or fields at Pulltrouser Swamp. Fish were abundant at the specialized chert workshop of Colha (Scott 1980). Notched sherds that ethnohistoric references suggest are netsinkers (Hellmuth 1977) were recovered at Late Classic period Lubaantun and at a Terminal Classic platform on the Hondo River near Nohmul (Pring 1975). A total of three fishhooks have been reported from Late Classic period contexts at Barton Ramie (Willey et al. 1965:494 and fig. 304c) and at Altar de Sacrificios (Willey 1972). The data on fishing are erratic and may suggest local differences in fish utilization.

Fishing at inland sites may have been practiced more regularly during the Preclassic, on the one hand, and Postclassic and historical periods, on the other. Fish bones occurred at Preclassic Cuello (Hammond et al. 1979) and Tikal (Moholy-Nagy, personal communication, 1974) and at Postclassic Flores (Pohl 1976) and Macal-Tipu. Weights have been found in Preclassic contexts at Yaxha and Sacnab and in

Postclassic occupational debris at Tayasal, Nohmul (D. Chase, personal communication, 1980), Barton Ramie, Mayapan (Willey et al. 1965:408), Topoxte, and Macanche (D. Rice, personal communication, 1980). When Cortés met Canek at Lake Petén, the Itza leader had fish in his canoe (López de Gómara in Simpson 1964). Later many fish from the lake were presented to priests who visited the same area (López de Cogolludo 1688, II:252–253).

Transportation

What impressed the Spaniards most was Maya commercial activity and the canoe transportation system associated with trade. The connection between transportation and storage facilities may also be significant.

Most foodstuffs seem to have been stored not in the settlements but in the fields. The Cortés expedition suffered food shortages. The Spanish soldiers found that the Indians had burned their towns. Cortés "discovered under the burnt houses, some granaries that contained small quanitities of maize." (MacNutt 1908:241) "Tamaztepec was deserted and destroyed.

Nevertheless, our men rested for six days, finding fruit and green maize in the fields, and grain in the bins." (López de Gómara in Simpson 1964:347)

The historic record suggests that Maya storehouses, possibly communal, were located throughout the countryside. After reaching Itzamkanac (perhaps the site of El Tigre where Siemens and Puleston [1972] investigated wetland fields), Díaz went out with Mazariegos and 80 soldiers to collect food from outlying settlements. They brought back 100 canoe loads of maize, fowl, honey, and salt (Puleston 1977:450). Canoes could be used to mobilize large amounts of produce quickly. A sixteenth-century illustration of Timucua Indians in north Florida may demonstrate the system (fig. 3.1). A canoe, loaded with food, approaches a round storehouse that may resemble the Maya "bins." A descriptive text remarks, "The reason

Figure 3.1. Wattle and daub storage facilities maintained by Timucua Indians of north Florida in the sixteenth century. Photograph courtesy of the Florida Photographic Collection of the Florida State Archives.

their granaries are always built near a cliff on the bank of a stream not far from the forest is that they should be accessible by water. Thus, if they are in need of food in their winter quarters, they are able to get supplies by canoe." (Lorant 1946:83)

A sixteenth-century *Relación* of Alta Verapaz indicates that maize was preserved by smoking for 10–15 days. Untreated maize would be attacked by insects in two or three months and would last less than four months in *tierra caliente* (Viana et al. 1955, quoted in Reina and Hill 1980:77).

Networks of canals and fields emerged in the Late Preclassic period (Freidel and Scarborough 1979; Turner and Harrison 1983). The elaboration of water

Figure 3.2. Method of preserving foodstuffs employed by Timucua Indians of north Florida in the sixteenth century. Present-day Maya hunters of northern Belize use a similar smoking rack to preserve meat. Photograph courtesy of Florida Photographic Collection of the Florida State Archives.

transportation technology together with the productivity of wetland fields and efficacy of food preservation techniques (fig. 3.2) may have encouraged the development of the large sedentary communities that appeared at that time in areas with access to wetlands.

Water Conservation in Yucatán

Although Yucatecan farmers did not have access to wetlands, they took advantage of the ability of stony soils to conserve moisture. The Spanish fathers observed this phenomenon in the sixteenth century. Bishop Landa (Tozzer 1941:86) remarked, "It is marvelous that the fertility of this land is so great on top of and between the stones, so that everything that there is and that grows in it grows better and more abundantly amongst the rocks than in the earth . . . The cause of this is, I believe, that there is more moisture and it is preserved more in the rocks than in the earth." Rocks reduce moisture losses from the soil. In addition, they may improve the environment for soil fauna, since worm and insect activity is often

higher under stones (Wilken 1972:555). Rocks keep down weeds that compete with crops. Ciudad Real (Noyes 1932:311) wrote:

> It seems impossible that this maize . . . is able to yield in that province because the Indians sow it among the rocks . . . with only the timely burning of the bush the land is left . . . well cultivated by the fire . . . and the more and the better burned the milpa is, the more and better corn it produces, because the fire and the ashes from it serve as dung that burns the insects and roots of the weeds, and when the milpa has been recently burned and the maize sowed thus and the rains approach [of which the Indians keep careful count], it sprouts quickly and grows with the showers and when the weeds start to grow, they find the maize already up, so that they cannot grow well before they are crushed and smothered, and the maize prospers and grows very fast until it reaches full size.

Ciudad Real thought that the fires killed the weeds, but the rocky soil no doubt contributed to the suppression of competitive vegetation. Historic period Maya living in dry regions recognized the virtues of natural stone mulches. Faced with similar conditions, prehistoric Maya might have chosen to make their milpas on rocky ground.

Summary

Wetland fields, both ditched and unditched, appear to have been cultivated in the sixteenth century, though we have no idea of the extent of such field complexes. Some may have already been abandoned when the Spaniards arrived. The evidence suggests that wetland cultivation was primarily a dry season activity. The principal crop grown in wetlands was maize. Cacao was grown in riverine areas, but we do not know whether the trees were located in wetland fields. Though wetland cultivation was not possible in the Yucatán Peninsula, farmers there devised their own means of water manipulation. They took advantage of the ability of rocky soils to conserve moisture.

References

Atsatt, P. R., and D. J. O'Dowd
1976   Plant Defence Guilds," *Science* 193:24–29.

Bradbury, J. P., and D. E. Puleston
1974   "The Use of Pollen Analysis in Investigations of Prehistoric Agriculture." Paper delivered at the 75th annual meeting of the American Anthropological Association, Mexico City.

Bronson, B.
1966   "Roots and the Subsistence of the Ancient Maya," *Southwestern Journal of Anthropology* 22:251–279.

Cowgill, U. M.
1961   "Soil Fertility and the Ancient Maya," *Transactions of the Connecticut Academy of Arts and Sciences* 42:1–56.

Cromartie, W. T.
1975   "The Effect of Stand Size and Vegetational Background on the Colonization of Cruciferous Plants by Herbivorous Insects," *Journal of Applied Ecology* 12:517–533.

Dahlin, B. H.
1979   "Cropping Cash in the Protoclassic: A Cultural Impact Statement." In *Maya Archaeology and Ethnohistory*, edited by N. Hammond and G. R. Willey. University of Texas Press, Austin, pp. 21–37.

Díaz del Castillo, B.
1956   *The Discovery and Conquest of Mexico*, translated by A. P. Maudslay. Grove Press, New York.

Diccionario de Motul
1929   *Maya-Español*. Attributed to Fray Antonio de Ciudad Real. Edited by J. M. Hernandez. Companía Tipográfica Yucateca, Mérida.

Dobyns, H. F.
1979   "Amaranth in Timucua Horticulture." Paper presented at the 27th annual meeting of the American Society for Ethnohistory, Albany, N.Y.

Fish, S. K.
1978   "Palynology of Edzna: Environment and Economy." Paper presented at the 43rd annual meeting of the Society for American Archaeology, Tucson.

Flannery, K. V.
1979   "Commentary." Presented at the History and Development of Maya Subsistence, a conference in memory of Dennis E. Puleston. St. Paul.

Freidel, D. A., and V. Scarborough
1979   "Subsistence, Trade and Development of the Coastal Maya." Paper presented at the History and Development of Maya Subsistence, a conference in memory of Dennis E. Puleston. St. Paul.

Glass, E. H., and H. D. Thurston
1978   "Traditional and Modern Crop Protection in Perspective," *Bioscience* 28:109–115.

Hammond, N., D. Pring, R. Wilk, S. Donaghey, F. P. Saul, E. S. Wing, A. V. Miller, and L. H. Feldman
1979   "The Earliest Lowland Maya: Definition of the Swasey Phase," *American Antiquity* 44:79–91.

Hellmuth, N.
1977   "Cholti-Lacandon (Chiapas) and Peten-Ytza Agriculture, Settlement Pattern and Population." In *Social Process in Maya Prehistory*, edited by N. Hammond. Academic Press, London, pp. 421–448.

Janzen, D. H.
1973a   "Interfield and Interplant Spacing in Tropical Insect Control," *Proceedings of the Tall Timbers Conference on Ecological Animal Control by Habitat Management*, 4:1–6.
1973b   "Tropical Agroecosystems," *Science* 182:1212–19.

Jones, G. D.
1982   "Agriculture and Trade in the Colonial Period Southern Maya Lowlands." In *Maya Subsistence*, edited by K. V. Flannery. University of Texas Press, Austin, pp. 275–293.

López de Cogolludo, D.
1688   *Los tres siglos de la dominación española en Yucatán o sea historia de esta provincia*, 2 vols. Akademische Druk-u, Verlagsanstalt, Graz (1971).

Lorant, S.
1946   *The New World: The First Pictures of America*. Duell, Sloan and Pearce, New York.

MacNutt, F. A.
1908   *Letters of Cortés*. Letter 5, vol. 2. G. P. Putnam's Sons, New York.

Marcus, J.
1976   *Emblem and State in the Classic Maya Lowlands*. Dumbarton Oaks, Washington, D.C.
1982   "The Plant World of the Sixteenth and Seventeenth Century Lowland Maya." In *Maya Subsistence*, edited by K. V. Flannery. Academic Press, New York, pp. 239–273.

Miksicek, C. H.
1983   "Macrofloral Remains of the Pulltrouser Area: Settlements and Fields." In *Pulltrouser Swamp: Ancient Maya Habitat, Agriculture, and Settlement in Northern Belize*, edited by B. L. Turner and P. D. Harrison. University of Texas Press, Austin, pp. 94–104.

Noyes, E., editor and translator
1932   *Fray Alonso Ponce in Yucatán, 1588*. Tulane University, Middle American Research Series 4, pp. 297–372.

Paso y Troncoso, F. del, compiler
1939   *Epistolario de Nueva España*. Vols. 5 and 6, *1547–1549*. Antigua Librería Robredo de José Porrua e Hijos, México.

Pohl, M.
1976   "The Ethnozoology of the Maya: An Analysis of Faunal Remains from Five Sites in Peten, Guatemala." Ph.D. dissertation, Department of Anthropology, Harvard University.

Pring, D. C.
1975   "Summary of the Ceramic Sequence in Northern Belize." In *Archaeology in Northern Belize, 1974–75, Interim Report of the British Museum—Cambridge University Corozal Project*, edited by N. Hammond. Centre of Latin American Studies, Cambridge, England, pp. 116–127.

Puleston, D. E.
1977   "The Art and Archaeology of Hydraulic Agriculture in the Maya Lowlands." In *Social Process in Maya Prehistory: Studies in Memory of Sir Eric Thompson*, edited by Norman Hammond. Academic Press, London, pp. 449–469.

Reina, R. E.
1967   "Milpas and Milperos," *American Anthropologist* 69:1–20.

Reina, R. E., and R. M. Hill II
1980   "Lowland Maya Subsistence: Notes from Ethnohistory and Ethnography," *American Antiquity* 45:74–79.

Roys, R. L.
1931   *The Ethno-Botany of the Maya*. Middle American Research Series 2, Tulane University.

Scholes, F., and R. L. Roys
1968   *The Maya Chontal Indians of Acalan-Tixchel*. University of Oklahoma Press, Norman. Originally published 1948.

Scott, R. F.
1980   "Faunal Remains from 1979–1980 Seasons, Colha, Belize." Paper presented at the 45th

annual meeting of the Society for American Archaeology, Philadelphia.

Siemens, A. H.
1978 "Karst and the Pre-Hispanic Maya in the Southern Lowlands." In *Pre-Hispanic Maya Agriculture*, edited by P. D. Harrison and B. L. Turner II. University of New Mexico Press, Albuquerque, pp. 117–143.

Siemens, A. H., and Dennis E. Puleston
1972 "Ridged Fields and Associated Features in Southern Campeche: New Perspectives on the Lowland Maya," *American Antiquity* 35:228–239.

Simpson, L. B., translator and editor
1964 *Cortés: The Life of the Conqueror by His Secretary Francisco López de Gómara*. University of California Press, Berkeley.

Steggerda, M.
1941 *Maya Indians of Yucatán*. Carnegie Institution of Washington, Publication 531.

Strong, D. R., Jr.
1979 "Biogeographic Dynamics of Insect-Host Plant Communities," *Annual Review of Entomology* 24:87–119.

Tahvanainen, J. O., and R. B. Root
1972 "The Influence of Vegetational Diversity on the Population Ecology of a Specialized Herbivore, *Phyllobreta cruciferae* (Coleoptera: Chrysomelidae)," *Oecologia* 10:321–346.

Thompson, J. E. S.
1974 "'Canals' of the Río Candelaria Basin, Campeche, Mexico." In *Mesoamerican Archaeology: New Approaches*, edited by N. Hammond. University of Texas Press, Austin, pp. 297–302.

Thompson, S.
1981 "Evidence for Pre-Columbian Use of Aroids." Paper presented at the 4th Ethnobiology Conference, Columbia, Mo.

Tozzer, A. M.
1941 *Landa's Relación de las cosas de Yucatán: A Translation*. Peabody Museum Papers, vol. 18, Harvard University.

Tsudaka, M.
1966 "The Pollen Sequence." In *The History of Laguna de Petenxil: A Small Lake in Northern Guatemala*. U. M. Cowgill, G. E. Hutchinson, H. A. Racek, C. E. Goulden, R. Patrick, and M. Tsukada. Memoirs of the Connecticut Academy of Arts and Sciences 17. New Haven.

Turner, B. L., II, and P. Harrison
1981 "Prehistoric Raised Field Agriculture in the Maya Lowlands: Pulltrouser Swamp, Northern Belize," *Science* 213:399–405.

Turner, B. L., II, and P. D. Harrison, editors
1983 *Pulltrouser Swamp: Ancient Maya Habitat, Agriculture and Settlement in Northern Belize*. University of Texas Press, Austin.

Urrutia R., V. M.
1967 "Corn Production and Soil Fertility Changes under Shifting Cultivation in Uaxactun, Guatemala." M.A. thesis, University of Florida.

Vaughan, H. H.
1979 "Prehistoric Disturbance of Vegetation in the Area of Lake Yaxha, Petén, Guatemala." Ph.D. dissertation, Department of Zoology, University of Florida.

Viana, F. de, L. Gallego, and G. Cadena
1955 "Relación de la provincia de la Verapaz hecha por los religiosos de Santo Domingo de Coban 1574," *Anales de la Sociedad Geografía e Historia* 28:18–31.

Villagutierre Soto-Mayer, J.
1701 *Historia de la conquista de la provincia del Itza*. Biblioteca "Goathemala" de la Sociedad de Geografía e Historia 9. (1933).

Wilken, G. C.
1972 "Microclimate Management by Traditional Farmers," *Geographical Review* 62:544–560.

Willey, G. R.
1972 *The Artifacts of Altar de Sacrificios*. Peabody Museum Papers, vol. 64, Harvard University.

Willey, G. R., W. R. Bullard, J. B. Glass, and J. C. Gifford
1965 *Prehistoric Settlements in the Belize Valley*. Peabody Museum Memoirs, vol. 13, Harvard University.

Wiseman, F. M.
1978 "Agricultural and Historical Ecology of the Maya Lowlands." In *Pre-Hispanic Maya Agriculture*, edited by P. D. Harrison and B. L. Turner II. University of New Mexico Press, Albuquerque, pp. 63–116.
1980 "Pollen Analysis of Raised Fields at Pulltrouser Swamp, Belize." Paper presented at the 45th annual meeting of the Society for American Archaeology, Philadelphia.
1983 "Analysis of Pollen from the Fields at Pulltrouser Swamp." In *Pulltrouser Swamp: Ancient Maya Habitat, Agriculture, and Settlement in Northern Belize*, edited by B. L. Turner, II, and P. D. Harrison. University of Texas Press, Austin, pp. 105–119.

Chapter 4

Dry Season Agriculture among the Kekchi Maya and Its Implications for Prehistory

Richard R. Wilk

Ethnographic studies of modern agricultural systems do more than provide simple analogies for what past farmers may have done. By studying the diversity and transformations of present agriculture we can derive general models of how productive systems are integrated with other aspects of society and the physical environment and of why they change. This kind of predictive model is essential because ancient agricultural systems leave only limited evidence in the archaeological record. We may find seeds, pollen, traces of burning or land modification and something of the material culture of the people who created and maintained the system. But when it comes to productivity, seasonality, the sexual division of labor, and such technical matters as weed and pest management, storage technology, and land tenure, the material record is silent. We must depend on our knowledge of agricultural systems to make inferences on these matters.

In this chapter I will outline the modern Kekchi dry season riverbank agricultural system as a potential direct analogy for ancient practices. I will also attempt to draw some general points from the Kekchi example that may have wider application for understanding the long-term transformations of the ancient Maya system. One point can be made at the outset: there is growing evidence that modern Maya agriculture is extremely diverse. Farming practices differ greatly from place to place in response to variation in the physical environment, local population densities, and market orientation. Just among the Kekchi villages of south-

Richard Wilk is rural sociologist/anthropologist, U.S. Agency for International Development Mission to Belize; research associate, Bureau for Applied Research in Anthropology, University of Arizona; and associate, Board of Studies in Anthropology, University of California, Santa Cruz.

The research on which this paper is based was funded by the University of Arizona, the Wenner-Gren Foundation for Anthropological Research, and a dissertation improvement grant from the National Science Foundation (ENS 7814205). A more thorough presentation of the data can be found in Wilk 1981a. Thanks are due to Catherine Borchert for reading and commenting on an earlier version of this chapter and to Laura Kosakowsky for assisting in the research.

ern Belize there are differences in crop mixtures, farming techniques, and scheduling of crop cycles. The variation is greater between the Belizean Kekchi, the Izabal (Guatemala) Kekchi studied by Carter (1969), and the Mopan, who live just north of the Kekchi in Belize. This should serve as a caution against speaking of Maya agriculture, ancient or modern, as a monolithic entity that can be characterized by a single set of crops, techniques, or cycles. If anything, ancient Maya agriculture was even more diverse and locally adapted than modern. By the Classic period there had been over 2,000 years of local adaptation to widely varying environments and to changing social and economic circumstances.

The Agricultural System

Floodwater recessional agriculture itself is not a unitary system that can be characterized by a single example. Denevan's summary of *varzea* systems in South America (1982) makes a clear case in this regard. He points out the great diversity of microzonation of biotopes within the floodplain and the diversity of agricultural uses of each zone. Unfortunately, detailed environmental studies of riverside habitats in Belize are lacking, and I was not able to conduct a large-scale survey. This chapter outlines an agricultural system in use in a single study village and does not attempt to document the diversity of the system within southern Belize.

The riverbank dry season farming system I studied among the Kekchi is not, however, unique in Mesoamerica. It can be compared to floodwater recessional systems studied by Orozco-Segovia and Gliessman in Tabasco (1979), and by Coe and Diehl in Veracruz (1980) and has much in common with floodplain agriculture in the Amazon and Orinoco drainages (see Roosevelt 1980; Denevan 1982). It is similar, except in location of fields, to the dry season re-use of low-lying *milpas* reported by Carter (1969) among the Izabal Kekchi, and by Culbert, Spencer, and Magers (1978) among Mopan in southeastern Petén. In some southern Belize Kekchi villages not located near cultivable riversides, similar double cropping of *milpas* is done in particularly moist areas in small alluvial pockets within rugged hill country.

As a cropping system, the system I shall describe is not unique to the riverine habitat, and it may be more accurately characterized by its seasonality. It is foremost a dry season phenomenon, adapted to the special circumstances of temporary rainfall shortage in an environment that receives more than 4,000 mm of rain in an average year.

The names for this dry season cropping method are expressive. *Matahambre*, the Spanish term, means literally "kills hunger," and the Kekchi term *sak'ecuaj* translates to "sun cornfield" or "dry season cornfield." The Spanish term expresses the colonial experience of many marginalized peasant farmers throughout Latin America, for whom wet season milpa farming was often insufficient for subsistence—the matahambre crop makes up for the corn shortages from the wet season productive cycle. This is the way most ethnographers have described the system, as a minor back-up crop (see Reina 1967; Reina and Hill 1980; Carter 1969; Kelley and Palerm 1952). The Kekchi term merely notes the time of year that the crop is grown and conveys nothing of its function. In fact, subsistence farming Kekchi consider the sak'ecuaj an important and sometimes essential element of an integrated yearly agricultural cycle. Recent studies of Maya farming have tended to acknowledge that dry season cropping is more than an appendage to the agricultural system and that it may have had a central role in the evolution of agroecosystems in the lowland neotropics (Culbert, Spencer, and Magers 1976; Culbert, Magers, and Spencer 1978; Coe and Diehl 1980; Coe 1974; Orozco-Segovia and Gliessman 1979; Roosevelt 1980). The minor importance and low yields of dry season cropping among modern Maya groups may be as deceptive a model for prehistory as the swidden hypothesis has proved to be (Hammond 1978; Turner 1978; Puleston 1982).

Physiography, Soils, and Fields

Southern Belize can be divided into two basic agricultural zones: rolling and sometimes rugged uplands and a swampy coastal plain (Wright et al. 1959; Wilk 1981a). Upland soils vary in fertility depending on local geology and topography but are generally of good to high quality. High yields are obtained on these soils during the wet season from May to September, through long-fallow shifting cultivation. At this time of year most lowland areas are inundated and unusable. When the rains begin to slack off in September and October, however, the permeability of the upland soils and the sloping terrain result in soils that do not have enough moisture for reliable cultivation. Only some kind of terracing system, like that

built by the ancient Maya in central Belize (Healey, van Waarden, and Anderson 1980; Healey 1982; Turner 1978), would make these upland soils usable during the dry season, by trapping moisture and storing it behind impermeable walls.

While large parts of the coastal plain stay swampy during the dry season, other areas, especially the banks of the major rivers, become dry enough for cultivation. Drainage is crucial in the choice of a dry season field. The dry season in this part of Belize is short (mid-January to the end of April) and is often punctuated by showers, with a mean of about 80 mm of rain falling in the driest month (Jenkins, Anderson, and Silva 1978). The timing of onset of the dry season and the amount of rain that falls then is variable; some years have virtually no dry season and in others no rain falls for four or five months. Microtopography is therefore important for successful cultivation; a field cannot flood or pond during unseasonal rains, nor can it drain too quickly in a drought. Small pockets in valleys within the upland areas and parts of the riverbanks are the only places that fit within these limits, though the water-retaining capabilities of soils can be modified through practices such as mulching, sowing cover crops, and interplanting.

The riverbanks themselves do not form a uniform zone. In some limestone areas the rivers are seasonal, and no cultivation is possible on their fast-draining banks. Close to the coast extensive levees grade into large ponding areas and bogs and can only be used late in the dry season because they dry so slowly. In the uplands most of the drainages have a high gradient and flow within narrow, deep channels and therefore rarely overflow their banks to create levees (floodplains) suitable for cultivation. The optimum combination of drainage and soil quality is found in the middle stretches of the rivers, more than 10 km inland but below the 125 m contour. Most of the 17 Kekchi villages in southern Belize are located in this zone. Villages that do not have access to cultivable riverbank soils tend to be small and ephemeral; those with large areas for sak'ecuaj are the largest and most stable over time (Wilk 1981a).

The zones I call riverbanks are actually a complex and variable mixture of areas differing in soil, drainage, and flora. Unfortunately, the range of variation is unknown because there have been no studies of riverbank ecology and seasonality. Most needed are studies of riverbank morphology, river hydrochemistry, and the seasonality and degree of flooding. My own untrained impression from river travel and hikes through the areas during the dry season is that landform and vegetation is considerably less complex and more stable than in the floodplain areas of the major rivers of South America as summarized by Denevan (1982). River channels seem stable; it is only in the area closest to the coast that complexes of new and old channels, oxbows, backswamps, and playas occur. Rather than exploit the full range of riverine habitats through a complex of finely adapted agricultural cycles, the Kekchi presently concentrate their efforts on the tops and backslopes of the levees, with some use of higher backswamps at the upland edge of the coastal plain.

Riverbank areas are highly valued by the Kekchi and are considered the property of the person who clears them from virgin forest. They can be inherited, are frequently loaned, but are not sold. This is a different practice from that applying to wet season milpa land, which is managed as a communal village resource to which all residents have access, a practical arrangement where population densities are low and fallow cycles are more than 15 years.[1]

Farming Methods

The natural vegetation of the riverbanks is a dense gallery forest dominated by huge fig trees and packed with Cohune palms, Quamwood, and Santa Maria. When a new field is cleared this growth is cut and burned like that of a wet season milpa, leaving a row of trees along the edge of the river as a wind-break and to minimize erosion during flooding. In subsequent years, during the wet season or when the field is fallowed, a low, retarded successional association called *vega* in Spanish and *sajal* in Kekchi becomes established in the fields.

Sajal consists of low shrubs dominated by *Melathera nivea* (*Piper umbellatum* and *Carica papaya* are also common.) vines (among them *Ipomoia* spp., *Calonyction* sp., and *Passiflora foetida*), and leafy succulents (including *Heliconia* spp. and *Xanthosoma* sp.). Though sajal includes many plants that produce itching and irritation or are armed with thorns and spines, farmers consider its growth essential for continuing cultivation. This is because the dense mat of vegetation shades out pernicious grasses, is easy to clear, and protects the soil from erosion and hardening. The field is considered unusable unless sajal vegetation becomes established.

The technique of cultivation can be labeled slash-and-mulch. Beginning in November and continuing into January, the sajal vegetation is slashed at the roots, chopped up, and spread to form a springy mat of decaying matter, into which corn is dibbled. This mulch protects the soil from erosion during wet season flooding and helps conserve soil moisture during the dry season. Carter (1969) says that Izabal Kekchi sow an inedible legume, the velvet bean (*Stitzolobium* sp.), with the corn, which then shades out most weeds and after harvest serves as fallow cover. Some Belizean Kekchi are experimenting with this technique at present.

The primary and often only crop sown is corn. Five native varieties and one recently introduced short growing-season variety are planted, though most farmers plant only one or two varieties per field. Instead of interplanting plantains, root crops, and vegetables among the corn, as is done in the wet season milpa, a separate plot or garden is sometimes established for these crops in an especially well-suited (and well-drained) portion of the riverbank field. Because the sak'ecuaj field is held in long-term tenure, farmers often use a part of it for crops that take more than a year to grow (like sugar cane) and for a few fruit trees.

Little weeding is done in the sak'ecuaj fields; for the most part the sajal is allowed to grow up beneath the corn, shading out grasses. As the corn grows, farmers devote a good deal of time to protecting the field from animals, which are the main cause of crop loss. The yearly shifting of wet season milpa prevents the establishment of a resident population of pests, but sak'ecuaj fields are plagued by coatimundi, rats, and some kinds of flocking birds. Tapirs frequent the riverbanks at night and like to roll on their backs in the green corn, leveling large areas but eating little. Since these fields are usually close to the village, they are also in danger from horses and mules.

Green corn is harvested beginning in late January, and dry corn is broken as early as the first week in February. The latest plantings are not ready for harvest until April or May. The corn is not stored in the field but is taken back to the village for immediate consumption and for storage in a special corn-crib built in the house.

Scheduling

Timing for clearing and planting sak'ecuaj is delicate and requires balancing of climate, regrowth of vegetation, and the farmer's other tasks. The corn must have a good start in growth before the dry season begins and soil moisture declines. Given the variation in the onset of the dry seasons, the earlier the corn is in the ground, the better. But farmers cannot begin the sak'ecuaj until they have finished harvesting the wet season crop. If wet season yield is high, they may not finish that harvest until the end of November. So a regulating mechanism operates: the higher the wet season yield of corn, the less time the farmer has to

---

1. According to Belizean law, most Kekchi live in designated Indian Reserves, in which no individual is allowed to own land and which remains the property of the government. In practice most villages regulate their own land tenure practices with little interference from the government, a situation that may soon change.

plant a dry season crop. If the wet season yield is low, plenty of time is available for clearing and planting a large area for sak'ecuaj, and the dry season yield makes up for the wet season shortfall. Local corn varieties have thick and tight husks, allowing farmers to leave them standing in the field long after ripening giving them some flexibility in the harvest.

Regrowth of slashed sajal vegetation imposes a tight schedule on the farmer once sak'ecuaj clearing has begun. If the field is not planted within a week after it is slashed and cleared, the weeds will have too much of a head start on the young corn. For this reason the clearing and planting of sak'ecuaj follows a cyclic pattern. The farmer clears a small plot and plants it, then continues clearing and planting more areas until he thinks the dry season is approaching too closely (usually about the middle of January). In Aguacate village farmers cleared and planted an average of 1.6 plots, totaling an average of about 0.99 hectares.

Fallow Cycles

Although wet season milpas are abandoned after a single corn crop because of weed infestation, the riverbank fields can be re-used annually for a number of years. In Aguacate village the average is 5.2 consecutive years of use followed by an average 2.8 years of fallow, though I recorded one field that had been

Table 4.1. Sak'ecuaj labor inputs by task.

Task	Mean man-hours per hectare
Clearing and mulching	205.1
Planting	77.7
Weeding	21.0
Guarding and checking[a]	56.2
Harvest	57.5
Transportation	30.2

a. Fields are often checked and guarded while other tasks are being performed nearby (i.e., fishing, hunting, working in garden, bathing). This figure is an estimate of the total time spent in formal visits and protection.

used continuously for 12 years. Farmers explained that after a number of years of use the soil in the fields gets "hard"—compacted in texture—and the field should then be rested.

Another reason that fields are sometimes fallowed or abandoned is that wet season flooding can deposit layers of sand and silt. The sand makes the soil too permeable and covers the mulch so the corn will wither at the peak of the dry season. An extended period of regrowth is required before the field will be usable once more. In choosing a site for a new sak'ecuaj field, sandy soils are avoided for this same reason.

Riverside fields are capable of sustained use for a number of reasons. The soils are on the whole more fertile than the hill soils used for milpa, and annual flooding deposits new soil. Perhaps of more direct importance to Kekchi farmers, the sajal vegetation prevents grass invasion, and the decaying mat of green mulch maintains soil texture and returns nutrients for use by crops. Catastrophic flooding or erosion was never mentioned by Kekchi farmers as a cause for abandonment of fields, despite the fact that the area is periodically hit by hurricanes.

Yield

The amount of corn harvested from dry season fields varies widely. The average yield in Aguacate was 839 kg/hectare. The minimum was 234, and the maximum was 1943, with a coefficient of variation (CV) of 59 percent. Part of the variability in yield is due to differences in the drainage properties of soils within the micro-relief of the riverside. In a short or rainy dry season, low-lying fields stay waterlogged, and the corn grows poorly. If the dry season is long and arid, the better-drained fields will dry out too much, and the corn will also suffer. Farmers cope with this variation at present by plot scattering; they try to plant one field in a wet area and another in a high and dry place, practicing a familiar form of risk minimization (McCloskey 1975). Active manipulation of the drainage of the fields would be another, more labor-intensive form of risk minimizing, a possibility I will return to later.

Another source of variation in corn yield is the difference in the amount of time and care that farmers devote to the crop. Those who need the corn most tend to spend more time chopping and spreading the mulch, weeding, and watching for pests and fencing trails to keep out horses and mules. This extra work was rewarded; for a sample of ten farmers the correlation between man hours per hectare and yield per hectare was high ($r = .962$, $p < .001$). This shows that the system can be intensified greatly without any new technology or land modification.

Table 4.2. Maize yields for a sample of Maya farmers.

Group/Area	Source	R value[a]	Average kg per hectare	Range of kg per hectare
Kekchi/Toledo	Present study	<7	1,515	1,097–2,820
Jacaltec/Highlands	Stadelman 1940	<9	1,845	1,024–3,102
Yucatec/Yucatán	Morley 1946	16.7	1,303	1,054–1,551
Ladino?/La Venta	Drucker and Heizer 1960	20.0	1,050	800–1,100
Mopan/Petén	Cowgill 1962	c. 30.0	877	not given
Kekchi/Izabal	Carter 1969	11.1–67.0	846	not given
Mam/Highlands	Stadelman 1940	c. 36.0	1,024	620–1,240
Kekchi/Toledo[b]	Present study	64.1	839	234–1,943

a. R as defined by Joosten (1962) is

$$R = \frac{\text{Number of years of cultivation of a plot} \times 100}{\text{Number of years of fallow} + \text{number of years of cultivation}}$$

The smaller the R value, the less intensive the agricultural system. A value of 1 means a field is rested for 100 years for each year of use, while the maximum value is 100, when a field is in continuous use.

b. These figures relate to the Kekchi practice of dry season corn farming.

A further source of variability in yield is crop damage from pests and from occasional wind storms, which blow down many corn plants. Because my yield data comes from a single season during which no great damage was reported, I cannot draw any conclusions on the magnitude of crop losses from these sources.

Where land is not a scarce resource, labor tends to be the limiting factor in agricultural production. Meaningful measures of yield must therefore be based on labor inputs and costs. Total labor inputs for the whole dry season crop cycle were high—an average of 448 man hours from each farmer who grew sak'ecuaj in Aguacate village in 1979. Table 4.1 breaks down labor inputs by task, based on a sample of 12 farmers.

Yield per man hour varied greatly ranging from 0.69 kg of shelled corn up to 2.92 kg, with an average of 1.83 kg and a CV of 43 percent. Again, some of this variation was the product of differences in the care and attention given the fields—there was a tendency for those who devoted more man hours to each hectare to later harvest more corn for their labor. This is not entirely a matter of choice, as some farmers have less time available at this time of year because they are still bringing in the wet season crop or have decided to

get an early start in clearing the next year's milpa. Cash cropping also conflicts with sak'ecuaj and takes labor away from it.

Another source of variation in yield per man hour is the size of the farmer's household. Large households with more than one adult male laborer are able to devote more time to caring for fields by dividing their labor between conflicting tasks. They can also coordinate the tricky timing of clearing and planting more effectively (see Wilk 1981b). Most large households own a draft animal, which cuts the amount of time spent carrying corn back to the village. Those with access to a draft animal averaged 2.06 kg/man hour, compared with 1.64 kg/man hour for those who had to carry their crop on their backs.

How do riverbank farming yields compare with yields from other farming systems in the Maya area? Unfortunately, yield per unit labor figures are not available for comparison. Table 4.2 places yield of shelled corn per hectare from Kekchi wet season and dry season farming in the context of some other Maya systems, scaled according to their ratio of cropping period to fallow length. As expected, there is a strong tendency for increased yield with longer fallow, regardless of seasonality or location. On the other

Table 4.3. Yield in shelled corn in wet and dry season farming.

Measure	High forest milpa	Low forest milpa	Dry season riverbank
Yield in kg per hectare	1,875	1,274	839
Yield in kg per man-hour	2.33	2.61	1.83
Coefficient of variation of yield in kg per man-hour (%)	12.6	33.4	42.6
Yield in total kg per hectare over 25 years of plot use	1,875	1,633	13,446

hand, it is clear that Kekchi dry season farming is about equal in yield per hectare with the wet season shifting cultivation practiced in the Petén and Izabal areas where fairly short fallow periods are used. More important, the sak'ecuaj system can be intensified to produce higher yields without shortening fallow cycles and without the danger of grass infestation; the wet season milpa system does not present any easy avenue toward increased yield (Vasey 1979).

Table 4.3 presents a comparison of yields from Kekchi wet and dry season corn farming, including a breakdown of wet season milpas into those planted in high forest (more than 15 years fallow) and those planted in low secondary forest (5–15 years fallow). These figures beg the question of why the Kekchi practice riverbank cultivation at all, given that they have abundant land suitable for long fallow, wet season farming, which produces a much higher average yield with much less variability.

For the farmer who has had a poor harvest from wet season farming, there is really no consideration of yield per hectare or of man hours invested. What he needs is corn to feed his family and pigs, and sak'ecuaj is the only way to ensure a steady supply until the next wet season crop is planted and harvested. At present, however, it is exceptional for farmers in most Kekchi villages to suffer a shortage from the wet season milpa, so the survival motive can rarely account for the growing of a sak'ecuaj crop.

The most common situation is for the farmer to schedule and balance the wet and dry season productive cycles. He will not grow a maximum size crop during the wet season and will count on the dry season crop to provide enough to get him through the rest of the year. Though he can produce more efficiently by putting maximum effort into the wet season crop and forgetting about sak'ecuaj, maximum labor efficiency is not an overriding concern. Rather, the farmer wants to even out his labor input throughout the year, neither overworking himself nor resting idle for too long. Maximizing the wet season corn yield

would leave him idle for the entire dry season, because there are few other productive activities to pursue at that time of year. The wet season, on the other hand, is a busy time when other activities, including the cash-cropping of rice, compete for his labor. Therefore, the farmer is willing to accept a lower yield for his labor in the sak'ecuaj, knowing that though it is less productive than wet season milpa, there is nothing else he can do with his labor during the dry season that will be more productive.[2]

A final motive for accepting lower average yields is that dry season farming is an attractive gamble. If we look at the range of yields rather than the averages, we find that the best case for sak'ecuaj fields is 1,943 kg/ha and 2.92 kg/man hour, well above the average for wet season milpa. For the farmer this means that there is always the prospect of a handsome payoff if everything goes well and if he has the time to care for the crop adequately. For the farmer who has an adequate corn supply for the rest of the year, an especially abundant sak'ecuaj yield is a windfall, which can be disposed of in a number of ways. The corn can be fed to pigs, a form of banking (the pigs can always be sold to buyers who truck them to Belize city), or it can be sold directly to the government marketing board for cash. It is because some men can view part of their sak'ecuaj as disposable surplus that they sometimes give it very little attention and care. If someone proposes a hunting trip or if they find a week or two of wage labor in town, they can leave the field untended and hope for the best.

How important is the matahambre crop in Kekchi subsistence? In villages where there is still plenty of primary forest within an hour's walk and where cash cropping does not draw labor away from wet season milpas, the matahambre crop plays a minor role. More than 80 percent of the year's corn supply will be obtained from the wet season milpa, and a number of

---

2. I am indebted to B. L. Turner II for helping me to clarify this point.

farmers will not plant any sak'ecuaj at all.[3] Much of the dry season crop will be surplus, which can be fed to pigs or sold. As the fallow status of the land around the village diminishes, however, and as cash crops take a larger and larger part of the farmers' time away from the wet season corn crop, the matahambre corn increases in importance. For some households in Aguacate, the matahambre field provides two-fifths to one-half of the years total corn field, though the average is closer to one-third. The average household expends 410 man hours on dry season corn (about 46 working days; this includes 5 out of 22 households that did not farm during the dry season), as opposed to 1,104 man hours (about 123 working days) on wet season production.

Of course, crop yield and energy investment are not always the best measure of importance in the overall subsistence pattern. For a few people each year and for many people in the rare bad years, sak'ecuaj cultivation is the difference between subsistence and starvation. With present technology and low population density, wet season milpa farming is still more productive than dry season riverbank farming, but this gap can close rapidly, as it seems to have done in some of the more densely settled Mopan villages to the north of the Kekchi area in Belize. There, high population density has led to shortening of fallow periods for wet season milpa areas to the point where most fields are cleared from five to ten years after they were last farmed. As fallow is shortened, grass invasion becomes a serious problem, yields decline, and the variability in yield (and therefore the farmer's risks) increases. At the same time, yields from sak'ecuaj can be increased through interplanting, weeding, and more careful tending of fields. Although the Kekchi farmers I worked with agreed that dry season yields were lower than their wet season amounts, Mopan farmers in San Antonio reported that they had better results from matahambre than from wet season milpa.

Evolutionary Implications

Dry season riverbank farming, as I have presented it here, is not an autonomous system but an integral part of a subsistence cycle. Rather than tear the technique out of its context for use as a template to match with the past (or worse, as a mold into which prehistoric data can be forced), I shall try to use the Kekchi agroecosystem as an example from which we can draw useful generalizations for understanding agricultural change in prehistory.

---

3. Corn is by far the most important component of the human diet and is the staple for livestock as well. Over 80 percent of calories are derived from corn; men consume an average of 996 gm per day, and women about 636 gm.

By far the most influential general model in studies of prehistoric agriculture has been that of agricultural intensification and population pressure, based on the formulations of Boserup (1965) and Dumond (1965). In simple terms, which do no justice to the complexity of the original work, this model states that population increase on a fixed land base requires people to extract ever greater amounts of food through agriculture, leading to shortening of fallow cycles and a consequent transition from shifting cultivation to permanent cropping. This transition has been labeled agricultural intensification.

This model has been extended by some to explain all prehistoric agricultural change as response to increased population pressure (Harner 1970; Cohen 1977). According to these theorists, progressive increases in prehistoric population size were accompanied by shortening of fallow cycles and then adoption of such techniques as terracing and irrigation in ever intensifying attempts to meet the food crisis. In Maya prehistory we might expect to find that long fallow swidden agriculture was the predominant technique through the Early and Middle Preclassic, with techniques like tree farming, drained fields, and terracing appearing later as population increased (see Harrison 1977).

The Kekchi case supports the basic point of this model—that population increase leads to changes in agricultural techniques aimed at increasing total production. But the same data contradict many of the more detailed predictions of the model and require us to take a more sophisticated view of the complex phenomenon of agricultural intensification.

First, it is useful to remember that population pressure is not the only cause of agricultural intensification. In the Kekchi area natural population growth has a negligible affect on agricultural techniques. Rather, it is the addition of cash crops to the subsistence system that promotes many intensifying measures. Also, people migrate to areas near markets where cash crops can be profitably grown, again causing pressure on land resources (see Smith 1975). The landscape is a mosaic of areas with higher and lower population densities, greater and lesser degrees of intensification. To speak of aggregate population densities for the whole of the Maya Lowlands and to relate them to pan-Maya agricultural techniques (Webster 1977) is meaningless. For any time after about 1000 B.C. in the Maya Lowlands, we must acknowledge the presence of central places, trade networks, and political boundaries, which must have affected population distributions and agricultural techniques.

Second, we must break away from the simple equation of fallow cycles with agricultural intensity. A more appropriate definition must preserve the economists' original meaning of the term intensification: the application of more labor, capital, technology, or skills to production (see Turner and Doolittle 1978). Shorter fallow cycles do not always mean less production, as in areas with soils with high natural fertility or in permanent arboriculture (Netting 1977). Intercropping, multicropping, switching to higher yielding cultivars, weeding, and applications of fertilizer or pesticides are all methods of intensifying agriculture and producing more food without shortening fallow cycles (Grigg 1980). Therefore, there is no reason why short fallow agriculture will necessarily follow shifting cultivation in an evolutionary sequence.

Third, the population pressure model rests on an unrealistic assumption of strict maximizing behavior on the part of farmers, who change agricultural techniques in order to prevent a decline in per capital production. Recent (and also older) work on subsistence and peasant farming has emphasized risk minimization, rather than yield maximization in agricultural decision making (Johnson 1971; Cancian 1972). Kekchi farmers who cultivate in long fallow forest at a distance from their village get lower average yields per man hour of labor than the farmers who use low secondary forest closer to the village, but they accept the lower yield because the higher forest yields are less variable and the risk of crop damage from pests or grass invasion is lower. Response to land shortages due to population pressure will include measures to minimize risk and yield variation instead of, or in addition to, measures aimed at maintaining a high average yield. A sure bet, even with lower average yield, may well be preferred over a technique that has high variability and higher average productivity. Further, a long-term reduction in average yield may be perceived by the farmer as an increase in variability and risk, and the measures taken in response may be designed to improve the stability of the system rather than maintain yield. For example, the farmer might decide to ditch part of the field to improve drainage during heavy rains rather than shorten fallow.

A common technique for minimizing risk is the use of a number of productive systems in different environments, each with different productivity and each with higher or lower risk from different kinds of environmental variation. Mixtures of long and short fallow farming, infield-outfield systems, and the use of subsidiary dooryard gardens are all common ways of dealing with risk (Netting 1977). We should expect to find mixtures of techniques among subsistence farmers rather than exclusive use of a single cropping system. Dependence on a single technique is usually the product of involvement in a regional marketing system, which allows farmers to specialize and to buffer their annual crop variation through the storage of goods or cash by the farmer or the state. This may have been the situation in the Late Classic period in the Maya Lowlands or even in the Early Classic, but it is not a likely scenario for the Preclassic.

Conclusions

The modern Kekchi take up short fallow cultivation of riverbank soils long before serious population pressure on wet season milpa land is felt, because they want to make use of their dry season labor, because dry season yields are not greatly below those of milpa, because of the desire for surplus corn for sale, and because it reduces their overall subsistence risk. I think that similar circumstances were present during the Early through Late Preclassic periods and that we should not expect to find a simple transition from early, long fallow systems to later, short fallow agriculture. From early on, many kinds of farming probably coexisted. Still, there must have been evolutionary changes in the mixture and predominance of techniques.

Predicting what these changes may have entailed cannot rest solely on our knowledge of modern farming. The yield per man hour of milpa, riverbank, and drained field farming in prehistory would have been different because a lithic-based technology was used. The amount of time spent clearing forest with stone tools is far greater than that required with steel axes and machetes (see Carneiro 1979), and this factor would have had an impact on the relative productivity of the systems. Clearing high forest for milpa with steel tools presently takes the Kekchi 151 man hours per hectare out of a total of 560 hours spent per hectare through the whole year. If stone tools were used and the clearing operation took three times as long, the annual harvest would return only 1.62 kg/man hour instead of the present 2.51. In contrast, dry season riverbank farming can be pursued without much clearing labor at all, by burning the sajal rather than slashing and mulching it. The Kekchi prefer not to do this because of the advantages of green mulching, but fires do sometimes occur in the sajal without doing permanent damage to the field. If we accept that regular burning would still require some slashing and spreading (say 80 hrs/ha), and that in the long run yields in such a system would be a third lower than in present sak'ecuaj, we arrive at a yield of 1.92 kg/man hour for a prehistoric riverbank system, well above that of the hypothetical prehistoric long fallow milpa.

I do not offer this example as a definite model for the past systems but to show that changes in technology could switch around the ranking of systems by productivity. Estimating how risks in prehistoric systems may have differed from the modern puts us on even softer ground. Both riverbank and milpa attract animals that are hunted as much for their meat as to protect crops (Linares 1976). Hunting in riverbank fields is easier, since it can be done by paddling a canoe silently down the river and because the field tends to be closer to the village. Crop damage from animals was therefore probably easier to control in riverbank fields.

All this points to a strong possibility that riverbank agriculture was in use just as early, if not earlier than long fallow swidden farming in the Maya Lowlands. Sauer (1958) and the Pulestons (1971) have already made this suggestion; recent archaeological evidence is consistent with this hypothesis (Bloom, Pohl and Stein, chap. 2). Likely analogies for the prehistoric practice exist among South American horticulturalists (Maybury-Lewis 1967). The relative scarcity of large land-clearing axes in the lithic assemblages from Early and Middle Preclassic Cuello in northern Belize support the idea that wet season milpa was not the predominant element of the subsistence system at that time (Hammond et al. 1979). But it should be stressed that riverbank farming was probably only a part of a much more complex yearly round of farming, hunting, and gathering.

If we accept the early predominance or at least presence of riverbank recessional farming, what happened later as population increased? What was the avenue that eventually led to the intensive drained and mounded fields or the vast systems of terraces? The answer must be that there were as many avenues as there were local variations in environment, population growth, and market networks. We must not ignore the possibility that in some areas there was a direct progression from riverbank farming into systems of canalization and mounding. While some drained field systems may have been built in a short period of time as a state-managed enterprise, others may have grown slowly, with little annual labor investment by the cultivators. Given that variation in drainage properties is a significant source of risk in riverbank farming, minor and then major land modification may have been seen as a simple means of reducing risk and of making more land available for use. Canalization would also have helped reduce the other main source of crop damage, animal predation, by allowing hunting by canoe through the field and by isolating fields from the mainland. Canoe access to all parts of the field and canals leading to the settlement would have allowed faster transportation of the crop, a major labor cost in unimproved fields. Any investment in canals would have been paid back in other labor savings within a finite period. Improved estimates of the labor costs of building canals and platforms, like those presented by Turner (1982), will help put this possibility into perspective.

After this theoretical discussion and my disclaimers about using Kekchi riverbank farming as a direct analogy for the past, I must admit to a belief that the riverbank fields of the Preclassic period must have looked much like the modern examples. They may have served a different function in the overall subsistence system, but it is reassuring to think that the practices of the modern Maya farmer are rooted in 4,000 years of accumulated wisdom.

References

Boserup, Esther
1965 *The Conditions of Agricultural Growth.* Aldine, Chicago.

Cancian, Frank
1972 *Change and Uncertainty in a Peasant Economy: The Maya Corn Farmers of Zinacantan.* Stanford University Press, Palo Alto.

Carneiro, Robert
1979 "Tree-Felling with the Stone Ax: An Experiment Carried Out among the Yanomamo Indians of Southern Venezuela." In *Ethnoarchaeology*, edited by Carol Kramer. Columbia University Press, New York, pp. 21–58.

Carter, William E.
1969 *New Lands and Old Traditions: Kekchi Cultivators in the Guatemalan Lowlands.* University of Florida Press, Gainesville.

Coe, Michael
1974 "Photogrammetry and the Ecology of Olmec Civilization." In *Aerial Photography and Anthropological Field Research*, edited by Evon Z. Vogt. Harvard University Press, Cambridge, pp. 1–14.

Coe, Michael, and Richard Diehl
1980 *In the Land of the Olmec.* University of Texas Press, Austin.

Cohen, M. N.
1977 *The Food Crisis in Prehistory: Overpopulation and the Origins of Agriculture.* Yale University Press, New Haven.

Cowgill, Ursula M.
1962 "An Agricultural Study of the Southern Maya Lowlands," *American Anthropologist* 64:273–286.

Culbert, T. P., P. Magers, and M. Spencer
1978 "Regional Variability in Maya Lowland Agriculture." In *Prehispanic Maya Agriculture*, edited by Peter Harrison and B. L. Turner. University of New Mexico Press, Albuquerque, pp. 157–163.

Culbert, T. P., M. Spencer, and P. Magers
1976 "Slash and Burn Agriculture in the Maya Lowlands," *Actes du XLII Congrès International des Américanistes*, 8:335–344.

Denevan, William M.
1982 "Ecological Heterogeneity and Horizontal Zonation of Agriculture in the Amazon Floodplain." Paper presented at the Conference on Frontier Expansion in Amazonia, University of Florida, Gainesville.

Drucker, Phillip, and Robert F. Heizer
1960   "A Study of the Milpa System of La Venta Island and Its Archaeological Implications," *Southwestern Journal of Anthropology* 16:36–45.

Dumond, D. E.
1965   "Population Growth and Agricultural Change," *Southwestern Journal of Anthropology* 16:36–45.

Grigg, David B.
1980   *Population Growth and Agrarian Change: An Historical Perspective.* Cambridge University Press, Cambridge.

Hammond, N. D.
1978   "The Myth of the Milpa: Agricultural Expansion in the Maya Lowlands." In *Prehispanic Maya Agriculture*, edited by Peter Harrison and B. L. Turner. University of New Mexico Press, Albuquerque, pp. 23–34.

Hammond, N., D. Pring, R. Wilk, S. Donaghey, E. Wing, A. Miller, F. Saul and L. Feldman
1979   "The Earliest Lowland Maya?" *American Antiquity* 44:92–110.

Harner, Michael
1970   "Population Pressure and the Social Evolution of Agriculturalists," *Southwestern Journal of Anthropology* 26:67–86.

Harrison, Peter D.
1977   "The Rise of the Bajos and the Fall of the Maya." In *Social Process and Maya Prehistory*, edited by Norman Hammond. Academic Press, London, pp. 470–507.

Healey, P.
1982   "Ancient Maya Terraces at Caracol, Belize." Paper presented at Conference on Lowland Maya Environment and Agriculture, Minneapolis.

Healey, P., C. van Waarden, and T. Anderson
1980   "Nueva Evidencia de Antiguas Terrazas Mayas en Belice," *América Indígena* 40.4:773–797.

Jenkins, R. N., I. P. Anderson, and G. L. Silva
1978   "Toledo Rural Development Project, Belize. Phase 1: Soil, Irrigation and Drainage Studies for the Selection of a Pilot Farm Site." Ministry of Overseas Development Land Resources Division, Project Report no. 41. Surbiton.

Johnson, Allen
1971   *Sharecroppers of the Sertao.* Stanford University Press, Palo Alto.

Joosten, J. H. L.
1962   *Wirtschaftliche und Agrarpolitische Aspekte Tropischer Land Bausysteme.* Institut für Landwirtschaftliche Betriebslehre, Gottingen.

Kelley, I., and A. Palerm
1952   *The Tajin Totonac*, pt. 1. Smithsonian Institution, Social Anthropology Publication 13. Washington, D.C.

Linares, Olga
1976   "'Garden Hunting' in the American Tropics," *Human Ecology*, 4.4:331–350.

Maybury-Lewis, D.
1967   *Akwĕ-Shavante Society.* Clarendon Press, Oxford.

McCloskey, Donald M.
1975   "The Persistence of English Common Fields." In *European Peasants and Their Markets*, edited by W. Parker and E. Jones. Princeton, pp. 73–123.

Morley, S. G.
1946   *The Ancient Maya.* Stanford University Press, Palo Alto.

Netting, Robert M.
1977   "Maya Subsistence: Mythologies, Analogies, Possibilities." In *The Origins of Maya Civilization*, edited by R. E. W. Adams. University of New Mexico Press, Albuquerque, pp. 299–334.

Orozco-Segovia, Alma, and Stephen Gliessman
1979   "The Marceño in Flood-Prone Regions of Tabasco, Mexico." Paper presented in Symposium on Mexican Agroecosystems, 43rd International Congress of Americanists, Vancouver.

Puleston, Dennis
1982   "The Role of Ramón in Maya Subsistence." In *Maya Subsistence*, edited by Kent Flannery. Academic Press, New York, pp. 353–366.

Puleston, Dennis, and Olga Puleston
1971   "An Ecological Approach to the Origins of Maya Civilization," *Archaeology* 24.4:330–337.

Reina, Ruben
1967   "Milpas and Milperos," *American Anthropologist* 69.1:1–20.

Reina, Ruben, and Robert Hill
1980   "Lowland Maya Subsistence: Notes from Ethnohistory and Ethnography," *American Antiquity* 45.1:74–79.

Roosevelt, Anna C.
1980   *Parmana*. Academic Press, New York.

Sauer, Carl
1958   "Man in the Ecology of Tropical America,"
        *Proceedings of the Ninth Pacific Science
        Congress, 1957* 20:105–110.

Smith, Carol
1975   "Production in Western Guatemala: A Test
        of von Thunen and Boserup." In *Formal
        Methods in Economic Anthropology*, edited
        by Stuart Plattner. Special Publication of
        the American Anthropological Association
        4.

Stadelman, Raymond
1940   *Maize Cultivation in Northwestern
        Guatemala*. Carnegie Institution of
        Washington, Contributions to American
        Anthropology and History 33, pp. 83–263.

Turner, B. L., II
1978   "The Development and Demise of the Swid-
        den Thesis of Maya Agriculture." In *Pre-
        Hispanic Maya Agriculture*, edited by Peter
        Harrison and B. L. Turner. University of
        New Mexico Press, Albuquerque, pp.
        13–22.
1982   "Raised Field Construction Techniques."
        Paper presented at Conference on Lowland
        Maya Environment and Agriculture, Min-
        neapolis.

Turner, B. L., II, and William Doolittle
1978   "The Concept and Measure of Agricultural
        Intensity," *Professional Geographer* 30.3:
        297–301.

Vasey, Daniel E.
1979   "Population and Agricultural Intensity in
        the Humid Tropics," *Human Ecology*
        7.3:269–285.

Webster, David
1977   "Warfare and the Evolution of Maya
        Civilization." In *The Origins of Maya
        Civilization*, edited by R. E. W. Adams.
        University of New Mexico Press, Albuquer-
        que, pp. 335–372.

Wilk, Richard R.
1981a   "Agriculture, Ecology and Domestic
        Organization among the Kekchi Maya."
        Ph.D. dissertation, University of Arizona.
        University Microfilms, Ann Arbor.
1981b   "Households in Process: Domestic
        Organization, Land Pressure and Cash
        Crops Among the Kekchi Maya of Belize."
        Paper presented at Wenner-Gren sym-
        posium, Households: Changing Form and
        Function, Mt. Kisco, New York.

Wright, A. C. S., D. H. Romney, R. H. Arbuckle,
and V. E. Vial
1959   *Land in British Honduras*. Colonial
        Research Publication 24. Her Majesty's Sta-
        tionery Office, London.

Part I
The Development and Impact of Ancient Maya Agriculture

Section B: Agriculture and the Environment

Mary Pohl

Limitations of the Environment

Although the positions taken are not so extreme as those in the past, researchers still have subtle differences in attitude about the environment. Turner (chap. 13) and Harrison (Harrison and Turner 1978) follow Denevan's (1982:181) view that agricultural potential is a cultural rather than an environmental phenomenon. Drawing on Boserup's (1965) theory of the relationship between agricultural intensification and population growth, they see the development of labor-intensive fields in swamps like Pulltrouser as an effective, though costly, means of maintaining a productive subsistence economy under the stress of increasing settlement density and concomitant demand for food.

Bloom, Pohl, and Stein (chap. 2) propose that cultivation in some areas like Albion Island involved problems that were hard to resolve at any cost. Rising water levels may have forced the Maya to abandon formerly productive wetland fields on the lower reaches of rivers such as the Hondo. If farmers later returned to cultivate wetlands, they probably found productivity significantly reduced because of infertile clay soils and perhaps also high levels of soluble salts, which characterize these areas today. Recent analysis of upland soils of Northern Belize conducted by Bloom and Crum have revealed deficiencies in certain nutrients, especially zinc, that would have made agricultural intensification (for example, by short fallow swiddening) difficult.

Other work suggests that agriculture, particularly swidden cultivation, caused environmental degradation. Although they hesitate to draw a causal connection with the Maya collapse, D. Rice, P. Rice, and Deevey (chap. 7) maintain that cores from central Petén lakes provide evidence for erosion and nutrient sequestering that may have had a significant effect on productivity. Working in the same area, Wiseman (chap. 5) interprets a maize pollen pulse as indicative of intensive monoculture that might have led to soil exhaustion. Sanders (1979:498–499), also under the influence of Boserup, suggests that with Classic period population pressure, the Maya found it necessary to reduce fallow periods increasingly and that the collapse may have resulted from problems consequent to such agricultural policy. Unfortunately, the data, especially problems with the radiocarbon dates, do not allow us to evaluate fully the effect of cultivation practices on the downfall of Maya civilization.

See chapter 1 for Mary Pohl's affiliation.

Technical Problems in Interdisciplinary Research

Many of the arguments about Maya agriculture and environment hinge on technical problems. The dating quandary caused by carbonate error or hard-water-lake effect has plagued analyses. Aquatic organisms get a substantial portion of their carbon not from the atmosphere but from the surrounding carbonate rock, which is infinitely old on a radiocarbon scale.

The dating problems have resulted in controversy. Wiseman (chap. 5) and Vaughan and colleagues (chap. 6) disagree about the effect of the collapse on vegetation at the end of the Classic period. Wiseman argues for relatively rapid reforestation, while Vaughan and colleagues believe that the process occurred much more slowly.

Pollen analysis promises to provide invaluable data on prehistoric landscape and economy, but we have yet to resolve basic problems of pollen identification. Wiseman has resorted to indirect evidence for his hypothesis that *Gossypium* occurring in pollen samples from the southern Lowlands is cultivated cotton. He points out that pollen of this type appears only in wetland field as opposed to lake contexts and that wild relatives with which cultivated cotton might be confused do not occur in the area.

Puleston (Bradbury and Puleston 1974) had proposed that Chenopodiaceae prevalent in all pollen cores might include cultivated amaranth. Nevertheless, pollen of Chenopodiaceae behaves like other weedy herbs in field contexts such as Pulltrouser Swamp (Wiseman, personal communication, 1981), and amaranth has been conspicuously absent in flotation samples from the southern Lowlands, including the well-preserved *chultun* samples from Cuello (Miksicek 1982). Miksicek suggests that amaranth use was characteristic of drier areas such as Yucatán.

Problems with pollen identifications extend beyond cultigens to forest types like Melastomataceae and Combretaceae (Hansen, in press), which are abundant in a wide variety of biotopes. In the literature these pollen types are referred to as *Terminalia* (Combretaceae), *Terminalia* type, and Melastomataceae. The work of various researchers is difficult to compare because of different methods of classification. Vaughan (chap. 6) has prominent curves for Melastomataceae in central Petén lakes Quexil, Sacnab, and Macanche. In an unpublished diagram, Yezdani has a strong *Terminalia* curve for Quexil but not Melastomataceae, a pattern also found in Tsukada's (1966) profile for nearby Lake Petenxil. In his diagrams for the latter two lakes, Wiseman has a curve he calls *Terminalia* type, and again no Melastomataceae. A great deal of further research in reference collections and examination with the scanning electron microscope is needed to help sort out pollen identification problems such as these.

Even the preservation of pollen is a problem in the tropical forest environment. Wiseman's (1982) tests indicate that soil fungi break down the exine of pollen stored in a plastic bag in six months. If such fungi contaminate ancient samples, they will destroy them too. Pollen samples from excavations should be refrigerated or treated with a preservative such as formalin until they can be studied.

Analogs

In interpreting evidence for past environments, we have a great need for analogs. In particular, we must have models of situations involving human activity or species that people exploit. Such contexts have by and large been ignored by biologists, but Wiseman (chap. 5) has broken new ground by sampling modern pollen rain in fields in various stages of succession.

References

Boserup, E.
1965   *The Conditions of Agricultural Growth.* Aldine, Chicago.

Bradbury, J. P., and D. E. Puleston
1974   "The Use of Pollen Analysis in Investigations of Prehistoric Agriculture." Paper delivered at the 75th annual meeting of the American Anthropological Association, Mexico City.

Denevan, W. M.
1982   "Hydraulic Agriculture in the American Tropics: Forms, Measures and Recent Research." In *Maya Subsistence*, edited by K. V. Flannery. Academic Press, New York, pp. 181–203.

Fish, S. K.
1978   "Palynology of Edzna: Environment and Economy." Paper presented at the 43rd annual meeting of the Society for American Archaeology, Tucson.

Hansen, B. S.
In press   "Pollen Stratigraphy of Laguna de Cocos, Belize." In *Ancient Maya Wetland Cultivation on Albion Island, Northern Belize*, edited by Mary Pohl. University of Minnesota, Publications in Anthropology 2.

Harrison, P. D., and B. L. Turner II
1978   *Pre-Hispanic Maya Agriculture.* University of New Mexico Press, Albuquerque.

Miksicek, C.
1982   "Plant Macrofossils from Northern Belize: A 3000 Year Record of Maya Agriculture and Its Impact on Local Environment." Paper presented at the conference Lowland Maya Environment and Agriculture, Minneapolis.

Sanders, W. T.
1979   "The Jolly Green Giant in Tenth Century Yucatán, or Fact and Fancy in Classic Maya Agriculture," *Reviews in Anthropology* 6:493–506.

Tsukada, M.
1966   "The Pollen Sequence." In *The History of Laguna de Petenxil: A Small Lake in Northern Guatemala*, U. M. Cowgill, G. E. Hutchinson, A. A. Racek, C. E. Goulden, R. Patrick, and M. Tsukada. Memoirs of the Connecticut Academy of Arts and Sciences 17, New Haven.

Wiseman, F. M.
1982   "Palynology in Northern Belize." Paper presented at the conference Lowland Maya Environment and Agriculture, Minneapolis.

Chapter 5

Agriculture and Vegetation Dynamics of the Maya Collapse in Central Petén, Guatemala

Frederick Matthew Wiseman

A major civilization, supported by a diverse agricultural system, arose in the central Maya Lowlands between 250 B.C. and A.D. 900. But by A.D. 1000 the area was almost deserted. Students of Mesoamerican prehistory have long pondered the causes of the abandonment of the central Maya Lowlands in the ninth century A.D.

Many disciplines have been applied to the study of past human and biotic fluctuations of the central Maya Lowlands. Archaeological survey and excavations have documented the slow rise and the rapid decline of prehistoric Maya populations (Puleston 1974:309; Rice 1978). Paleomalacology (Covich and Stuiver 1974:682–691), zooarchaeology (Pohl 1980), and palynology (Tsukada 1966:63–66) have been used to outline biotic changes that have occurred during the last few thousand years. This chapter employs pollen analysis to reconstruct the nature of vegetation response to cultural collapse in the Lowland Maya zone.

Pollen Analysis and the Maya Collapse

Pollen analysis has long been used to measure the response of temperate zone plant communities to the changing climates of the Pleistocene and Holocene. Palynology has only recently been applied to the American tropics, however (Graham 1973:316–360). The first pollen diagrams from the Maya area came from Lake Petenxil, south of Lake Petén. Tsukada (1966:63–66) published two cores, labeled numbers 2

and 3, in which he distinguished three pollen zones: (1) a pre-Maya savanna zone, characterized by the pollen of grassland plants; (2) a Maya zone, inferred from spectra dominated by forb (weed) pollen; and (3) a zone of high forest pollen.

The juncture between the Maya and forest zones was dated by C-14 to 1040 ± 200 B.P. (910 B.C.) in Core 2 and to 1305 ± 140 B.P. (A.D. 645) in Core 3. Carbonate error may effect the C-14 dates from these lakes, which are surrounded by limestone (Deevey 1976:6; Stuiver and Deevey 1961:126–140; Stuiver, Deevey, and Rouse 1963:312–341). The C-14 dates nevertheless tend to agree with the cessation of elite construction dated by stelae to around A.D. 750–900.

The contemporaneity of vegetational change and cultural collapse has been challenged by recent research in nearby Lake Quexil and at the neighboring basin of Yaxha (Deevey et al. 1979:303). The pollen diagram produced by these researchers presents the juncture as a late Postclassic event. The collapse itself is associated with the zone characterized by weeds.

We have two competing interpretations of the pollen dating. In the first interpretation, the catastrophic cultural events of the ninth century A.D. had a profound effect on the vegetation and hence on the pollen. In Deevey and his associates' reconstruction, the collapse had little effect. If the second model is correct, fossil pollen probably cannot be used to study the ecology of the downfall.

Zooarchaeological data can throw light on the problem of dating ambiguity. Hunters were probably exploiting what was available, though the factor of cultural selection should be kept in mind. Instituto de Antropología e Historia de Guatemala excavations in Group G at Tikal produced a faunal sample that can probably be dated to the Terminal Late Classic period. The fauna contains some high forest species, but the fauna is primarily indicative of clearance or emergent secondary forest (Pohl 1980). The Postclassic fauna obtained by G. Cowgill (1963) at Flores (Pohl 1976), now believed to date to the Middle Postclassic period (Arlen Chase, personal communication to Pohl, 1979), may most closely approximate the faunal biomass of modern, relatively undisturbed forest as observed in Surinam and in Panama (Eisenberg and Thorington 1973). Flores is but a few

Frederick Matthew Wiseman is principal research scientist, Center for Materials Research in Archaeology and Ethnology, Massachusetts Institute of Technology, Cambridge.

Partial support for the initial fieldwork was provided by NSF Grant BMS 72-01859 to E. S. Deevey, Jr., and NSF Grant DEB 75-13944 to P. S. Martin and the Department of Geosciences, University of Arizona. Support for reexamination of the pollen cores came from Louisiana State University Advanced Studies and Research Summer Faculty Award. I would like to acknowledge Mary Pohl, the late Dennis Puleston, and B. L. Turner for comments on previous drafts of this chapter.

kilometers from Petenxil basin, and biota must have been very similar at the two locations during the Postclassic period. High forest fauna is also well represented in a Terminal Postclassic – early historic sample from Macal-Tipu, eastern Belize (Pohl 1981).

If the second dating system is valid, one would expect that the animals hunted in the region of Lake Petén during the Postclassic period would reflect open, weedy habitats. They do not. We may suggest, therefore, that the area contained a mature forest fauna by Middle Postclassic times, and by extension, a suite of forest habitats. These data are hard to reconcile with the assumption that the Postclassic vegetation of the lake region was dominated by herbs.

Another argument against the second dating interpretation is that if we accept it, then most of the zone with the highest percentages of maize and disturbance indicators (Wiseman 1978a:109) is Postclassic in age. On the other hand, the Preclassic and Classic period sediments would contain little indication of human agriculture or disturbance.

Analyses of modern agricultural and successional pollen, as well as the results of computer simulation of Precolumbian Maya agriculture, have been applied to this issue (Wiseman 1978a and 1978b). The data indicate that the agricultural systems necessary to support a large Classic period population, in excess of 200 persons per km^2, produced quantities of maize, high- and low-spine compositae and other disturbance indicators. I therefore believe that the present balance of the evidence favors the hypothesis that the archaeological collapse and the radical shift from herb-dominated spectra to forest spectra in the pollen diagrams represent two symptoms of the same process.

Pollen Analysis and the Shift

Seven cores were collected by me from Lakes Petenxil and Ekixil (also known as Quexil) in 1975. The resultant cores were resampled in 1977 and in 1978 for study of the field-forest shift (Wiseman 1978b). The sediment cores were first sampled in 5 cm increments for preparation of standard pollen diagrams (Wiseman 1978a:109). This sampling technique proved too coarse for analyses of vegetation changes that occurred during the cessation of regional agriculture. A second suite of samples, taken at 1 cm intervals, pinpointed the transition from a herbaceous agricultural flora to a forest-dominated pollen spectrum in three of the cores that did not have evidence of significant bioturbation. The other four cores were characterized by a "blurring" of major transitions, probably due to mixing by bottom-dwelling fauna and were rejected. Once the transition had been located by subsampling, it was bracketed by a series of 2 mm samples taken with a core sectioning device. The fine-scale sample set was

then treated with acids to distill the pollen from the sediment. (See Wiseman [1983] for extraction method.) The resulting residues were counted under a microscope using 400X and 1,000X magnifications.

Percentage data were calculated from the counts instead of absolute pollen influx rates. Sedimentary rates, necessary for the influx calculation, were impossible to derive without C-14 dating as a control. Earlier analysis had used reconstructed prehistoric events or ethnohistory as horizon markers (Wiseman 1974), but this approach is fraught with assumptions about cross-dating, problems with palynological seriation and one's own bias. These factors multiply the error inherent in the use of tracers and simple counting error. An alternate strategy was used to reduce the error.

Three pollen sums comprised the final data set. The first sum was fixed at 500 grains of all recognizable pollen. Recognizable pollen consisted of grains identified to biological taxon, as well as those grains distinctive enough to be classified but that have not been matched with a living genus or family ("unknowns"). A second sum, the statistical set, consisted of 500 grains of 17 pollen types that have been shown to contain the greatest information on local vegetation while producing the least statistical noise (Wiseman 1978a). The third sum was variable. It consisted of two taxa: maize (*Zea mays*) and all other pollen grains lumped together.

Maize pollen is uncommon in lake sediments, usually less than 2 percent of the statistical set. The statistical noise in such percentages is large and hinders interpretation of changes in those percentages (Adam 1974:728). The error can be decreased by increasing the pollen sum. For small percentages such as maize, however, the sum needed may be huge. A useful statistic for estimating the effect of sample size on a pollen percentage is the confidence interval.

$$\text{CI pollen} = P + \frac{(3.84)}{(2n)} \pm 1.96\, p\sqrt{1-p+\frac{3.84}{4n^2}}$$

p = percent expressed as tenths;
n = pollen sum.

The variability of maize pollen at the juncture between herb and forest zones was found to be about 3–3.5 percent, based on the second, 1 cm sample. A confidence interval of ± 0.75 percent on maize pollen will separate the two populations and was established as a requirement to allow a sounder interpretation of small changes in this taxon. This restriction required high pollen counts, upwards of 5,000 grains in some cases. Maize pollen was easily recognized, however, and a Veeder Vary tally was used as a mechanical counting aid for the combined taxon. Thus large counts were easily completed.

Some sediment samples lacked sufficient pollen for such counts. This pollen scarcity was probably caused by rapid sedimentation characteristic of lakes during the Classic period (Deevey et al. 1979:302). In these cases, neighboring samples were combined, or exotic tracer pollen was used to increase the sample size.

Preliminary Interpretation of the Core Data

The palynologist uses a pollen diagram as the basis for reconstructing vegetation. Reconstructions are equivocal without some knowledge of the habitat, niche, and pollen productivity of each taxon in the diagram, the mechanics of pollen transport from plant to sediment, and post-depositional processes. Investigation of pollen productivity in vegetation types characteristic of the environs of Lakes Ekixil and Petenxil was conducted in 1973, 1975, and 1979 (Wiseman 1974, 1976, 1978a, and 1978b). While much of the data is not directly applicable to land use change, the information does guide in reconstructing succession.

Pollen samples from 1/10 ha plots were taken in successional areas where the date of clearance was known. The samples indicate that several taxa and groups of taxa accurately discriminate between stages in succession. The first indicator taxon is maize,, which is produced in active fields. This pollen type would not occur in natural plant communities, since maize cannot reproduce itself without human aid. Following abandonment of active fields, a herbaceous flora producing pollen of Chenopodiaceae (Cheno-Am), high spine Compositae, low spine Compositae, Gramineae, and other types quickly replace maize. This weedy flora persists for several years until overshadowed by an arborescent scrub, including the pollen-producing *Trema* and *Acacia*. After a decade or more, depending on characteristics of soil and drainage, secondary forest plants, including producers of the pollen types *Bursera, Manilkara,* and *Zanthoxylum,* recolonize the scrub. From these data, estimators of active plots, newly abandoned fields, successional scrub, and secondary forest were derived.

Fossil pollen spectra may have been produced by communities under decidedly different climatic or agricultural conditions. Application of modern data to fossil pollen spectra must proceed with caution. In order to test the validity of the application, principal components analysis was performed on the modern data. The first principal component had high factor loadings for *Zea* and weeds and negative loadings for secondary trees. This factor was used as a hypothesis to test against the core data.

Pollen data from several cores in Lakes Petenxil and Ekixil were analyzed by principal components analysis. Their first eigenvectors served as the test set

for the modern eigenvector using Pearson's product-moment correlation coefficient. In all cases the modern and fossil data were similar at the .01 confidence level (Wiseman 1978a:109). The structuring within the fossil successional pollen data is sufficiently similar to the modern pollen to allow use of the modern analogs for reconstruction of agricultural collapse (Wiseman 1978a and 1978b).

The estimators that resulted were the following: *Zea* = agriculture; Cheno-*Am,* Compositae, and Gramineae = recently abandoned fields and active disturbance; *Trema* = successional scrub; and *Bursera, Manilkara, Moraceae,* and *Zanthoxylum* = secondary forest. These estimators were examined in the second fossil pollen sum, which consisted of the 17 statistically significant taxa, from cores in Lakes Petenxil and Ekixil. The results of one such analysis are summarized in fig. 5.1.

The main feature, common to all cores that intercepted Classic period sediment, was a replacement of agricultural weeds by secondary forest trees. This event can be placed about 57–61 cm in Core E-5a. In most previously published pollen diagrams from Petén, the sampling interval was so coarse that this transition was expressed only by a line connecting two samples. Use of a finer interval has made the characteristics of this change easier to analyze, although it led to rejection of some cores due to problems in sediment mixing.

The lower portions of the critical transition zone have been termed the "agricultural zone." This division corresponds to Zone G2 in Tsukada's pollen diagrams (1966:64–65) and to the Late Preclassic, Early Classic, and Late and Postclassic zones presented by Deevey et al. (1979:303). Maize pollen is low, at about 1.5 percent. *Trema* is also low at 5 percent. Forest represents about 15 percent of the pollen, while percentages of weeds are high, about 50 percent.

This agricultural zone is palynologically similar to samples taken today from areas under swidden cultivation in central Petén. The pollen indicate that maize was raised in the ancient fields, and several other crops were undoubtedly grown as well (Wiseman 1978a:86). These spectra reflect the widespread suppression of lakeside and upland trees and their replacement by weedy agricultural plots characteristic of the Preclassic and Classic period in the Maya Lowlands. The pollen spectra are similar from sample to sample and from core to core. This fact probably indicates that conditions in the basin were in spatial equilibrium.

The first break in this equilibrium appears at 64 cm in fig. 5.1. A decline in maize pollen that is sustained for three samples, the beginning of a decline in weed pollen, and a resurgence in *Trema* and forest pollen are evident. This change ushers in the second pollen zone, in which evidence for a decline in agriculture can be found.

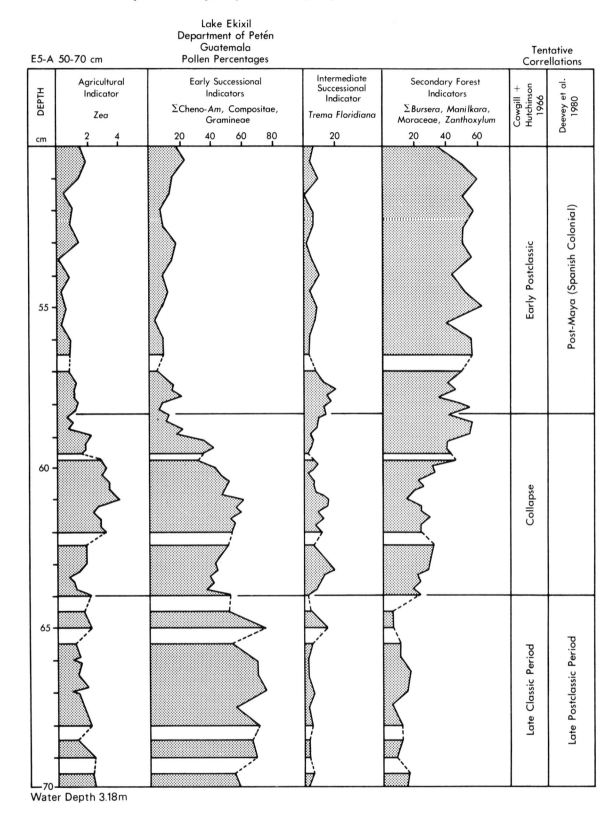

Figure 5.1. Pollen diagram from
Lake Ekixil (Quexil), Petén,
Guatemala.

In many ways, this zone is the most intriguing part of the entire profile. The observed change might be a palynological indicator of a crisis in the agricultural system. The effect could also be a product of bias, statistical problems, or counting error. The latter explanation is unlikely for three reasons. First, the event has been replicated by resampling on either side of the minimum *Zea* sample at 63.4 cm to eliminate the "single minimum" source of error (Faegri and Iversen 1975:125). Second, the counts are large enough that erratic tendencies of minor constitutents in the pollen sum have been eliminated (Halsten, quoted in Faegri and Iversen 1975:124). Third, the effect is systemic; it shows up in several taxa and cores. This pulse may thus represent a social, economic, or ecological event that curtailed local maize production and allowed scrub and secondary forest to colonize fields. The duration of this event could have been as short as one to two years, although sediment mixing by bottom dwelling organisms undoubtedly diffused pollen from this event into immediately adjacent strata.

A marked reversal occurs at 61 cm with a maximum of *Zea* pollen at about 4 percent. This *Zea* maximum can also be seen in Tsukada's core diagrams at about 130 cm in Core 2 and at 185 cm in Core 3 (Tsukada 1966:64–65). The maize maximum was tested for error in the same manner as the maize minimum. The maximum was shown to be a valid pulse. Weed pollen recovers, but forest trees retain higher percentages through the lower half of this zone. The upper half of the zone features a decline in agricultural indicators and an increase in scrub and forest pollen. By the end of the zone, maize pollen is almost absent, and weed pollen reaches its minimum.

The last zone above 58.4 cm reflects ephemeral but persistent agriculture. This zone is characterized by consistently low percentages of maize, by weed and scrub indicators, and by high percentages of forest taxa. These data contain only the sparsest evidence for agriculture in the lowest sections. Agriculture increases in the upper portion, perhaps indicating a slight recolonization of the lake's environs by agriculturalists.

In sum, fine-scale sampling has clarified the history of a crisis in Maya agriculture. A train of events can be followed. First, a rapid decline in maize agriculture occurred. Maize subsequently reappeared in a dramatic fashion. A rise of scrub and forest indicators followed. The application of these data to the issue of the Maya collapse will now be discussed.

The Maya Collapse in the Environs of the Twin Basins

The most complete archaeological sequences in the region of Lakes Petenxil and Ekixil come from Tikal, 70 km to the north (Culbert 1973:66–71), and from the Yaxha region (Rice 1978:35) to the east. An examination of pottery at Tikal provides an outline of the problem. Late Classic period Imix ceramics are associated with the population peak. An estimated 1,000 to 2,000 persons were living in high status residences at Tikal. The distribution of sherds in the Terminal Late Classic Eznab phase indicates a significantly smaller population, about 500 persons. Inhabitants were not living in palaces but camping on top of them. After a hiatus, an apparently ephemeral occupation is represented by the Postclassic Caban phase. This final occupation may have been intrusive, possibly the result of sporadic ceremonial visits to the once-great center (Culbert 1973:66–71).

The question arises whether the phenomenon that affected those living in elite residences at Tikal penetrated to lower levels of Maya society. In his survey of housemounds in the Lake Yaxha and Sacnab basins, Rice (1978:144) found a dramatic change in population density from 210 persons per km² to 21.6 persons per km² during the Terminal Classic period. Ford (1980) has found that intersite areas between Tikal and Yaxha continued to be occupied, though at population levels lower than those attained during the climax of Maya civilization in Petén.

The sites of Tayasal and Ixlu are located in the area where the pollen cores were taken. They were small Maya centers that enjoyed a brief ascent to elite status during the Late Classic and Terminal Late Classic periods. Stela dedications dated from A.D. 854 to A.D. 879 at Ixlu and A.D. 790 to A.D. 869 at Tayasal (Morley 1956:64). The sites persisted longer than the larger elite center of Tikal where the last dedication date is A.D. 869. The Ixlu stelae feature intrusive Mexican elements (J. Graham 1973:213). Non-Maya traits are also found at Jimbal, which is close to Tikal, in the Terminal Late Classic period and at Tayasal and Flores in the Early Postclassic period (Chase and Chase 1980).

The fields surrounding the Petenxil-Ekixil basins were farmed by persons under the political influence of these sites. Pollen analysis indicates that these agriculturalists raised maize and that fields contained significant numbers of weeds. The inhabitants probably practiced swidden agriculture with a definite fallow cycle during the Late Classic period. This Late Classic agricultural regime is statistically indistinguishable from modern swidden agriculture in the same area (Wiseman 1978a).

These agriculturalists may have had a variety of food sources in addition to conventional agriculture, but we have no specific evidence for exploitation of other resources. Intensive systems of tree cropping, such as artificial rain forest (Wiseman 1973) and sylviculture (Puleston 1968), would have been rendered palynologically invisible by weedy fallow or border zones.

After this period, the agricultural system in the area was apparently briefly interrupted. Maize plots and associated weed-infested, fallow fields declined. Scrub and forest plants made significant inroads on old field surfaces. Forest plants were probably never cut back to levels characteristic of the Late Classic period.

The sequel to this agricultural minimum was the reappearance of maize cultivation, hinted at by the maize pollen maximum of the seven sediment cores from Lakes Petenxil and Ekixil that contained Classic period deposits. The maize episode is indistinct in one and absent in one. More than a localized, highly productive field is indicated. The reason for this event is unclear, but its magnitude may be roughly estimated.

Modern pollen was gathered from the mud-water interface at Lakes Petenxil and Ekixil. This pollen was compared with the prehistoric maize pollen maximum. The intensity of the latter was measured by the deviation between the maximum percentage of the ancient maize and the modern sample in each core, summed and divided by the number of cores (Wiseman 1978b):

$$M_m = \frac{(P_e - P_m)}{n} = 9.74$$

P_e = maximum *Zea* pollen during maize event;
P_m = maximum *Zea* pollen in modern sample;
n = number of cores.

Today 25–30 percent of the area around the cored lakes is covered with agricultural plots and young second growth. The pollen evidence suggests that maize agriculture was ten times as great during the maize maximum. While this figure is geographically unrealistic and indicative of the problems inherent in the comparison of modern and fossil data, the results must nevertheless be taken as evidence for agriculture that was more intensive than that practiced today. The watershed may have been completely covered by maize plots.

The basins of Ekixil and Petenxil were converted to such cultivation for only a short time according to the pollen record. Productivity probably exceeded the subsistence needs of the residents of Tayasal, Ixlu or other hamlets within the watersheds of the basins. Surplus maize may have been exported.

The maize maximum appears to have been ecologically disastrous. Its effects can be seen in the agricultural collapse of the basins. Maize and open-field indicators decrease sharply, and secondary scrub shows a minor maximum soon after. These data indicate that recolonization by forest was occurring. Secondary forest, which had been increasing its pollen productivity throughout the maize maximum, soon reached post-collapse levels. This change is certain evidence for depopulation. We do not know whether the change occurred during the collapse or during the subsequent Postclassic period. As in the neighboring Tikal and Yaxha areas, population levels may have decreased by emigration or by death.

A small group of agriculturalists persisted in the region of the two basins. These farmers are palynologically visible by some maize and weed indicators (fig. 5.1). These people probably made the Postclassic ceramics found in the area of Lake Petén. During this period, swamp and upland forest reestablished itself in the area.

Sharer (1977:531) has contended that Maya elites recognized the existence of problems that could have led to societal collapse and that they made every effort to reduce its impact. He suggests that agricultural production was intensified and that ceremonial construction was accelerated during the Late Classic period. In Sharer's view, these measures were a response to social stress, not simply a cause of it. The concept of response to stress is intriguing. Pollen may provide evidence for Maya agrarian policies as adaptive strategies.

During the Early Classic period, coercion probably replaced economic incentives as the motivation for agricultural productivity. The reasons are manifold. They include higher "prices" for goods and produce, increasing levels of consumption by the growing elite bureaucracy, and sporadic scarcities (Culbert 1973:527). The result would have been a highly regulated system of production, perhaps including prescribed cultivars and agricultural systems, and of tightly controlled distribution, including trade and storage. The system must have been managed by some segment of the hierarchy roughly corresponding to the U.S. Department of Agriculture, with similar coercive powers. Agriculture must have become a tool of the hierarchy. Agrarian policy could have been used to meet any crises perceived by the elite.

The pollen data from the two basins indicate a slow decrease in maize and weed indicators throughout the Classic period prior to the collapse (Wiseman 1978a:109). This pattern may be evidence for an expansion of trade and a change from swidden plots managed by farmers to intensive agriculture managed by elites.

By the Late Classic period, Maya elites were participants in a fully civilized, sociopolitical system. A secure, intensive agricultural base probably contributed to the development of Maya civilization.

Contra Sharer (1977:544), intensification was probably not developed as a result of Classic period stress. Evidence for intensive agriculture dates as early as the Preclassic period (Puleston 1977; Turner and Harrison 1981). Highly productive cultivation systems were widely used by the Early Classic Maya and no doubt contributed to the population densities of the Late Classic period. We have archaeological and paleoecological evidence for a variety of subsistence techniques, including swidden agriculture, wetland field and canal systems, terracing, and artificial rain-forest (Wiseman 1978a). These options must have contributed to the stability of the Maya economy.

The increase in elite construction during the Late Classic period must have had profound effects upon subsistence. Agriculturalists were removed from their fields. They would have become masons and builders. Newly conscripted urban laborers would have to have been fed by the remaining agriculturalists. Labor shortages during critical times in the agricultural cycle may have occurred. Intensive agrarian systems, such as terraces and raised fields, require more work than extensive methods of agriculture. Intensive systems would therefore have been more vulnerable to labor shortages, and the limits of the Maya system of production and distribution may have been approached.

As the Terminal Classic crisis loomed, increasing interruption of trade in foodstuffs may have occurred. Causes probably lay in interference from outsiders (Ball 1977; Chase and Chase 1982) as well as internal problems in elite centers. The shunting of manpower into ceremonial construction must have been a particular problem.

Pollen provides some evidence for interruptions. Such an event may be recorded in the agricultural minimum and in the distinctive rise of secondary forest pollen. Secondary scrub recolonization probably occurred first in the least productive plots or in lands planted in crops for export.

The character of this recolonization is problematic. The source of each recolonizing sere is progressively harder to explain. Present-day succession in Petén progresses through herb, scrub, and tree stages. Taxa quickly following abandonment of a field include grasses (e.g., *Olyra* sp.), *Irsine* sp., *Solanum nigrum*, and the composites *Zexmenia* and *Eupatorium*. Today the seed reservoir for this first stage is present as infield and boundary weeds in agricultural plots. The same source is assumed for early successional plants that appeared at the end of the Late Classic period.

The seed sources for the later secondary scrub plants, such as the genera *Cecropia, Cassia, Alvaradoa, Croton, Guazuma, Piper,* and *Acacia,* would not have been in the fields or in border habitats. These are large plants, usually over 2 m high. They have no place in a well-tended field system. They would have been repeatedly cut for firewood or removed to reduce competition with cultivars. They may have resided in long fallowing plots, on hill crests too steep to crop, along pathways, or in areas under legal dispute. The secondary forest stage, as seen in the Terminal Classic pollen data, probably occurred on hill slopes or in edaphic microhabitats unsuitable for agriculture, such as the oak woodlands or savannas.

Habitats with the best potential for mesic forest (Wiseman 1978a:67) must certainly have been used for agriculture at this time. The more mesic plants may

have had but a few ravine microhabitats as refuges. Most mesic forest taxa have insect-pollinated flowers. Seeds are dispensed by gravity or with the aid of animals. Such species include *Manilkara* (*zapote*) and *Brosimum* (*ramón*). Other taxa with wind-dispersed seeds, *Swietenia* (mahogany) for example, use inefficient samaras or wings. Thus mesic forest species have a small seed shadow compared to the secondary plants, such as those in the sunflower family with their more efficient, wind-dispersed seeds. The migration rate for large, woody plants would have been slow. Hundreds of years may have been required to reach a mesic forest equilibrium in the Petenxil-Ekixil area. The recolonizing forest that began at this time must have had a xeric, semi-deciduous character because such forest probably covered the poorest slopes of Petén hills, the exhausted soils of the lowlands, or the margin of the oak forest to the south of the lakes.

With forest encroaching on abandoned plots and supplies of imported foodstuffs becoming sporadic, elites would probably have concentrated on obtaining food for themselves and on maintaining their status. Elites at Ixlu and Tayasal may have forced this strategy on agriculturalists in the Petenxil-Ekixil watersheds. The Petén agriculturalists who had been planting well-adapted combinations of crops may have had to focus their efforts on a very few species. Heavy maize production may have had something to do with Ixlu's brief rise to elite status during the collapse. This hypothesis is supported by evidence for increase in maize pollen.

Shifts may have been made quickly and without consideration of local conditions or long-term effects. Monoculture of a crop such as maize is deleterious to the nutrient balance of the soil (Wiseman 1973). Intensive maize cultivation must have resulted in nutrient strain. Soil exhaustion must have occurred, first in marginal fields, later in the most productive habitats. Once environmental degradation had taken place, a return to earlier, productive techniques would have been difficult, if not impossible. The encroaching scrub forest and grasslands would have been more difficult to deal with than the previous vegetation.

The agrarian population may eventually have broken under increased demands for labor coupled with diminishing agricultural returns. The resulting revitalization movements postulated in the Maya Lowlands (Sharer 1977:547) may have been a final response on the part of the people. Agricultural reform may have alleviated soil depletion in the best sites, such as those around lakes. Most of the land would have been ruined, however. The Maya would have had to move away or face starvation.

At this point the secondary forest, which had been increasing during the Late Classic period, quickly expanded into former upland fields. Agriculture may still have been practiced in those few areas unaffected by soil depletion. Former farming settlements and elite centers must have been engulfed by an increasing tide of scrub and dry monsoon forest, however. The remaining agriculturalists probably kept some paths open through the scrub for ceremonial visits to the old temple complexes as part of their revitalization effort. Eventually, the vegetative recolonization of ancient cultural surfaces was complete. Natural processes of vegetational succession replaced agricultural management.

Many habitats, although deficient in nutrients, had the potential for mesic forest. As time passed, pioneering plants would have altered the soil, added organic nutrients, and provided protection from solar insolation and erosion. The beneficial effects of the early plant colonists would have provided favorable conditions for more mesic species. Mesic forest slowly recolonized Petén to produce the forests that occur there today.

Sometime following the collapse a small re-emergence of maize cultivation appeared in the Petenxil and Ekixil basins. We do have archaeological evidence for Postclassic use of the sites of Tayasal and Ixlu. While the collapse was devastating, it did not eliminate the Maya entirely.

Summary

There is a drastic shift in pollen spectra in the upper portions of pollen diagrams from the Maya Lowlands. This shift is believed to have been culturally caused, either as a result of the Maya collapse or a Late Postclassic decline. Independent faunal evidence supports the first interpretation. A fine-scale sampling strategy was devised to render this shift amenable to analysis as a process rather than an abrupt transition between two states. Several episodes lie within the major shift, including a decline in agricultural indicators, a rapid resurgence of maize pollen, and finally an agricultural collapse. Combining the meager Terminal Late Classic archaeological data from the watersheds of the pollen core sites with the pollen data, a hypothetical land use sequence is derived. This scenario includes a conversion of land from diverse intensive agriculture to maize monoculture with its attendant denudation, reinforcing the social chaos attending the Maya collapse.

References

Adam, D. P.
1974   "Palynological Applications of Principal Component and Cluster Analyses," *Journal of Research, United States Geological Survey* 2:727–742.

Adams, R. E. W.
1973   "The Collapse of Maya Civilization: A Review of Previous Theories." In *The Classic Maya Collapse*, edited by T. P. Culbert. University of New Mexico Press, Albuquerque, pp. 21–34.

Ball, J. W.
1977   "A Hypothetical Outline of Coastal Maya Prehistory: 300 B.C. – A.D. 1200." In *Social Processes in Maya Prehistory*, edited by N. Hammond. Academic Press, London. pp. 167–196.

Bullard, W. L.
1973   Postclassic Culture in Central Peten and Adjacent British Honduras. In *The Classic Maya Collapse*, edited by T. P. Culbert. University of New Mexico Press, Albuquerque, pp. 221–242.

Chase, D. Z., and A. Chase
1982   "Yucatec Influence in Terminal Classic Northern Belize," *American Antiquity* 47:596–614.

Covich, A., and M. Stuiver
1974   "Changes in Oxygen 18 as a Measure of Long-Term Fluctuations in Tropical Lake Levels and Molluscan Populations," *Limnology and Oceanography* 19:682–691.

Cowgill, G. L.
1963   "Postclassic Period Culture in the Vicinity of Flores, Petén, Guatemala." Ph.D. dissertation, Department of Anthropology, Harvard University.

Culbert, T. P.
1973   "The Maya Downfall at Tikal." In *The Classic Maya Collapse*, edited by T. P. Culbert. University of New Mexico Press, Albuquerque, pp. 63–92.

Culbert, T. P., editor
1973   *The Classic Maya Collapse.* University of New Mexico Press, Albuquerque.

Deevey, E. S.
1976   "Holocene Forests and Maya Disturbance near Lake Quexil, Petén, Guatemala." Revised version of a paper delivered at the 2nd International Symposium on Paleolimnology, Mikolaiki, Poland.

Deevey, E. S., D. Rice, P. Rice, H. Vaughan, M. Brenner, and M. Flannery
1979 "Mayan Urbanism: Impact on a Tropical Karst Environment," *Science* 206:298–306.

Eisenberg, J. F., and R. W. Thornington, Jr.
1973 "A Preliminary Analysis of Neotropical Mammal Faunas," *Biotropica* 5:150–161.

Faegri, K., and J. Iversen
1975 *Textbook of Pollen Analysis.* 2nd ed. Hafner Press, New York.

Ford, A.
1980 "Classic Maya Settlement Patterns and Problems of Economic and Political Complexity." Paper presented at the 45th annual meeting of the Society for American Archaeology, Philadelphia.

Graham, A.
1973 "Literature on Vegetational History in Latin America." In *Vegetation and Vegetational History of Northern Latin America*, edited by A. Graham. Elsevier, Amsterdam.

Graham, J.
1973 "Aspects of Non-Classic Presences, Inscriptions and Sculptural Art at Seibal." In *The Classic Maya Collapse*, edited by T. P. Culbert. University of New Mexico Press, Albuquerque, pp. 207–220.

Morley, S. G.
1956 *The Ancient Maya.* 3rd ed. Stanford University Press, Stanford.

Pohl, M.
1976 "Ethnozoology of the Maya." Ph.D. dissertation, Department of Anthropology, Harvard University.
1980 "The Terminal Classic Period Economy at Tikal." Paper presented at 45th annual meeting of the Society for American Archaeology, Philadelphia.
1981 "Faunal Remains from Macal-Tipu: 1981 Season." Manuscript in Tallahassee, Florida.

Puleston, Dennis E.
1968 "*Brosimum alicastrum* as a subsistence alternative for the Classic Maya of the Central Southern Lowlands:." M.A. thesis, University of Pennsylvania. University Microfilms, Ann Arbor.
1974 "Intersite Areas in the Vicinity of Tikal and Uaxactun." In *Mesoamerican Archaeology: New Approaches*, edited by N. Hammond. University of Texas Press, Austin, pp. 303–312.
1977 "The Art and Archaeology of Hydraulic Agriculture in the Maya Lowlands." In *Social Processes in Maya Prehistory*, edited by N. Hammond. Academic Press, London, pp. 449–469.

Rice, D. S.
1978 "Population Growth and Subsistence Alternatives in a Tropical Lacustrine Environment." In *Prehispanic Maya Agriculture*, edited by P. D. Harrison and B. L. Turner. University of New Mexico Press, Albuquerque, pp. 35–62.

Sharer, R. M.
1977 "The Maya Collapse Revisited: Internal and External Perspectives." In *Social Processes in Maya Prehistory*, edited by N. Hammond. Academic Press, New York, pp. 532–552.

Stevens, J. L.
1963 *Incidents of Travel in Yucatan.* 2 vols. Dover, New York. Originally published 1841.

Stuiver, M., and E. S. Deevey
1961 "Yale Natural Radiocarbon Measurements VI." *Radiocarbon*, 3:126–146.

Stuiver, M. E., S. Deevey, and I. Rouse
1963 "Yale Natural Radiocarbon Measurements VIII," *Radiocarbon* 5:312–341.

Tsukada, M.
1966 "The Pollen Sequence." In *The History of Laguna de Petenxil*, by U. Cowgill and G. E. Hutchinson. Memoirs of the Connecticut Academy of Arts and Sciences 17, pp. 63–66.

Turner, B. L., II, and P. D. Harrison
1981 "Prehistoric Raised-Field Agriculture in the Maya Lowlands," *Science* 213:399–405.

Wiseman, F. M.
1973 "The Artificial Rainforest." Paper presented at the 38th annual meeting of the Society for American Archaeology, San Francisco.
1974 "Paleoecology and the Prehistoric Maya." M.S. thesis, Department of Geosciences, University of Arizona.
1975 "The Earliest Maya." Paper presented at the 40th annual meeting of the Society for American Archaeology, Dallas.
1978a Agricultural and Historical Ecology of the Maya Lowlands. In *Prehispanic Maya Agriculture*, edited by P. D. Harrison and B. L. Turner II. University of New Mexico Press, Albuquerque, pp. 63–116.
1978b "The Terminal Classic Maize Episode." Paper delivered at 43rd annual meeting of the Society for American Archaeology, Tucson.
1983 "Analysis of Pollen from the Fields at Pulltrouser Swamp." In *Pulltrouser Swamp: Ancient Maya Habitat, Agriculture, and Settlement in Northern Belize*, edited by B. L. Turner II and P. D. Harrison. University of Texas Press, Austin, pp. 105–119.

Chapter 6

Pollen Stratigraphy of Two Cores from the Petén Lake District, with an Appendix on Two Deep-water Cores

Hague H. Vaughan, Edward S. Deevey, Jr., and S. E. Garrett-Jones

During reconnaissance in the Petén lake district in 1972, inaugurating the University of Florida project Historical Ecology of the Maya Area (see Rice, Rice, and Deevey, chap. 7), Vaughan and G. H. Yezdani cored the sediments under 7.2 m of water in the western part of Lake Quexil (Ekixil). Preliminary study of pollen and sediment chemistry (Vaughan 1976, 1978b; Deevey 1978) showed that the period spanned, about 8,400 radiocarbon years, was at least twice as long as that previously known from nearby Lake Petenxil (Tsukada 1966). In 1973 and 1974, however, when H. K. Brooks and Vaughan raised several longer but stratigraphically less complete cores from Lakes Yaxha and Sacnab, correlations between lakes were less straightforward. In addition to the usual problems of palynology—identification of pollen from a huge, little-studied tropical flora; statistical

Hague H. Vaughan is head, Monitoring and Agreements, Inland Waters Directorate, Environment Canada, Western and Northern Region, Regina, Saskatchewan, Canada. Edward S. Deevey, Jr., is graduate research professor, The Florida State Museum, University of Florida, Gainesville. S. E. Garrett-Jones was research associate, Department of Natural Sciences, Florida State University, at the time he wrote this paper and is now senior project officer, (Australian Federal) Department of Science and Technology, Belconnen.

In revising this chapter, a short version of Vaughan's Ph.D. dissertation (1979), Vaughan and Deevey profited greatly from consultation with S. E. Garrett-Jones, who joined the Florida group for the drilling campaigns of 1978 and 1980. His new pollen diagrams, exhibited but not previously published (Deevey, Garrett-Jones, and Vaughan 1980), are given in his appendix to this chapter. All three authors have had the benefit of discussions with Don S. Rice and Prudence M. Rice and with Mark Brenner, who has examined the same sediment cores for fossils other than pollen and whose Ph.D. dissertation has now been completed. Thanks are also due to F. M. Wiseman and Mary Pohl, cochairmen and contributors to the Society for American Archaeology symposium at Tucson in 1978, and to other readers of various versions of this work. Our project has been supported by the National Science Foundation under grants BMS 72-01859, DEB 77-06629, EAR 79-26330, and EAR 82-14308.

uncertainty and ecological ambiguity of pollen percentages; local or perhaps regional differences of vegetation and of pollen rain in study areas 50 km apart— the special sedimentology of the Petén lakes poses special difficulties, both for correlation and for environmental interpretations. This account of our results emphasizes the difficulties, because Mayanists need to understand what can and what cannot be inferred from pollen.

Sedimentological Problems

Some of the difficulties experienced in this work are traceable to the little-known mechanism, colluviation, by which much Petén lake sediment was emplaced. Offshore deposits of inland lakes are mixtures, more or less re-sorted by particle size, of organic and inorganic, airborne and waterborne materials of aquatic (autochthonous) and terrestrial (allochthonous) provenance. Limnologists generally emphasize the organic, especially the identifiable fossil constituents, among which airborne pollen grains carry ecological information far out of proportion to their abundance. The source of the inorganic matrix of silt and clay, normally at least half and often over 90 percent of the total, is the soils of the drainage basin; but what is seen microscopically is no longer soil but detrital minerals and rock fragments, presumably delivered as alluvium, that is, by running water, and redistributed over the lake bottom. Although much soil also moves downhill in bulk, by gravity, entering a lake as colluvium, colluvial and alluvial soil particles are not distinguishable after redeposition in standing water.

Under exceptional geologic circumstances, in high latitudes, lake sediments of colluvial origin can be distinguished by their abnormal pollen content. The varved glaciolacustrine clays of Scandinavia are colluvially deposited rock flour, unfossiliferous except for pollen derived from pre-Pleistocene lignite beds (Iversen 1936). Masses of mull soil, rich in heather (*Calluna*) pollen, are known to have slid from steep hillsides in the English Lake District (Mackereth 1966; Pennington 1969). Among criteria for recognition of "secondary" or "rebedded" pollen, when anomalous geologic age cannot be proved, are differential destruction of all but the most resistant types, such as heather, and microscopic evidence of bacterial or other oxidative attack on surfaces of grains that survive two-stage deposition.

In the heavily forested Petén lake district, so different in character from glaciated landscapes, we did not anticipate extensive colluviation. The soil-stabilizing forest is a post-Maya phenomenon, however, and thin karst soils are now known, on several lines of indirect evidence, to have been more mobile during Maya times (Deevey et al. 1979, 1980; Deevey and Rice 1980). The first such indication appeared in the 1973 core from Lake Yaxha, where the thick Maya clay proved to contain few microfossils other than obviously secondary pollen. Some evidence of surface attack on pollen grains was then detected in the Maya clay zones of the Sacnab core, but pollen in the (more organic) clay-gyttja zones of the Quexil core, thought to be in part colluvial because of their relatively high carbonate content, shows no signs of rebedding.

Later, in a study of lacustrine animal and plant microfossils, Brenner (1978) found all fossils suspiciously scarce in clay zones of all cores, including Quexil. All planktonic fossils are subject to at least some diagenetic (post-depositional) loss of structure, even in freshly deposited sediments (Deevey, Vaughan, and Deevey 1977); Brenner suggested that exceptionally severe loss results from mechanical abrasion by sand-size (volcanic glass?) particles dispersed in clay. In any case, whether most abrasion occurs during soil movement or during transport of mineral detritus within the lake, Brenner's data support our finding that Quexil pollen is least affected, as Yaxha pollen is most affected, by diagenesis in the Maya clay.

As was proved by sediment-trap experiments in Lakes Yaxha and Sacnab (Deevey, Vaughan, and Deevey 1977), the sediment sampled by coring is not a uniform blanket that settles evenly on a lake bottom. After repeated resuspension, indicated by the present-day turbidity of Petén lakes, sediments move across the lake bottom, and before final burial there is a net centripetal transport (sediment focusing) that tends to fill deep sinkholes and trenches while shoals retain less sediment or none (Lehman 1975; Deevey, Vaughan, and Deevey 1977; Deevey et al. 1980). Raising of complete or fully representative stratigraphic sections in an unmapped and topographically complex basin is therefore often a matter of luck.

Because of apparatus limitations all the 1972–74 cores were taken in relatively shallow water; the Sacnab core alone was near the present-day maximum depth. Now (1980) that deep-water cores are available from Lakes Quexil, Macanche, and Salpeten, we can see that our first Quexil core was our luckiest hit. It is short (6.5 m) compared with the 9.2 m length of core

Quexil H (1978), taken in 30 m of water, but stratigraphically fully representative. Within the period spanned, about 8,400 C-14 years in both cores, the principal difference is that the Maya clay is thicker and more homogeneous in the deep basin. The pollen diagrams of both cores are closely similar, and Garrett-Jones reports no evidence of surface attack on pollen in the Maya clay. Presumably our initial success in shallow water reflects the fact that the core is not on an exposed shoal but near the center of a shallow subsidiary basin, which would be an independent lake if water level were 4 m lower than at present.

Substantial place-to-place differences in thickness of the Maya clay, from about 1.6 m in our Quexil core to more than 6.3 m in Lake Yaxha, imply changes of sedimentation rate over time that are at least as large; deposition of silicious sediment in Lake Yaxha, during a time thought to be Early Classic, was amplified over earlier rates by about 500 times (Deevey and Rice 1980). Ordinarily, because the instrumental and statistical uncertainties of C-14 assay amount to a few percent (a few decades), large variations of sedimentation rate are easier to establish than small variations. To our regret, after repeated attempts, some 29 C-14 measurements by three laboratories have been rejected as meaningless. Two kinds of uncertainty, both geochemical in origin, invalidate all dates on Petén lake sediments except DAL 198, 8410 ± 180 (Ogden and Hart 1977), a sample of terrestrial wood from near the bottom of the Quexil core.

The first difficulty, the "hard-water-lake effect" (Deevey et al. 1954; Deevey and Stuiver 1964), stems from metabolic incorporation, in tissues as well as shells of lacustrine organisms, of carbon dissolved as bicarbonate from ancient (C-14-free) limestone. Dates from Tsukada's Petenxil cores (Stuiver and Deevey 1961; Stuiver et al. 1963) were not corrected for limestone carbon; valid correction is in fact impossible when, as in these lakes, siltation has caused exposure of lake water to limestone to diminish irregularly over time. Dating errors in excess of 30 percent of the C-14 assay, or about 2,500 years, can be expected from this source alone.

The other, even more serious, difficulty is that colluvium, especially when composed of carbonate-rich soil, can enter a lake with any isotopic composition or apparent age, from "modern" to "infinitely old." Bulk samples of lake sediment formed in this way give a jumble of meaningless dates, while carbonate fractions are sometimes "older" and sometimes "younger" than organic fractions of the same sample.

Unlike redeposited pollen, which can affect the interpretation of pollen as samples of vegetation but is believed not to do so in the Quexil cores, uncontrolled variations of C-14 abundance affect only the chronologic, not the paleoecological inferences regularly drawn from pollen sequences. This crucial distinction, rarely made explicit by palynologists, is often misunderstood by archaeologists. The reason is probably that the "pollen chronology" of European archaeology, before radiocarbon, was a true though imprecise chronology, dated by reference to climate changes of known age. Outside this context, a pollen "event" is not a date but a layer in a stratigraphic sequence. Having neither C-14 dates nor a known climatic chronology, we date these layers by reference to phases of human occupation, which we believe to have caused the pollen events. Reversing archaeological practice in this way is not circular for us but is circular for any archaeologist tempted to use our dates as independent evidence of age. These chronologic and stratigraphic questions need further discussion before we turn to ecological interpretations.

Stratigraphic Problems

With C-14 dating of lake sediments precluded, we are forced to rely on pollen assemblages and their sequences for any useful subdivision of our cores. In adopting this approach we stress that assemblages are first defined objectively and arbitrarily, their botanical meaning being, for the moment, irrelevant. What matters for stratigraphy is that definable sequences of changing composition be reproducible in other sections. Water-laid pollen assemblages come from airsheds of indefinite area, containing unspecifiable proportions of distant, low-growing, or nonwind-pollinated plants, and are at best strongly biased representatives of upland vegetation. Moreover, pollen counts are laborious, identification is rarely possible below the level of the genus, and statistical (binomial) variance is high, especially for types of low percentage frequency. Once distinctive pollen-stratigraphic zones have been established within any one core or lake, however, as was done by Tsukada in Lake Petenxil, equivalent zones can be looked for in other lakes. The working assumptions are that major changes of terrestrial vegetation have been of similar character and therefore approximately synchronous over broad upland areas surrounding both lakes. High binomial variance can be discounted, even for infrequent types, if even nonsignificant trends of percentages are consistently reproduced in two or more sections.

These assumptions have regularly been validated by independent evidence where climatic change has been the major control over vegetation and the regional pollen rain. Equivalence of pollen zones is thereby easily demonstrated between widely separated and dissimilar deposits. Such equivalence is very general and is arrived at by setting aside local differences arising from intraregional variations of topography, microclimate, specific composition of vegetation, and mechanics of sedimentation. Even when refined by independent dating, such a broad-brush chrono-

stratigraphy has low resolution. For example, if a 10 m thick, 10,000 year long section has ten pollen zones, stratigraphic assignment is accurate only to about a meter or one millennium. Similarly, Tsukada's three pollen zones, which overlie three others in the Quexil sections, do not take us very far toward resolving events a few *katuns* apart.

Human interference with vegetation inevitably alters pollen assemblages, masking responses to climate and violating the assumption of synchrony. Selective attack on supposed climatic indicators, such as elm in Neolithic Europe, distorts pollen evidence in subtle ways (Godwin 1961). Pueblo shamans, ceremonially blowing maize pollen to the six directions, have been accused of "[playing] fast and loose with history" (Martin 1963:*v*). Wholesale forest clearance, at least in regions where a few tall tree species produce most of the regional pollen rain, can mimic a major climatic shift toward savanna, steppe, or even tundra. Reduction of forest-tree pollen is then proportionate to rises of pollen of herbs and shrubs of open country, that is, savanna or grassland; but the cereal (grass) and weed pollen characteristic of landscapes cleared for agriculture is seldom distinguishable, except perhaps by stratigraphic context, from pollen of native grassland.

Extensive forest clearance in Petén is now proved stratigraphically by intercalation of dominantly clay sediments, almost devoid of arboreal pollen, between younger and older organic layers containing much pollen of tropical forest. The older forest-pollen zones, first seen in Lakes Quexil and Sacnab, and now known also from Lake Macanche, were not reached in the Yaxha core and may not exist in shallower Lake Petenxil. Tsukada could not surmise their existence. His division of the oldest sediments accessible to him into two zones, interpreted as savanna, probably induced by agriculture, was based on sequences of nonarboreal, putative weed pollen, which were consistent and consistently overlain by forest-tree pollen in his two Petenxil cores. Archaeological considerations, roughly supported by a few C-14 dates, converted the tripartite sequence into a chronostratigraphy. As such, it was and is of strictly local applicability, for a change of upland vegetation, if not a response to changing climate, need not have been synchronous over the lake district. Our first Quexil section, however, lies only a kilometer away from Lake Petenxil, within the same airshed. Thus we take the upper three pollen zones in the two lakes to be locally coeval (within a century or so) as well as stratigraphically equivalent.

In the presence of overwhelming evidence of human disturbance, pollen correlations across the 50 km distance between the Quexil and Yaxha districts need not carry the same implication of contemporaneity. The usual advantage of comparison over such a distance, that it separates local from regional dif-

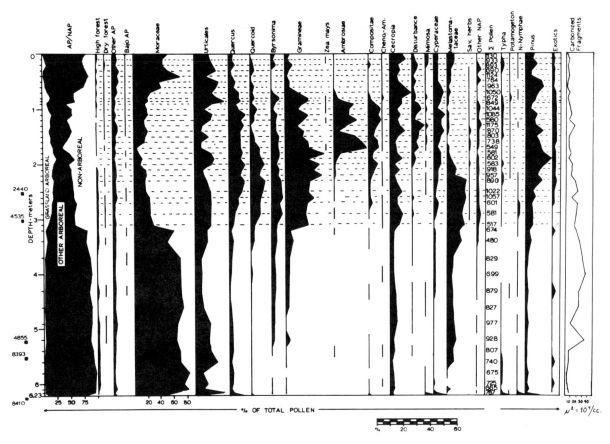

Figure 6.1. Pollen percentage
diagram for the 1972 core from Lake
Quexil in 7.2 m of water. Total
numbers counted range from 600 to
1,000 at most levels. Carbonized
vegetable fragments, at right, are not
percentages, but concentrations (in
areal units, μ^2) per unit volume of
wet sediment. Radiocarbon dates, at
left, are rejected except for the bot-
tommost, which was based on terrestrial wood.

ferences, is offset here by evidence of poor preservation of pollen, particularly in the Yaxha sediments.
Nevertheless, the Maya collapse was both abrupt and
widespread; if we could detect it in the pollen, we
could use it for correlation between distant sections. If
the mean sedimentation rate was 1 mm per year, a
century-long regional collapse of agriculture ought to
be detectable palynologically between two levels 10 cm
apart. We find, however, that no collapse is surely
marked by a pollen change, either in our cores (figs.
6.1 and 6.2) or in Tsukada's. Instead, a prominent
stratigraphic boundary (Tsukada's G1/G2, our
P4/P5), marked in all cores by rises of most
agricultural indicators, is clearly not a collapse of any
sort; both from its character and from its position in

our regional sequence we suppose it to represent the
transition from Early to Late Classic. Cultural changes
at this level were approximately contemporaneous
throughout the Maya area, a fact that supports our
age assignment but falls short of proving it.

Similarly, the youngest prominent boundary, marking strong resurgence of forest trees, need not be synchronous at all sites. Reforestation, if it began in
some districts with the collapse, may have been
delayed by several centuries near Postclassic foci, such
as Topoxte in the Yaxha basin. A 100 year difference
in time of reforestation between Lake Quexil and
Lake Sacnab, in the Yaxha airshed, might be detectable, if the stratigraphic position of some other event
were securely fixed. As Postclassic populations are
known archaeologically throughout the lake district,
the difference in timing of reforestation between any
two sections is probably not as great as 100 years.
Still, without dates, volcanic ash beds, or other
stratigraphic reference points, we have extended
Tsukada's stratigraphy both downward and outward
but have improved neither its precision nor its accuracy as a chronology. Moreover, the imprecision is
such that we expect no differences in pollen rain between Lakes Yaxha and Sacnab; absence of
Postclassic populations from the Sacnab sub-basin is
not demonstrable in the pollen.

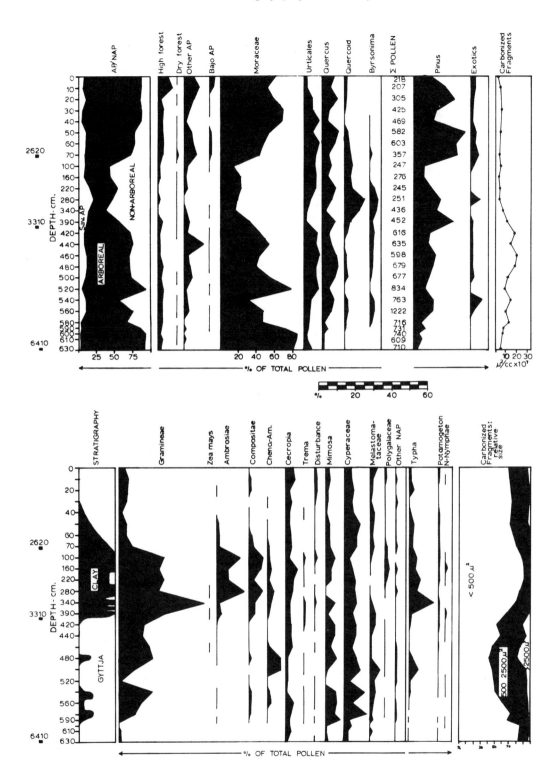

Figure 6.2. Arboreal (above) and nonarboreal (below) pollen percentage diagrams for a core from Lake Sacnab in 7.5 m of water. Counts at levels particularly rich in clay are less reliable than others, as microscopic examination shows evidence of abrasion or oxidative (microbial) attack on surfaces of some grains. At right, above, concentrations of carbonized fragments are shown as in figure 6.1; at right, below, large and intermediate-sized fragments are shown as percentages of total fragments. The three radiocarbon dates, at left, are rejected as meaningless; all Petén lake sediments contain large amounts of carbon derived from C-14-free limestone.

Attempts to make pollen stratigraphy more precise take one or both of two forms. First, concentrations of pollen types in specified amounts (milliliters or grams) of sediment need not be cast as percentages, in which all rare and all common types are forced statistically to interact with each other (Davis 1963, 1969). If the rate of sedimentation can be estimated, preferably over short intervals, division of total amounts or concentrations by a time interval yields estimates of input or influx,[1] expressed in units of volume, mass, or numbers of grains of a given type per unit area and year. So calculated over intervals of about a *baktun* or half a millennium, inputs of carbonates, silicates, and phosphorus to three Petén lakes provide the best evidence of colluviation, changes of nutrient loading, and population-specific outputs within the basins (Deevey et al. 1979). Such estimates are at best gross approximations, defensible only because order-of-magnitude changes of inputs from zone to zone seem much too large to be generated by large uncertainties, either in mean concentrations or in the relative ages of zone boundaries.

Escape from the statistical constraint of percentages frees the palynologist to consider real changes in abundance of any pollen type, independent of those of any other type. When influx rates of grass pollen rise, one knows that there were more grasses and not simply fewer trees or shrubs. Unfortunately, when influxes of individual pollen types are calculated for the Quexil core, the approximations to sedimentation rate are so gross as to defeat the purpose of the calculation. Influxes of carbonized vegetable fragments (fig. 6.3) are informative, particularly when they are compared with the unreduced (volume- and depth-specific but not time-specific) concentrations in fig. 6.1. We do not present the influx diagram of individual pollen types (Vaughan 1979) because readers are sure to find it more confusing than we do. What defeats us, of course, is wild variations in rate of sedimentation, uncontrolled by close-interval dating. Sedimentation has been so constant in some lakes (Stuiver 1971) as to provide, as tree rings do, a known-age standard for measuring the C-14 content of the biosphere. Plainly, such lakes are not to be found in the Maya area.

The other approach to stratigraphic refinement is microstratigraphic. If the mean sedimentation rate is 1 mm per year, events recorded 10 cm apart in one core are separated by about a century. If half-century precision is attainable by halving the sampling interval, why not sample at centimeter (10 year) or millimeter (1 year) intervals? The short answer is that average sedimentation is like the average weight of persons of all ages; skewed variances, many times

larger than the mean, arise from local and temporal inequalities of deposition.

We have measured some of these inequalities in Lakes Yaxha and Sacnab (Deevey, Vaughan, and Deevey 1977). At the surface of short cores, before compaction, about a milliliter of fresh sediment (0.2–10 ml/cm² or 2–100 mm thickness on each square centimeter, depending on the method of estimate) is formed annually. In sediment traps, because of horizontal transport toward deeper water, thicknesses of accumulation range from 5 to 160 mm in six months, depending on location. Moreover, during and after deposition of the top 10 cm or so, pollen grains are proved experimentally to undergo stratigraphic smearing (bioturbation) by burrowing animals (R. Davis 1974). Clearly, pollen sampled at centimeter intervals is unlikely to give a meaningful microstratigraphy. Except where annual laminae are present (they are normally obliterated by bioturbation), any precision gained by sampling closer than 5 cm is likely to be spurious.

These limitations on microstratigraphic precision have led us to question Wiseman's analysis (chap. 5) of pollen in short cores from Lakes Petenxil and Quexil. Apparently, all cores (Wiseman 1978) were a meter or so long; stratigraphic details are unpublished. In one Quexil core (E-5) the transition from weed-pollen to forest-pollen abundance lies between 58.4 and 64 cm depth, a little closer to the mud surface than in any core we know but readily correlatable with Tsukada's G2/G3 (our P5/P6) boundary. Relying heavily on two C-14 dates from Petenxil, Wiseman believes this level to be that of the Maya collapse.

Reassigning the rise of forest pollen to the end of the Postclassic, on ampler evidence from five lakes, we can still welcome Wiseman's close look at botanical details of the decline of Maya agriculture. If the nonarboreal-arboreal transition was as recent as the seventeenth century, Wiseman's earlier studies of present-day soils, pollen, and plant succession are that much more likely to be helpful. Wiseman claims to see the botanical details in samples spaced 2 mm apart in a zone 5.6 cm thick. We think that such details, however similar statistically to those of plant succession on abandoned fields, are misleading. Especially when recorded in sediments like these, the regional pollen rain, drawn over several years from an indefinitely large mosaic of vegetation, cannot be sensitive to short-term successional changes on particular plots.

The most interesting "event" within the half-century-long transition in Wiseman's core is the maximum of maize pollen about half way up, at 61 cm. Highly polyploid maize is the one cereal that is distinguishable from other grasses, by the large size of its pollen and also electron-micrographically (Tsukada and Rowley 1964). Large grains travel short distances

_____
1. Incorrectly and confusingly called "absolute frequencies" by palynologists (see Colinvaux 1978).

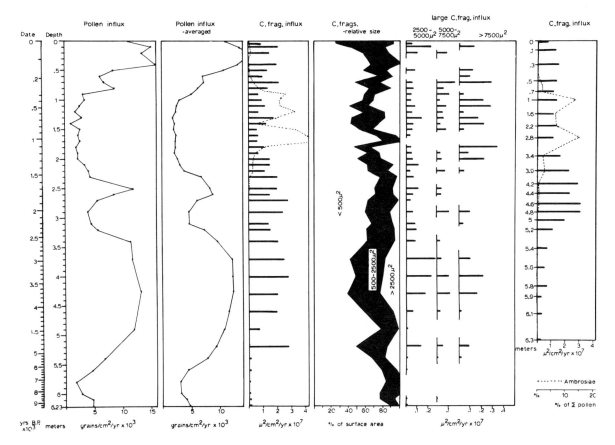

Figure 6.3. Influx rates, shown here for total pollen and carbonized fragments in the Lake Quexil core, are concentrations (per unit volume of sediment) divided by estimated time-intervals spanned by short segments of the core. The estimates of time-duration, shown as a continuously interpolated time-scale at the left, give gross approximations to sedimentation rate, which increased dramatically in middle sections of the core. Proportions and influx rates of large and intermediate-sized fragments are shown, and the double maximum of Ambrosiae pollen (Zone P5, figs. 6.1 and 6.2) is plotted for comparison. Data for the Sacnab core, at right, are similarly calculated influxes of carbonized fragments and percentages of Ambrosiae.

in air, however, and whereas maize pollen occurs in offshore deposits in proportions of a few per thousand, absence of types so infrequent cannot be relied on. By increasing numbers counted to several thousand and counting maize against "all others," Wiseman escapes the ordinary constraints of binomial variance. (The penalty for focusing on one rare type is loss of information about all others, and we have not attempted it.) Statistically, then, the maize maximum at 61 cm is certainly "real." Rejuvenation of Maya agriculture is not provable by such evidence, in our opinion; we think it at least as probable that the zone centered on 61 cm is a block of soil from some riparian milpa.

Interpretation of Pollen Sequences

The full pollen diagrams from the Quexil and Sacnab cores, drawn from Vaughan's thesis (1979), have been presented as slides at various meetings (Vaughan 1976, 1978a and b) and were summarized by Deevey et al. (1979) but are published here for the first time (figs. 6.1, 6.2). They show, as convincingly as pollen stratigraphy can ever show, the overriding influence of human disturbance on vegetation. Archaeologists may need little convincing on this point, but palynologists have different preconceptions. (If Neolithic disturbance could have been seen as interpolated between records of undisturbed mixed-oak forest, much botanical discussion of Holocene climatology might have been dispensed with.) The extended stratigraphy proves what Tsukada could not surmise in 1966: that Maya occupation of the Petén was an episode, a kind of artifact that converted tropical forest to savanna in at least two places 50 km apart.

Reiterating that this is a coarse-grained stratigraphy for which dates are inferential, we discuss its paleoenvironmental interpretation, zone by zone, in general terms. For a fuller discussion of botanical details, which are inevitably clouded by identification problems and by the ecological and stratigraphic uncertainties of pollen assemblages, Vaughan's dissertation may be consulted. For insight into which botanical features are of local rather than regional significance, two pollen diagrams are better than one, but our evidence for local differences is made ambiguous by indications of pollen degradation in some segments of the Sacnab core. Lakes Quexil and Petenxil lie closer to the problematic modern savannas south and southwest of the lake district, and the relative luxuriance of modern forest near Yaxha and Sacnab appears to be reflected in the modern pollen rain; but the origin of modern savannas cannot be intelligently discussed until cores are obtained from savanna lakes. Because the forest-savanna-forest sequence is now known at Lake Macanche, we dare to designate our pollen zones (P1–P6) as Petén zones, but their plant-ecological correlatives may not exist outside the lake district.

Zone P1: Pre-Maya

The oldest forest-pollen zone is less than a meter thick in the Quexil core and appears not to have been reached in Lake Sacnab. At its lower end, where the core contained limestone fragments and was approaching bedrock, pollen spectra are distorted by abundant pollen of aquatics (pond weeds, cat-tail), recording the first rise of water level to an altitude some 13 m below the present-day lake surface. Our only acceptable C-14 date, 8410 ± 180 radiocarbon years (about 7000 B.C. after various debatable corrections) was obtained from a piece of wood at 6.23 m in this zone.

Earlier stages of the rise of water level and of the accompanying invasion (or synthesis) of high forest that evidently marks the beginning of the Holocene are recorded in the 1980 deep-water cores. Until these can be analyzed, ecological discussion of early Holocene vegetation is premature. From the limited data of figure 6.1, we can say that most pollen in Zone P1 is of Moraceae, an ecologically heterogeneous family that includes *Brosimum* (*ramón*) and *Ficus* (*amate*). The "high forest" component graphed in the diagram is a separate group, composed of *Achras* (*chico sapote*), *Bombax* (*amapola*), *Thouinia*, and *Sapium* and excluding one moraceous indicator of clearings (*Cecropia, guarumo*). Being insect-pollinated, some of the most characteristic forest-tree species are almost unrepresented in pollen assemblages. Collectively, these high-forest indicators are noticeably more abundant throughout the Sacnab

core than in Lake Quexil. Their relative abundance below 5.0 m in the Quexil core is interesting but may not be significant; what distinguishes the zone from sediments above 5.3 m is the near absence of carbonized fragments and of pollen of all nonarboreal upland plants.

Zone P2: Early and Middle Preclassic

Of the two older zones containing signs of human disturbance, both of which antedate Tsukada's Petenxil sections, the first is strongly dominated by arboreal pollen. The second, which records extensive deforestation, we take to coincide with Late Preclassic expansion of population, civic architecture, and ceremonialism. On this assumption, the validity of which is discussed in a later section, the arboreal pollen zone, P2, is 2.2 m thick in the Quexil core. If its lower boundary is as old as the late third millennium B.C., as implied by dates for the Swasey ceramic phase at Cuello, Belize (Hammond et al. 1979), the forest near Lake Quexil, though rather open, was not much altered by disturbance during nearly two millennia or not until the third century B.C.

The openness of this forest is suggested by the regular occurrence of three indicators of clearings or of open savanna: *Cecropia*, *Byrsonima* (*nance*), and Melastomataceae, a family containing several common shrubs. (Like the pollen group referred to the large order Urticales, melastomataceous pollen is difficult to identify to genus. Tsukada reported *Terminalia* (*canxan*), a high-forest component with similar pollen, but we are unable to confirm the identification.) The group we separate as "savanna arboreal" consists of *Byrsonima*, *Quercus* (oak), and an unidentified "quercoid" type that tends to follow oak stratigraphically. The main expansion of all these savanna indicators defines Zone P3, where all other arboreal pollen is sharply reduced by rises of grassland types (Gramineae, high-spine Compositae, Cyperaceae, the chenopod-amaranth group). Above this clear boundary, therefore, all evidence points to culturally induced savanna with at least some agricultural weeds; below it, moderate but long-continued disturbance, perhaps by swiddening, is implied by abundant carbonized fragments and small quantities of pollen of *Cecropia* and the shrubs expected in clearings.

We have drawn these data and inferences from Zone P2 in the Quexil core; in the lower part of the Sacnab core, although forest openings are evident at all levels, the stratigraphic relations are different. Savanna shrubs and grassland herbs tend to rise and fall together, rather than in the P2–P3 sequence of Lake Quexil. We must resist the temptation to overinterpret such differences, if only because oscillations in the proportion of arboreal pollen generate

reciprocal oscillations in all other percentages. As all
Sacnab sediments are poorer in organic matter than
most Quexil sediments, the oscillations may result
from diagenetic loss of pollen in clay. Direct evidence
of degraded pollen was seen only higher up in the section, in purer clay, but the congruence of thin bands
of clay with prominent minima of Moraceae may not
be accidental. In view of this possibility and the
related possibility of stratigraphic mixing by colluvium, we hesitate to draw zone boundaries within
the lower Sacnab segment. The deforestation and expansion of savanna types observed above 4.0 m can
hardly be later than Early Classic; on that assumption
Deevey et al. (1979) drew the Late Preclassic (P3)
boundary at 5.20 m. At the lower end of the core,
there being no indication that pre-Maya sediments
were reached, we set the local boundary for purposes
of calculation at 2650 B.C. This guess-date is given by
subtracting 2,000 years from the corrected C-14 age of
6410 ± 100 (QL 1029) (Deevey, Vaughan, and Deevey
1977).

Despite stratigraphic uncertainties, the fact remains
that all indicators of disturbance, including carbonized
fragments, occur throughout the lower Sacnab
sediments. To infer that Preclassic Maya people
caused the disturbance would strain such evidence,
were it not that Middle Preclassic settlement is amply
documented in the Sacnab basin and elsewhere in the
lake district (Rice 1976; Rice and Rice 1980). This settlement is the oldest so far known in the lake district,
but substantially older cultures are known not far
away. Are there indications of two early phases of
disturbance, the older perhaps corresponding to a
hypothetical Early Preclassic? Scanning the pollen sequence in Quexil Zone P2, we see a possible Middle
Preclassic rise of *Byrsonima* and Melastomataceae at
3.75 m, conceivably correlated with similar percentage
changes at 5.90 m in the Sacnab core. Such "evidence"
recalls the ironic motto of the Friends of the
Pleistocene—"I wouldn't have seen it if I hadn't
believed it"—and supports no legitimate ecological inferences. A supposititious boundary was drawn by
Deevey et al. (1979, figs. 4, 5) solely so that sedimentation rates and phosphorus inputs could be estimated
for periods known archaeologically in the lake district
and for which chemical differences were detectable in
the sediments.

The Maya Zones: P3, P4, and P5

Clay-rich sediments in which no more than 30 percent
of the pollen is arboreal are intercalated between
organic zones in four long cores from three lakes,
Quexil, Macanche, and Sacnab. The same lithologic
sequence is seen in eight other deep-water cores in
which pollen has not been studied: five in Quexil, one

in Macanche, and two in Salpeten. Informally, we
refer to the intercalated unit as the Maya clay. (As a
formation it is better named Quexil clay, for the
locality of the type section.) Both within the formation and below it, in a transitional clay-gyttja zone,
the uniformity of pollen assemblages points clearly to
extensive deforestation by the Maya and the spread of
their agriculture. The period of dominance by nonarboreal pollen began before deposition of the purest
clay and must then have lasted about two millennia,
from the beginning of the Late Preclassic in the third
century B.C. through the end of the Petén Postclassic
in the seventeenth century A.D.

Modest differences in nonarboreal pollen permit
recognition of a sequence of three zones, which we
call Late Preclassic (P3), Early Classic (P4), and Late
Classic plus Postclassic (P5). The chronology implied
is purely inferential (and some alternatives are discussed in a later section), but stratigraphic validity is
guaranteed by reduplication of this sequence in all
four long cores. The diagnostic differences are these:
savanna trees and shrubs (*Byrsonima*, Melastomataceae) and *Cecropia* have their maxima in
the transitional Zone P3; all grassland types expand in
Zone P4, with one exception; the exception is low-
spine Compositae, conventionally referred to the tribe
Ambrosieae,[2] which are scarce below and rise to two
successive maxima in Zone P5. Perfect consistency in
all these features is marred by two departures: maxima
of *Byrsonima* and *Cecropia* fall in Zone P5 in the
unreliable Sacnab core.

Such differences in the regional pollen rain tell us
very little about the intensity, agronomic practice, or
geographic deployment of Maya agriculture.
Agricultural weeds are undoubtedly concealed within
the grassland assemblage, but the only crop plant attested by identifiable pollen is maize. We have no
ecological explanation for the deferred rise of Ambrosiae, a group that includes such familiar weeds as
ragweed, sagebrush, wormwood, and cocklebur. Many
plants that may have been deliberately cultivated or
whose pollen percentages may be raised by sparing living plants in clearings have been recognized in these
sediments but only by their families: Myrtaceae,
Solanaceae, Caryophyllaceae, Polygalaceae, Ulmaceae
and other Urticales, Ericaceae. Little definite information is given by these identifications, for very few
plants of the Maya area are likely to have had no
economic, ritual, or ornamental use. The Solanaceae,
a family that includes potato, tomato, tobacco, night-
shade, and chili peppers, must have been of great importance. Our "disturbance" group as graphed in

---

2. The tribal name ending *-eae* is mandated by the taxonomic code. Considering Ambrosiae to be a form name,
for low-spine composites, we have not changed the spelling
where the reference to a tribe is not explicit.

figure 6.1 consists of *Trema* (*capolin*), Myrtaceae (doubtless including *Pimenta*, allspice), Caryophyllaceae, and Solanaceae. "Savanna nonarboreal" lumps Ericaceae and Polygalaceae. As percentage frequencies of all these types automatically rise where arboreal percentages fall, their stratigraphic restriction to the Maya zones proves neither deliberate nor inadvertent propagation by the Maya.

Similarly, where trees were reduced but not exterminated, percentages of arboreal pollen can give no indication either of arboriculture or of sparing. If any trees were spared by the Maya, some Mayanists might expect ramón (*Brosimum*) to be among them, while botanists observing modern milpas could not fail to notice that palms are often spared. Palm pollen is almost unknown in sediments, however, whereas *Brosimum* may be the dominant arboreal type, within as well as above and below the Maya zones. As far as we can see, *Brosimum* pollen is a nearly constant fraction of total Moraceae (other than *Cecropia*), and its maxima and minima coincide with those of another moraceous genus, *Pseudolmedia* (*manax*). Minima falling in Zones P4 and P5, recently confirmed as minima of *Brosimum* and as recurring at those levels in deep-water cores, do not suggest sparing of *ramón*. Recognizable grains of other forest trees occur so infrequently as barely to hint at the famous diversity of Petén forests. In addition to the four "high forest" types already listed, they include *Matayba* (*zacuayum*) and *Alchornea*, grouped as "dry forest" in our diagrams, and the "*bajo* forest" genera *Haematoxylon* (*tinta*, logwood) and *Coccoloba* (*cholob*). *Spondias* (*jobo*) and *Bursera* (*chacaj*) are included with "other arboreal."

The one forest component that rises where Moraceae decline is "savanna arboreal" (*Byrsonima*, *Quercus*). Relative abundance of these types in the Maya zones is confirmed in the deep-water cores, but this consistency does not remove the ecological ambiguity. Oak-*nance* savannas (the encinal and nanzal of Wiseman 1978) grow today within a kilometer of Lake Quexil, but the Quexil-Petenxil pollen rain, at the mud surface and throughout post-Maya sediments, is dominated by Moraceae. Where moraceous pollen is suppressed, the oak pollen that takes its place can have come from anywhere in the Northern Hemisphere whereas *Byrsonima* pollen, if not local, is at least Central American. In the absence of a pollen-influx diagram, expansion of nanzal is no more probable than the alternative: influx of savanna pollen remained constant through Maya times, while mesic forest was replaced by villages and milpas.

Carbonized vegetable fragments are abundant in Petén lake sediments (Hutchinson and Goulden 1966). Concentrations of these fossils in the Quexil and Sacnab cores are graphed in figures 6.1 and 6.2. (Most fragments are plates of grass epidermis; their areal dimensions were not converted to volumes. Units

graphed are square micrometers (μm^2, μ^2 in diagrams) per cubic centimeter of wet sediment.) If fragments are mainly produced during burning of milpa, higher concentrations observed below the Maya zones may seem anomalous. However, one expects concentrations to be enriched, perhaps by large factors, where bulk sedimentation rates were slower. Using the approximations applied to calculation of phosphorus inputs (Deevey et al. 1979), influxes of carbonized fragments were estimated as shown in figure 6.3. In Quexil Zone P2, where the mean concentration is about five times the mean for the Maya zones, the mean influx differs by less than twofold. Interestingly, maximal influxes appear at Late Preclassic levels in both cores.

As is true for total pollen influxes (fig. 6.3), these differences are too uncertain to throw light on modes or intensities of Maya agriculture. The only safe conclusion is that carbonized fragments come mainly from fires that people set. But the fragments, being larger and less regular in shape than pollen grains, travel shorter distances in air and are much more likely to be of local origin. Fragments larger than 7,500 μm^2 which are 10-30 times larger than typical pollen grains, appear to be significantly more abundant in the Maya zones of the Quexil core. Large fragments are scarcer in the Sacnab core, perhaps because they are ground to smaller sizes in clay; the largest fragments seen in this core (fig. 6.2) are restricted to the supposed Late Preclassic zone. Unfortunately, even if we take this evidence to mean that fires burned closer to the lakes during Maya times, the trees that supplied the pollen were probably farther away. It is well known that the opening of forest enhances the representation of far-traveled grains, notably of oak and pine (Tsukada and Deevey 1967).

The Late Classic Collapse

Pollen assemblages of the Maya zones are dominated by grassland types: sequential percentage rises that characterize the zones are shown by savanna trees, grasses and other herbs, and Ambrosiae. Granting ecological ambiguity, is stratigraphic resolution really so low that 2-5 m of sediment, deposited over two millennia, contain no more than three recognizable zones? In fact there are at least four, for the maximum of Ambrosiae is double in all sections—five cores from four lakes, counting Petenxil Core 3—that are now known to span Zone P5. Figure 6.3 gives a suggestion that large carbonized fragments increase and decrease with Ambrosiae in Quexil Zone P5; this correlation is absent in Lake Sacnab, where Rice (1978; Rice and Rice 1980) found no Postclassic settlement.

Presumably, then, the end of the Maya Late Classic brought an interruption, perhaps a century long, in the spread of agricultural weeds. Slight but consistent rises of *Cecropia* and other Moraceae at this level imply some reforestation, which was reversed during the next several centuries of Postclassic occupation. Deevey et al. (1979) did not use such exiguous evidence for stratigraphic subdivision because the zonation of Yaxha sediments was problematic and the deep-water cores had not been analyzed. We now assign the minimum of Ambrosiae (1.40 m in Quexil, 2.20 m in the Sacnab core) to the Classic Maya collapse.

Anthropologists must find it disappointing, if not incredible, that one of the most dramatic episodes in human history was so feebly echoed in the pollen rain. Our perspective gives the point a different emphasis. Arboreal pollen assemblages are so sensitive to forest clearance that regionally developed agriculture is easily distinguished from local swiddening. Once established, however, a nonarboreal pollen rain is so insensitive to changing population density that tenfold increases and decreases are almost imperceptible. The useful point that emerges is that a system's damped responses to external forcing ("complacency" of tree-ring widths, "resilience" of ecosystems under different degrees of stress) can vary measurably, though not yet predictably, in degree of damping. What disappoints us is not that Maya-zone pollen percentages are more complacent than architectural or ceramic styles; it is our inability to measure sedimentation rates with precision sufficient to improve our estimates of sensitivity.

Post-Maya Reforestation: Zone P6

With relaxation of disturbance by agricultural people, forests reoccupied the Petén lake district as if two millennia of urban development had been "a watch in the night." Considering the uniformity of the underlying nonarboreal pollen assemblages, the sharp rise of moraceous pollen in the topmost meter of sediment in five lakes implies regional depopulation by a factor much larger than ten; this stratigraphic boundary seems to us clear and unambiguous. We have already discussed its probable synchrony and its assignment to the end of the Postclassic.

Until recently, so late a date would have troubled botanists even more than Mayanists. (The persistent notion that tropical forests have been stable since the Eocene arose from confusion of flora, a taxonomic construct, with vegetation, which is what an observer sees.) Botanical evidence is still scanty, especially in the New World, but geologic data prove tropical Pleistocene climates to have been too arid, during glacial ages, to permit the existence of rain forests (Street and Grove 1976, 1979; Peterson et al. 1979). If the Petén forest, like the Amazonian rainforest (van der Hammen 1972), was synthesized from savanna in the early Holocene, there is no reason to doubt its reassembly within two centuries after depopulation.

Discussion

Climatic Changes

Theoretical climatology (Kraus 1973; Gates 1976; Manabe and Hahn 1977) deduces that Pleistocene glacial ages were dry in the tropics but makes no useful inferences about Holocene tropical climates or about distribution of rainfall in Central America (Deevey 1978). Geologic data, most of which are dated high and low stands of African lakes, show undisputed evidence of an early Holocene moist period, from about 10,000 to about 5,000 radiocarbon years ago; thereafter, minor and less consistent rises interrupted the long decline of lake levels. In the American tropics, closely similar hydrologic histories are inferred from isotopic measurements in two lakes: Chichancanab, Yucatán (Covich and Stuiver 1974), and Valencia, Venezuela (Tamers and Thielen 1966). The moist period, long familiar to Africanists as "Leakey's Gamblian pluvial" and proved to be of Holocene age by Kendall (1969) and Richardson and Richardson (1972), brought mesic forest to the shores of deeper lakes as far from Lake Nakuru (Leakey's locality) as Guyana (Wijmstra and van der Hammen 1966), Venezuela (Bradbury et al. 1981), Florida (Watts 1975; Watts and Stuiver 1980), and Queensland (Kershaw 1974; Bowler et al. 1976). The episode was evidently pantropical. To our regret, although we have referred to it elsewhere (Deevey, Brenner, and Binford 1983) as Gamblian, this term has been dropped by Africanists (Bishop 1967). Thus the Early Holocene pantropical moist period lacks an accepted time-stratigraphic name; to avoid making semantic problems for other stratigraphers, we refer to it by the informal time-term "pre-Maya moist period."

The forest-pollen Zone P1 being an obvious equivalent of an East African episode, signs of later Holocene fluctuations of rainfall are to be looked for in Petén. To scrutinize pollen assemblages for such indications is to invite self-deception, but Petén lakes are closed, and records of high and low levels can be expected in their basins. Perhaps because geomorphic evidence is obscured by dense forest, there are no known strand lines much higher than those of 1980, which were about 5 m above 1973–74 levels of Lakes Peten-Itza, Salpeten, Yaxha, and Sacnab. Lakes Yaxha and Sacnab were joined in 1980, as they have not been since 1933 (Deevey, Garrett-Jones, and Vaughan 1980); but the disastrous 1980 rise was not so evident at Lake Quexil. Pleistocene low-water stages are recorded in sediments below 40 m depth in Lakes Quexil and Salpeten. Higher up in the shallow-water Quexil core, between 1.8 and 3.0 m (9.0–10.2 m below the 1973 water level), fluctuations of lithology and of lacustrine fossils suggest lake-level and climatic instability. Shelly and peaty layers, alternating with clayey and organic layers containing planktonic animals and water-lily pollen, indicate permanent but very shallow water, fluctuating seasonally or over longer periods between 1 and 3–5 m depth at the coring site. If Lake Quexil's level stood around −5 m, falling perhaps as low as −8 m during the Late Preclassic, the western basin would appear to have been a separate pond, like Lake Petenxil today.

If we accept this as evidence of reduced rainfall during Maya times, we can deduce various botanical and cultural concomitants, as discussed in Vaughan's dissertation (1979). The range of rainfall figures is suggested by modern observations at Flores: the wettest year (1938) recorded 2,598 mm, more than twice that of the driest year (1974, with 1,213 mm). If the rainfall during and after pre-Maya Holocene time averaged over 2,000 mm, the earliest swidden agriculture, confined to karst uplands as the settlements were, would not have disturbed much forest. Later, as increasing population required more extensive and intensive cultivation, rainfall averaging 1,200 mm would have favored savanna on flatter areas, including bajos, and so account for the rise of *Byrsonima* pollen.

Plausible as such scenarios may be, they are purely deductive, and the limnological evidence is amenable to other interpretations. Preclassic cultivation in the immediate vicinity of the coring site, suggested by abundance of carbonized fragments, raised the possbility that some peaty or clayey layers are nonlacustrine colluvium. Near-shore littoral and swampy supralittoral deposits are difficult to distinguish and could be commingled by wave action near the shore of an astatic lake. Moreover, if Lake Quexil was 5 m lower when these deposits were formed, the inference of climatic change is not compelling. At best, a stand at −5 m is compatible with a climate favoring savanna. More exactly, it implies a different hydrologic balance, with mean net rainfall substantially below a normal gross of 1,600 mm, the modern average for ten Petén stations. Forest clearance, by increasing evapotranspiration, can reduce net rainfall; thus savannization could be the cause of an altered hydrology and not the consequence of climatic change.

We consider it likely but unproved that episodes of drier and moister climate have alternated once or twice during Maya time in the Petén. If fluctuations of rainfall were comparable in amplitude and duration to African fluctuations, they are sure to have influenced agriculture, especially in a karst region. Our skepticism about such episodes is aroused not merely by the scarcity and ambiguity of the data but by the neat way in which our evidence fits our long-standing preconceptions (Deevey 1953), notions ultimately derived from the history of Lake Nakuru.

An Alternative Interpretation

Setting aside climatic interpretations as unprovable, we have to consider alternative chronologies for phases of cultural disturbance. The pivotal assumption of our chronostratigraphy is that suppression of forest-tree pollen dates from expansion of agriculture in Late Preclassic times. If one follows Wiseman's assignment of reforestation (the P5/P6 boundary) to the end of the Late Classic, all other boundaries could also be older by about a baktun than we have assumed. All the Maya zones would still correspond to known cultural phases; deforestation would be attributed to Middle Preclassic people, and the subzones of Zone P5, separated by the minimum of Ambrosiae, would be of Early and Late Classic age. A population decline in Early Classic time is well established at several localities within the lake district, and a Late Classic dating of the second Ambrosiae rise is defensible, particularly at Lake Sacnab where no later population is known.

Like the Maya calendar before its calibration, any stratigraphic chronology floats in time, and 8,400 radiocarbon years is a long time in which to float; we are in no position to be dogmatic. We have noted, however, that the only positive evidence for Wiseman's correlation is the C-14 dating of Petenxil sediments, and we have given reasons for rejecting those dates. We doubt that reforestation began as long as a millennium ago for two other reasons: sedimentation of the topmost half-meter or meter, at least as measured in sediment traps in Lakes Yaxha and Sacnab, is much more rapid than a Late Classic dating would imply; and the absence of any palynological sign of the Postclassic, though a permissible interpretation of the Sacnab core, seems generally incompatible with the archaeological evidence.

The age of the P2/P3 boundary is a separable problem. Throughout the Maya area the Late Preclassic was the time of construction of many major and innumerable minor ceremonial centers. Many were built on Middle Preclassic habitation sites, and many others were not. Late Preclassic expansion of populations, documented quantitatively in the Yaxha-Sacnab basin (Rice and Rice 1980), has long seemed self-evident to most Mayanists, and the literature is replete with deductive arguments about expanding or intensified agriculture. The one deduction we can verify is that expansion of some population required clearance of much forest. Accelerated soil erosion and siltation of lakes are deducible consequences of forest clearance, also supported by data, but our lake sediments, contrary to our expectations, provide no independent evidence of the timing of deforestation. We cannot deny that Middle Preclassic people were capable of felling trees; what little we know of their population density and economy suggests no compelling need to deforest the Petén.

Summary and Conclusions

Sediment cores collected from two Petén lakes in 1972 and 1973 extended Tsukada's Lake Petenxil pollen stratigraphy in two ways: outward by 50 km to Lake Sacnab and downward to sediments at least four millennia older in Lake Quexil. The oldest deposits, C-14 dated on terrestrial wood fragments at 8410 ± 180 B.P., were first studied palynologically in Lake Quexil, but in 1977 and 1978 (see appendix) they were encountered and studied in deep-water cores from lakes Quexil and Macanche. Nearly devoid of carbonized fragments and nonarboreal pollen, they record an early Holocene (pre-Maya) time of rising lake levels when mesic forest replaced more xeric vegetation in the tropics of all continents. Poorly as water-laid pollen can represent the composition of that forest, deposits of Zone P1 anchor the vegetational history of the Petén lake district in a time of closed high forest, undisturbed by people. In 1980, when still older (Pleistocene, pre-pre-Maya) deposits were found below Zone P1 in lakes Quexil, Macanche, and Salpeten, the stratigraphic interpretation was confirmed and extended (Deevey, Brenner and Binford 1983), but the palynology of the 1980 cores has not yet been studied. As twice revised since its first presentation in 1978, this chapter, with its appendix, discusses the pollen stratigraphy of shallow-water cores from lakes Quexil and Sacnab and of deep-water cores from lakes Quexil and Macanche.

As stratigraphic practice requires, we first describe Holocene pollen assemblages objectively. Accepting as definitive only those trends of percentages that Garrett-Jones also observed in deep-water cores, we recognize six pollen zones, of which five overlie the pre-Maya zone P1. All five contain carbonized fragments and some pollen of savanna and grassland plants, and zones P5, P4, and part of Zone P3 are also lithologically distinct; they constitute a formation we call the Maya clay. Clay is overlain by more organic sediments (Zone P6) in all six lakes that have been cored (counting lakes Petenxil and Salpeten), and is intercalated between organic zones in 12 sufficiently long cores from four of the six (Quexil, Sacnab, Macanche, Salpeten). Both underlying and overlying organic zones are known to be forest-pollen zones in four cores from three lakes (Quexil, Sacnab, Macanche). Pollen in the oldest of the five zones, P2, is

dominantly of Moraceae, with low percentages of savanna trees (*Byrsonima, Quercus*) and shrubs (Melastomataceae). As all arboreal pollen is sharply reduced at the top of the zone, rises of these savanna types characterize the lithologically transitional Zone P3, the oldest of the three Maya zones. Zone P4 contains more pollen of most grassland herbaceous types, but among these Ambrosiae increase farther up to a double maximum and characterize Zone P5. Arboreal (moraceous) pollen then rises, in Zone P6, to percentages similar to those of Zone P2.

Correlation of pollen zones between separate lake deposits implies nothing but regionally consistent changes in composition of the pollen rain. Where such changes have clearly resulted from response of upland vegetation to climatic change, correlation also implies contemporaneity. Pollen then provides a chronostratigraphy, susceptible to calibration and microstratigraphic refinement, for example, by C-14 dating of pollen-bearing sediments. When rates of sedimentation can be estimated, the intrinsic ambiguity of percentage changes can be removed by calculating pollen-influx and other input rates.

None of these advantages is available for interpretation of our pollen diagrams. If the openness of forest (Zone P2) implies swiddening, and if arboreal pollen was reduced by deforestation (Zone P3), culminating in the Early Classic (Zone P4), post-Maya reforestation reflects relaxation of disturbance; but savannization is then a Maya artifact, neither climatic in origin nor necessarily synchronous throughout the lake district. Radiocarbon dating of these sediments is invalidated by large and probably variable additions of C-14-free carbonate to lake waters. The Maya clay, formed by accelerated erosion and redeposition of basin soils, confirms the existence and intensifying impact of human disturbance; but soils redeposited by gravitational creep (colluviation) contain both humus and carbonates of vastly different isotopic composition.

Likely as we may think it that savannization was favored by drier climate in the first millennium B.C. or that other climatic changes influenced Maya agriculture, *percentage changes of pollen composition, when not proved to be changes of pollen-influx rates, imply nothing about climate and very little about vegetation,* except that forest trees were notably scarce during deposition of the Maya zones. We see some evidence of lowered lake levels in the shallow-water sediments of Lake Quexil, but this evidence too is ambiguous; savannization, by increasing evapotranspiration, can alter the hydrologic balance of a region. As to agriculture, we can say nothing new, for weed pollen is grassland or savanna pollen, and maize is the only demonstrable crop plant.

Despite ambiguities, we argue that phases of increasingly severe disturbance imposed roughly synchronous changes in lithology and in composition of pollen assemblages in several lakes; the zones constitute a stratigraphic chronology of Maya interference with forests. The chronology floats in time; but if most Moraceae were cut before they pollinated in the Late Preclassic and if most forests were cleared for agriculture by Early Classic time, we can read "Preclassic swiddening" in the declining arboreal percentages of Zone P2, and the reforestation in Zone P6 is indubitably post-Postclassic. Supported by new data from deep-water cores, we can even detect the Late Classic collapse as the minimum between two maxima of Ambrosiae in Zone P5.

To date pollen zone boundaries by known historical events inverts archaeological reasoning as practiced in Europe before 1950 when radiocarbon made it obsolete, but it is not circular as applied to dating lake sediments. Obviously, such inferential dates must not be re-used for their own purposes by archaeologists; but the low precision of our chronostratigraphy—about 5 katuns in the Maya clay and about a baktun in the Preclassic—tends to make such a precaution unnecessary.

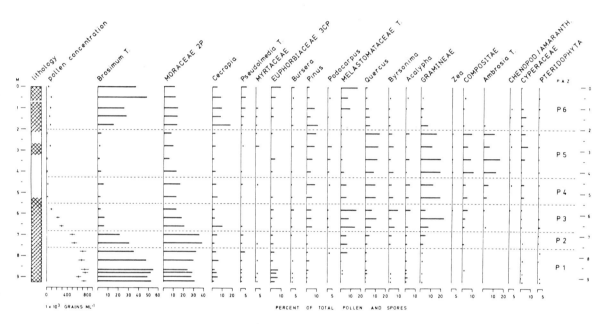

Figure 6.4. Pollen percentage diagram for core Quexil H, collected in 1978 by Kullenberg corer in 27.7 m of water. Analyses by S. E. Garrett-Jones.

Figure 6.5. Pollen percentage diagram for core Macanche D, collected in 1977 by Kullenberg corer in 54.5 m of water. Analyses by S. E. Garrett-Jones.

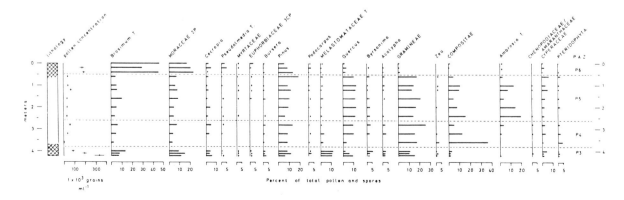

Appendix: Palynology of Deep-Water Cores Quexil H and Macanche D

S. E. Garrett-Jones, Florida State Museum

The Kullenberg corer used on Lake Macanche in 1977 and on Lake Quexil in 1978 is a messenger-released gravity-driven piston corer, built at the University of Florida under the guidance of D. A. Livingstone, Duke University. In lakes such devices rarely penetrate as far as 10 m in soft but sticky sediments, and our longest core—Quexil H, 9.23 m long under 27.7 m of water—failed by a few centimeters to reach the Pleistocene sediments that were finally encountered in 1980 (Deevey, Brenner, and Binford 1983). At and just above the bottom of this core, two samples of organic mud gave Smithsonian Institution C-14 dates averaging 8350 ± 900 B.P. (SI-3773 and SI-3774) (Stuckenrath and Deevey n.d.), indistinguishable from the terrestrial-wood age (DAL-198, 8410 ± 180) (Ogden and Hart 1977) of the bottom of Vaughan's shallow-water core. Thus the deep-water core Quexil H is longer, as a result of sediment focusing, but stratigraphically no more complete than its shallow-water counterpart.

The best core obtained in Lake Macanche—Macanche D, 4.2 m long under 54.5 m of water—penetrated below the Maya clay but appears to have bottomed in Zone P3. Radiocarbon measurements of organic and calcareous samples from this core are made ambiguous by hard-water-lake effects and by colluviation and are discussed elsewhere (Stuckenrath and Deevey n.d.).

Pollen diagrams from cores Quexil H (fig. 6.4) and Macanche D (fig. 6.5) were exhibited at the Fifth International Palynological Congress (Deevey, Garrett-Jones, and Vaughan 1980) but have not been published before. Although the sampling interval is rather wide, the diagrams confirm Vaughan's pollen stratigraphy in all essential respects. Formal designation of pollen zones P1–P6 does not appear in Vaughan's dissertation and is applied here in the light of results from Quexil H (fig. 6.4). The nearly complete section of Zone P1 adds substantially to our knowledge of pre-Maya pollen assemblages. In the light of results from the 1980 drilling campaign (Deevey, Brenner, and Binford 1983), proof that Zone P1 is nearly complete in both Quexil cores indicates that nearly all of the 30 m rise of lake level occurred soon after the opening of the Holocene.

References

Bishop, W. W.
1967   "Annotated Lexicon of Quaternary Stratigraphical Nomenclature in East Africa." In *Background to Evolution in Africa*, edited by W. W. Bishop and J. D. Clark. University of Chicago Press, pp. 375–395.

Bowler, J. M., G. S. Hope, J. N. Jennings, G. Singh, and D. Walker
1976   "Late Quaternary Climates of Australia and New Guinea," *Quaternary Research* 6:359–394.

Bradbury, J. P., B. Leyden, M. Salgado-Labouriau, W. M. Lewis, C. Schubert, M. W. Binford, D. G. Frey, D. R. Whitehead and F. H. Weibezahn
1981   "Late Quaternary Environmental History of Lake Valencia, Venezuela," *Science* 214:1299–1305.

Brenner, M.
1978   "Paleolimnological Assessment of Human Disturbance in the Drainage Basins of Three Northern Guatemalan Lakes." M.S. thesis, Department of Zoology, University of Florida.
1983   "Paleolimnology of the Maya Region." Ph.D. dissertation, Department of Zoology, University of Florida.

Colinvaux, P. A.
1978   "On the Use of the Word 'Absolute' in Pollen Statistics," *Quaternary Research* 9:132–133.

Covich, A., and M. Stuiver
1974   "Changes in Oxygen 18 as a Measure of Long-Term Fluctuations in Tropical Lake Levels and Molluscan Populations," *Limnology and Oceanography* 19:682–691.

Davis, M. B.
1963   "On the Theory of Pollen Analysis," *American Journal of Science* 261:897–912.
1969   "Climatic Changes in Southern Connecticut Recorded by Pollen Deposition at Rogers Lake," *Ecology* 50:409–422.

Davis, R. B.
1974   "Stratigraphic Effects of Tubificids in Profundal Lake Sediments," *Limnology and Oceanography* 19:466–488.

Deevey, E. S.
1953   "Paleolimnology and Climate." In *Climatic Change: Evidence, Causes, and Effects*, edited by Harlow Shapley. Harvard University Press, Cambridge, pp. 273–318.

1978   "Holocene Forests and Maya Disturbance near Quexil Lake, Peten, Guatemala," *Polskie Archiwum Hydrobiologii* 25:117–129.

Deevey, E. S., M. Brenner, and M. W. Binford
1983   "Paleolimnology of the Peten Lake District, Guatemala, III: Late Pleistocene and Gamblian Environments of the Maya Area," *Hydrobiologia* 103:211–216.

Deevey, E. S., M. Brenner, M. S. Flannery, and G. H. Yezdani
1980   "Lakes Yaxha and Sacnab, Peten, Guatemala: Limnology and Hydrology," *Archiv für Hydrobiologie*, Supplement-Band 57:419–460.

Deevey, E. S., S. E. Garrett-Jones, and H. H. Vaughan
1980   "Impact of Mayan Civilization on Tropical Lowland Forest" [abstract, poster presentation], Fifth International Palynological Congress, Cambridge, 1980, *Abstracts*, p. 107.

Deevey, E. S., M. S. Gross, G. E. Hutchinson, and H. L. Kraybill
1954   "The Natural C-14 Contents of Materials from Hard-Water Lakes," *Proceedings of the National Academy of Sciences* 40:285–288.

Deevey, E. S., D. S. Rice
1980   "Coluviación y retención de nutrientes en el distrito lacustre del Petén central, Guatemala," *Biotica* 5.3:129–144.

Deevey, E. S., D. S. Rice, P. M. Rice, H. H. Vaughan, M. Brenner, and M. S. Flannery
1979   "Mayan Urbanism: Impact on a Tropical Karst Environment," *Science* 206:298–306.

Deevey, E. S., and M. Stuiver
1964   "Distribution of Natural Isotopes of Carbon in Linsley Pond and Other New England Lakes," *Limnology and Oceanography*, 9:1–11.

Deevey, E. S., H. Vaughan, and G. B. Deevey
1977   "Lakes Yaxha and Sacnab, Peten, Guatemala: Planktonic Fossils and Sediment Focusing." In *Interactions between Sediments and Fresh Water*, edited by H. L. Golterman. Junk, The Hague, pp. 189–196.

Gates, W. L.
1976   "Modeling the Ice-Age Climate," *Science* 191:1138–44.

Godwin, H.
1961   "The Croonian Lecture: Radiocarbon Dating and Quaternary History in Britain," *Proceedings of the Royal Society of London* B, 153:287–320.

Hammond, N., D. Pring, R. Wilk, S. Donaghey, F. P. Saul, E. S. Wing, A. V. Miller, and L. H. Feldman
1979   "The Earliest Lowland Maya? Definition of the Swasey Phase, *American Antiquity* 44:92–110.

Hutchinson, G. E., and C. E. Goulden
1966   "The Plant Microfossils." In *The History of Laguna de Petenxil: A Small Lake in Northern Guatemala*, by U. M. Cowgill, G. E. Hutchinson, et al. Memoirs of the Connecticut Academy of Arts and Sciences 17, pp. 67–73.

Iversen, J.
1936   "Sekundäres Pollen als Fehlerquelle," *Danmarks Geologiske Undersøgelse* ser. 4, 2, no. 15.

Kendall, R. L.
1969   "An Ecological History of the Lake Victoria Basin," *Ecological Monographs* 39:121–176.

Kershaw, A. P.
1974   "A Long Continuous Pollen Sequence from North-Eastern Australia," *Nature* 251:222–223.

Kraus, E. B.
1973   "Comparison between Ice Age and Present General Circulation," *Nature* 245:129–133.

Lehman, J. T.
1975   "Reconstructing the Rate of Accumulation of Lake Sediment: The Effect of Sediment Focusing," *Quaternary Research* 5:541–550.

Mackereth, F. J. H.
1966   "Some Chemical Observations on Post-Glacial Lake Sediments," *Philosophical Transactions of the Royal Society of London* B, 250:165–213.

Manabe, S., and D. G. Hahn
1977   "Simulation of the Tropical Climate of an Ice Age," *Journal of Geophysical Research* 82:3889–3911.

Martin, P. S.
1963   *The Last 10,000 Years: A Fossil Pollen Record of the American Southwest.* University of Arizona Press, Tucson.

Ogden, J. G., and W. C. Hart
1977   "Dalhousie Natural Radiocarbon Measurements II," *Radiocarbon* 19:392–399.

Pennington, Winifred
1969   "The Usefulness of Pollen Analysis in Interpretation of Stratigraphic Horizons, Both Late-Glacial and Post-Glacial," *International Vereinigung der Limnologie, Mitteilungen* 17:154–164.

Peterson, G. M., T. Webb, J. E. Kutzbach,
T. van der Hammen, T. A. Wijmstra, and
F. A. Street
  1979   "The Continental Record of Environmental
         Conditions at 18,000 Yr B.P.: An Initial
         Evaluation." *Quaternary Research* 12:47–
         82.

Rice, D. S.
  1976   "Middle Preclassic Maya Settlement in the
         Central Maya Lowlands," *Journal of Field
         Archaeology* 3:425–445.
  1978   "Population Growth and Subsistence Alter-
         natives in a Tropical Lacustrine Environ-
         ment. In *Pre-Hispanic Maya Agriculture*,
         edited by P. D. Harrison and B. L. Turner.
         University of New Mexico Press, Albuquer-
         que, pp. 35–61.

Rice, D. S., and P. M. Rice
  1980   "The Northeast Peten Revisited," *American
         Antiquity* 45:432–454.

Richardson, J. L., and A. E. Richardson
  1972   "History of an African Rift Lake and Its
         Climatic Implications," *Ecological
         Monographs* 42:499–534.

Street, F. A., and A. T. Grove
  1976   "Environmental and Climatic Implications
         of Late Quaternary Lake-Level Fluctuations
         in Africa," *Nature* 261:385–390.
  1979   "Global Maps of Lake-Level Fluctuations
         since 30,000 Yr B.P.," *Quaternary Research*
         12:83–118.

Stuiver, M.
  1971   "Evidence for the Variation of Atmospheric
         C¹⁴ Content in the Late Quaternary." In
         The Late Cenozoic Glacial Ages, edited by
         K. K. Turekian. Yale University Press, New
         Haven, pp. 57–70.

Stuiver, M., and E. S. Deevey
  1961   "Yale Natural Radiocarbon Measurements
         VI," *Radiocarbon* 3:126–140.

Stuiver, M., E. S. Deevey, and B. I. Rouse
  1963   "Yale Natural Radiocarbon Measurements
         VIII," *Radiocarbon* 5:312–341.

Tamers, M. A., and C. Thielen
  1966   "Radiocarbon Ages of Ground Water Flow-
         ing into a Desiccating Lake, *Acta Científica
         Venezolana* 17:150–157.

Tsukada, Matsuo
  1966   "The Pollen Sequence." In *The History of
         Laguna de Petenxil: A Small Lake in
         Northern Guatemala*, by U. M. Cowgill, G.
         E. Hutchinson, et al. Memoirs of the
         Connecticut Academy of Arts and Sciences
         17, pp. 63–66.

Tsukada, M., and E. S. Deevey
  1967   "Pollen Analyses from Four Lakes in the
         Southern Maya Area of Guatemala and El
         Salvador. In *Quaternary Paleoecology*,
         edited by E. J. Cushing and H. E. Wright.
         Yale University Press, New Haven, pp.
         303–331.

Tsukada, M., and J. R. Rowley
  1964   "Identification of Modern and Fossil Maize
         Pollen," *Grana Palynologica* 5:406–412.

van der Hammen, T.
  1972   "Changes in Vegetation and Climate in the
         Amazon Basin and Surrounding Areas dur-
         ing the Pleistocene," *Geologie en Mijnbouw*
         51:641–643.

Vaughan, H. H.
  1976   [Abstract] "Prehistoric Disturbance: The
         Area of Flores, Peten, Guatemala," *Bulletin
         of the Ecological Society of America* 57:9.
  1978a [Abstract] "Interpretation of Prehistoric
         Disturbance of Vegetation in the Area of
         Lake Quexil, Peten, Guatemala." Program
         abstracts, 43rd Annual Meeting, Society of
         American Archaeology, Tucson, p. 81.
  1978b [Abstract] "An Absolute Pollen Diagram
         from Lake Quexil, Peten, Guatemala,"
         *Bulletin of the Ecological Society of
         America* 59:97.
  1979   "Prehistoric Disturbance of Vegetation in
         the Area of Lake Yaxha, Peten,
         Guatemala." Ph.D. dissertation, Depart-
         ment of Zoology, University of Florida.

Watts, W. A.
  1975   "A Late Quaternary Record of Vegetation
         from Lake Annie, South-Central Florida,"
         Geology 3:344–346.

Watts, W. A., and M. Stuiver
  1980   "Late Wisconsin Climate of Northern
         Florida and the Origin of Species-Rich
         Deciduous Forest," *Science* 210:325–327.

Wijmstra, T. A., and T. van der Hammen
  1966   "Palynological Data on the History of
         Tropical Savannas in Northern South
         America," *Leidse Geologische Mededel-
         ingen* 38:71–90.

Wiseman, F. M.
  1978   "Agricultural and Historical Ecology of the
         Maya Lowlands." In *Pre-Hispanic Maya
         Agriculture*, edited by P. D. Harrison and
         B. L. Turner. University of New Mexico
         Press, Albuquerque, pp. 63–115.

Chapter 7

Paradise Lost: Classic Maya Impact on a Lacustrine Environment

Don S. Rice, Prudence M. Rice, and Edward S. Deevey, Jr.

Since 1972 we have been engaged in research that focuses on exploitation of a tropical forest environment by the aboriginal Maya. In the project we attempt to integrate geochemical, biological, and anthropological studies within an area of major Maya occupation for the purpose of studying land use and sociopolitical evolution. In its design, the study has taken a quantitative approach couched in the research terms of tropical ecology: what was the effect of Maya occupation on the tropical forest ecosystem?

The locus of our study has been the lowland Guatemalan Department of Petén. As the Petén was the locale of dense and extensive Maya settlement from approximately 1000 B.C. to the Spanish conquest in A.D. 1697, that archaeologically identifiable occupation can be looked upon as a set of quantifiable treatments of tropical forest ecosystems, over several thousand years. From this perspective, the Maya represent a large-scale experiment in the use of tropical forest. The definition of the conditions of the experiment and the measurement of the consequences become the objectives of the research (Deevey 1969). Those conditions and consequences should be evident in both human settlement characteristics and paleoenvironmental variables. The Central Petén Historical Ecology Project (see also chap. 6) was instituted to search the cultural and natural records of Maya history for qualitative and quantitative data on these quasi-experimental parameters of environmental impact.

Don S. Rice is associate professor, Department of Anthropology, University of Chicago, Illinois. Prudence M. Rice is associate professor, Department of Anthropology, University of Florida, Gainesville. See chapter 6 for Edward S. Deevey, Jr.'s, affiliation.

Our work in Petén has been supported by the National Science Foundation through grants BMS 72-01859 and DEB 77-06629 to E. S. Deevey and grant BNS 78-13736 to Don and Prudence Rice. We are grateful to Wendy Ashmore, Rutgers University, David Freidel, Southern Methodist University, and Mary Pohl, Florida State University, for their critical comments on an earlier version of this chapter. Figure 7.1 is reproduced with permission courtesy of the *Journal of Field Archaeology*, Boston University.

The Central Petén Lakes Region

As a laboratory for the Maya environment, the Department of Petén can be characterized environmentally as a series of east-west folds and ridges of karsted Miocene and Eocene limestone, which form a low, uneven surface varying between 100 m and 300 m above sea level that generally rises from north to south. Rainfall also varies in a north-to-south trend from less than 2,000 mm to more than 3,000 mm annually.

Variable lithology and rainfall regimes, together with variable microtopography, have produced soil suites with different properties of fertility, permeability, and erodability. The significance of this soil heterogeneity cannot be overstated, as soils have a great influence on the natural vegetation of the region, on the food production capabilities of populations, on the characteristics of standing water resources, and on the character of natural and human-induced perturbations in resources.

In spite of adequate, albeit seasonal, rainfall, the Petén lowlands are characterized by a paucity of perennial water sources. Several rivers drain in the direction of the Gulf of Mexico or Caribbean Sea, but for the most part streams are seasonal. Standing water includes sinkholes and *bajos*. Bajos are perched depressions lined with residual, partly alluvial clays and are only inundated during the rainy season.

The most conspicuous water sources in Petén lie in a line of troughs formed by an east-west fault zone roughly coinciding with 17° north latitude. This fault lies between the two geological regions of Petén, a karst area to the north and an orogenic piedmont region in the south. With the close of the Pleistocene these depressions filled with water and became the central Petén lake system (fig. 7.1). The lakes occupy the deeper parts of elongate, fairly shallow basins of interior drainage. Within the fault-line depression small streams may discharge into the large bodies of water, but no permanently flowing external outlets exist. Like the bajos, some lakes have perched water tables and drain down very slowly to the underlying aquifer (Deevey, Brenner, Flannery, and Yezdani 1980).

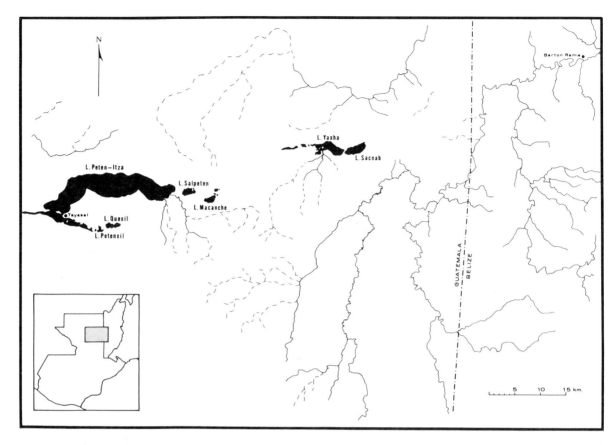

Figure 7.1. The central Petén lakes region, Guatemala, and portions of adjacent western Belize, showing major drainages.

The central Petén lake region is particularly amenable to the study of the adaptation of an agricultural society to a lowland tropical forest environment. Although this region is not the location of the most spectacular Maya civic-ceremonial centers, its documented span of continuous Maya settlement makes it an appropriate area for investigating long-term demographic trends, land-use patterns, and Maya societal development. In addition, the lakes themselves are a source of data on the environmental impact of Maya populations.

Lakes are only partially self-contained ecosystems, and their internal dynamics and accumulating sediments reflect processes taking place in the larger lake-basin ecosystem for which they serve as catchments. Free from the ambiguity of significant export by effluent streams, closed lakes like those of the Petén chain preserve evidence of natural and artificial changes in the larger ecosystem. Such evidence includes lacustrine animal and algal fossils, pollen grains and carbonized fragments from terrestrial vegetation, and mineral and ionic inputs from terrestrial sources and rainfall.

One pair of lakes, Yaxha and Sacnab, was chosen for our initial attempts to correlate population and natural histories because information from earlier archaeological work there suggested the existence of Preclassic, Classic, and Postclassic occupation with the basins (Bullard 1960, 1970). At the same time, the Lake Yaxha basin was suggested to have supported heavier settlement during all periods, including the large architectural center of Yaxha, than that of Lake Sacnab. Experimentally, the sedimentary records of the two lakes could be investigated singly, for conditions before, during, and after Maya occupation and, comparatively, in terms of a high-low pair of occupation intensities. Archaeological surveys and paleolimnological studies were carried out within the basins to provide data for the description and correlation of the lakes' cultural and natural histories.

The Historical Ecology Project: Archaeology

The archaeological research was designed to recover data on the relative size and density of Maya populations in the Yaxha and Sacnab basins, the qualitative parameters of that settlement, and the gross changes in occupation through time. These data were recovered by way of combined programs of survey and test-excavation. Because the research design of the historical ecology project dictated a focus on the hydrologically defined lake basins, the archaeological sampling universe was defined by an imaginary 2 km strip of terrain encircling the lakes. This zone embraced the immediate sediment- and chemical-producing area of the lakes' drainage basins.

A multistage probability sampling procedure was employed within this universe. The sampling units were transects (operations) 500 m wide, radiating out north or south from the lake shore to the boundary of the 2 km wide strip. These units crossed all physiographic and vegetational changes within the east-west trending topography. The number of transects on each lake was chosen arbitrarily to equal 25 percent of the total possible 500 m wide divisions of the lake shoreline lengths, distributed proportionately on the north and south shores. The area of the civic-ceremonial center of Yaxha, on the north shore of Lake Yaxha, was eliminated from the universe to avoid duplication of previous mapping at that locale (Hellmuth 1972). This sampling procedure resulted in six survey transects randomly placed around Lake Yaxha and four on Lake Sacnab. In addition to this strategy, a survey line was judgmentally placed across Cante Island, one of the Topoxte Islands in Lake Yaxha, where a Postclassic community was known to have existed (Bullard 1970). This was done to ensure that a sample of Postclassic construction and artifact material would be included in the study.

All transects were searched for structural remains, and of the total of 586 mounds located and mapped within the mainland transects, 148 loci (a 25.2 percent sample) were chosen for test-pit excavation by means of a random numbers table (Rice and Rice 1980). Another 19 loci were sampled on Cante Island. Test pits were located within structure areas in order to recover datable material, primarily pottery and lithic refuse, from construction fill (D. Rice 1976a:132–134). The ceramic chronology used to date constructions was not as fine-grained as might be desired, since it was obtained through limited excavation exposures of structures, and inventories of datable material were therefore restricted. This excavation strategy allowed for greater geographical sampling within the basins than would otherwise have been possible, however.

Chronological ordering of data was based on comparisons with sequences established at other sites in the Maya Lowlands. The settlement history of the Lake Yaxha and Lake Sacnab basins has been divided into the Middle Preclassic (1000–250 B.C.), Late Preclassic (250 B.C.–A.D. 250), Early Classic (A.D. 250–550), Late Classic (A.D. 550–900), and Postclassic (A.D. 900–1525) periods. In the discussion of the natural histories of Lakes Yaxha and Sacnab we have also considered a pre-Maya period, that span of time

prior to the occupation of the basins, and a post-Maya period, which encompasses the Postclassic abandonment of the basins through modern times. We also discuss the Classic and Postclassic periods together as one environmental episode because of the difficulty in distinguishing palynologically or geochemically the boundary between the two (see Vaughan, Deevey, and Garrett-Jones, chap. 6).

A substantive discussion of settlement history in the Yaxha and Sacnab basins has been presented elsewhere (Rice 1976b, 1978; Rice and Rice 1980; Jones, Rice, and Rice 1981), and it is not our purpose to review those data in detail here. Suffice it to say that the number of discrete architectural units constructed in the basins increased from the Middle Preclassic through the Late Classic period. The greatest number of settlement units were identifiable as Late Classic and, as anticipated from Bullard's earlier surveys (1960, 1970), the density of Late Classic settlement loci in the Yaxha basins was on the order of three times greater than that around Lake Sacnab. The Maya "collapse" is manifest in a dramatic decline in settlement remains in the mainland transects and an apparent reorientation of architectural activities toward the Topoxte Islands.

Assuming that the majority of settlement loci mapped in the basins were residential in nature, several factors can account for the fluctuations in their numbers. The most obvious is change in the actual number of basin occupants, with settlement size a direct reflection of population size. Structure numbers may also be contingent on the social and economic decisions of the resident group, however. Household structure, wealth, status, access to land, and generational continuity of occupation all affect the degree to which residents will invest in domestic architecture and the degree to which occupation will leave archaeological traces recoverable by surface survey and test excavation (Netting 1982; Wilk and Rathje 1982).

Population numbers and the social and economic organization of residence groups are obviously interrelated on many levels, and relative impact of each on the structure of the archaeological record is difficult to sort out, particularly for a project with survey and excavation strategies like our own. The magnitudes of settlement change from period to period and the environmental data to be discussed herein convince us that the structure numbers and occupation percentages recovered during our archaeological work are a reasonable estimate of population dynamics.

It is apparent from our survey data that the number of loci of construction in the basins increased through the Late Classic period, and we interpret this rise as indicative of population growth. Because periodization based on ceramic assemblages has not yielded fine chronological control, it is difficult to suggest growth rates or their constancy. Nevertheless, if we accept the tally of occupation loci per period as a measure of population size and if we assume both a constant annual increment to some maximum at the end of the period and contemporaneity of structures at that peak, then we can integrate our occupation numbers over the span of the periods to arrive at an estimate for the average rate of population growth (Rice 1978). This procedure yields a figure for a rate of sustained increase that can be evaluated comparatively.

Although the chronological intervals are rather coarse and the dynamics of growth from one period to the next may have been highly variable, overall growth in settlement projects to approximately 0.17 percent per year or an approximate doubling time of 408 years. For purposes of comparison, the average growth rate for Ixtapalapa populations in the Valley of Mexico from 1200 B.C. to A.D. 1520 has been estimated at 0.13 percent, with rates as high as 0.59 percent (Blanton 1972). Hassan (1981:140) has suggested a probable maximal rate of natural increase for prehistoric populations of 0.52 percent, with rates possibly as high as 2.65 percent per year under special conditions (Hassan 1973). The doubling time for a growth rate of 0.1 percent, the time it would take that population to double in size, is on the order of 700 years. The Preclassic and Classic growth rate of 0.17 percent for the combined Yaxha-Sacnab basins is below Hassan's average maximum for Neolithic cultivators and well below his upper limit. Considered alone, the Late Classic period was a time of accelerated population growth, which may be attributed either to unchecked natural increase or to in-migration. In the case of the former, the annual growth rate in the Yaxha-Sacnab basins would rise to 0.24 percent per year (0.34 percent for Yaxha and 0.14 percent for Sacnab). There is no archaeological evidence for in-migration.

The growth curve for recovered structures can be converted to a population profile by adjusting the total number of structures per phase to reflect the actual number of residences and by multiplying the resulting figure by an estimated constant population per residence (Rice 1978:42–46). In computing population figures we have assumed that by the end of each period the structures constructed during that period were contemporaneous (Haviland 1970:191); that approximately 84.0 percent of the total number of structures occupied during a period were actual residences (Haviland 1970:193); and that 5.4 persons per structure is a stable average for Preclassic and Classic period population estimates (Puleston 1973:183). These assumptions are based on the results of intensive archaeological analysis at the major Petén site of Tikal, and they are not necessarily valid for other contemporary site regions in the Petén. There are no data presently available by which to test their universality, however. While it is doubtful that the derived constants were invariant from area to area or through time, they do allow us to propose an approx-

imate magnitude of population density per square kilometer within the basins per time period: Middle Preclassic: 25 persons/km²; Late Preclassic: 61 persons/km²; Early Classic: 102 persons/km²; Late Classic: 211 persons/km². Such a conversion adds no new information on the rate of demographic change within the Yaxha-Sacnab basins, but population estimates become significant in an evaluation of regional environmental utilization and the carrying capacity of agricultural systems. They are also necessary for estimating the per capita impact of exponential growth within the lacustrine ecosystem.

While minor fluctuations of population remain undefined, the overall demographic trend for the Yaxha-Sacnab basins suggests no physical limits to growth until the end of the Late Classic period or at least no problems that could not be overcome by technological or social means. Nonetheless, the continued growth of agrarian population in the basins during approximately 2,000 years of Maya occupation preceding the collapse undoubtedly had an effect on the tropical forest environment. The paleolimnological aspect of the project was designed to measure that impact.

The Historical Ecology Project: Paleolimnology

Any ecosystem sustains itself on a flow of chemical elements drawn by vegetation from rocks, soil, and air and carried either in dissolved or suspended form by water. Elements that are mobilized and cycled by terrestrial plants and animals become components of waterborne outputs from the watershed. In closed lake basins, which have no outlets to the sea, elements that enter the lakes find their ultimate repository in accumulating sediments and ground water. Functionally, lakes can be thought of as nutrient and sediment traps, with their fresh waters being reflections of the terrestrial components of their catchment basins.

In undisturbed ecosystems, the specific elemental composition of a lake mirrors the relative concentration of elements in the terrestrial environment. Anomalies in the lacustrine occurrence of particular elements, such as large concentrations or rapidly changing rates of elemental input, are most likely the result of urbanization, agriculture, or both. Indeed, lakes are one of the best indicators of the activities of humans in drainage basins.

In tropical areas, forest clearance by agrarian populations deflects much of the terrestrial nutrient pool to soils. Nutrients are later captured for human nutrition through cropping. Deforestation, establishment of standing agricultural crops, field or garden abandonment, and subsequent natural plant succession are reflected in an altered rain of pollen and particulate matter—changes in the quantity and species composition of windblown pollens and other plant remains that find their way to the lake and into the lake sediments.

In addition to depriving the soil surface of protective forest cover, architectural and agricultural engineering can also rapidly accelerate the processes of alluviation and colluviation, thus increasing the rates of erosion and deposition of organic and inorganic materials. This deposition alters the quality and chemistry of lacustrine waters and in turn influences the species composition and growth characteristics of aquatic flora and fauna. Inputs to the lakes and the changes they effect likewise become incorporated into accumulating lacustrine sediments.

Paleolimnological studies provide a way of measuring the impact of riparian human populations on their environment over time, taking advantage of the fact that lake sediments form a record of the natural and cultural history of the associated basin. The paleolimnological research program at Yaxha-Sacnab was undertaken in order to recover quantitative evidence of the sequence of sedimentary, chemical, palynological, and microzoological and microbotanical inputs into the lakes. In 1972 and 1973 sediment cores were obtained with a hand-operated Livingstone piston corer from Lakes Yaxha and Sacnab and from the smaller Lake Quexil approximately 65 km to the southwest. The cores were transported to the Florida State Museum, where they were extruded, described, and sampled for pollen, chemical composition, aquatic fossils, and radioactive carbon assay.

The sediments of all three lakes contain thick layers of silty montmorillonitic clay dating from the period of Maya occupation. The thickness of the layers is related to the extent of local Maya disturbance. Clay minerals are silicates, conventionally expressed as SiO_2 (silica). The Maya clay, as seen in these lakes, also contains increasing proportions of limestone ($CaCo_3$) toward the tops of the sections. Both silicates and carbonates here are clastics, fragments of preexisting rocks, and not autochthonous (aquatic) precipitates of the lake water. Their accelerating inputs resulted from human activity around the basins. Sedimentation in Lakes Yaxha and Sacnab was so great during the Maya period that clay deposited in both lakes still seals their basins and insulates the exceptionally fresh lake waters from harder ground waters.

This layer of Maya clay prohibited penetration of the coring apparatus into pre-Maya sediments in Lake Yaxha. The Yaxha core sequence is therefore younger than that from Sacnab, beginning at some time during what we believe to have been the Late Preclassic period. The Lake Sacnab core contains a complete record of the Maya episode, with layers of organic mud evident both above and below the Maya clay. Although the oldest Yaxha sediments recovered were younger than those of Sacnab, the Yaxha core is more

than 1 m longer. This high sediment yield is attributable to the greater human activity around Lake Yaxha.

Broadly speaking, the Yaxha and Sacnab cores suggest a pattern of increased sedimentation resulting from Maya disturbance. The major problem associated with interpretation of the core material, however, is one of dating. Quantitative evidence for environmental stability or change depends on the measurement of rates of sedimentation, and such rates are ordinarily calculated from differences in sediment accumulation between radiocarbon-dated levels in the cores. A method relying on radiocarbon dates proves inapplicable in the Yaxha-Sacnab basins because of large carbonate error in hard-water lakes, redeposition of soil carbon of various ages, and inadequate amounts of carbon for dating in the sediments. For these reasons, we can make little sense of the 29 radiocarbon measurements from Petén lake sediments and must reject all but the oldest (DAL 198, 8410 ± 180); (Ogden and Hart 1977), a sample of wood from near the bottom of the Lake Quexil core. Because this sample consisted of woody tissue of terrestrial origin, no carbonate contribution and thus no carbonate error was involved (Deevey 1978).

Fortunately, enough is now known of pollen stratigraphy in Petén to permit division of the cores into a smaller number of distinctive pollen zones. These zones can be correlated between cores because pollen assemblages recording Maya deforestation and agricultural disturbance are similar in lakes Yaxha, Sacnab, Macanche, and Quexil (Deevey, Garrett-Jones, and Vaughan 1980; Vaughan 1979; Vaughan, Deevey, and Garrett-Jones, chap. 6), and Quexil's sister lake, Petenxil (Tsukada 1966), and very different from high-forest assemblages of zones above and below the Maya period.

Any relative stratigraphic chronology floats in time, and to anchor this one in historic time we have assigned archaeological dates to significant changes in pollen composition shared between cores. In matching the pollen stratigraphy with the events of Maya prehistory, we rely on the accepted radiocarbon date from Quexil as an absolute anchor for the commonalities of the various cores and on the corpus of archaeological data as a basis for assumptions on the beginning and ending dates of Maya occupation in the southern Maya Lowlands. Pollen zones in each of the sedimentary profiles that contained similar percentages of various indicator pollen types were attributed to similar archaeological periods (see Vaughan, Deevey, and Garrett-Jones, chap. 6).

Within this framework, the general trend of pollen sequences is one of a decline in arboreal pollen through the Maya Preclassic periods and a concomitant increase in pollen of disturbance species. Weed pollen of the composite tribe Ambrosieae, the most specific indicator of human presence, increases exponentially through the Classic period, while all indicators of primary and secondary forest decline dramatically. There is a subsequent interruption in the spread of cultivation weeds, particularly Ambrosieae, accompanied by pollen evidence for slight reforestation, which we correlate with the Classic collapse. This episode is followed in turn by renewed deflection of arboreal pollens and increase of savanna types, attributable to Postclassic Maya activity in the basins. Finally, with the close of the Postclassic period, disturbance indicators decline, successional species increase, and reforestation of the basins begins (Vaughan 1979; Vaughan, Deevey, and Garrett-Jones, chap. 6).

Once the pollen sequence has been established and temporally grounded by correlation with archaeological phases, drainage input rates can be estimated. Influx rates are calculated by dividing average sedimentary concentrations of phosphorus, organic and carbonate carbon and the remainder (chemically expressed as SiO_2) by the time intervals between major changes of pollen composition (Deevey et al. 1979).

In considering possible errors in this procedure, it is useful to separate questions of the precision of zone definition from those of the accuracy with which those zones are placed in real time. The stratigraphic precision of the pollen zone definitions is within about 10 cm depth, because of the blurring of pollen zone boundaries by the mechanics of deposition. The pollen zones designated by us are approximately 1 m thick, and uncertainty as to their boundaries makes their time-duration imprecise by about 14 percent (the root-mean-square of two 10 percent errors). Calculated elemental influxes, then, are ratios of imprecise mean concentrations, with confidence limits of 5–20 percent, to imprecise durations. Being ratios, the precision of the influx rates cannot be specified exactly but may be no better than 50–100 percent. Factor-of-two differences in influx rates from zone to zone therefore may not be meaningful, but the differences found in the Yaxha and Sacnab cores and described below are by factors of five or ten. Such large differences require explanation, the stratigraphic problems notwithstanding.

The question of accuracy, the true age of the zonation, arises when matching the zonal influx rates with populations assumed to be coeval with the zones. What we defend as highly probable but cannot yet verify by independent dating is our assignment of the first major deforestation to the Late Preclassic period. The Late Preclassic was a time of considerable construction and population growth in the Yaxha and Sacnab basins (Rice and Rice 1980). Estimates of Lowland Maya population densities suggest that land shortages would have existed under a swidden agricultural system by Late Preclassic period, alleviation of which undoubtedly would have included diversification of crops and cropping strategies and max-

imal utilization of the landscape (D. Rice 1978; Webster 1977). Correlation of a pollen zone characterized by sharp reduction of arboreal pollen and significant increases of disturbance types with Late Preclassic population expansion reflects deductive arguments about the environmental impact of expanding or intensified agriculture. If this pivotal date is wrong, our whole stratigraphic chronology could be wrong (inaccurate) by two to four centuries. The above, and alternative correlations and chronologies, are discussed in chap. 6. Here we note only that some population during its expansion and contraction caused a sequence of vegetational changes and a parallel sequence of changing rates of sedimentation in several lakes. A different correlation of the stratigraphy and Maya history, pivoting on Middle Preclassic or Early Classic dates, for example, will alter neither the parallelism of these sequences nor the rates of change within them. What would be altered is the degree of human impact computed from the sequence data. Mathematically, that is, a different matching of population sizes with rates of sedimentary influx gives a different numerical value to the estimate of influx per capita.

We further rationalize our approach by reasoning that, in dividing lacustrine history so coarsely, dating errors of a century or more cannot drastically affect the palynologically calculated sedimentation rates. The stratigraphic validity of the sediment zones is equal to that of the ceramic periods utilized in discriminating population change and is therefore appropriate for evaluating relative elemental input rates as indicators of population impact on environment.

In determining the effect of exponential population growth, we are particularly interested in two elements, silicon and phosphorus, because they are not recycled through the atmosphere. Unlike the biological elements carbon, nitrogen, sulfur, and dihydrogen oxide (water), silicon and phosphorus have no volatile compounds at ordinary temperatures. Their net flow is into the lakes, and we can assume that final delivery rates to lacustrine sediments indicate their rates of extraction and flow within the drainage basin. Moreover, as human residence and exploitation modify patterns and rates of element flow, final delivery rates in the basins are also measures of environmental impact.

As silica (SiO_2, quartz) or as alumino-silicate clay minerals, silicon is the most abundant element (after oxygen) on earth and is the main constituent of soil. It is virtually insoluble in water, and at ordinary temperatures its reactions are so slow that it has no chemistry, practically speaking. In lake sediments, except for quantitatively unimportant diatom skeletons, one can be fairly sure that a majority of silica and silicates were pre-existing soils that had been transported and redeposited without chemical change. As such, under conditions of human settlement silica influxes can be interpreted as a manifestation of societal output—a nonbiological expression of the impact of architectural and agricultural engineering on environment.

At Yaxha-Sacnab one external (nonbasinal) source of silica has been tentatively identified, volcanic dust (tephra) from the geologically active highlands to the south. A suite of ten concentrated sediment samples representing the Late Preclassic through Postclassic zones in four of the Petén lakes, including Yaxha and Sacnab, has been analyzed for tephra by Virginia Steen McIntyre at the University of Colorado. Nine samples had small to minute amounts of coarse silt-size particles and, of these, seven contained volcanic ash shards. No studies have yet been undertaken to identify the sources of the ash, but physical characteristics of the shards suggest tephra from more than one eruption. There is no information on quantities or rates of deposition or on the characteristics of rebedding during deposition. At present we can only assume that the tephra component of the silica influx is a minimal one, potentially useful for establishing absolute dates for the core zones.

The ecological role of phosphorus is different from that of silica. Phosphorus is a highly reactive biological element that is geochemically scarce. Phosphorus occurs naturally in the environment as a form of phosphate, either as soluble inorganic phosphate ions or as a part of other organic or inorganic molecules of varying solubility. No life is possible without phosphorus because energy required for protein synthesis and all other metabolic processes of living cells is handled by the reversible phosphorylation of adenosine diphosphate (ADP) to the triphosphate (ATP). To enter living cells and perform its essential functions, phosphorus must be absorbed from a watery medium as phosphate ions. The ultimate source of these ions is some form of rock, and these nutrients are first made available to living organisms through the weathering of sedimentary deposits. These ions are more than ordinarily scarce in calcium-rich alkaline limestone regions such as Petén.

Plants obtain soluble phosphate ions through their roots and incorporate them into living tissue. These tissues are consumed by human or nonhuman herbivores, who then utilize the captured phosphorus in their own organic processes. Excess phosphate in the diets of members of the food chain is excreted by them. As this detritus and dead plant and animal tissues decompose, the phosphate component of organic molecules is liberated in the form of inorganic ions. These ions may be taken up by plants or incorporated into sediments. Phosphate ions in the soil may react with other chemicals, such as calcium, to form insoluble compounds or become physically incorporated into clay minerals, thereby reducing their availability to living organisms. Because some phosphate compounds are not very soluble,

phosphorus is not readily removed from sediments once incorporated into them.

Since phosphorus is rare in the Petén environment and is immobilized by calcium, its movement in the system above normal minimal levels is largely from human inputs (fertilizers, food wastes, sewage, and burials) or through human-aided processes such as deforestation. During periods of landscape disturbance, when erosion, leaching, and watershed outputs are thus increased, losses of phosphorus are also increased. In the central Petén lacustrine areas, much phosphorus is immobilized by limestone-derived soils and removed from the terrestrial environment through soil transport to lakes, then permanently buried in lake sediments. Consequently, it is no longer available in any form to sustain human population or its crops. This nutrient sequestering or removal from biological cycling could be a particularly insidious form of environmental strain with negative impact on agricultural productivity (Deevey and Rice 1980).

In our Yaxha-Sacnab study we have detected variability in the phosphorus input rates in the two lacustrine systems through the various Maya periods (table 7.1). In Lake Sacnab, phosphorus influx rises exponentially from Middle Preclassic through Late Preclassic times, reaching a peak in the Early Classic period. The rate of phosphorus input declines in the Late Classic and Postclassic periods, then levels off at a slightly lower value in the post-Maya period. In Lake Yaxha, both phosphorus concentrations and rate of phosphorus input to the lake are low in the oldest sediments, which date to the Late Preclassic period. This finding suggests that the sediment largely consists of mineral soil, perhaps reflecting the stripping of soil and rock during major construction of the civic-cermonial center of Yaxha. By the Early Classic period, inputs had greatly increased, and an exponential growth in the rate of phosphorus was maintained into the Late Classic and Postclassic periods. Yaxha's post-Maya influx rates drop to a level comparable to that which characterizes Lake Sacnab in the same period (Brenner 1978).

Excluding the phosphorus-deficient zones from Lake Yaxha, very high correlations ($r = 0.74 - 0.91$, $p < .001$) are found between the influxes of silica and phosphorus, silica and carbonates, and phosphorus and carbonates (Deevey et al. 1979:303). As all silica is allochthonous (derived from outside the lake), we suggest that most phosphorus and carbonates were also redeposited as part of the soil rather than through flow of phosphate and bicarbonate ions. Because the high influxes of phosphorus continue into the post-Maya period, when leaching should have been diminished by regrowth of forests, we infer that a great deal of soil was injected directly into the lakes as colluvium (by gravity) and to a lesser extent as alluvium (by running water). This inference is reinforced by the chemical similarity between most lake

Table 7.1. Populations and influxes of phosphorus and silica to lakes Yaxha and Sacnab, Petén, Guatemala.

Archaeological-pollen time units	Duration (years)	Phosphorus influx ($\mu g/cm^2/yr$)	Silica influx ($mg/cm^2/yr$)	Maximum population on transects ($no./km^2$)	Mean riparian population ($no./km^2$ of lake area)	Number of shells per house mound (both lakes)
LAKE SACNAB, area 3.897 km²; land area 12.41 km² ("2-km basin")						
Post-Maya	420	8.05	34.73	0	0	
Late Classic + Postclassic	1,000	9.57	36.59	168[a]	167.6	
Early Classic	300	22.38	159.27	102	239.5	
Late Preclassic	500	13.65	29.04	51	128.3	
Middle Preclassic	1,250	3.14	8.16	34	85.5	
Early Preclassic	1,280	1.70	4.43	0	0	
LAKE YAXHA, area 7.4 km²; land area 26.51 km² ("2-km basin")						
Post-Maya	420	8.58	29.50	0	0	28.26
Late Classic + Postclassic	1,000	11.02	72.99	256	244.0	2.99
Early Classic	300	3.25	282.06	101	319.0	3.69
Late Preclassic	300	1.29	244.09	70	173.0	10.70
Middle Preclassic	-	-	-	22	67.7	24.95

Note: Numbers of shells per house mound are reported for the combined lake basin.

a. Late Classic only; Sacnab had no Postclassic settlement.

sediments and the topsoils within the basins. Analyses of soils from the drainages indicate that most phosphorus does in fact remain in the topsoil, whereas highly soluble sodium or potassium are distributed throughout the profiles. Also, phosphorus, alone among the elements subject to leaching, is currently moving downhill toward the lakes from the ridges that form the basin perimeters (Brenner 1983).

Influxes of phosphorus and silica run parallel to the growth of the Yaxha-Sacnab population, but the deposition of silica is more accelerated than that of phosphorus. On the logarithmic scales of figure 7.2, phosphorus influxes, like population densities, increase by one order of magnitude by Late Classic time. At the same time, silica influxes rise by two orders of magnitude in Lake Yaxha. Land areas within the basins were altered at rates so closely correlated with population densities that disturbance is adequately indexed by population sizes. For phosphorus, if the quantity delivered with the disturbed soil is largely anthropogenic, population sizes are not merely indicative of influx rates but causal, and an input-output model suggests itself.

If phosphorus influxes and populations increased at the same exponential rates, no formal treatment by calculus is needed to see that the relationship between rates is some constant per capita output. Its numerical value is of special interest because the phosphorus output of any human population at physiological steady state, with excretion balancing intake, is 550 gm per capita-year. In the limnological literature, the quantity that today includes outputs of garbage, fertilizers, and detergents is commonly taken as 800 gm, and many lakes are threatened by societal outputs of 1,500 gm per capita or more (Wetzel 1975:215–245).

The harmonic mean of phosphorus output by Yaxha-Sacnab populations is 570 gm per capita per year, again excluding the phosphorus-poor zones from Lake Yaxha. This figure approximately matches the physiological steady state figure. The Late Classic and Postclassic delivery rate of phosphorus to Lake Yaxha from riparian populations exceeds 1,400 gm per capita, however, approaching levels that might be considered dangerous in temperate lakes of comparable depth in modern Europe or North America (Vollenweider 1968). There are no data available that allow similar comparison with other tropical lakes. Extra-physiological outputs by the Yaxha-Sacnab populations would have come from decomposing forest products, food consumption and human biological processes, food wastes, and mortuary disposal.

The danger of high phosphorus inputs lies in the fact that the support capability of lakes, also referred to as biological productivity, is so closely attuned to a normally tiny supply of phosphorus that even small increments by way of culturally induced inputs

(sewage, food wastes, fertilizers) can easily double or treble production. The term cultural eutrophication has come to be widely used to denote this type of organic pollution from human activities—the accelerated input of nutrients to a freshwater system that leads to increased growth rates of lake biota (algae, plants, and animals). In advanced stages of cultural eutrophication, damage to the lake occurs when excess production leads to oxygen depletion, creation of anaerobic conditions, and the drastic alteration of the composition of aquatic floral and faunal communities.

We know that influxes of phosphorus to lacustrine sediments were accelerated by Maya occupation in the Yaxha-Sacnab basins, but we find no unequivocal indications of eutrophication. Evidence of enhanced production was sought in the sedimentary record by counting fossil remains of lacustrine animals and plants and by chemical measurement of organic carbon. Microscopic examination of microfossils shows that preservation is extremely poor in the clay sediments (Brenner 1978; Deevey, Vaughan, and Deevey 1977). Organic carbon follows no discernible pattern in lakes Yaxha and Sacnab.

Several factors lead us to believe that the probability of eutrophication in lakes Yaxha and Sacnab was low. If colluvium, or redeposited soil, is the principal source of phosphorus in lacustrine sediments, the highly insoluble calcium phosphate that entered the lakes is unlikely to have enhanced biotic growth. Most of the calcium phosphate probably settled to the bottom without contributing to the available nutrient pool. In addition, lakes Yaxha and Sacnab were probably frequently made turbid by the influx of soil, and lower rates of biological productivity might be attributable to reduced penetration of sunlight as an energy source for photosynthesis.

We also note that the numbers of lacustrine mollusc shells recovered from excavations in Maya constructions around the lakes declined in frequency from the Middle Preclassic to Late Classic period (table 7.1), suggesting a decline in consumption of the animals. The decline in mollusc shells from archaeological contexts may reflect reduced populations of molluscs in the lakes (as opposed to gustatory preferences), a reduction that could have resulted either from siltation or from overfishing. While Maya activity within the lake basins undoubtedly altered the biotic constituents of the lakes, any negative impact on available lacustrine resources may well have been the result of siltation, rather than eutrophication.

Implications of Environmental Change

The importance of the documented environmental impact of Maya populations at Yaxha-Sacnab lies in its implications for the nature and success of Maya sub-

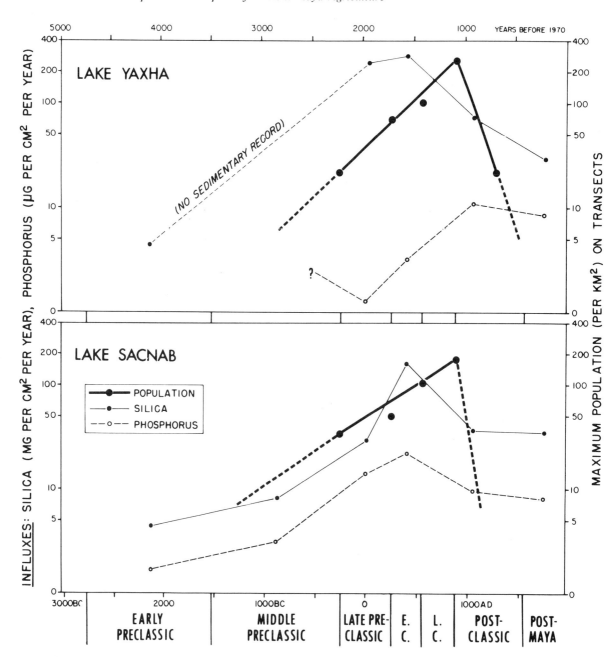

Figure 7.2. The relationship between
phosphorus and silica influxes and
population growth in the basins of
Lakes Yaxha and Sacnab
(logarithmic scale).

sistence patterns there. The possible consequences of lacustrine pollution, for example, can be seen in the mollusc data discussed above. If a disturbance of aquatic habitats is causally related to the decline of mollusc populations, similar problems in the procurement of fish and other lacustrine resources might be anticipated.

Lacustrine changes have their origin in the terrestrial component of the forest-lake ecosystem, and the perturbing influence of activity would be similar there, although more direct. The pollen sequence reflects a progressive deforestation of the region in which the basins sit, while accelerated deposition of sediments indicates technological manipulation of the basin terrain. These modifications would severely diminish natural habitats, which would in turn have a negative impact on the availability of terrestrial botanical and zoological resources. Predation and harvesting by growing Maya populations would undoubtedly hasten such declines.

It is likely, then, that wild food procurement systems became increasingly stressed and unproductive through time, as would the collection of botanical resources for fuel, crafts, and construction. We expect that pressures on lacustrine and terrestrial biota would reinforce any propensities the Maya might have had toward selective protection of useful plant species, pisciculture, and animal husbandry.

Terrestrial perturbations could also have had an effect on the character of Maya agriculture in the region. Although the specific modes of agriculture are open to question, archaeologically and paleo-limnologically defined processes suggest potential constraints on agricultural practices. Increasing amounts of upland soil were covered by buildings and plazas, effectively removing well-drained upland areas from production and altering terrain so as to acclerate erosion. Agriculture can have a similar geophysical impact, increasing soil degradation by larger factors than do residences. Unfortunately, we cannot distinguish the differential effects of architecture and agriculture easily.

We do know, however, that after initial clearing, agriculture, in contrast to architecture, modifies the rates of mobilization and flow of phosphorus within the system. Because phosphorus is a nutrient, first for plants and then for people, the linear relationship between population growth and phosphorus was expectable: agricultural production, ingestion, excretion, mortality and decomposition, and down-hill delivery were in long-term balance. The potential problem for agricultural production lies in the fact that phosphorus is naturally rare, released only slowly from rock, and the ultimate fate of at least a portion of that reservoir is down-hill delivery and sequestering in lacustrine sediments.

The Maya agriculturalists of Yaxha-Sacnab had to cope with declining access to upland soils on which to crop, deterioration of the soil matrix on the remainder, and constant diminution of essential nutrients within the system. This is not to say that these processes progressed to a level where subsistence agriculture was not practicable, only to suggest that these were processes with which the Maya had to cope. There is sufficient evidence for sophisticated agro-engineering in the Maya Lowlands (Puleston 1978; Turner 1978) to indicate that the Maya recognized such problems, and we would expect farmers in the Yaxha-Sacnab region to have responded with agricultural practices designed to compensate for these processes. Documentation of those practices assumes that the Maya of Yaxha-Sacnab actually pursued subsistence activities within the surveyed drainage basins.

Possible conservation features include terraces (Turner 1974, 1979), raised fields (Harrison 1977; Siemens and Puleston 1972; Turner and Harrison 1981), and kitchen garden arboriculture (Puleston

1968, 1973). Terraces check the down-hill movement of soils and in so doing increase the amount of land available while impeding the effects of erosion and chemical weathering. Raised fields (Turner and Harrison 1981) are constructions in which soils are essentially recycled, dug and piled up onto a platform to enhance drainage in inundated areas. Like agricultural terraces, raised fields allow for expansion of the area and frequency of cropping in an improved medium for cultivation. In kitchen gardens, the garden structure, a complex pattern of foliage distribution and canopy heights, rather than technological structure, reduces the impact of physical forces on soil surfaces. Kitchen gardens allow for cropping in areas too confined for open-field agriculture.

All three modes are potential foci of intensive production, although the intensity may vary, and they are susceptible to nutrient and structural rejuvenation through fertilization and mulching. The application of night soil and organic detritus, combined with inter-cropping and multiple cropping techniques to enhance soil nutrient utilization, would delay the loss of phosphorus ions through leaching or their immobilization by calcium-rich sediments and forestall to some degree the effect of nutrient sequestering.

The plausibility of various local subsistence options of different cropping foci and intensities through time in the Yaxha-Sacnab region has been evaluated by modeling the quantities and qualities of available land and the land requirements of estimated populations under various staple crops and levels of agricultural intensification (D. Rice 1978). The conclusions are not surprising given a condition of exponential population growth within the basins; it would have been necessary for Yaxha-Sacnab populations to practice increasingly intensive agriculture on ever larger percentages of the total landscape. We are inclined to view Maya agriculture as a complex of component systems, each adapted for maximal production and conservation within specific micro-environmental zones. In the absence of evidence for agro-engineering from surveyed areas, however, it is difficult to speculate on the components involved or their integration.

The lack of agricultural terracing on sloping upland terrain in the survey samples may suggest that open-field agriculture was not a prominent subsistence mode within the basins by the Classic period. The lack may also be the result of the Yaxha-Sacnab Maya not farming within the basins or of the inability of the survey to detect the remains of such terracing. The modest nature of visible archaeological traces of terracing at the gradually sloping savanna site of El Fango (Rice and Rice 1979), Petén, suggests that such evidence might be disintegrated and imperceptible on the 20° + slopes of the Yaxha and Sacnab basins.

It is equally difficult to verify the practice of kitchen garden arboriculture in these same areas. We do not have the absolute chronological control over the

Yaxha-Sacnab pollen sequences nor the necessary pollen preservation or species determinations to substantiate the presence of this or other modes of subsistence production.

There were also no survey data to support the likelihood of raised field production, but here it is possible that human impact on the landscape may be an obfuscating factor. Soils moving within the basins would gravitate toward the lake shores and bajo areas south and east of both lakes. Outside the immediate basins, soils would have collected in depressions and in bajos to the north of Yaxha's north shore. If the lake shores and bajos suffered alluviation and colluviation on a scale comparable to that measured in the lakes, physical evidence for raised fields in the region may well be buried in sediments.

Only one of the transects surveyed during the Yaxha-Sacnab field work sampled a bajo area within the drainage basins (Operation 7 on the south shore of Lake Yaxha), and there was no evidence of agro-engineering found, either for reasons of transect location or the problem of sedimentation mentioned above. Recent results reported by the Jet Propulsion Laboratory of NASA from their Synthetic Aperture Radar survey of Central America indicate, however, the possibility of vast networks of canals and raised fields in Petén, Guatemala, and Belize (*The Times*, June 4, 1980; *The New York Times*, June 4, 1980; Adams 1980; Adams, Brown, and Culbert 1981). Included in the areas identified by the radar analyses as probable loci of raised fields are the bajos within and surrounding the Yaxha and Sacnab basins (Adams 1980, fig. 2; B. L. Turner, personal communication, 1981). While the existence of a system of canals has not yet been verified on the ground at Yaxha-Sacnab, surveys in Petén in 1980 confirmed the presence of raised fields depicted by the radar in the vicinities of the sites of Aguateca, Seibal, and Tikal (Adams 1980:208–209).

If the Maya practiced agriculture in the bajo areas around Lakes Yaxha and Sacnab, they could with appropriate techniques take some advantage of redeposited soils from the uplands as a cultivation medium rather than suffer the loss. This is not to say that such recycling would have altered natural field fertility, however. Bajo soils, like lake sediments, are poor in available phosphorus (Cowgill and Hutchinson 1963), and it is unlikely that the raised field technology would increase amounts of usable phosphorus, although phosphorus locked in insoluble compounds may be gradually released over a number of years. In addition, alluviation and colluviation would probably have presented a problem in that the siltation would have forced continual retrenching of fields. While raised field agriculture is a conservation measure, with intentional movement of soil to cultivable plots, raised field engineering must also

have increased the rate of sediment and nutrient transfer to the lake from normally undisturbed littoral zones.

In sum, it is at present easier to hypothesize appropriate agricultural practices for the Yaxha-Sacnab region than it is to demonstrate their existence. More difficult still is any determination of the success of these conservation measures or the degree to which and the duration for which they could offset the processes of environmental degradation. Slow but constant (over the long term) population growth for several millennia indicates that the Maya of Yaxha-Sacnab either experienced no decline in productive capacities or recognized and responded to the exigencies of food production. Evidence from the side-looking radar surveys of possible field and canal systems in the area provides a clue that the response was in part technological. We also recognize that the Maya of Yaxha-Sacnab functioned within a broader pan-Maya community. Responses to local production problems were undoubtedly also social and political, involving interregional interaction and the trade of foodstuffs. This realization takes us beyond our data and beyond the scope of this chapter, except to suggest that the fate of Yaxha-Sacnab populations and institutions may not have rested completely on local production.

Summary

The Central Petén Historical Ecology Project is a quantitative investigation of human interaction with a tropical environment, using as its laboratory the Maya-occupied lake basins of Petén, Guatemala. The combined archaeological and paleoecological approach employed at lakes Yaxha and Sacnab recovered data on relative size and density of settlement through time and chemical and pollen evidence of changes in the forest-lake ecosystem. In ecological terms the problem is one of deducing environmental stress from a measured amount of strain. Strain is defined as a measurable change in rates of flow of certain chemical elements from drainage basins to lake and is measured by final rates of deposition of these elements in accumulating sediments.

Drainage basins exploited differently yield different, culturally modified influxes of two elements in particular: phosphorus, the scarcest and therefore most essential of biological nutrients, and silicon, the chemically unreactive framework element of rocks and soil. Both are delivered to lakes by erosion of soils, and neither element can escape to the air or from the lake basin that lacks an outlet. The palynological evidence for deforestation in central Petén is conclusive. We argue from several lines of limnological evidence that most sediments in Lake Sacnab are in fact redeposited soils, delivered by colluviation after erosion was sharply accelerated by Preclassic deforestation. Late Preclassic and Early Classic sediments of Lake Yaxha are exceptionally deficient in phosphorus; they appear to be mineral soil, stripped during construction of the civic-ceremonial center.

Archaeological data show that mainland settlement and population densities increased over at least 17 centuries, only to undergo an abrupt decline and reorientation in location during Postclassic times. Influxes of total phosphorus and silica (SiO_2) increased exponentially through the Early Classic period, though at different rates, and declined only slightly thereafter. Influxes of these elements continue today at rates many times higher than before disturbance and higher than expected after reforestation.

The principal result of comparative study of differently exploited basins is that deposition of phosphorus and of silica were both amplified by Maya disturbance but by factors that differed numerically according to the mode of exploitation. Phosphorus, moving through crops and people and deposited within the basins at a constant per capita rate, was eventually immobilized in lake sediments in direct linear proportion to the size of the riparian population. That is, both population densities and phosphorus influxes increased by about one order of magnitude through Late Classic time. Silica deposition, reflecting the technological component of stress on environment, was accelerated by larger factors: by about two orders of magnitude in Lake Sacnab and by nearly three orders of magnitude in Lake Yaxha, where engineering activities were most intense.

Deforestation, agricultural cultivation, and urban construction are generally known to enhance erosion rates by one, two to three, and three to four orders of magnitude, respectively (Deevey and Rice 1980). Our measurements of silica deposition follow a similar trend. Geological studies have not previously revealed that phosphorus eroded from soils and buried in lake sediments is permanently removed from agricultural use. If such nutrient sequestering inhibits agricultural production while demand continues to rise, a negative feedback mechanism may be set in motion, contributing to the damping of population growth.

The Maya of the Yaxha-Sacnab region drastically altered the terrestrial and aquatic components of the ecosystem, and it is tempting to see some relationship between this degradation and the Maya collapse. To say that environmental strain, measured by accelerated erosion rates and consequent sequestering of nutrients, could have been a causative factor in the collapse is not to prove that it was, however. Without more data on crops, cropping strategies, and cropping locations we cannot suggest that productive limits were in fact reached. It is presently not possible to extrapolate from the Yaxha-Sacnab basins to any other lacustrine or nonlacustrine regions of Petén, where population profiles are unknown and micro-environmental characteristics are different, and we are particularly reluctant to generalize to the southern Maya Lowlands as a whole.

The fragility of lowland tropical forests is manifest in the rapidity with which the soil matrix loses its structure and nutrients are lost from the system. The rate and extent to which these processes can occur varies from location to location, as do the characteristics of geological parent material, soil, topography, and water sources. The conspicuous success of the Maya utilization of tropical forests was undoubtedly due in part to their recognition of the mechanisms and consequences of environmental perturbation and to their ability to integrate a range of crops and conservation techniques into a productive agricultural system on both the local and interregional levels. The specific characteristics of such a system and the degree to which degradation contributed to pan-Maya subsistence stress and concomitant sociopolitical problems remain foci for future environmental research in the Maya Lowlands.

References

Adams, R. E. W.
1980   "Swamps, Canals, and the Locations of Ancient Maya Cities," *Antiquity* 54:206–214.

Adams, R. E. W., W. E. Brown, Jr., and T. P. Culbert
1981   "Radar Mapping, Archaeology, and Ancient Maya Land Use," *Science* 213:457–463.

Brenner, M.
1978   "Paleolimnological Assessment of Human Disturbance in the Drainage Basins of Three Northern Guatemalan Lakes." M.S. thesis, Department of Zoology, University of Florida, Gainesville.
1983   "Paleolimnology of the Maya Region." Ph.D. dissertation, Department of Zoology, University of Florida, Gainesville.

Bullard, W. R.
1960   "Maya Settlement Patterns in Northeastern Peten, Guatemala," *American Antiquity* 25:355–372.
1970   "Topoxte: A Postclassic Maya Site in Peten, Guatemala." In *Monographs and Papers in Maya Archaeology*, edited by W. R. Bullard, Jr. Peabody Museum Papers, 61, Harvard University, Cambridge.

Cowgill, U., and G. E. Hutchinson
1963   *El Bajo de Santa Fe.* Transactions of the American Philosophical Society 53. Philadelphia.

Deevey, E. S.
1969   "Coaxing History to Conduct Experiments," *Bioscience* 19:40–43.
1978   "Holocene Forests and Maya Disturbance near Quexil Lake, Peten, Guatemala," *Polskie Archiwum Hydrobiologii* 25:117–129.

Deevey, E. S., H. H. Vaughan, and G. B. Deevey
1977   "Lakes Yaxha and Sacnab, Peten, Guatemala: Planktonic Fossils and Sediment Focusing." In *Interactions between Sediments and Fresh Water*, edited by H. L. Golterman. Junk, Wageningen.

Deevey, E. S., D. S. Rice, P. M. Rice, H. H. Vaughan, M. Brenner, and M. Flannery
1979   "Maya Urbanism: Impact on a Tropical Karst Environment," *Science* 206:298–306.

Deevey, E. S., M. Brenner, M. Flannery, and H. Yezdani
1980   "Lakes Yaxha and Sacnab, Peten, Guatemala: Limnology and Hydrology," *Archiwum Hydrobiologii Supplement* 57:419–460.

Deevey, E. S., S. E. Garrett-Jones, and H. H. Vaughan
1980   "Impact of Mayan Civilization on Tropical Lowland Forest," Paper presented at the 5th International Palynological Congress, Cambridge (abstract).

Deevey, E. S., and D. S. Rice
1980   "Coluviación y retención de nutrientes en el distrito lacustre del Petén central, Guatemala," *Biotica* 5:129–144.

Farnworth, E., and F. Golley
1974   *Fragile Eco-systems: Evaluation of Research and Applications in the Neotropics.* Springer-Verlag, New York.

Harrison, P. D.
1977   "The Rise of the *Bajos* and the Fall of the Maya." In *Social Process in Maya Prehistory*, edited by N. Hammond. Academic Press, New York.

Hassan, F.
1973   "On Mechanisms of Population Growth during the Neolithic," *Current Anthropology* 14:535–542.
1981   *Demographic Archaeology.* Academic Press, New York.

Haviland, W. A.
1970   "Tikal, Guatemala and Mesoamerican Urbanism," *World Archaeology* 2:186–198.

Hellmuth, N.
1972   "Excavations Begin at Maya Site in Guatemala," *Archaeology* 25:148–149.

Jones, G. D., D. S. Rice, and P. M. Rice
1981   "The Location of Tayasal: A Reconsideration in Light of Peten Maya Ethnohistory and Archaeology," *American Antiquity* 46:530–547.

Netting, R. McC.
1982   "Some Truths on Household Size and Wealth," *American Behavioral Scientist* 25:641–662.

Odum, E.
1971   *Fundamentals of Ecology.* Saunders, Philadelphia.

Ogden, J. G., III, and W. C. Hart
1977   "Dalhousie University Natural Radiocarbon Measurements II," *Radiocarbon* 19:392–399.

Puleston, D. E.
1968   *"Brosimum alicastrum* as a Subsistence Alternative for the Classic Maya of the Central Southern Lowlands." M.A. thesis, Department of Anthropology, University of Pennsylvania.
1973   "Ancient Maya Settlement and Environment at Tikal, Guatemala: Implications for

Subsistence Models." Ph.D. dissertation, Department of Anthropology, University of Pennsylvania.

1978 "Terracing, Raised Fields, and Tree Cropping in the Maya Lowlands: A New Perspective on the Geography of Power." In *Prehispanic Maya Agriculture*, edited by P. Harrison and B. L. Turner. University of New Mexico Press, Albuquerque.

Rice, D. S.
1976a "The Historical Ecology of Lakes Yaxha and Sacnab, El Peten, Guatemala." Ph.D. dissertation, Department of Anthropology, Pennsylvania State University.

1976b "Middle Preclassic Maya Settlement in the Central Maya Lowlands," *Journal of Field Archaeology* 3:425–445.

1978 "Population Growth and Subsistence Alternatives in a Tropical Lacustrine Environment." In *Prehispanic Maya Agriculture*, edited by P. D. Harrison and B. L. Turner. University of New Mexico Press, Albuquerque.

Rice, D. S., and P. M. Rice
1980 "The Northeast Peten Revisited," *American Antiquity* 45:432–454.

Rice, P. M., and D. S. Rice
1979 "Home on the Range: Aboriginal Maya Settlement in the Central Peten Savannas," *Archaeology* 32:16–25.

Siemens, A. H., and D. E. Puleston
1972 "Ridged Fields and Associated Features in Southern Campeche: New Perspectives on the Lowland Maya," *American Antiquity* 37:228–239.

Tsukada, M.
1966 "The Pollen Sequence." In *The History of Laguna de Petenxil*, by U. Cowgill, G. E. Hutchinson, A. A. Racek, C. E. Goulden, R. Patrick, and M. Tsukada. Memoirs of the Connecticut Academy of Arts and Sciences 17.

Turner, B. L.
1974 "Prehistoric Intensive Agriculture in the Mayan Lowlands," *Science* 185:118–124.

1978 "Ancient Agricultural Land Use in the Central Maya Lowlands." In *Prehispanic Maya Agriculture*, edited by P. Harrison and B. L. Turner II. University of New Mexico Press, Albuquerque.

1979 "Prehispanic Terracing in the Central Maya Lowlands: Problems of Agricultural Intensification." In *Maya Archaeology and Ethnohistory*, edited by N. Hammond and G. R. Willey. University of Texas Press, Austin.

Turner, B. L., and P. D. Harrison
1981 "Prehistoric Raised-Field Agriculture in the Maya Lowlands," *Science* 213:399–405.

Vaughan, H. H.
1979 "Prehistoric Disturbance of Vegetation in the Area of Lake Yaxha, Petén, Guatemala." Ph.D. dissertation, Department of Zoology, University of Florida, Gainesville.

Vollenweider, R. A.
1968 *Scientific Fundamentals of the Eutrophication of Lakes and Flowing Waters, with Particular Reference to Nitrogen and Phosphorus as Factors in Eutrophication.* Organisation de Coopération et de Développement Economiques report no. DAS/CSI/68.27, Paris.

Webster, D.
1977 "Warfare and the Evolution of Maya Civilization." In *The Origins of Maya Civilization*, edited by R. E. W. Adams. University of New Mexico Press, Albuquerque.

Wetzel, R. G.
1975 *Limnology.* W. B. Saunders, Philadelphia.

Wilk, R., and W. Rathje
1982 "Household Archaeology," *American Behavioral Scientist* 25:617–640.

Part II
Osteological Evidence for Subsistence and Status

Mary Pohl

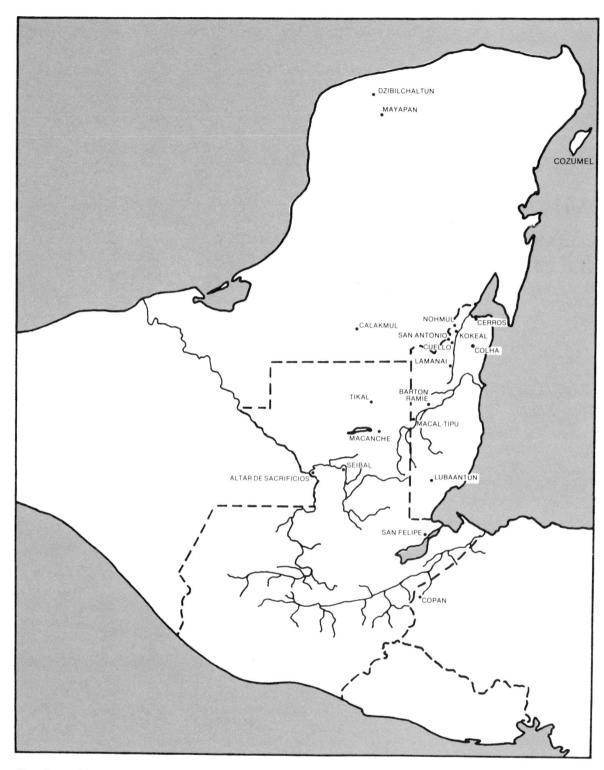

Sites discussed in part II.

Regional Patterns in Animal Resource Utilization

We now have faunal data from a number of tropical lowland sites, and using the global view provided by cluster analysis, Wing (1981) has defined regional food consumption patterns in the Maya Lowlands as well as on the Gulf Coast. She has demonstrated that domestic dogs (*Canis familiaris*) were prominent in the Preclassic diet of both areas. They comprise 12–16 percent of Olmec bone assemblages (calculated according to minimum numbers of individuals) and 10–23 percent of Maya faunas. Preclassic Maya sites are characterized by higher percentages of deer (*Odocoileus virginianus* and *Mazama* sp.), but musk turtles (*Kinosternon* spp. and *Claudius angustatus*) and snook (*Centropomus* spp.) are more typical of Olmec sites.

In the Classic period most Maya sites show a marked predominance of deer and turtle. Wing (1981) notes that fewer dog remains occur at ceremonial centers, but Pendergast (1974) found dog teeth representing 124 individuals in Terminal Late Classic deposits at the cave of Polbilche, demonstrating that the Maya continued to use many dogs in rituals. In the Gulf Coast region, dogs continued to occur at Classic period centers, and terrestrial mammals as a group played a greater role in the diet, while the exploitation of fish and turtles declined.

Regional differences are evident within the Lowland Maya region. Ocellated turkey (*Meleagris ocellata*) is more abundant at the Preclassic to Postclassic Yucatecan sites of Dzibilchaltun (Wing 1981), Mayapan (Pollock and Ray 1957), and Cozumel (Hamblin 1984) than at most southern lowland sites such as Seibal, Altar de Sacrificios, Lubaantun, Cerros, and Cuello (Pohl 1976; Wing 1975a; Hammond et al. 1979; Carr, chap. 8). The Late Preclassic sites of Cerros (Carr, chap. 8) and Cancun (Wing 1975b) as well as Postclassic Cozumel (Hamblin, chap. 11) demonstrate that coastal inhabitants were always heavily dependent on resources from the sea.

As yet we do not know the extent of regional variability. The specialized flint production site of Colha has a markedly different fauna, resembling Gulf Coast sites much more than other Maya centers (Wing 1981). Aquatic animals, fish (including peripheral types), crocodilians, and turtles (*Chrysemys* sp. and *Staurotypus* spp.), are characteristic (Scott 1981, 1982). Among terrestrial fauna, turkey is abundant, but peccary is rare (Wing 1981).

Temporal Trends

As evidence on fauna gradually accumulates, temporal trends in animal resource utilization are becoming evident. A shift in mollusc utilization occurred between the Preclassic and Classic periods. Quantities of freshwater molluscs, including *Pomacea, Pachychilus,* and *Nephronaias,* occurred in Preclassic refuse deposits at Cuello (Feldman, personal communication, 1980), Lamanai (Pendergast 1981), Tikal (Moholy-Nagy 1978), Barton Ramie (Willey et al. 1965:525–528), and Copan (Longyear 1952:16–17). In the Classic period, such molluscs were used for ritual and ornamental purposes. *Pomacea tristami,* possibly imported from Lake Petén, occurred with lake turtle (*Dermatemys mawei*) and crocodile in special votive offerings at Early Classic Tikal (Moholy-Nagy 1978:660–70). The *Pomacea* are larger than those from Preclassic midden, and kitchen tests (Miksicek 1980) indicate that such individuals are less palatable than the smaller ones found in early refuse. At Barton Ramie, *Nephronaias* shells, perforated for suspension, were put in three Late Classic burials. Late Classic Maya at Lubaantun deposited large quantities of *Pachychilus* in ceremonial caches associated with the ball courts at the site. Though *Pachychilus* also occurs in midden, specimens from the ritual deposit were larger, suggesting that they had been specifically selected for size (Hammond 1975:384–385).

The reason for this change is a mystery. It may have to do with a change in food processing or refuse disposal. The use of snails for social rather than dietary purposes in the Classic period may also have been a deliberate decision. Excavations in wetlands at San Antonio Río Hondo revealed that molluscs such as *Pomacea* were abundant throughout the profile from Preclassic times to the present. In northern Belize the animals did not decrease in number because the Maya were destroying their habitat with wetland cultivation. Rice, Rice, and Deevey (chap. 7) argue that siltation in central Petén might have resulted in a Classic period decline in lacustrine resources, including molluscs. Nevertheless, recent analysis has shown that in the Hondo River the concentration of dissolved ions is such that small-sized particles flocculate; they do not stay in suspension for long unless large amounts of water are supplied to the system as, for example, during hurricane floods (Stein, in prep.). Obviously, the situation is complex, and each area will have to be examined carefully. One might argue, however, that even if Petén lakes were silty, turbidity might have increased rather than decreased productivity (S. Flannery, personal communication, 1984).

The Maya dined on snails again in the Postclassic period though this food was less popular than in Preclassic times. *Pomacea* has been found in the final

---

See chapter 1 for Mary Pohl's affiliation.

stages of occupation at Tikal (Moholy-Nagy, personal communication, 1974) as well as at Postclassic sites in central Petén (D. Rice, personal communication, 1975). Spanish records indicate that the Maya were still eating snails in the early historic period. When soldiers destroyed the fields of the Cholti-Lacandon of lowland Chiapas, they remarked on "mountains of snail shells that they (the Indians) had gathered together to eat." (Hellmuth 1977:424)

Small game, such as armadillo (*Dasypus novemcinctus*), rabbit (*Sylvilagus* spp.), agouti (*Dasyprocta punctata*), and paca (*Agouti paca*), as well as fish, are more characteristic of Preclassic faunas at Cuello (Wing n.d.; Hammond et al. 1979) and Terminal Late Classic through Postclassic faunas at Tikal, Macanche (Pohl 1976), and Macal-Tipu (Pohl 1981a) than Classic faunas (Pohl 1976). Excavators might have missed small bones in Classic deposits, however, and we will have to fine-screen soils from these contexts before we can determine whether the scarcity of small game and especially of fish is real.

Catchment Areas

The marine fauna suggest that the Maya generally ate what they procured near the site (Wing 1977). Sites located 10 km or more from the coast have only small amounts of marine materials. At Tikal, for example, traces of parrotfish (*Sparisoma*) occurred in a Late Preclassic context on the North Acropolis (Moholy-Nagy, personal communication, 1974) and in the Terminal Classic as well (Wing 1977:54). A parrotfish maxilla also turned up in Late Classic Kokeal. One grunt (cf. *Haemulon*) bone may date to Late Preclassic or Late Classic times at Seibal (Pohl 1976), and a quantity of unmodified shells might represent food refuse at Dzibilchaltun (Andrews 1969:59). Marine organisms at Early Preclassic Cuello testify to the fact that importation began very early (Wing, personal communication, 1984).

Sites near the mouths of rivers and coastal lagoons have considerable numbers of peripheral and some marine fish bones in spite of being 25–30 km from the sea (Wing 1977, table 3). Wing believes that easy access to the coast influenced exploitation patterns. At San Felipe, Guatemala, peripheral fish account for 59 percent of the Late Preclassic minimum numbers and 56 percent of the Classic fauna. Marine fish constituted 15 percent of the Late Preclassic and 7 percent of the Classic faunas, while freshwater types made up only 7 percent of the individuals of both time periods. For Late Classic Lubaantun, the figures are 25 percent peripheral, 18 percent marine, and 5 percent freshwater. At Lubaantun parrotfish, which are confined to coral reefs, and Scombridae (tuna

family), which inhabit deeper waters, indicate that fishermen were frequenting the cays and perhaps even the barrier reef 55 km offshore (Wing and Hammond 1974:134). The fact that grouper (Serranidae) gather in great numbers to mate off the coast of southern Belize was probably one of the factors that lured the Maya to the sea.

The fauna suggest that the Maya regularly imported significant quantities of marine organisms for purposes other than food. Marine materials are common in ritual deposits. At Dzibilchaltun, five Early Period caches contained shark teeth, ray spines, sea trout (*Cynoscion* sp.), and spiny boxfish (*Chilomycterus* sp.). Over one-half the individual animals represented in these caches is marine, a proportion far higher than in domestic refuse (Wing 1977). At Postclassic Mayapan, marine fish occurred in the cenote deposits, which were the focus of the rain cult, and freshwater fish were found in high status domestic contexts (Pohl 1983). The Maya particularly favored marine molluscs for votive offerings at sites like Tikal, including contexts emphasizing the power of the elite (Andrews 1969; Moholy-Nagy, chap. 10).

The terrestrial vertebrate fauna appear to follow the same pattern. The deer is a case in point. On Cozumel Island (Hamblin 1984), where deer may not have occurred naturally, *Odocoileus virginianus* comprise only 1.4 percent of the fauna. The locally available peccary (26 percent) as well as the domestic dog (13 percent) evidently took the place of the deer. Of the deer elements, 79 percent were head or foot and ankle bones, some burned and one occurring in a burial, suggesting that residents of Cozumel occasionally imported deer for votive offerings.

Human Sacrifice and Cannibalism

Human bones frequently occur in Maya ritual offerings, as well as in midden deposits. At Cuello (Hammond 1981) a Late Preclassic multiple burial included at least 23 people, all but one adolescent. An unhealed puncture wound testifies to slaughter, and evidence indicates that the victims had subsequently been chopped up. This massacre appears to have been a high status activity. Three carved bone tubes in the burial may have been handles for fans, an insignia of rank in Precolumbian Mesoamerica; in fact, one tube displayed the mat design associated with rulership. The presence of mass burials as well as of fortifications in the Late Preclassic period suggests that raiding for sacrificial victims was an established practice by that time. At Tikal human remains from Terminal Late Classic midden showed signs of burning and chewing that point to cannibalism (Harrison, personal communication, 1974).

Status Differences

In tracing the development of complex society, we must study distribution, as well as production. The faunal remains provide evidence for the distribution of both meat and status paraphernalia within and between sites. Carr (chap. 8) found that a civic-ceremonial context at Late Preclassic Cerros had more mammals than a provenience of lesser status. Pohl (chap. 9) has demonstrated that the Late Classic rulers of Seibal ate more meat than lower class inhabitants at the same site, and elites apparently controlled the use of scarce resources such as cats. On Postclassic Cozumel Island, high status sites yielded more diverse bird faunas, probably reflecting greater ritual activity as well as food consumption (Hamblin chap. 12).

The Role of Ceremony in the Subsistence Economy

The chapters on fauna in this book demonstrate that ritual was a significant element in stimulating production and defining patterns of distribution. Ceremonialism was closely connected with status and power. Wetlands may have been a factor in the development of social stratification during the Preclassic period. The San Antonio excavations indicate that Preclassic wetland fields were fertile (chap. 2). Using ethnographic analogy, Wilk (chap. 4) emphasizes that such fields provide security. The archaeological data suggest that those who controlled wetland fields were able to risk cultivation of nonsubsistence crops such as cotton which was probably woven into cloth for elites. Sites with access to wetlands like Nohmul and Cerros prospered.

The presence of fortifications suggests that competition had developed by the Late Preclassic period (Webster 1977). Ceremonialism also flowered in the Late Preclassic period, and rituals must have been one of the means by which those who were gaining power and wealth attracted followers and coerced their support. Although many Mayanists believe that population pressure emerged by the Late Preclassic period, labor scarcity might in fact have been a problem. Maya agriculture appears to have demanded many workers, and craft industries such as cotton textile production are labor-intensive.

Adams (1977:99) has traced the development of a royal cult emphasizing divine elite ancestry and religiously sanctioned status (Adams and Smith 1981:340) beginning in the Late Preclassic period. The cult is marked by thatched roof temples over burial platforms (such as Burial 105, Structure B-111 at Altar de Sacrificios), later changing to stone and mortar temples housing tombs (e.g., Tikal Burial 85). Research on ceremonialism explicitly depicted in Late Classic art, and probably originating much earlier, suggests that the ruler assumed the burden (*cuch*) of responsibility for guiding his followers through cycles of time and assuring economic well-being (Pohl 1981b).

Elites consolidated their control in the Classic period. Adams (Adams and Smith 1981:341) has pointed out that at least 90 percent of formal architecture in Maya centers was for elite use in contrast to many central Mexican cities where upper class structures make up the minority of buildings. The size of the elite ranks may have been smaller than archaeologists have previously thought if the elites periodically moved around from ceremonial centers to residences in the countryside, as Adams (Adams and Smith 1981:348) suggests on the basis of Río Bec settlement data together with ethnohistoric accounts. Fortifications, such as the earthwork at Tikal, possibly dating to the Classic period (Puleston and Callender 1967), together with scenes of sacrifice in the art from which we can infer raiding activity may reflect a struggle for economic power, probably including the appropriation of both land and labor, as well as for status enhancement.

Fauna provided the metaphorical expression for economic and class concerns. In Classic Maya art, deer are closely associated with water and rain, on the one hand, and with fire, sun, and drought, on the other (Pohl 1982). Judging from early historical observations, communal deer hunts may have symbolized the gathering of a successful maize harvest (Pohl chap. 9). The parallelism between deer and human sacrifices in the art suggests that human sacrifical victims may have substituted for deer in some ceremonies (Pohl 1982). Deer iconography associated with the *cuch* rite appears on monuments marking the investiture of authority (Pohl 1981b). Marine shells placed in tombs may have reinforced the immortality of the rulers (Moholy-Nagy chap. 10), who claimed to control the destiny of the community.

Evidence for ritualism declines in the archaeological record of the Postclassic period. Elites stopped constructing pyramids glorifying dead rulers and dedicated ceremonial architecture to deity cults. An example is the pyramid at Mayapan, which ethnohistoric data indicate was devoted to Kukulcan. The Maya by and large dropped representations of ceremonies validating rulership on ceramics and on stone stelae. In Postclassic times military interests may have become so powerful that ceremonialism as a means of coercion was no longer necessary.

References

Adams, R. E. W.
  1977   "Río Bec Archaeology and the Rise of
          Maya Civilization." In *The Origins of Maya
          Civilization*, edited by R. E. W. Adams.
          University of New Mexico Press, Albuquer-
          que, pp. 77–100.
  1982   "Ancient Maya Canals, Grids and Lattices
          in the Maya Jungle," *Archaeology 35*:28–35.

Adams, R. E. W., and W. D. Smith
  1981   "Feudal Models for Classic Maya Civiliza-
          tion. In *Lowland Maya Settlement Pat-
          terns*, edited by Wendy Ashmore. Universi-
          ty of New Mexico Press, Albuquerque, pp.
          335–349.

Andrews, E. W., IV
  1969   *The Archaeological Use and Distribution of
          Mollusca in the Maya Lowlands*. Tulane
          University, Middle American Research In-
          stitute 34.

Hamblin, N.
  1984   *Animal Use by the Cozumel Maya*. Univer-
          sity of Arizona Press, Tucson.

Hammond, N.
  1975   *Lubaantun: A Classic Maya Realm*.
          Peabody Museum Monographs, no. 2, Har-
          vard University.
  1981   "The Earliest Maya." Lecture delivered to
          the Department of Anthropology, Florida
          State University.

Hammond, N., D. Pring, R. Wilk, S. Donaghey,
F. P. Saul, E. S. Wing, A. V. Miller, and
L. H. Feldman
  1979   "The Earliest Lowland Maya? Definition of
          the Swasey Phase," *American Antiquity*
          44:92–110.

Hellmuth, N.
  1977   "Cholti-Lacandon (Chiapas) and Peten-Ytza
          Agriculture, Settlement Pattern and
          Population." In *Social Process in Maya
          Prehistory*, edited by N. Hammond.
          Academic Press, London, pp. 421–448.

Longyear, J. M.
  1952   *Copan Ceramics: A Study of Southeastern
          Maya Pottery*. Carnegie Institution of
          Washington 597.

Miksicek, C.
  1980   *Botanical Remains from Pulltrouser
          Swamp*. Paper presented at the 45th annual
          meeting of the Society for American Ar-
          chaeology, Philadelphia.

Moholy-Nagy, H.
  1978   "The Utilization of *Pomacea* Snails at
          Tikal, Guatemala," *American Antiquity*
          43:65–73.

Pendergast, D. M.
  1974   *Excavations at Actun Polbilche, Belize*.
          Royal Ontario Museum, Archaeology
          Monograph 1.
  1981   "Lamanai 1981: A Regular Three-Ring Cir-
          cus," *Royal Ontario Museum, Archaeo-
          logical Newsletter* 192.

Pohl, M. E. D.
  1976   "The Ethnozoology of the Maya: An
          Analysis of Faunal Remains from Five Sites
          in Petén, Guatemala." Ph.D. dissertation,
          Department of Anthropology, Harvard
          University.
  1981a   "Faunal Remains from Macal-Tipu: 1981
          Season." Manuscript in the files of the
          author.
  1981b   "Ritual Continuity and Transformation in
          Mesoamerica. Reconstructing the Ancient
          Maya *Cuch* Ritual," *American Antiquity*
          46:513–529.
  1982   "The Precolumbian Ritual Role of the
          Deer." Manuscript.

Pohl, M.
  1983   "Maya Ritual Faunas: Animal Remains
          from Burials, Caches, Caves, and Cenotes
          in the Maya Lowlands." In *Civilization in
          the Ancient Americas*, edited by Richard
          Leventhal and Alan Kolata. University of
          New Mexico Press, Albuquerque.

Pohl, M. and L. H. Feldman
  1982   "The Traditional Role of Women and
          Animals in Lowland Maya Economy." In
          Maya Subsistence, edited by K. V. Flan-
          nery. Academic Press, New York, pp. 295–
          311.

Pollock, H. E. D., and C. E. Ray
  1957   *Notes on Vertebrate Animal Remains from
          Mayapan*. Carnegie Institution of
          Washington, Report 41.

Puleston, D. E., and D. W. Callender
  1967   "Defensive Earthworks at Tikal," *Expedi-
          tion* 9:40–48.

Scott, R. F., IV
  1981   "Vertebrate Faunal Remains from Colha,
          Belize: The Analysis of the 1980 Materials."
          Paper delivered at the 46th annual meeting
          of the Society for American Archaeology,
          San Diego.

1982   "Notes on the Continuing Faunal Analysis for the Site of Colha, Belize: Data from the Early Postclassic." In *Archaeology at Colha, Belize: The 1981 Interim Report*, edited by T. R. Hester, H. J. Shafer, and J. D. Eaton. Center for Archaeological Research, the University of Texas at San Antonio and Centro Studi e Ricerche Ligabue, Venice, pp. 203–207.

Stein, J.
In   "Sedimentation and Maya Agriculture along
Prep.   Río Hondo, Belize." In *Ancient Maya Wetland Cultivation on Albion Island, Northern Belize*, edited by Mary Pohl. University of Minnesota, Papers in Anthropology 2.

Vaughan, H. H.
1979   "Prehistoric Disturbance of Vegetation in the Area of Lake Yaxha, Petén Guatemala." Ph.D. dissertation, University of Florida. University Microfilms, Ann Arbor.

Webster, D. L.
1977   "Warfare and the Evolution of Maya Civilization." In *The Origins of Maya Civilization*, edited by R. E. W. Adams. University of New Mexico Press, Albuquerque, pp. 335–372.

Willey, G. R., W. R. Bullard, Jr., J. B. Glass, and J. C. Gifford
1965   *Prehistoric Maya Settlements in the Belize Valley*. Peabody Museum Papers, vol. 54, Harvard University.

Wing, E. S.
1975a   "Animal Remains from Lubaantun." In *Lubaantun: A Classic Maya Realm*, by Norman Hammond. Peabody Museum Monographs, no. 2, Harvard University.
1975b   "Vertebrate Faunal Remains." In *Archaeological Investigations on the Yucatán Peninsula* by E. W. Andrews, IV, et al. Tulane University, Middle American Research Institute 31, pp. 186–188.
1977   "Factors Influencing Exploitation of Marine Resources." In *The Sea in the Pre-Columbian World*, edited by E. P. Benson. Dumbarton Oaks, Washington, D.C., pp. 47–66.
1981   "A Comparison of Olmec and Maya Foodways." In *The Olmec and Their Neighbors. Essays in Memory of Matthew W. Stirling*, organized by M. D. Coe and D. Grove, edited by E. P. Benson. Dumbarton Oaks, Washington, D.C., pp. 21–28.

Wing, E. S.
n.d.   "Animal Remains Associated with the Formative Occupation at Cuello in Northern Belize." Manuscript in the files of the author.

Wing, E. S., and N. Hammond
1974   "Fish Remains in Archaeology: A Comment on Casteel," *American Antiquity* 39:133–134.

Chapter 8

Subsistence and Ceremony: Faunal Utilization in a Late Preclassic Community at Cerros, Belize

Helen Sorayya Carr

In recent years, excavations at several sites have yielded data concerning the Preclassic period in the Maya Lowlands. One of these sites is Cerros, located on the Southeastern shore of Corozal Bay in northern Belize (fig. 8.1). This site was the subject of survey and excavation from 1974 to 1981 under the direction of David A. Freidel. All major architecture and habitational remains are dated by ceramics and C-14 to the Late Preclassic period (Robertson-Freidel 1980:1). Within this period, three phases have been distinguished: Ixtabai, estimated at 300–200 B.C., C'oh, 200–50 B.C., and Tulix, 50 B.C.–A.D. 150 (Robertson-Freidel 1980:307–318).[1] With its minimal overburden of Classic and later material, Cerros offers an excellent opportunity to focus attention on various aspects of Maya life in the Late Preclassic.

As preserved, the site consists of a civic-ceremonial precinct located on the coast and a settlement zone surrounding it and extending inland (fig. 8.2). The latter includes both residential and nonresidential structures. A canal system demarcates the zone of densest occupation and monumental architecture, as well as serving for drainage and irrigation of wetland fields (Scarborough 1980:270; Freidel and Scarborough 1982:133). There is also a nucleated village area adjacent to the central precinct and covered by its latest structures.

The relationship of the site to the coast in Late Preclassic times differed from the present situation to an as yet undetermined degree. The shore of Corozal Bay has eroded, cutting into the nucleated village remains. The presence of a dock-like structure in a

matrix of water-laid clay and silt indicates that at the time of occupation at least a part of the site was close to the shore, but what type of shore remains uncertain. The soil underlying the cultural deposits in the nucleated village together with *Melongena* shells in the midden layers were initially interpreted as indicative of a lagoon environment (Scarborough 1980:36, 37). The implication was that the New River mouth was closer to the site at the time of occupation, with its present position some 3.5 km to the south resulting from the same erosion that opened the lagoon up into what is now Corozal Bay. A recent reconsideration of the evidence by the excavator in charge of the nucleated village area (Cliff, personal communication, 1982) suggests that the adjacent water body may already have been a bay.

Despite this unresolved question, the occupants of Cerros had access to a variety of aquatic habitats. Modern residents of the area exploit streams, seasonally flooded savannas, fresh to brackish mangrove-lined lagoons such as Laguna Seca (approximately 3 km east of Cerros), and the sea, including the barrier reef forming the Belizean cays.

The terrestrial environment of the peninsula on which Cerros is located includes well-drained areas in which the climax vegetation is a deciduous tropical forest. How much of this vegetation was present at the time of occupation would have depended on the extent of agricultural land clearing. The environs of Cerros probably included a substantial amount of thick, brushy successional vegetation that would grow in fallow fields. This type of "low bush" may also have occurred naturally, as it does today, in low-lying, poorly drained *bajo* areas. Nevertheless, it appears that the bajos at Cerros are partly the result of human manipulation of the landscape (Scarborough 1980:60, 63). Therefore the vegetation in undisturbed areas throughout most of the Late Preclassic would have been largely the tropical forest mentioned above.

Excavations at Cerros have yielded a substantial sample of faunal remains. Most of these came from the nucleated village area, which is characterized by a complex stratigraphy of superimposed floors, burial pits, and midden layers, all overlain by the rubble fill of the main plaza built in the latest phase of Preclassic

Helen Sorayya Carr is a doctoral candidate, Tulane University, New Orleans, Louisiana.

I am grateful to David A. Freidel and the staff of the Cerros Project for giving me the opportunity to excavate and analyze the Cerros fauna and for discussing with me their interpretations of the archaeological contexts. Elizabeth S. Wing has generously made the resources of the zooarchaeology collection at the Florida State Museum available to me. Robin Robertson and Charles A. Schwartz provided helpful comments on a draft of this chapter. Arlene Fradkin assisted in redrawing the figures.

1. The precise dating may be subject to revision (Cliff 1982:195-198); however, all dates are solidly Preclassic.

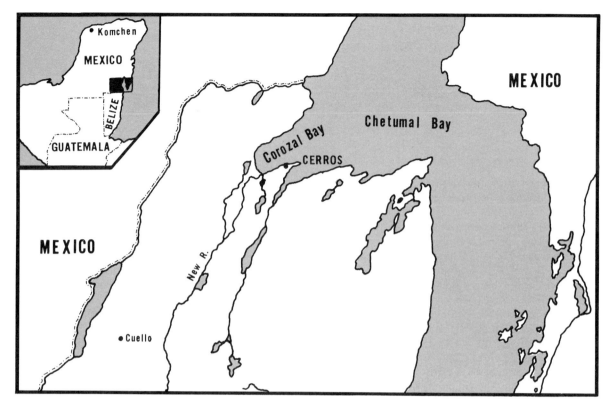

Figure 8.1. Northern Belize, with
sites mentioned in text. Based on
Cliff 1982, figure 11, and Freidel and
Scarborough 1982, figure 1.

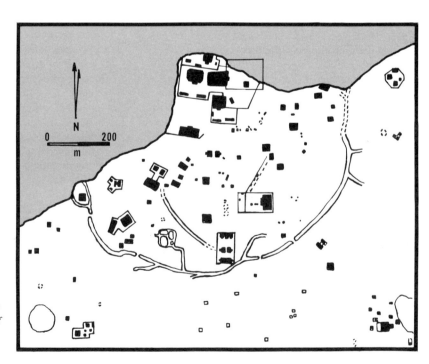

Figure 8.2. Central portion of Cerros. Rectangle at top center indicates
the area of figure 8.3. Based on Cliff
1982, figure 12, and Freidel and
Scarborough 1982, figure 2.

occupation. The identification of these remains has not been completed as yet; however, a preliminary characterization of the faunal assemblage may be made, based on the material from parts of two operations in the nucleated village (fig. 8.3).

To date, suboperations a–h of Operation (Op.) 1, located near the eastern edge of the village, have been analyzed. These suboperations are a series of contiguous squares of approximately 2 m × 2 m. (The exact north-south dimension of each varies with the form of the natural erosional profile forming the northern edge of the operation.) A much smaller proportion of Op. 34 has been analyzed to date: 31 lots from Op. 34a, a 24 m² excavation some 50 m to the west of Op. 1. Op. 34 contains the dock as well as two other structures, midden materials, beach deposits, and the overlying plaza fill.

The ultimate goal of the faunal analysis is to delineate the pattern of faunal procurement and use at Cerros and its changes through time. In order to understand this pattern as well as to facilitate comparisons with other faunal analyses the material is being quantified in terms of fragment counts, minimum numbers of individuals (MNI) represented, and biomass estimates derived from bone weights. In order to minimize the effects of arbitrary excavation unit divisions on the MNI count, individual lots are grouped following correlations established by the excavator in charge of the area (Cliff, personal communication, 1982). Thus, materials from adjacent

parts of a single midden stratum, for example, are combined in order to arrive at the most archaeologically valid estimate of MNI.

Subsistence Activities at Cerros

To date, a total of 4,670 fragments from Op. 1 and 34 have been examined, approximately 80 percent of which are identifiable to the class level or beyond. The taxa identified and their distribution are listed in tables 8.1 and 8.2.[2]

The assemblage from Op. 1, which has been interpreted as a nonelite residential locus (Robertson-Freidel 1980:267), probably provides the best indication of the role of fauna in the subsistence of most of

---

2. Included here are remains of vertebrates and crustaceans. The molluscs are the subject of a separate analysis. General surface collection and mixed lots are not included in these tables. Biomass estimates are based on formulas in the Florida State Museum files. These estimates are not provided for taxa for which formulas have not yet been developed (or for *Homo sapiens*, on the assumption that these bones do not represent food).

Figure 8.3. Locations of Operations 1, 34, and 41. From Cliff 1982, figures 14, 16, and 81.

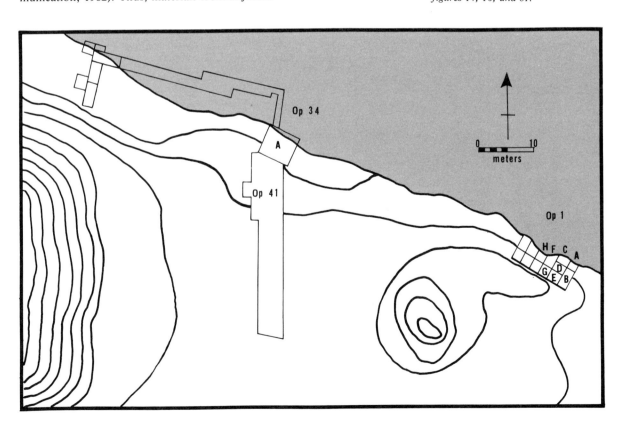

Table 8.1. Fauna of Operation 1a-h.

Species	C'oh/Tulix transition (1,224 fragments)			Early Tulix (2,446 fragments)			Late Tulix (Main Plaza fill, 5 fragments)		
	% fragment	% MNI	% biomass	% fragment	% MNI	% biomass	% fragment	% MNI	% biomass
CRUSTACEA									
Callinectes sp. (blue crab)	2.3	6.7	–	5.3	8.5	–	20.0	50.0	–
Menippe mercenaria (stone crab)	–	–	–	0.1	0.4	–	–	–	–
Unidentified crustacean	0.9	–	–	1.8	1.2	–	20.0	–	–
CHONDRICHTHYES									
Carcharhinidae (requiem sharks)	0.5	1.3	1.6	0.6	2.7	3.0	–	–	–
cf. *Mustelus* sp. (smooth dogfish)	–	–	–	(<0.1)	0.4	0.2	–	–	–
Sphyrnidae (hammerhead sharks)	0.1	0.7	9.4	0.2	1.2	2.8	–	–	–
Carcharhinidae/ Sphyrnidae	0.1	–	0.1	0.2	0.4	0.7	–	–	–
Pristis sp. (sawfish)	0.1	0.7	0.1	(<0.1)	0.4	0.1	–	–	–
cf. *Rhinobatus* sp. (guitarfish)	0.1	0.7	0.3	(<0.1)	0.4	0.1	–	–	–
Urolophus jamaicensis (yellow stingray)	0.1	0.7	0.3	–	–	–	–	–	–

Table 8.1 (continued).

Species	% fragment	% MNI	% biomass	% fragment	% MNI	% biomass	% fragment	% MNI	% biomass
Rajiformes (rays)	–	–	–	(<0.1)	0.4	0.1	–	–	–
Unidentified chondrichthyes	0.3	0.7	1.7	0.5	0.4	1.1	–	–	–
OSTEICHTHYES									
Elops saurus (ladyfish)	0.1	0.7	(<0.1)	–	–		–	–	–
Megalops atlantica (tarpon)	0.1	0.7	0.5	0.4	2.3	2.0	–	–	–
E. saurus/ M. atlantica	–	–	–	(<0.1)	0.4	(<0.1)	–	–	–
Albula vulpes (bonefish)	1.7	6.0	0.7	1.1	4.6	0.8	–	–	–
Muraenidae (moray eels)	0.2	2.0	0.2	0.2	1.2	0.1	–	–	–
Ariidae (sea catfishes)	–	–	–	0.1	0.8	0.1	–	–	–
Belonidae (needlefishes)	0.1	0.7	0.1	0.1	0.8	0.1	–	–	–
Serranidae (groupers and sea basses)	1.4	4.7	9.9	1.4	5.4	5.5	–	–	–
cf. Echeneidae (remoras)	0.1	0.7	0.1	–	–	–	–	–	–
Carangidae (jacks)	1.4	6.0	4.3	1.7	4.6	6.4	–	–	–
Lutjanidae (snappers)	3.4	8.7	2.1	1.6	5.0	2.1	–	–	–

Table 8.1 (continued).

Species	% fragment	% MNI	% biomass	% fragment	% MNI	% biomass	% fragment	% MNI	% biomass
Gerreidae (mojarras)	1.6	6.0	0.9	1.1	5.4	0.7	–	–	–
Pomadasyidae (grunts)	1.3	6.0	1.0	1.3	5.0	1.7	–	–	–
cf. Sparidae (porgies)	0.1	0.7	(<0.1)	–	–	–	–	–	–
Sciaenidae (drums)	–	–	–	0.1	0.8	0.1	–	–	–
Cichlidae (cichlids)	0.1	0.7	(<0.1)	0.2	0.8	0.1	–	–	–
Mugilidae (mullets)	1.1	3.4	0.5	1.7	3.8	0.9	–	–	–
Sphyraena sp. (barracudas)	1.2	5.4	0.5	1.3	4.6	0.8	–	–	–
Sphyraena sp./ Echeneidae	–	–	–	0.1	0.4	(<0.1)	–	–	–
Sphyraena sp./ *Scomberomorus* sp.	0.1	–	(<0.1)	(<0.1)	–	(<0.1)	–	–	–
Labridae (wrasses)	0.4	2.0	2.4	0.1	0.8	0.3	–	–	–
Scaridae (parrotfishes)	1.2	4.7	2.6	1.3	6.2	3.0	–	–	–
Acanthurus sp. (surgeonfishes)	1.9	6.7	0.9	2.1	5.4	1.3	–	–	–
Balistidae (triggerfishes, filefishes)	–	–	–	0.1	0.8	0.1	–	–	–
Perciformes	0.6	1.3	1.6	0.2	–	0.4	–	–	–
Unidentified teleost	56.9	1.3	13.5	36.6	–	14.9	–	–	–

Table 8.1 (continued).

Species	% fragment	% MNI	% biomass	% fragment	% MNI	% biomass	% fragment	% MNI	% biomass	% fragment	% MNI	% biomass
AMPHIBIA												
Bufo marinus (marine toad)	–	–	–	0.2	0.8	–	–	–	–	–	–	–
Unidentified anuran (frog/toad)	0.1	0.7	–	0.1	0.4	–	–	–	–	–	–	–
REPTILIA												
Emydidae (pond turtles)	0.2	1.3	0.7	0.4	0.8	0.8	–	–	–	–	–	–
Emydidae/Dermatemydae	0.1	0.7	0.3	–	–	–	–	–	–	–	–	–
Kinosternidae (mud and musk turtles)	0.1	0.7	0.3	0.8	1.5	2.1	–	–	–	–	–	–
Cheloniidae (sea turtles)	–	–	–	0.2	0.8	2.3	–	–	–	–	–	–
Unidentified turtle	0.6	2.7	2.6	0.3	0.8	0.7	–	–	–	–	–	–
Unidentified lizard	–	–	–	(<0.1)	0.4	–	–	–	–	–	–	–
Crocodylus sp.	–	–	–	(<0.1)	0.4	–	–	–	–	–	–	–
Unidentified reptile	0.4	1.3	–	0.1	0.4	–	–	–	–	–	–	–
AVES												
Ortalis vetula/Phasianidae (chachalaca/quail)	–	–	–	(<0.1)	0.4	(<0.1)	–	–	–	–	–	–
Meleagrididae (turkeys)	–	–	–	0.1	0.8	0.1	–	–	–	–	–	–

Table 8.1 (continued).

Species	% fragment	% MNI	% biomass	% fragment	% MNI	% biomass
Medium to large bird	–	–	–	0.4	–	0.3
Unidentified bird	–	–	–	2.2	1.2	0.2
MAMMALIA						
Sylvilagus sp. (rabbit)	–	–	–	(<0.1)	0.4	(<0.1)
Cricetidae (rats, mice)	0.2	1.3	0.1	1.0	2.3	0.1
Dasyprocta punctata (agouti)	0.1	0.7	0.2	–	–	–
Dasyprocta punctata/Coendu mexicanus (agouti/ Mexican porcupine)	–	–	–	(<0.1)	0.4	(<0.1)
cf. *Agouti paca* (paca)	–	–	–	(<0.1)	0.4	0.1
Unidentified rodent	0.2	0.7	(<0.1)	1.7	0.4	0.2
cf. Procyonidae (raccoon, coati, etc.)	–	–	–	(<0.1)	0.4	(<0.1)
Canis familiaris (domestic dog)	1.1	3.4	7.1	1.2	3.8	8.6
Urocyon cinereoargenteus (grey fox)	–	–	–	(<0.1)	0.4	0.1
Medium to large carnivore	–	–	–	(<0.1)	–	(<0.1)

Table 8.1 (continued).

Species	% fragment	% MNI	% biomass	% fragment	% MNI	% biomass	% fragment	% MNI	% biomass
Tayassu (Dicotyles) tajacu (collared peccary)	0.1	0.7	2.2	–	–	–	–	–	–
Tayassuidae/Cervidae	–	–	–	(<0.1)	–	0.4	–	–	–
Odocoileus virginianus (white-tailed deer)	0.2	2.0	20.8	0.9	3.1	13.6	–	–	–
Mazama americana (red brocket)	0.1	0.7	0.1	0.3	1.5	1.4	–	–	–
Cervidae (deer)	0.4	0.7	1.5	0.3	–	3.3	–	–	–
Homo sapiens	–	–	–	0.1	0.8	–	–	–	–
Small mammal	–	–	–	0.1	–	0.1	–	–	–
Small to medium mammal	–	–	–	(<0.1)	–	0.1	–	–	–
Medium and large mammals	1.3	2.0	7.3	3.1	1.9	13.4	40.0	50.0	100.0
Unidentified mammal	2.0	0.7	1.3	1.9	0.8	2.7	–	–	–
UNIDENTIFIED FRAGMENTS	13.4	–	–	22.5	–	–	20.0	–	–
TOTAL	100.1	100.2	99.8	99.4	100.8	100.1	100.0	100.0	100.0

Table 8.2. Fauna of Operation 34a.

Species	Ixtabai (3 fragments)			Early Tulix (471 fragments)			Late Tulix (16 fragments)		
	% fragment	% MNI	% biomass	% fragment	% MNI	% biomass	% fragment	% MNI	% biomass
CRUSTACEA									
Callinectes sp.	33.3	33.3	–	0.6	3.3	–	6.3	14.3	–
Unidentified crustacean	–	–	–	0.6	3.3	–	6.3	–	–
CHONDRICHTHYES									
Carcharhinidae	–	–	–	0.6	6.7	1.0	–	–	–
OSTEICHTHYES									
Megalops atlantica	–	–	–	0.2	3.3	0.2	–	–	–
Albula vulpes	–	–	–	–	–	–	6.3	14.3	1.4
Ariidae	–	–	–	0.2	3.3	0.1	–	–	–
Lutjanidae	–	–	–	0.8	3.3	1.1	–	–	–
Gerreidae	–	–	–	0.6	3.3	0.4	–	–	–
Pomadasyidae	–	–	–	0.4	3.3	0.5	–	–	–
Sciaenidae	–	–	–	–	–	–	6.3	14.3	10.1
Mugilidae	–	–	–	0.4	3.3	0.2	–	–	–
Sphyraena sp.	–	–	–	0.2	3.3	0.1	–	–	–
Scaridae	–	–	–	1.1	6.7	1.1	–	–	–
Unidentified teleost	–	–	–	3.8	–	1.8	6.3	–	10.1
REPTILIA									
Kinosternidae	–	–	–	0.2	3.3	0.1	–	–	–
Unidentified turtle	–	–	–	5.7	3.3	12.5	–	–	–

Table 8.2 (continued).

Species	% fragment	% MNI	% biomass	% fragment	% MNI	% biomass	% fragment	% MNI	% biomass
AVES									
cf. large bird	–	–	–	0.2	3.3	0.1	–	–	–
MAMMALIA									
Dasyprocta punctata	–	–	–	0.2	3.3	0.2	–	–	–
Agouti paca	–	–	–	0.2	3.3	0.1	–	–	–
Canis familiaris	33.3	33.3	26.0	7.2	13.3	14.0	12.5	14.3	20.1
Canidae	–	–	–	1.3	–	4.3	–	–	–
Felis concolor/onca (puma/jaguar)	–	–	–	0.2	3.3	0.1	–	–	–
Tayassu (Dicotyles) tajacu	–	–	–	1.7	3.3	3.4	–	–	–
Tayassu sp.	–	–	–	0.6	3.3	0.6	6.3	14.3	3.2
Odocoileus virginianus	–	–	–	1.9	6.7	20.0	6.3	14.3	19.6
Mazama americana	33.3	33.3	74.0	0.2	3.3	0.3	–	–	–
Cervidae	–	–	–	1.7	3.3	12.0	–	–	–
Homo sapiens	–	–	–	0.4	3.3	–	6.3	14.3	–
Small to medium mammal	–	–	–	0.2	–	(<0.1)	–	–	–
Medium to large mammal	–	–	–	8.5	–	12.1	12.5	–	17.8
Unidentified mammal	–	–	–	53.3	–	13.8	18.8	–	17.8
UNIDENTIFIED FRAGMENTS	–	–	–	6.4	–	–	6.3	–	–
TOTAL	99.9	99.9	100.0	99.6	99.4	100.1	100.5	100.1	100.1

the Cerros population. An examination of the taxa identified reveals the variety of resources provided by the aquatic habitats near Cerros and suggests that the exploitation of these habitats was a vital aspect of the subsistence economy. It is difficult to pinpoint the source of many of the aquatic fauna because of the estuarine nature of this area. Many species tolerate a fairly wide range of salinities. Estuarine fish may move between the bay and river as the salinity levels fluctuate between the rainy and dry seasons; in addition, severe storms may push normally nonestuarine species from the reefs into the bay (Gibson, Belize Department of Forestry and Fisheries, personal communication, 1979). According to modern residents of the Cerros area, a number of fish can occur in everything from savanna to rivers and lagoons to Corozal Bay.

Despite these features of fish distribution, there are indications in the faunal collection that the inhabitants of Cerros regularly exploited a variety of fishing grounds. The majority of fish are euryhaline types that may have been procured from one or more sources within the estuarine system. Nevertheless, there is a substantial and regularly occurring component of reef fish, which seems to represent more than occasional catches of fish blown into the bay by hurricanes. Their presence implies fishing trips to the cays, although the importation of reef fish as part of a coastal trading system is also a possibility.

The species represented at Cerros include types today normally taken with nets (mojarras) or with hooks or spears (barracudas). The ranges in size and behavioral pattern of the fish represented suggest more than one procurement technique. Unfortunately, there are few indications in the material culture at Cerros of the techniques used in aquatic resource procurement. Although notched sherds (*mariposas*), interpreted as net or line weights, are common at the site, virtually all of them date to the relatively ephemeral Classic and Postclassic occupations (Garber 1981:205). No artifacts interpretable as hooks or harpoons have been recovered. Most fishing was probably accomplished through the use of traps and nets of perishable materials, with the probable additional use of some spears or hooks, which have not been recovered or simply have not been recognized. (For instance, unmodified stingray spines might have served as spear points.)

Although marine fauna predominate in Op. 1, terrestrial fauna also contribute significantly to the Cerros collection, particularly in terms of biomass (table 8.3). By far the most abundant are the domestic dog and the deer, mainly the white-tailed deer. Discounting the rats and mice, which are interpreted as natural intrusions into the deposit, and the human remains, canids and cervids constitute approximately 90 percent of the mammals identified beyond the class

level (table 8.4). This proportion is consistent whether the collection is viewed in terms of fragments, MNI, or biomass. Other species occur, but their numbers do not suggest a practice of regularly seeking them out. Rather, they may have been hunted or trapped in a casual manner, as when a paca hole was discovered while clearing land for a field. The procurement of reptiles and birds (and amphibians, if they are not intrusive) seems to have followed a similar pattern.

In sum, the faunal procurement activities of the Cerros Maya comprised four aspects. (1) *Marine faunal procurement* took place in more than one habitat and yielded a wide variety of species (although in the case of crabs one species is predominant). Fishing was probably one primary focus of the subsistence economy. (2) *Dog raising* provided a steady source of meat and could be relied upon when fishermen and hunters were "grounded" by agricultural work requirements or by the weather (such as the frequent winter *nortes*, which drastically change water levels and make transportation by water difficult or impossible). This role of dogs in estuarine economies in Mesoamerica has been pointed out by Wing (1978). Dog raising did not involve the time and labor inputs required by fishing and hunting and may have been handled by the women (Pohl and Feldman 1982:295). The faunal data suggest that the other domesticate, the turkey, was not raised at this time. (3) *Deer-hunting activities* provided a large amount of meat, and deer were probably common in forest and field-edge habitats. The raising of deer in households, while difficult to document, is also a possibility (Pohl and Feldman 1982:295). (4) *Hunting and trapping of other terrestrial animals* was probably an occasional activity that added variety to the diet but did not play a major economic role.

The total pattern of narrow-spectrum terrestrial hunting combined with fishing and agriculture fits the picture of "garden hunting" as described by Linares (1976) for coastal peoples of Panama, although different terrestrial species were stressed in each case.[3]

Social Aspects of Faunal Use

At the time of the conquest, and still today, animals have played a role in the social life of the Maya (Pohl and Feldman 1982:295-302). Landa (Tozzer 1941) records the use of animals for sacrifice in rituals, and differential access to meats by elites and commoners is also recorded (Pohl 1976:159). That these social

---

3. In addition to the faunal analysis, a study of botanical remains is currently being conducted by Cathy Crane of Southern Methodist University. When completed, this study will provide a better-rounded view of subsistence in the Late Preclassic period at Cerros.

Table 8.3. Relative contribution of marine fauna and mammals in Operation 1a-h.

	C'oh/Tulix transition			Early Tulix			Late Tulix		
	% fragment	% MNI	% biomass	% fragment	% MNI	% biomass	% fragment	% MNI	% biomass
Marine fauna	79.5	79.2	55.3	61.5	75.5	49.5	40.0	50.0	–
Mammal[a]	5.3	10.7	40.6	8.1	13.1	43.9	40.0	50.0	100.0

a. Not including small rodents or *H. sapiens*.

Table 8.4. Relative contribution of canids and cervids among identified mammals in Operation 1a-h.

	C'oh/Tulix transition			Early Tulix			Late Tulix[b]		
	% fragment	% MNI	% biomass	% fragment	% MNI	% biomass	% fragment	% MNI	% biomass
Canids	56.0	41.7	22.3	42.3	40.7	31.7	–	–	–
Cervids	36.0	41.7	70.3	49.3	44.4	66.2	–	–	–
Other identified mammals[a]	8.0	16.7	7.5	8.5	14.8	2.1	–	–	–

a. Not including small rodents or *H. sapiens*.

b. Late Tulix mammals could not be identified.

aspects of faunal procurement and use may be reflected in the archaeological record has been demonstrated repeatedly (Pohl 1976:158-185; Hamblin 1980:305-310).

The area of Op. 1 at Cerros has been interpreted as a nonelite residential locus. Nevertheless, there occur several burials, contexts that deserve special attention because of their ritual nature. The burials in Op. 1 were in simple pits dug into house yards. In such a case, the fauna found in the burial pit may be associated with the burial (e.g., offerings or remains of ritual meals), fortuitously included in the burial by being in the soil used to fill it, or intrusive. All these sources of fauna may be represented in the burials in Op. 1.

In general, the fauna of the seven burial contexts analyzed are comparable to the assemblage found in other contexts in Op. 1. Prominent in the burial assemblages are bony fish (twelve taxa), and crabs, chondrichthyes, turtles, one bird bone, and mammals also occur. Most of the fauna in the burials can be explained as fortuitous inclusions from the midden layers into which the pits were excavated.

Two burials, B1 and B16, are distinguished from other contexts in Op. 1 by the presence of a significant number of small rodent bones. These remains are likely to be natural intrusions into the deposit.

Two animals may be more directly associated with the burials. One is a kinosternid turtle in B16. The better part of the carapace and three plastron elements were recovered. In addition to several separate fragments, a number of bones were held together by cemented dirt, forming a chunk comprising nearly a quarter of the carapace, crushed by the weight of the soil. This is more complete than any turtle specimen found to date in midden contexts at Cerros. Some of the breaks that occur could be due to butchery rather than postdepositional factors. It is possible, however, that the shell was kept intact, perhaps for use as a rattle or drum. A perforated turtle carapace in a Late Preclassic burial at Seibal (Willey 1978:171) provides a parallel to this find.

The second noteworthy animal found in a burial at Cerros is the grey fox, *Urocyon cinereoargenteus*. Although some of the unidentified mammal bone fragments elsewhere in Op. 1 could belong to this species, the only element identifiable as *Urocyon* is a left frontal found in B3. A small round hole behind the orbit appears to have been drilled, as for suspension. To my knowledge, the only comparable item found elsewhere in the Maya area is a drilled partial tayra skull found at Seibal (Willey 1978:170).[4] The

two species are similar in terms of the size, form, and even surface texture of the cranial bones. The Seibal specimen was found in a temple context. This parallel at Seibal supports the notion of a magico-religious or even a lineage-related significance for the drilled fox skull at Cerros. There is no indication that the context here is elite.

A type of bone commonly associated with ritual contexts in the Maya area is the stringray spine, used at the time of conquest in ritual bloodletting (Tozzer 1941:191). Although rays are edible and may also have been collected for the purpose of ridding fishing grounds of a menace to wading fishermen, the presence of ray spines in archaeological contexts in the Maya area has traditionally been interpreted as an indication of ritual activity. This interpretation is generally justified by the context: ray spines are most frequently found in caches and burials, often in inland sites to which they must have been imported (Coe 1959:64-66; Willey 1972:239-241).

At Cerros, one ray spine (*Urolophus jamaicensis*) has been identified from Op. 1. It is in a midden context with no recognized ritual associations. Also from the nucleated village, another ray spine (identified only to order, Myliobatoidea) was recovered from Op. 30a, a salvage operation of a burial visible in the coastal erosion profile. Although the possibility of accidental incorporation of midden materials into the burial should be kept in mind, the presence of this spine in such a context suggests that the ritual significance of stingray spines attested to elsewhere was present in the Late Preclassic at Cerros.

In Classic Maya sites and Preclassic sites located inland (Coe 1959:66), stingray spines have been recovered from contexts that suggest an association with community- or wider-level ceremonialism (e.g., in stela caches). Comparable contexts at Cerros, such as dedicatory caches and termination rituals for public buildings, have not yielded any stingray spines. One reason could be taphonomic: the dry-laid rubble construction fill covering these ritual deposits did not serve to protect bones as well as the compact soil of the nucleated village (Garber 1981:139). Nevertheless, the possibility also exists that during the Late Preclassic at this coastal site, where fish of all sorts were commonplace, stingray spines were used in family-level rituals but not in community-level ones.

Shark teeth, another item found in ritual contexts in the Maya area (Borhegyi 1961:281), occur in a Postclassic cache associated with later reuse of one of the major mounds at Cerros. (Their poor preservation supports Garber's observation cited above.) In Preclassic contexts three shark teeth have been examined to date. One unmodified specimen and one drilled with two holes were recovered from domestic refuse in Op. 1, while the third, also drilled, is from a context described as domestic debris (Garber 1981:143) in Op. 34. Although the debris in Op. 34 is probably

---

4. I have since learned (Scudder, personal communication, 1983) of a drilled *Galictis* (grison) mandible found at Cuello, in Swasey Phase sub-floor fill. This find may be somewhat analogous to the drilled skull fragments of small carnivores found at Seibal and Cerros.

from an elite source and could in addition have ritual associations, there is no clear-cut association between shark teeth and ritual contexts in the Preclassic period at Cerros.

The relative value placed on aquatic and terrestrial resources by the Cerros Maya is germane to the interpretation of the features excavated in Op. 34, the westernmost of the major excavations into the nucleated village. The presence in this operation of the feature interpreted as a dock implies some functional differences from Op. 1. In addition, the excavation of Op. 41, extending 31 m inland from Op. 34, revealed a platform whose architecture and associated artifacts indicated that it had a public civic-ceremonial function.

The expectation that materials recovered from Op. 34 would be different from those in Op. 1 is borne out: a difference was revealed in ceramics, nonceramic artifacts, and faunal remains. Op. 34 has been interpreted as including both elite domestic and ceremonial areas (Robertson-Freidel 1980:267). A large number of broken jade beads fits the pattern of a termination ritual, which was normally performed on civic-ceremonial structures at Cerros (Garber 1981:130-132).

The fauna identified to date from Op. 34 are listed in table 8.2. A comparison of tables 8.1 and 8.2 illustrates the differences between the faunal assemblages of Ops. 1 and 34. Although the same species are represented in both areas, their relative contributions to the assemblages differ markedly. In Op. 34, mammals are dominant in terms of fragment counts and biomass and at least equal to the marine fauna in terms of MNI (table 8.5). Although dog and deer are the most common mammals (table 8.6), as they are in Op. 1, peccary assumes a more prominent role in Op. 34, being represented by several fragments in more than one level, as opposed to the single drilled canine identified in Op. 1a-h (Garber 1981:143).

In view of the smaller number of bones identified to date from Op. 34, in contrast to Op. 1, sampling problems might be posited as a source of the apparent discrepancy between the assemblages. A thorough inspection of the remaining lots shows that this is not the case, however.

I would argue that the fauna in Op. 34 constitute a largely elite or ceremonial assemblage derived from activities taking place in the civic and religious hub of the site. More than one activity involving fauna is represented. Several fragments of cervid long bones are artifacts or by-products of artifact manufacture (an activity attested in Op. 1 as well). The proportion of burned bones is not unlike that in Op. 1, and these bones are likely to represent food remains. Much of the unburned bone is thought to represent food remains as well, the meat having been boiled or cut off the bones prior to cooking.

Greater access to preferred meats by elite elements of the population has been documented at Classic period Maya sites (Pohl 1976:158-161). The intrasite distribution of mammal remains at Cerros may demonstrate the same custom for the Late Preclassic. Terrestrial fauna as a whole may have been particularly valued at this coastal site. A parallel situation is documented for the Postclassic period on Cozumel Island, where a greater percentage of terrestrial fauna occurs in assemblages from what are interpreted as elite or ceremonial contexts, although here this is thought to reflect different activities more than status distinctions per se (Hamblin 1980:216, 305-310).

A further item of note in Op. 34 is the presence of *Homo sapiens* remains outside a recognized burial context. Unlike the three human elements in the faunal collection of Op. 1, these are not teeth, which can be lost in life, or relatively small elements, which may easily become scattered if an old burial is disturbed by later digging. Rather, they are large shaft sections of major long bones (two femora, one humerus). Cut human long bones, sometimes elaborately carved, have been recovered from ritual contexts at contemporary and later Maya sites, for example, Chiapa de Corzo (Lee 1969:162-164) and Piedras Negras (Coe 1959:67). Although the human long bone shafts examined to date from Op. 34 are not worked in any way, they may be analogous to these finds.

Comparisons

The findings at Cerros can be compared with faunal analyses at other sites to determine to what extent Cerros mirrors a wider Preclassic Maya pattern of faunal use. The site of Cuello, south of Cerros in Orange Walk District, has aroused attention because of its 3,000 year Preclassic sequence preceding the Classic period levels (Hammond et al. 1979:92). In addition to an impressive archaeological stratigraphy, the site has yielded approximately 8,000 animal bone fragments identifiable at least to the class level (Scudder, personal communication, 1982).[5] Of these identified fragments, 966 are derived from Late Preclassic (Chicanel) contexts.

The Cuello assemblage is characterized by a high proportion of mammals (approximately 53 percent of the MNI calculated for the Late Preclassic). Although the collection as a whole contains more mammalian species than have been identified at Cerros, the Late Preclassic portion of the collection contains a comparable range of species. There are indications that the exploitation of species other than dog and deer was on

5. Although I have observed a portion of the Cuello collection, all details on the faunal assemblage are courtesy of Elizabeth S. Wing and Sylvia Scudder of the Florida State Museum. Their analysis of the fauna will be published as chapter 12 in *Excavations at the Cuello Site, Belize*, by Norman Hammond (Academic Press).

Table 8.5. Relative contribution of marine fauna and mammals in Operation 34a.

	Ixtabai			Early Tulix			Late Tulix		
	% fragment	% MNI	% biomass	% fragment	% MNI	% biomass	% fragment	% MNI	% biomass
Marine fauna	33.3	33.3	-	9.5	43.1	6.5	31.5	42.9	21.6
Mammal[a]	66.6	66.6	100.0	77.2	43.1	80.9	56.4	42.9	78.5

a. Not including small rodents or *H. sapiens*.

Table 8.6. Relative contribution of canids and cervids among identified mammals in Operation 34a.

	Ixtabai			Early Tulix			Late Tulix		
	% fragment	% MNI	% biomass	% fragment	% MNI	% biomass	% fragment	% MNI	% biomass
Canids	50.0	50.0	50.0	55.6	30.8	33.3	50.0	33.3	47.0
Cervids	50.0	50.0	50.0	25.0	30.8	58.7	25.0	33.3	45.6
Other identified mammals[a]	0.0	0.0	0.0	19.4	38.5	8.0	25.0	33.3	7.4

a. Not including small rodents or *H. sapiens*.

a more regular basis than is documented at Cerros: nearly one-third of the fragments, half the MNI, and 10 percent of the biomass of identified mammals (discounting man and the small rodents) are contributed by these other species. Nevertheless, cervids and canids still predominate among the mammals, with cervids forming a comparable proportion and canids a smaller proportion of the identified mammals in comparison to Cerros.

In addition to mammals, pond turtles form a significant component of the Cuello assemblage. Most of the same types occur at Cerros, but here, probably because of the variety provided by marine resources, they were not collected in large numbers.

An additional variation in Preclassic Lowland Maya faunal procurement and use may be seen at Dzibilchaltun (Wing and Steadman 1980) and the nearby site of Komchen (Carr 1981) in northern Yucatán.[6] Although located some 20 km from the coast, Dzibilchaltun yielded a large collection of marine molluscs (Andrews 1969). The marine exploitation pattern here is more specialized than that of coastal Cerros; marine animals other than molluscs are rare in the collection. The variety of terrestrial fauna identified is comparable to that at Cerros and Cuello, with the exception of the birds, which form a much larger proportion of the assemblage at Dzibilchaltun. In Preclassic contexts, however, the assemblage is largely mammalian, and dog and deer predominate.

The recently studied evidence discussed here lends further substantiation to Wing's (1981) findings concerning the importance of dog and deer in the economies of Maya Lowland sites in the Late Preclassic. This pattern crosscuts a variety of habitats, appearing even at Cerros, which is heavily marine oriented. Variations on this theme appear at each site, in accordance with its immediate environment.

Conclusions

The site of Cerros on Corozal Bay, northern Belize, was a trading center whose demise at the end of the Preclassic period was followed by minimal later construction, and thus it provides an opportunity for the study of Late Preclassic Maya culture. Preliminary results of faunal analysis suggest that the subsistence economy stressed fishing in a variety of habitats. Terrestrial hunting activities focused on the procurement of deer, which, together with domestic dogs, provided a significant contribution to the diet. Although marine fauna were often of ceremonial importance among the Maya, at this coastal site terrestrial fauna were favored for ceremonial use.

---

6. Since Komchen was treated as a part of Dzibilchaltun at the time of early excavations there (Andrews et al. 1981:20), the two are here considered as a unit.

References

Andrews, E. Wyllys IV
1969   *The Archaeological Use and Distribution of Mollusca in the Maya Lowlands.* Tulane University, Middle American Research Institute 34.

Andrews, E. Wyllys, V, William M. Ringle III, Philip J. Barnes, Alfredo Barrera Rubio, and Tomas Gallareta N.
1981   "Komchen: An Early Maya Community in Northwest Yucatan." Paper presented at the 1981 meeting of the Sociedad Mexicana de Antropología, San Cristobal, Chiapas.

Borhegyi, Stephan F. de
1961   "Shark Teeth, Stingray Spines, and Shark Fishing in Ancient Mexico and Central America," *Southwestern Journal of Anthropology* 17:273-296.

Carr, Helen Sorayya
1981   "Analysis of the Fauna from Komchen, Yucatan." Manuscript.

Cliff, Maynard B.
1982   "Lowland Maya Nucleation: A Case Study from Northern Belize." Ph.D. dissertation, Southern Methodist University.

Coe, William R.
1959   *Piedras Negras Archaeology: Artifacts, Caches, and Burials.* Museum monograph, the University Museum, University of Pennsylvania.

Freidel, David A., and Vernon Scarborough
1982   "Subsistence, Trade, and Development of the Coastal Maya." In *Maya Subsistence: Studies in Memory of Dennis E. Puleston,* edited by Kent V. Flannery, New York, Academic Press, 131-155.

Garber, James F.
1981   "Material Culture and Patterns of Artifact Consumption and Disposal at the Maya Site of Cerros in Northern Belize." Ph.D. dissertation, Southern Methodist University.

Hamblin, Nancy L.
1980   "Animal Utilization by the Cozumel Maya: Interpretation through Faunal Analysis." Ph.D. dissertation, University of Arizona.

Hammond, Norman, Duncan Pring, Richard Wilk, Sara Donaghey, Frank P. Saul, Elizabeth S. Wing, Arlene V. Miller, and Lawrence H. Feldman
1979   "The Earliest Lowland Maya? Definition of the Swasey Phase," *American Antiquity* 44:92-110.

Lee, Thomas A., Jr.
1969   *The Artifacts of Chiapa de Corzo, Chiapas, Mexico.* Papers of the New World Archaeological Foundation 26.

Linares, Olga F.
1976   " 'Garden Hunting' in the American Tropics," *Human Ecology* 4:331-349.

Olsen, Stanley J.
1978   "Vertebrate Faunal Remains." In *Excavations at Seibal: Artifacts*, edited by Gordon R. Willey, Peabody Museum Memoirs, vol. 14, no. 1, Harvard University, pp. 172-176.

Pohl, Mary E. D.
1976   "Ethnozoology of the Maya: An Analysis of Fauna from Five Sites in Petén, Guatemala." Ph.D. dissertation, Harvard University.

Pohl, Mary, and Lawrence H. Feldman
1982   "The Traditional Role of Women and Animals in Lowland Maya Economy." In *Maya Subsistence: Studies in Memory of Dennis E. Puleston*, edited by Kent V. Flannery, New York, Academic Press, pp. 295-311.

Robertson-Freidel, Robin A.
1980   "The Ceramics from Cerros: A Late Preclassic Site in Northern Belize." Ph.D. dissertation, Harvard University.

Scarborough, Vernon L.
1980   "The Settlement System in a Late Preclassic Maya Community: Cerros, Northern Belize." Ph.D. dissertation, Southern Methodist University.

Tozzer, Alfred M.
1941   *Landa's Relación de las cosas de Yucatán*. Peabody Museum Papers, vol. 18, Harvard University.

Willey, Gordon R.
1972   *The Artifacts of Altar de Sacrificios*. Peabody Museum Papers, vol. 64, no. 1, Harvard University.
1978   *Excavations at Seibal: Artifacts*. Peabody Museum Memoirs, vol. 14, no. 1, Harvard University.

Wing, Elizabeth S.
1978   "Use of Dogs for Food: An Adaptation to the Coastal Environment." In *Prehistoric Coastal Adaptations*, edited by Barbara L. Stark and Barbara Voorhies, New York, Academic Press, pp. 29-42.
1981   "A Comparison of Olmec and Maya Foodways." In *The Olmec and Their Neighbors: Essays in Memory of Matthew W. Stirling*, edited by Elizabeth P. Benson, Dumbarton Oaks, Washington, D.C., pp. 20-28.

Wing, Elizabeth S., and David Steadman
1980   "Vertebrate Faunal Remains from Dzibilchaltun." In *Excavations at Dzibilchaltun, Yucatan, Mexico*, by E. Wyllys Andrews IV and E. Wyllys Andrews V. Tulane University, Middle American Research Institute 48, pp. 326-331.

Chapter 9

The Privileges of Maya Elites: Prehistoric Vertebrate Fauna from Seibal

Mary Pohl

At the height of Maya civilization, during the Late Classic period, elites enjoyed unprecedented privilege. Ruling families may have imposed a royal cult, which conferred on them the status of divinity (Adams 1977) and constructed pyramids for the worship of dead rulers. Analysis of human skeletons and grave goods found in burials indicates that social mobility was restricted (Rathje 1971; Haviland 1967, 1977). While alive, these elites differentiated themselves from those of lesser rank by their patterns of consumption. Privileged access to many goods such as maize and cotton textiles cannot be traced archaeologically because of the lack of preservation. Nevertheless, ethnohistoric data indicate that one traditional social marker was the right to exploit animals for food, costume, and ritual sacrifices. The study of faunal remains from archaeological sites can, therefore, reveal a great deal about status.

In this chapter, bones from different contexts at Seibal are examined for evidence of social differences in animal exploitation and consumption. Elite activities are reconstructed with the aid of ancient art and ethnohistoric records in addition to the faunal remains. These data provide hypotheses to be tested at other sites.

The Site of Seibal

During the Late Classic Tepejilote and especially Bayal phases, Seibal became a flourishing ceremonial center, perhaps because of its location on the Pasión River. In the Bayal phase, differences in material culture and skeletal traits have suggested to some researchers that new elites, perhaps from the Puuc region of western Yucatán, ascended the river and installed themselves as the rulers of Seibal (Sabloff and Willey 1967; Ball 1974, 1977; Chase and Chase 1982; Saul 1975). Whether these elites were foreigners, their archaeological remains display Mexican traits (Graham 1973; Ball 1974).

The heart of Seibal is the ceremonial center covering 1 km². Groups A, C, and D occupy separate hilltops

connected by a system of artifical causeways. This area was the elite precinct probably combining both political and religious elements of Maya culture (see Bricker 1979).

At Seibal, smaller structures are densely distributed for at least 1 km along the river on either side of the central zone as well as inland, an area designated as the peripheral zone (Willey 1975:3; Tourtellot 1970). Within the peripheral area, a distinction was made between plain and fancy buildings. Peripheral plain structures are unprepossessing dwellings, and peripheral fancy buildings are elaborate, often range-type structures (Tourtellot, personal communication, 1978). One peripheral fancy building adjacent to Group D contained what appeared to be an altar.

The Seibal Fauna

At Seibal, refuse was not used for structure fill to the extent that it was at sites like Tikal; Seibal residents let their garbage accumulate. Middens lay in sheets around structures (Tourtellot 1970), and much of the evidence for animal exploitation comes from in situ deposit.

Late Classic period excavation lots generally contained pottery of both Tepejilote and Bayal phases, and since bones must be dated by associated artifacts, a distinction between these two occupational episodes could not be made. Thus, the Late Classic period is treated as a single unit here. This analysis contains limitations in chronological depth, but horizontal distinctions in archaeological contexts noted above provide a unique view of the privileges of Maya elites.

Fauna from late Classic period deposits at Seibal are presented in table 9.1. The totals for both the number of individual fragments and the minimum numbers of individuals (calculated by the minimum distinction method) are given. Bone weights were not measured because different conditions of preservation at Lowland Maya sites have produced marked variability in this trait.

In tabulating the fragments, certain modifications were made. Those bones that articulated and were obviously part of a single animal were counted as one

See chapter 1 for Mary Pohl's affiliation.

Table 9.1. Fauna from Seibal.

	High status		Low status	
	Cache	Elite ceremonial center	Peripheral fancy	Peripheral plain
MAMMALS				
Didelphis (opossum)		4/2[a]	1/1	2/1
Philander opossum (four-eyed opossum)				2/2
Alouatta villosa (howler monkey)		1/1		
Ateles geoffroyi (spider monkey)				1/1
Dasypus novemcinctus (armadillo)				1/1
Sylvilagus cf. *floridanus* (cottontail rabbit)		3/1		
Heterogeomys hispidis (pocket gopher)		1/1		
Cuniculus paca (paca)		6/2		2/1
Dasyprocta punctata (agouti)		3/1		1/1
Canis familiaris (domestic dog)		8/2		3/2
Urocyon cinereoargenteus (gray fox)		2/2		
Felidae (puma or jaguar)		2/1		
Felis cf. *onca* (jaguar)		1/1	1/1	
Felis cf. *pardalis* (ocelot)		2/2		
Felis cf. *concolor* (puma)		1/1		
Tapirus bairdii (tapir)				1/1
Tayassidae (peccaries)		6/2		2/1
cf. *Dicotyles (Tayassu) tajacu* (collared peccary)		2/1	1/1	
cf. *Tayassu pecari* (white-lipped peccary)		4/1		4/3

a. The figure on the left represents fragments, and the figure on the right is minimum number of individuals.

Table 9.1 (continued).

	High status		Low status	
	Cache	Elite ceremonial center	Peripheral fancy	Peripheral plain
Cervidae (deer)		3/1		1/1
Odocoileus virginianus (white-tailed deer)		181/18	13/2	95/6
Mazama (brocket deer)		2/1		
BIRDS				
Anhinga anhinga (anhinga)				1/1
Large raptorial bird cf. *Spitzaetus ornatus* (hawk eagle)		1/1		
Meleagris ocellata (ocellated turkey)		4/2		3/1
cf. *Amazona* (parrot)		1/1		
REPTILES				
Turtle		3/2		
Dermatemys mawii (hicotea blanca)		89/4	18/2	28/2
Staurotypus (musk turtle)				18/2
Chrysemys scripta[b] (pond turtle)		8/1	16/2	27/5
Kinosternon (mud turtle)				2/1
Crocodylus (crocodile)		1/1		2/1
Crotalus (rattlesnake)	1/1			
FISH				
Cichlidae cf. *Petenia splendida*		1/1		
Siluriformes (catfish)		1/1		
AMPHIBIANS				
Bufo marinus (marine toad)	1 (partial skeleton)			
TOTAL	2	341/55	50/9	196/34

b. *Chrysemys* is now *Pseudemys*.

fragment. The splintered condition of mandibles, notably of deer, suggested that these bones were cracked open to obtain marrow. Loose teeth, particularly numerous in the kitchen debris of Structure D-26, were judged to be sources of sample inflation and were not counted. An exception was made in the case of canines. Ethnohistoric descriptions, together with the presence of drilled roots and paste on prehistoric canines, indicate that animals were hunted specifically to obtain these teeth for personal adornment.

Antler fragments may not be representative of the animals actually hunted. Maya artisans may have brought shed antler found in the forest back to the site for use in craft production. Only those antler fragments that were clearly cut from the skull were included in the fragment frequency tabulations.

Turtle shell is very distinctive, and an identification can be made from tiny pieces of carapace or plastron. In contrast, the bones of the other animals represented in the faunal assemblage can be identified only when a reasonable amount of the element is preserved. In order to make counts as comparable as possible, only those fragments of turtle shell large enough to be identified to element were tabulated.

The differences in frequency representation discussed above do not affect the minimum number of individuals (MNI) method, which is based on the most commonly occurring element of any given species. The minimum numbers approach has other limitations, however. In large and small samples, the correspondence between the real number of individual species and their archaeological frequencies may be close (Hesse and Perkins 1974; Wing, personal communication, 1979). In moderate sized samples, such as that available for Seibal, infrequently represented species may assume greater importance than they should when calculated according to minimum numbers.

Zooarchaeologists do not have perfect means of deriving relative frequencies of animals. In this chapter conclusions are drawn from a judicious examination of the results obtained by both the minimum numbers and fragment methods.

At many Maya sites, sample size has been a problem. Preservation is poor, excavation has been directed toward the delineation of structures rather than the investigation of middens, and rigorous recovery techniques have not been employed. The Seibal faunal sample of 589 bones is respectable. Nevertheless, the assemblage must be regarded as representing the larger species because deposits were not screened.

The low frequency of fish remains is a particularly perplexing question, since the site of Seibal is located in the Pasión River. Fish bones tend to be small and fragile and are often missed. Nonetheless, in Group G

at Tikal, where Terminal Late Classic midden was sealed in rooms providing protection from scavenging dogs and the weather, I water-sieved samples of deposit through window screen and recovered only one tiny catfish spine. Theoretically, fish would have been available in *aguadas* at the site or perhaps in canals in the adjacent Bajo de Santa Fe (Adams, personal communication, 1980) even though these facilities may have been in a delapidated state by Terminal Late Classic times when the site was in decline. Further research must be done on the problem of Maya utilization of aquatic resources.

Zooarchaeologists must be wary of biases that may have resulted from the activities of the ancient Maya. In this century, Maya have traditionally gathered up bones and offered them to the gods. A. W. Anthony, who collected zoological specimens for the American Museum in the 1920s, noted wistfully:

> In many parts of Guatemala one finds little shelters, built of sticks and thatched with grass, where the natives build their altar fires to make sure of good crops. These houses of worship are in or near cornfields, and on the altar, slightly raised above the platform, where fires have been built for generations, one finds an excellent index to the larger mammals of the section. Skulls, so black with smoke that they might have been painted, are side by side with those taken but yesterday. It seems a shame to leave so many good specimens, but it would not have been safe to molest them.
>
> (Quoted in Goodwin 1934:2)

Anthony's observation demonstrates how bones get separated and are destroyed or incorporated into the earth in different ways. The representation of elements in the prehistoric faunal assemblage may be similarly skewed.

Seibal Procurement Patterns

One of the most significant problems in the interpretation of the fauna at Seibal lies in the reconstruction of the past ecology of the ceremonial center. No palynological data are available for southern Petén. Molluscs recovered in Seibal excavations are little help. For example, *Orthalicus princeps* (Feldman 1978:167) is characteristic of forested regions, but it has a high tolerance for disturbed conditions (Thompson, personal communication, 1980).

Some evidence for habitation around Seibal has been reported but not in the detail we need. In the western reaches of the Seibal upland, occupation appears to extend at least 4 km from the main ceremonial center, reaching the lesser ceremonial center of Anonal (Willey 1975:3-5). Settlement surveys have not been conducted to the east and north of the site.

The swampy margin of the Pasión River may have been transformed by ditched fields. Siemens has observed such fields in *bajo* areas adjacent to the river through aerial reconnaissance and photography (personal communication, 1976). On the basis of patterns recorded by side-looking airborne radar backed up by ground checks in the vicinity of Seibal, Adams (1980) has recently proposed that much of southern Petén was altered for agricultural use. An estimated 404 km² of swampy terrain around Seibal are thought to have been cut by canals, and radar indicates that such patterns may extend over 60 km from Tres Islas to Altar de Sacrificios. These constructions may have been associated with at least 12 other centers that are known to exist in the area (Adams, personal communication, 1980). As yet no chronology has been established for the proposed wetland agriculture in southern Petén, and Siemens (personal communication, 1980) warns that we must be cautious in accepting all of Adams's findings until further ground investigation is done.

Pollen from lake sediments in northern Belize and central Petén, where evidence for ditched fields and terraces is emerging, suggest that few trees were left standing by the end of the Classic period (Vaughan 1979; Wiseman Chap. 5; Hansen, in press). Food and shelter for game may have been scarce in southern Petén as well, though we have no specific evidence that this was the case.

The Late Classic Seibal fauna contains species from different biotopes. A number of high forest animals can be found (table 9.1). These consist of tapir (*Tapirus bairdii*), spider monkey (*Ateles*), howler monkey (*Alouatta*), brocket deer (*Mazama*), paca (*Cuniculus paca*), agouti (*Dasyprocta punctata*), and what are probably white-tipped peccary (cf. *Tayassu pecari*), jaguar (*Felis* cf. *onca*), and hawk eagle (cf. *Spitzaetus ornatus*). Other species, such as ocellated turkey (*Meleagris ocellata*), collared peccary (*Dicotyles tajacu*), ocelot (*Felis* cf. *pardalis*), puma (*Felis* cf. *concolor*), and white-tailed deer (*Odocoileus virginianus*), would have been procured in forested areas subject to varying degrees of disturbance.

Elite and ceremonial contexts at Seibal had 12 of the forest species listed above, comprising 65 percent of the total MNI. Peripheral plain refuse contained 7 species or 47 percent of the MNI. The evidence suggests that high status Maya tended to eat more game obtained on hunting trips to forested areas, perhaps located at a distance from the site of Seibal.

Relative percentages of turtles indicated the orientation of low status inhabitants toward animals that could be procured close to the site. Both the fragments and minimum numbers methods of frequency representation suggest that turtles were more common in the peripheral zone. Calculated according to MNI, turtles comprise only 13 percent of the elite

ceremonial center fauna. These reptiles amount to 33 percent of the peripheral bones. All the species of turtle recovered would have been available directly from the Pasión River, which flows in front of Seibal or from land around the site.

The turtles provide evidence for distinctions in species utilization. Turtles were not only more abundant in the peripheral zone, they were also more diverse. Only low status, peripheral plain residents ate the musk turtle (*Staurotypus*) and mud turtle (*Kinosternon*). The upper class displayed a preference for *Dermatemys*.

Of all meats, the ancient Maya loved venison best, and wealthy individuals got their share. Elite refuse contained a minimum of 33 percent of individuals of white-tailed deer, while peripheral dwellings yielded only 19 percent of this species. The association between venison and class was widespread in Precolumbian Mesoamerica. In Oaxaca, at the time of Spanish contact, status determined the amount of deer meat a household received (Spores 1965:969).

Maya demand for venison may have put stress on populations of white-tailed deer. The Maya were also exploiting the natural predators of deer, the felines, and removal of predators would have caused deer populations to increase, but this factor may have been offset by other activities of the Maya. One Late Classic period polychrome plate (fig. 9.1) depicts several hunters disguised in deerskins, luring does by

Figure 9.1. Late Classic period polychrome from Yucatán depicting hunters luring does with whistles. Drawing of plate in the Museo Nacional, Mexico City, by Janet Walters.

imitating the sound of stags or fawns (see Inkeles 1956). This hunting method removes females from the breeding population. Another plate painted in Late Classic style shows a hunter with deer headdress and blowgun, surrounded by a pack of dogs. Dogs pursue deer relentlessly, even in thick second growth, and those animals that are not killed usually move away. Even dogs cannot effectively chase deer in swampland, however. The destruction of protective vegetation for the construction of wetland fields would therefore have been very detrimental to deer populations.

When deer experience hunting pressure, the age structure of the population may display a bias toward young individuals because fewer and fewer animals survive into old age. Hunting pressure might be gauged by the proportion of juveniles to adults in the faunal sample (table 9.2). At Seibal the number of *Odocoileus* bones exhibiting signs of immaturity was low. This fact, together with the relative abundance of deer in the faunal sample as a whole, suggests that animals were available.

One explanation for the characteristics of deer bones at Seibal might be that the ancient Maya imposed restrictions on deer hunting as well as on the consumption of venison. Ethnohistoric evidence might be found in the story of Cortés's journey across Petén in 1525. According to Cortés's own account (MacNutt 1908:275), the Spaniards found many deer in a savanna south of Lake Petén. The deer were very tame, and the Spanish soldiers were able to kill a number of the animals. When the soldiers inquired about the strange behavior of the deer, their guides answered that "in those villages the deer were treated like gods because their main god had appeared to them in that form." Their god had ordered them not to molest the deer (López de Cogolludo, Book 1, chap. 15, quoted in Tozzer and Allen 1910:349, Díaz del Castillo, quoted in Thompson 1977:12). Most likely the deer did not flee the hunters because the animals were not accustomed to being pursued regularly.

Table 9.2. Late Classic period Seibal: fused/unfused elements of white-tailed deer (*Odocoileus virginianus*).

Element	Seibal elite zone	Seibal peripheral zone
Fused	69	49
Unfused	18	12
Percentage of adults	79	80

Source: Pohl 1976.

The institution of the deer cult is recounted in the Popol Vuh, the sacred book embodying the ancient traditions of the Quiche Maya:

And keep the Deerskin with care.
   They are the things to hide one's face
And to deceive
   And that will be the Deerskin
And also that will be our substitute from now on
   Before the Tribes.
When you are asked,
   Where is Storm?
That is when to point out the deerskin to them.
                                  (Edmonson 1971:186-187)

The Maya were directed to conduct hunts and to perform blood sacrifices on specific ceremonial occasions:

...give us
Those who are the children of grass,
   The children of weeds,
And in fact the young of deer,
   The young of birds.
Come then and give us a little of their blood.
   Have pity on our face.

And then began the hunting
Of the young birds,
   The young deer,
Trapped
   And hunted
By the sacrificers
   The worshippers.
So that was when they found birds
   And young deer.
Then they could go
   And anoint
The deer's blood
   And the birds' on the mouth of the idol
Of Storm
   And Lord Jaguar.
And it would be drunk;
   The blood would be drunk by the gods.
And at once the stone would speak.
                                  (Edmonson 1971:186-187)

In the early historic era, the Spaniards in Yucatán made numerous references to the fact that meat was eaten only at fiestas. In response to the royal questionnaire sent out in 1577, priests in Isamal, Santa Marta, Tecauto, Tepacan, Cuçal, and Chalaute (Relaciones de Yucatán 1898-1900; I:224, 271; II:122) reported that the consumption of flesh was a ritual affair. The seventeenth-century historian López de Cogolludo (1971, I:228, 235, 296) made the same observation.

In order to ensure that deer and other game were available for ritual sacrifices, the Maya may have maintained refuges or game parks for the animals. Cortés's account hints that the central Petén savanna might have been the location of such a refuge at the time of conquest, and the practice may have originated in Classic times. Settlement in savanna most accessible to Seibal dates to the Late Preclassic period (D. Rice, personal communication, 1980); the area does not appear to have been used for habitation during the Late Classic period.

The presence of two animals at Seibal, rattlesnake (*Crotalus*) and ocellated turkey (*Meleagris ocellata*), might suggest that at least some hunting was conducted to the north of the site, perhaps in central Petén savanna. Neither of these animals occurs in southern Petén now (Duellman 1963; Lee, personal communication, 1978), though both can be found in central Petén savanna (Stuart and Steadman, personal communications, 1977, 1978). Paynter (personal communication, 1975) thinks that southern Petén is too wet for the turkey, and the rattlesnake in particular likes dry areas.

It might be argued that past environment differed and that turkey and rattlesnake did occur in southern Petén during the Late Classic period. Deforestation would have increased evapotranspiration resulting in drier conditions. As noted above, we have no specific palynological data on the forests of southern Petén yet.

Sixteenth-century records indicate that the Maya, like many native New World cultures (Bourke 1892), conducted animal round-ups (Relaciones de Yucatán 1898, I:301). Landa wrote: "They also joined together for hunting in companies of fifty, more or less, and they roast the flesh of the deer on gridirons, so that it shall not be wasted, and when they reach the town, they make their presents to their lord and distribute the rest as among friends." (Tozzer 1941:57)

The Late Classic period Actun Balam vase (fig. 9.2), depicting several hunters pursuing deer with spear throwers, may show a prehistoric round-up in the Maya Lowlands. Some aspects of the scene suggest that this is a mythical hunt. A female deity rides a rearing stag, and two of the hunters are associated with glyphs that might be interpreted as referring to water and the rain god (Pendergast 1971:50). This painting may be an allegorical depiction of ceremonial drives that were actually enacted by the Maya, perhaps as part of an agricultural ritual.

Other evidence points to the use of nets as well as spear throwers in hunts. Nets are shown associated with white-tailed deer on Classic-style pottery, and the Popol Vuh mentions nets in connection with ceremonial hunting (see Edmonson 1971: note 6203).

The illustration of the Maya group hunt is remarkably like those pictured on prehistoric Moche pottery from coastal Peru (Donnan 1978), where deer are shown pursued with nets and spear throwers, as well as with dogs. Inca nobility were still conducting massive drives when the Spaniards arrived in the Peruvian Highlands. Thousands of drivers would surround areas sometimes more than 30 km in diameter. As many as 10,000–15,000 animals might be captured. Deer, birds, and small game were taken for food; camelids were shorn of wool and released, killed for meat, or led away for use as pack animals. These round-ups were held approximately every four years. The care taken with guanacos is noteworthy. Females were clipped and set free to breed. The largest and handsomest males were released as sires. Individuals that were getting old or were too "smart" were culled. Predators such as puma, bear, and fox were also eliminated. Although the guanacos were technically wild, they were managed in much the same way as domestic flocks (Browman 1974:194, personal communication, 1979). Perhaps the strange tameness of the Maya deer encountered by Cortés was due in part to selection of the kind practiced by the Inca.

Figure 9.2. Late Classic period vase from Actun Balam illustrating a deer hunt. Reproduced by permission from David M. Pendergast, The Prehistory of Actun Balam, British Honduras. *Royal Ontario Museum Art and Archaeology Occasional Papers 16, 1969.*

The behavior of the Maya deer might also be attributed to the fact that some individuals had been coddled when young. In sixteenth-century Yucatán, Bishop Landa (Tozzer 1941:127) reported that women "let the deer suck their breasts, by which means they raise them and make them so tame that they never go into the woods, although they take them and carry them through the woods and raise them there." The Motul dictionary (1929) defines *ah may* as *venadillo pequeño criado en casa* (a little deer raised in a house). Deer raising may have a long history among the Maya. At Seibal a peripheral zone building (D-36) adjacent to D Group was connected to a walled structure that resembled a pen (Tourtellot, personal communication, 1975), and two fragments of antler tine were associated with the refuse. Unfortunately, no definitive evidence that this structure might actually have been used for raising deer is at hand.

The ancient Maya may have used tame deer in their ceremonies, possibly conducted at the temples as in Moche Peru (Donnan, personal communication, 1981). García de Palacio described the following scene, which may have taken place in the southern Maya zone in the sixteenth century:

> They took a live deer to the courtyard of the *cu* or temple which they had outside the town and there they throttled and skinned him, collecting all his blood in a vessel and cutting the liver, lungs and stomach into small pieces. They divided the heart, head and legs. They cooked the deer by itself and the blood, by itself, and while these were cooking, they had their dances . . . When the dance was finished, the head and feet were scorched in the fire before the idol as an offering and afterwards taken to the house of the high priest and eaten.
>
> (Tozzer and Allen 1910:349)

The Calcehtok polychrome vessel (Morley 1946) from Yucatán may depict a Late Classic period ceremony (Pohl 1981) in which celebrants first decorated a stag with a cloth mantle and removed its antlers, probably subsequently sacrificing the animal. Cuello may provide evidence that tamed or managed animals were used in rituals as early as the Preclassic period. Two caches of deer mandibles (fig. 9.3) were deposited when the surface of a Late Preclassic period platform was renewed (Hammond, personal communication, 1980). Mandibles in the cache analyzed so far (Wing, personal communication, 1980) consist primarily of juveniles: of a total of 30 MNI, 20 were immature. The young age of the Cuello deer might indicate that certain individuals had been culled from a breeding stock, perhaps constituting the "young of deer" that the gods demanded in the Popol Vuh.

Patterns of Distribution and Consumption

The distribution of bones at Seibal may reflect ancient patterns of food consumption and ritual, but interpretation of the data is difficult. Patterns may be confounded by the selective removal of bones in ancient times, and one must judge whether a particular configuration of elements can be taken for what it appears to be.

The distribution of elements of white-tailed deer is illustrated in fig. 9.4. Bones of the forelimb (humerus, radius, ulna) were concentrated in elite contexts. Peripheral midden produced somewhat higher percentages of vertebrae. Since the trunk yields more meat

Figure 9.3. One of two caches of deer mandibles located approximately on the east-west axis of Late Preclassic period platform 34 at Cuello. Drawing courtesy of Norman Hammond.

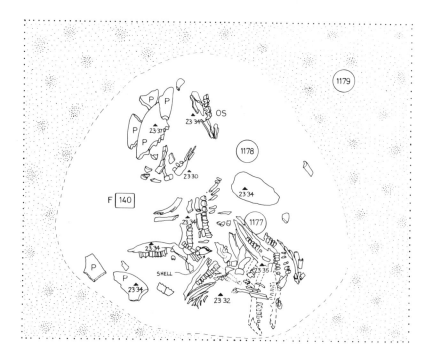

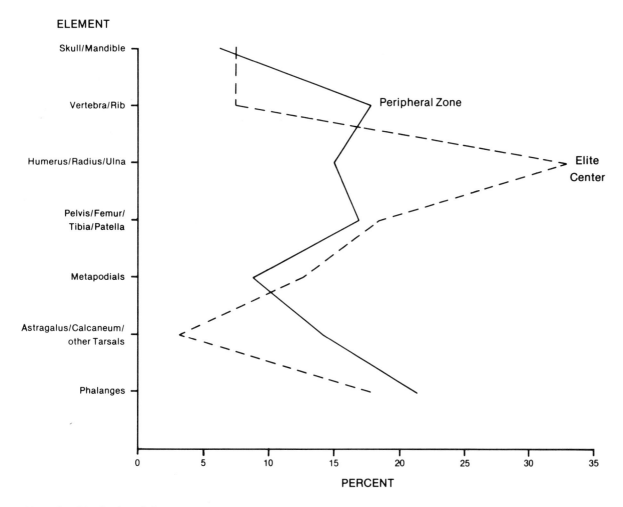

ELEMENT

PERCENT

Figure 9.4. Distribution of elements of white-tailed deer (Odocoileus virginianus) *according to context at Seibal. Total elements for elite contexts 158; peripheral zone 113.*

than the front leg, the suggestion that low status families got better cuts of meat is contrary to what one would expect.

The answer may lie in the relatively low numbers of bones of the hind leg (femur, tibia, patella, metapodial, astragalus, calcaneum, and other tarsals). The haunch is the hunter's prize. The Dresden and Madrid Codices, Postclassic ritual books that preserve traditions rooted in the Classic period, frequently depict bound haunches offered in sacrifices (Tozzer and Allen 1910, plate 31). Landa reports that in New Year's rites, "They divided these offerings among the strangers who were present and they gave the priest the leg of a deer." (Tozzer 1941:141) The haunch may be missing from elite refuse at Seibal because it was used in religious ceremonies.

The larger bones of the back leg would also have served as raw material for implements of various

kinds. The higher percentages of tarsals in the peripheral zone may indicate that the limbs were disassembled for tool production there.

Although in early historic times most Maya reportedly ate meat only at fiestas, elites were often served stews containing meat or fish for their daily meals (Roys 1943:44). The distribution of animal bones at Seibal suggests that class differences in meat consumption were maintained in prehistoric times. Bone was heavily concentrated in D-Group in the area of Court A and its associated buildings: D-26, D-27, D-28, D-29. A total of 265 identifiable fragments was recovered from this complex. Only 246 identifiable pieces of bone were retrieved from the entire peripheral zone excavation. Similar observations have been made at other sites. At Altun Ha (Pendergast 1979:66), for example, a single palace structure yielded the majority of bone refuse. Elite structures at Postclassic Mayapan produced 4,600 bones, and only 119 bones came from lower status buildings.

The differences at Seibal are magnified when the amount of meat represented by the bones is taken into consideration. The average white-tailed deer (*Odocoileus virginianus*) shot today at San Antonio

Río Hondo, northern Belize, weighs about 40 kg, of which about 65.5 percent or 26.2 kg is edible meat (see Wing and Brown 1979:132). On the other hand, a pond turtle (*Chrysemys scripta*) might produce only about 0.68 kg of flesh (Parmalee, personal communication, 1975). As a rough approximation, the minimum numbers of deer and turtles in elite contexts at Seibal represent about 478 kg of meat compared to about 166 kg from peripheral plain dwellings. Thus, high status individuals appear to have eaten substantially more meat, and they probably had better all-around diets.

I have already suggested that the white-tailed deer held a special place in Maya religion (Pohl 1981). A pattern is discernible in the side of the deer bones represented in Seibal refuse. Elite areas yielded 32 bones from the right side of the white-tailed deer and 100 from the left. In the peripheral zone, 28 bones came from the right side and 36 from the left. Left elements were concentrated in the elite zone. According to the Fisher exact test, the probability of such an association is very small ($p = 0.002$). This finding recalls Savage's (Pendergast 1971:82) demonstration that bones of the left wings of birds occurred in greater numbers at Eduardo Quiroz Cave than one would expect by chance. Also in the Late Classic period, a left deer haunch was buried beside a building in Copan, and a left human leg was laid over a prepared area of sascab beneath the floor of a monumental building at Chicanna (Eaton, personal communication, 1981).

The predominance of left elements, particularly front limb bones, in elite contexts at Seibal might reflect codes of meat distribution. White (1956:401) found a discrepancy in the side of limb bones from earth lodge villages of the Missouri Valley, and he sought an explanation in the fact that a couple customarily presented their parents or grandparents with the left front limb of a carcass.

The Seibal phenomenon may represent the observance of directional symbolism that apparently pervaded ancient Maya life. For example, in vase paintings the central character in any scene nearly always faces left, and the heads of people and animals that make up glyphs generally point the same way. In traditional Maya thought, left is closely associated with the underworld, the place where the sun sets.

Directional observance was common throughout aboriginal Mesoamerica. Most of our data on Precolumbian ritual come from early historic descriptions of central Mexico. At the Aztec feast to the sun god, Nauholin, the ceremony ended with participants piercing their left arms with blades, passing reeds through the holes, and casting the bloody offerings in front of the image of the sun (Durán 1971:191). At the Great Feast of Lords, captains tied deer hooves on their left legs with buckskin thongs (Sahagún 1951:94,

145). These rites were performed long after Seibal was abandoned, but the existence of this tradition in central Mexico is noteworthy because Terminal Late Classic Maya culture at Seibal was "Mexicanized."

Archaeological and ethnographic evidence indicates that related beliefs occurred in many areas of the New World. The left bones of a woman and a paca had been manipulated in a prehistoric burial in Panama (Cooke, personal communication, 1978). A preponderance of left wing elements of ducks was found in the excavation of a Middle Mississippian temple mound in northwest Mississippi (Gilbert, personal communication, 1979).

The Maya may have focused on left deer elements for their rituals at Seibal. Alternatively, they may have emphasized the right side. Today right is the dominant direction in conservative Highland Maya communities (Bricker, personal communication, 1977), and a modern Peruvian shaman uses the right leg of a deer in his rites (Donnan 1978:134). In the course of ancient Maya ceremonies, the right deer elements may have been removed, and the left bones found in midden might only be those that were discarded. Although the bones demonstrate that directional symbolism ruled at Seibal, the details of these prehistoric religious activities remain hazy.

In addition to the deer, the Maya revered felines, and the jaguar was a powerful supernatural being in the Maya pantheon. Late Classic period art demonstrates that these animals were ritually sacrificed. Pelts, teeth, and claws were essential for elite paraphernalia like throne cushions, sacred bundles, clothing, and other items of personal adornment. In the Lineage of the Lords of Totonicapan, "All these titles/And ranks/Had their insignia/And these were claws/Of jaguars,/Panthers." (Edmonson 1971:7708)

Cats were probably rare in Petén during the Late Classic period. The Maya were exploiting both the carnivores and their prey. Research on predator-prey relationships (Wilson and Bossert 1971) demonstrates that when hunters kill both predator and prey, the predator suffers a relative decline in numbers.

At Seibal, cat bones were scarce in the faunal sample, but they did occur in elite contexts. Six bones were recovered from two cuts around Structure D-26. The other structure that yielded cat remains was D-66, a peripheral building associated with D Group. A jaguar sacrum and three articulating vertebrae were found along the wall of what the excavators thought was an altar. The cat bones suggest that elites exercised tight control over precious resources.

Elites may have successfully monopolized the raw materials for status paraphernalia, but demand may not always have been satisfied. In a number of Late Classic period drawings, characters wear textiles that are decorated with spots resembling jaguar skin.

Similarly, in central Mexico, Sahagún (1951:82) noticed that lesser Aztec priests carried paper bags painted to look like ocelot skin. Although Mesoamerican elites appear very grand to us in their paintings, they may have had some difficulty keeping up appearances in real life.

Summary

Faunal remains, together with ancient paintings and ethnohistorical data, have been used to reconstruct patterns of animal exploitation at Seibal during the Late Classic period. The evidence suggests that elites ate more meat than those of lesser status. High status areas yielded higher percentages of white-tailed deer, an animal the Maya relished and frequently used as ceremonial offerings in agricultural rituals. Elites may have reserved felines for themselves for use as status paraphernalia. Demand for game must have been high while Maya agricultural and architectural projects were destroying animal habitats, and scarcities may have been felt. To ensure that enough game was available, elites might have maintained refuges, most likely in nearby savannas. Here game may have been managed and periodically rounded up by groups of men with nets and spear throwers. Maya women might also have reared deer in their houses, perhaps for elaborate fertility ceremonies.

This reconstruction is offered as a hypothesis. Analysis of fauna from other Maya sites will provide perspective on ancient hunting and ritual practices. Archaeologists will have to probe midden deposits and apply rigorous recovery procedures to obtain the necessary data. One of the greatest problems remains that of determining what information might be missing or skewed due to the activities of the ancient Maya themselves.

References

Adams, R. E. W.
1977   *Prehistoric Mesoamerica*. Little, Brown, Boston.
1980   "Ancient Land Use and Culture History in the Pasión River Region." Paper presented at Burg Wartenstein.

Anders, F.
1963   *Das Pantheon der Maya*. Akademische Druck-u Verlagsanstalt, Graz.

Ball, J. W.
1974   "A Coordinate Approach to Northern Maya Prehistory: A.D. 700–1200," *American Antiquity* 39:85–93.
1977   "A Hypothetical Outline of Coastal Maya Prehistory, 300 B.C.–A.D. 1200." In *Social Process in Maya Prehistory*, edited by N. Hammond. Academic Press, London, pp. 167–196.

Bourke, J. G.
1892   "Sacred Hunts of the American Indian," *Proceedings of the 8th International Congress of Americanists*. Paris, 1890, pp. 357–368.

Bricker, V. R.
1979   "Symbolic Representations of Protohistoric Social Stratification and Religious Organization in a Modern Maya Community." In *Codex Wauchope: Human Mosaic* 12:39–56.

Browman, D. L.
1974   "Pastoral Nomadism in the Andes," *Current Anthropology* 15:188–196.

Chase, D. Z., and A. Chase
1982   "Yucatec Influence in Terminal Classic Northern Belize," *American Antiquity*, 47:596–614.

Diccionario de Motul
1929   *Maya-Español. Atribuido a Fray Antonio de Ciudad Real*, edited by J. M. Hernandez. Talleres de la Compañía Tipográfica Yucateca, Mérida.

Donnan, C. B.
1978   *Moche Art of Peru: Pre-Columbian Symbolic Communication*. Museum of Cultural History, University of California, Los Angeles.

Duellman, W. E.
1963   *Amphibians and Reptiles of the Rainforests of Southern El Peten, Guatemala*. University of Kansas, Museum of Natural History Occasional Papers 15, pp. 205–249.

Durán, D.
 1971 *Book of the Gods and Rites and the An-cient Calendar*, translated and edited by F. Horcasitas and D. Heyden. University of Oklahoma Press, Norman.

Edmonson, M. S.
 1971 *The Book of Counsel: The Popol Vuh of the Quiche Maya of Guatemala.* Tulane University, Middle American Research Institute 35.

Feldman, L. H.
 1978 "Seibal and the Mollusks of the Usumacinta Valley." In *Excavations at Seibal*, edited by G. R. Willey. Peabody Museum Memoirs, vol. 14, Harvard University, pp. 166–167.

Goodwin, G. G.
 1934 "Mammals Collected by A. W. Anthony in Guatemala, 1924–1928," *Bulletin of the American Museum of Natural History* 68:1–60.

Graham, J. A.
 1973 "Aspects of Non-Classic Presences in the Inscriptions and Sculptural Art of Seibal." In *The Classic Maya Collapse*, edited by T. P. Culbert. University of New Mexico Press, Albuquerque, pp. 207–219.

Hansen, B. S.
 In "Pollen Stratigraphy of Laguna de Cocos."
 press In *Ancient Maya Wetland Cultivation on Albion Island, Northern Belize*, edited by Mary Pohl. University of Minnesota, Publications in Anthropology 2.

Haviland, W. A.
 1967 "Stature at Tikal, Guatemala: Implications for Ancient Maya Demography and Social Organization," *American Antiquity* 32:316–325.
 1977 "Dynastic Genealogies from Tikal, Guatemala: Implications for Descent and Political Organization," *American Antiquity* 42:61–67.

Hesse, B., and D. Perkins, Jr.
 1974 "Faunal Remains from Karataš-Semayuk in Southwestern Anatolia: An Interim Report, *Journal of Field Archaeology* 1:145–160.

Hooton, E. A.
 1940 "Skeletons from the Cenote of Sacrifice at Chichen Itza." In *The Maya and Their Neighbors*, edited by C. L. Hay, R. L. Linton, S. K. Lothrop, H. L. Shapiro and G. C. Vaillant. Appleton-Century, New York, pp. 272–280.

Inkeles, L. G.
 1956 "Meat for Mayan Tables," *Pacific Discovery* 9:4–12.

López de Cogolludo, D.
 1971 *Los tres siglos de la dominacíon española en Yucatán o sea historia de esta provincia.* 2 vols. Akademische Druk-u Verlagsanstalt, Graz.

MacNutt, F. A.
 1908 *Letters of Cortés.* Letter 5, vol. 2. G. P. Putnam's Sons, New York.

Morley, S. G.
 1946 *The Ancient Maya.* Stanford University Press, Stanford.

Pendergast, D. M.
 1969 *The Prehistory of Actun Balam, British Honduras.* Royal Ontario Museum, Art and Archaeology Occasional Papers 16.
 1971 *Excavations at Eduardo Quiroz Cave, British Honduras (Belize).* Royal Ontario Museum, Art and Archaeology Occasional Papers 21.
 1979 *Excavations at Altun Ha, Belize, 1964–1970.* Vol. 1. Royal Ontario Museum, Toronto.

Pohl, M. E. D.
 1976 "Ethnozoology of the Maya." Ph.D. dissertation, Department of Anthropology, Harvard University.
 1981 "Ritual Continuity and Change in Mesoamerica: Reconstructing the Ancient Maya *Cuch* Rite," *American Antiquity* 46:513–529.

Rathje, W. L.
 1971 "Lowland Classic Maya Socio-Political Organization: Degree and Form through Space and Time." Ph.D. dissertation, Department of Anthropology, Harvard University.

Relaciones de Yucatán
 1898– *Colección de documentos ineditos relativos*
 1900 *al descubrimiento, conquista y organización de las antiguas posesiones españolas de Ultramar.* 2nd series. 2 vols. Madrid.

Roys, R. L.
 1933 *The Book of Chilam Balam of Chumayel.* Carnegie Institution of Washington 438.
 1943 *The Indian Background of Colonial Yucatan*, Carnegie Institution of Washington, 548.

Sabloff, J. A., and G. R. Willey
 1967 "The Collapse of Maya Civilization in the Southern Lowlands: A Consideration of History and Process," *Southwestern Journal of Anthropology* 23:311–336.

Sahagún, Fray Bernardino de
 1951 *General History of the Things of New Spain.* Book 2 *The Ceremonies*, translated

by A. J. O. Anderson and C. E. Dibble. University of Utah and the School of American Research, Santa Fe.

Saul, F. P.
1972   *The Human Skeletal Remains of Altar de Sacrificios: An Osteobiographic Analysis.* Peabody Museum Papers, vol. 63, Harvard University.

1975   "The Maya and Their Neighbors (1974): As Recorded in Their Skeletons." In *The Maya and Their Neighbors.* Peabody Museum Publication no. 5, Harvard University.

Scholes, F. V., and R. L. Roys
1938   *Fray Diego de Landa and the Problem of Idolatry in Yucatan.* Carnegie Institution, Cooperation in Research, pp. 585–620.

1968   *The Maya Chontal Indians of Acalan-Tixchel.* University of Oklahoma Press, Norman. Originally published 1948.

Scott, R. F.
1980   "Faunal Remains from 1979–1980 Seasons, Colha, Belize." Paper presented at the 45th annual meeting of the Society for American Archaeology, Philadelphia.

Siemens, A.
1978   "Karst and the Pre-Hispanic Maya in the Southern Lowlands." In *Pre-Hispanic Maya Agriculture*, edited by P. D. Harrison and B. L. Turner II. University of New Mexico Press, Albuquerque, pp. 117–143.

Simpson, L. B. translator and editor
1964   *Cortés: The Life of the Conqueror by His Secretary Francisco López de Gómara.* University of California Press, Berkeley.

Spores, R.
1965   "The Zapotec and Mixtec at Spanish Contact." In *Handbook of Middle American Indians*, vol. 3, edited by R. Wauchope and G. R. Willey. University of Texas Press, Austin, pp. 962–990.

Stuart, L. C.
1935   *A Contribution to Knowledge of the Herpetology of a Portion of the Savanna Region of Central Peten, Guatemala.*

University of Michigan, Museum of Zoology, miscellaneous publication 29.

Thompson, J. E. S.
1970   *Maya History and Religion.* University of Oklahoma Press, Norman.

1977   "A Proposal for Constituting a Maya Subgroup, Cultural and Linguistic, in the Petén and Adjacent Regions." In *Anthropology and History in Yucatán*, edited by G. D. Jones. University of Texas Press, Austin, pp. 3–42.

Tourtellot, G.
1970   "The Peripheries of Seibal: An Interim Report." In *Monographs and Papers in Maya Archaeology*, edited by W. R. Bullard, Jr. Peabody Museum Papers, vol. 61, Harvard University.

Tozzer, A. M.
1941   *Landa's relación de las cosas de Yucatan.* Peabody Museum Papers, vol. 18, Harvard University.

Tozzer, A. M., and G. M. Allen
1910   *Animal Figures in the Maya Codices.* Peabody Museum Papers, vol. 4, Harvard University.

Vaughan, H. H.
1979   "Prehistoric Disturbance of Vegetation in the Area of Lake Yaxha, Petén, Guatemala." Ph.D. dissertation, Department of Zoology, University of Florida.

Villa Rojas, A.
1945   *The Maya of East Central Quintana Roo.* Carnegie Institution of Washington 559.

White, T. E.
1956   "The Study of Osteological Materials in the Plains," *American Antiquity* 21:401–404.

Willey, G. R., editor
1975   *Excavations at Seibal.* Peabody Museum Memoirs, vol. 13, Harvard University.

Wilson, E. O., and W. H. Bossert
1971   *A Primer of Population Biology.* Sinauer Associates, Stamford, Conn.

Wing, E. S., and Brown
1979   *Paleonutrition.* Academic Press, New York.

Chapter 10
The Social and Ceremonial Uses of Marine Molluscs at Tikal

Hattula Moholy-Nagy

The ancient inhabitants of Tikal gathered some molluscs for the animal and others for the shell. Certain kinds of molluscs, notably freshwater snails, were eaten and their shells discarded (Moholy-Nagy 1978). Other molluscs were valued for their shells, which were used in unmodified form or worked into artifacts. Marine molluscs would fall into this latter category under the assumption that Tikal is far enough from either seacoast to preclude their arrival in edible condition. Freshwater mussels might be considered a third category in that the shells were often utilized and the animals probably eaten as well. At present not enough is known about the archaeological land molluscs to fit them into this scheme, and they will not be discussed here.

In contrast to many other kinds of material culture recovered from Tikal, a large proportion of the known shells and shell artifacts were found where they had been specially deposited by their users. A consideration of this unusually good archaeological context, as well as spatial distribution and the kinds of shells and artifacts themselves, indicates primarily social and ceremonial use. Although some kinds of molluscs were eaten, there is no evidence of any well-established utilitarian use of shells. If any existed, it was probably casual, such as the occasional use of a mussel shell as a spoon or a scraper. The subject of this chapter, then, is the social and ceremonial use of marine and freshwater shell at Tikal.

Social Use

The most long-lived and significant use of shell was as personal adornment and other kinds of status indicators. By the Terminal Preclassic, if not long

Hattula Moholy-Nagy is a doctoral candidate, Department of Anthropology, University of Michigan, Ann Arbor.

This chapter is a revised version of a paper presented at the 43rd Annual Meeting of the Society for American Archaeology, May 4–6, 1978, in Tucson, Arizona. I wish to thank L. G. Löffler, head of the Ethnological Seminar of the University of Zurich, and the Jubiläumsspende für die Universität Zürich for enabling me to attend the meetings. I am grateful to W. R. Coe for his critical comments on an earlier draft.

before, different types of shell artifacts had come to indicate social status in what seems to have been a true stratified society. In Binford's terminology (1962:220) these artifacts had a sociotechnic function.

Primarily through a study of burials but also taking into consideration distribution in various types of architectural groups (see Moholy-Nagy 1976:91–92 for a trial classification), it is possible to make a general distinction between higher status and lower status sociotechnic shell artifacts (table 10.1). Finer distinctions were undoubtedly made by the Tikaleños themselves.

Artifacts from tomb burials are considered to have been of higher status. This group includes scarcely-altered shells, spangles, most kinds of beads, earflares and pipe-shaped ear ornaments, and shell mosaic work (almost always combined with jade), especially when any of these are of thorny oyster shell, *Spondylus* spp. (tables 10.2 and 10.3). This large marine bivalve, with its distinctive orange, red, or purple color, was valued almost as highly as jade (fig. 10.1). Also highly valued were pearl bead-pendants and composite pendants pieced together of pearls, blister pearl, or nacreous shell (fig. 10.2). *Spondylus* shell and pearl ornaments were often combined with those of jade to form elaborate necklaces, bracelets, anklets, ear ornaments, and so forth, known not only from tomb burials but also from Classic period monuments and pictorial ceramics. *Spondylus* shell, pearls, and jade were the prerogatives of the elite, and their appearance in burials may be taken as indicating an elevated social status of the deceased. Many of the higher-status artifact types occur now and then in Early and Middle Classic structure caches, a point to which we will return.

One characteristic of the thorny oyster is a thick white inner lining. In what I have called scarcely-altered shells, as much as possible of this inner lining was removed to expose the colored part of the shell (cf. W. R. Coe 1959, fig. 52, o). Alternatively, immature valves were not scraped out but ground and polished on the exterior to bring up the color (cf. Kidder 1947, fig. 82, a). At Tikal the exterior ground *Spondylus* shells seem to be limited to the time of the Middle and Late Manik ceramic complex (middle and late Early Classic period). The overall form of such

Table 10.1. Type and context of Tikal shells.

	Tomb burials	Other elite burials	Lower-class burials	Problematical deposits: burial-like	Stela caches	Structure caches	Problematical deposits: cache-like	General excavations	TOTAL
Horse collar	1								1
Mask elements	30								30
Spangles	78								78
(Fan?) handle	1								1
(Fan?) handle overlays	46						1?	18	65
Pearl pendants, composites, etc.	~224		1?	5				1	~236
Beads	~2,146	~476	1?	3	7	52	3	35	~2,723
Scarcely-altered shells	~279	23	1	~56		114	~20	148	~641
Earflares	2	2				3		2	9
Pipe-shaped ear ornaments	4	4						3	11
Uncut tinklers		26		>8					>34
Small narrow rings		7	1					6	14
Flat broad rings		3						4	7
Pendants	~18	8		9		7		28	~70
Rosettes and pegs		9	2					13	24
Cut tinklers		2	1	6			11	70	90
Cut conch artifacts							2	4	6
Miscellaneous cut fragments				5			4	65	74
Trumpets							1	1	2
Miscellaneous forms	1							5	6
Mosaic elements, simple forms	43	5	1	39	>124	>550	32	37	>831
Mosaic assemblages	2	~35		1		35	1		~74
Charlie Chaplins	8			3	25	505	9	2	552
Spondylus fragments	16	~36		12	50	>2,568	22	2	>2,704
Unworked shells	66	>348		180	>36	>2,176	150	>1,370	>4,326
TOTAL	~2,965	>984	8	~327	>242	6,015	~256	>1,812	>12,609

Note: Counts include fragments. All counts are preliminary.

Table 10.2. Type and material of Tikal shells.

	Spondylus	Other marine	Unidentified nacreous	Freshwater mussels	Freshwater snails	Land snails	Pearls or blister pearl	Combined counts or no data	TOTAL
Horse collar	–	1							1
Mask elements	26		4						30
Spangles	78								78
(Fan?) handle			1						1
(Fan?) handle overlays		7	58						65
Pearl pendants, composites, etc.	1	4	6				~225		~236
Beads	~2,644	24	7					48	~2,723
Scarcely-altered shells	206	~352	4	71	6	2			~641
Earflares	3	4						2	9
Pipe-shaped ear ornaments		11							11
Uncut tinklers		34							34
Small narrow rings		14							14
Flat broad rings		3	4						7
Pendants	19	34	~17						~70
Rosettes and pegs		24							24
Cut tinklers		90							90
Cut conch artifacts		6							6
Miscellaneous cut fragments	2	53	16		1?			2	74
Trumpets		2							2
Miscellaneous forms		6							6
Mosaic elements, simple forms, etc.								>831	>831
Mosaic assemblages								~74	~74
Charlie Chaplins	494	35	6					17	552
Spondylus fragments	>2,704								>2,704
Unworked shells	63	>2,583	>24	>159	>756	>510	7	>224	>4,326
TOTAL	>6,240	>3,287	>147	>230	>763	>512	~232	>1,198	>12,609

Note: Counts include fragments. All counts preliminary.

Table 10.3. Material and context of Tikal shells.

Material	Tomb burials	Other elite burials	Lower-class burials	Problematical deposits: burial-like	Stela caches	Structure caches	Problematical deposits: cache-like	General excavations	TOTAL
SPONDYLUS	~2,404	~474	1	~32	76	>3,170	31	55	>6,243
Worked	~2,378	~432	1?	~20	26	561	9	49	>3,476
Fragments	16	~36		12	50	>2,568	22		>2,704
Unworked	10	6				41		6	63
OTHER MARINE	~204	>328	7	156	>38	>2,051	138	389	>3,311
Worked	~178	67	7	43	6	96	39	292	~728
Unworked	26	>261		113	>32	>1,955	99	97	>2,583
UNIDENTIFIED NACREOUS	~59	>6		7		>16	2	69	>159
Worked	~58	3		6		8	1?	59	~135
Unworked	1	~3		1		~8	1	10	>24
FRESHWATER MUSSELS	4	13		~35		11	~9	~158	~230
Worked	4	6		~24			~2	35	~71
Unworked		7		11		11	7	>123	>159
FRESHWATER SNAILS	15	15		10		94	4	>624	>762
Worked		2				1		3	6
Unworked	15	13		10		93	4	>621	>756
LAND SNAILS	10	>57		41	4	64	35	>301	>512
Worked								2	2
Unworked	10	>57		41	4	64	35	>299	>510
PEARLS, BLISTER PEARLS	~224			2		6			~232
Worked	~220			2		3			~225
Unworked	4					3		7	7
COMBINED/NO DATA	45	~91	8	44	>124	>603	37	>216	>1,160
Worked	45	~90	8	40	>124	>602	33	2	~936
Unworked		1		4	1	1	4	>214	>224
TOTAL	~2,965	>984	8	~327	>242	>6,015	~256	>1,812	>12,609
Worked	~2,883	>600	8	~135	>156	>1,271	~84	442	>5,579
Spondylus fragments	16	~36		12	50	>2,568	22		>2,704
Unworked	66	>348		180	>36	>2,176	150	>1,370	>4,326

shells was scarcely altered; however, nearly all have two small drilled perforations, presumably for suspension.

Artifacts deposited in simple burials or never specially deposited and encountered only in general excavations are considered to have been of lower status. Cut tinklers, that is, perforated *Oliva* or *Conus* shells from which the spire has been removed (fig. 10.3), most kinds of pendants, and pairs of composite ornaments consisting of a rosette with a peg are included in this group (fig. 10.4). Most are made of the

Figure 10.1. The thorny oyster. The shell shown here is Spondylus princeps unicolor *Sowerby 1847, found in the Gulf of California southwards to Jalisco, Mexico. After Keene 1971, plate II.*

Figure 10.3. Cut tinklers made of Oliva *shells and, more rarely, of* Conus sp. *Three of these were drilled for suspension, one was sawn. Length of largest, 7.5 cm. After Kidder 1947, figure 85, d, but identical to tinklers from Tikal.*

Figure 10.2. (1) One-piece imitation pearl pendants of nacreous, dull white, and Spondylus *shell. (2) A complete, two-part, composite pendant and one element of another, cut of blister pearl. (1) and (2) to same scale, length of (1) 3.4 cm. (3) A pendant composed of two free pearls pegged together with bone. The uppermost pearl has the characteristic V-shaped suspension hole. Next to it are two views of the same large, hollow blister pearl. (3) and (4) to the same scale, height of (4), 2.2 cm.*

Figure 10.4. To the left are a pair of rosettes and their associated pegs from an "elite" burial, including Imix complex ceramics. Three other rosettes give an indication of the formal variety of these attractive artifacts. Length of longest peg, 2.4 cm.

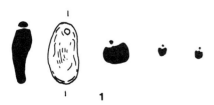
1

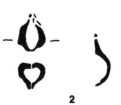
2

3

4

dull white shell of various genera of thick-walled conchs (*Strombus, Turbinella, Melongena*). Others are of thick pearly shell, which could be pearl oyster (*Isognomon, Pinctada,* or *Pteria*) or large top snail shells, *Cittarium pica* [L.]). A few artifacts were definitely made of freshwater mussels, such as *Nephronaias* and *Psoronaias*.

The earliest known occurrence of *Spondylus* shell as well as of jade at Tikal dates to the early Late Preclassic period, the time of the Chuen ceramic complex (Culbert 1977, fig. 2.1). Burial 121, although of an adolescent (W. A. Haviland, personal communication, 1973), had been interred with a necklace made of three small subspherical beads of *Spondylus* shell, three small subspherical beads of jade, and eight pendants of conch shell (fig. 10.5).

Toward the end of the Late Preclassic period, during the time of the Cauac ceramic complex, another manner of using *Spondylus* shell as a marker of social status appeared at Tikal. Among the many offerings placed in the tomb of Burial 85 was a large, scarcely-altered *Spondylus* shell. The size of this valve suggests it is *Spondylus calcifer* Carpenter, a Pacific coast species. This tentative identification is supported by a shell of *S. calcifer* of the same or somewhat later age from a tomb at Altun Ha in Belize, even farther from the Pacific coast than Tikal (Pendergast 1971:456).

The association of scarcely-altered *Spondylus* valves with tomb burials was elaborated upon during the Early Classic period, when such shells were often deposited in sets. Nine perforated shells, always matched in size and manner of working, were distributed around and over the body or principal body, with another larger, usually unperforated, shell placed over the top of the head like a skullcap (fig. 10.6). Jade pebble beads are often also distributed around the tomb in the same manner, but it is not clear how the beads were associated with the shells.

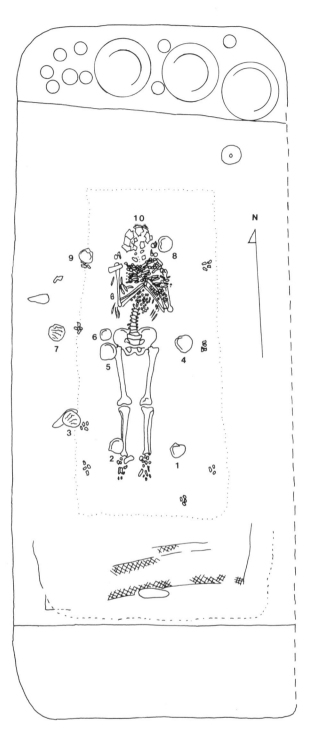

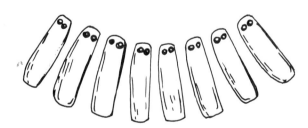

Figure 10.5. *Eight pendants cut from the lips of conch shells. Together with three* Spondylus *and three jade beads they formed a necklace buried with Burial 121, a North Acropolis burial probably contemporary with the Chuen ceramic complex. Length of longest, 4.4 cm.*

Figure 10.6. *Plan of Burial 23, including Ik complex ceramics. This tomb burial included a set of nine plus one scarcely-altered* Spondylus *shells. Nine were placed around and over the body; the tenth was placed over the top of the head.*

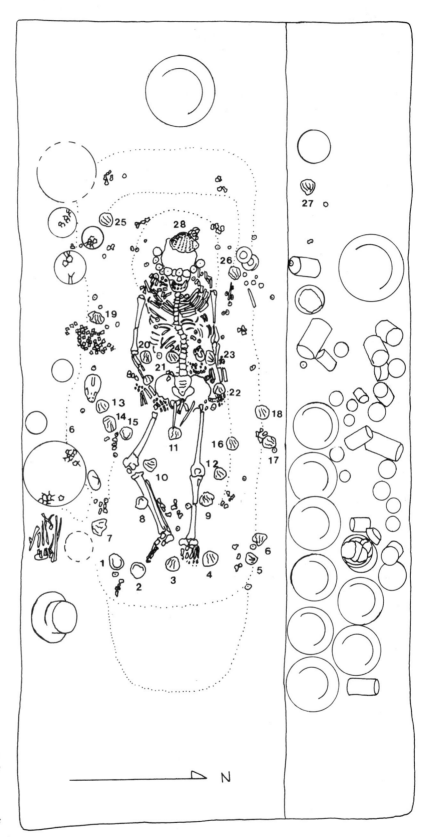

Figure 10.7. Plan of Burial 196, including Imix complex ceramics. This is the latest tomb burial known from Tikal. It and the somewhat earlier Burial 116 included 28 scarcely-altered Spondylus *shells, most likely a triple set of nine "body" shells plus the shell over the top of the head.*

The earliest known example of such a nine-plus-one *Spondylus* shell set is from Burial 10, interred during the time of the Late Manik ceramic complex. The latest is from Burial 196 (fig. 10.7), which dates to the middle of the Late Classic period, during the time of the Imix ceramic complex. Burial 196 and the somewhat earlier Burial 116 each included 28 shells, which I interpret as three sets of nine "body" shells and one "head" shell. Altogether, seven of the nine undisturbed Classic Period tomb burials known from Tikal included such sets. Burials 10, 23, 24, 48, 116, 160, and 196 had them; Burials 77 and 195 did not. Because they seem to occur only with males (Haviland, personal communication, 1973), such sets may have been given only to rulers. One or more *Spondylus* valves often occur in burials dating from the Terminal Preclassic into the Late Classic Period in the Central Lowlands, for example at Holmul (Merwin and Vaillant 1932), Uaxactun (Kidder 1947; Smith 1950), Piedras Negras (W.R. Coe 1959), and Altar de Sacrificios (Smith 1972). I have not been able to identify these special sets anywhere but at Tikal, however.

The circumstance that the shells occur in sets is noteworthy. Feldman (personal communication, 1974) has suggested that such sets were assembled at the seacoast, where the coastal folk had been informed of what was wanted. The general implication is that the importation of *Spondylus* shell and presumably of other marine materials was firmly in the hands of the elite.

Fragments of shell showing either no working or unsmoothed cut edges (the latter listed as "miscellaneous cut fragments" on the tables) occurred predominantly in the Late Classic period occupation debris of Smaller Structure Groups, thought to be lower-class residences. I would interpret such fragments as workshop debris. Possibly, at least by the time of the Imix ceramic complex, shell working was a specialized, and low status, occupation carried on in some of the Smaller Structure Groups.

Most of these fragments are of conch shell and some are of pearly shell, including freshwater mussel. As mentioned above, these are the same kinds of shell from which lower-status ornaments were made. Nevertheless, small fragments of worked *Spondylus* shell also turn up now and then in occupation debris, and I am uncertain as to how they should be interpreted.

That at least some scarcely-altered *Spondylus* shells were prepared at Tikal is attested by the presence of hundreds of chips, spines, and fragments of the white inner lining. These fragments were not found in occupation debris but had been gathered up and deposited in caches, similar to the special deposition of obsidian workshop debris suggested elsewhere (Moholy-Nagy 1976:100).

At present it is hard to be sure if other types of *Spondylus* artifacts were manufactured at Tikal or even if all of the shell artifacts of lower status were.

During the Classic period, several types of shell artifacts, such as scarcely-altered *Spondylus* shells, pipe-shaped ear ornaments, cut tinklers, rosettes and pegs, and simple pendants show such a widespread distribution throughout the Central Lowlands that an exchange network, including some finished products as well as unworked shell, seems to be a reasonable hypothesis.

Ceremonial Uses

From the Early Classic period to the middle of the Late Classic period, unworked shells and shell artifacts occur in contexts usually interpreted as "ceremonial." Certain kinds of shells and certain types of artifacts were frequently placed in structure caches, occasionally in stela caches, but only rarely in burials. They may be considered as having had an ideotechnic function (Binford 1962:220).

Ideotechnic artifacts include cutouts of geometric and anthropomorphic form, the so-called Charlie Chaplins (fig. 10.8), shell and jade mosaic figurines (Moholy-Nagy 1966), and the debris from the working of *Spondylus* shell. Cached unworked shells are almost entirely of marine origin. Most are small, thin-

Figure 10.8. Anthropomorphic cutouts (Charlie Chaplins), usually of Spondylus *shell but sometimes also of dull white and nacreous shell, with details added in incised line or, rarely, in dull black paint. The cutouts shown here are quite realistic. Usually the faces and limbs are more abstract, as illustrated in Coe 1959, figure 51, f–h. Length of largest, 3.4 cm.*

walled, weathered, oddly shaped, or otherwise un-suitable for any other purpose. Scarcely-altered and unworked *Spondylus* shells are the only common exceptions. Sometimes at Tikal and elsewhere, unworked pairs of thorny oyster were used as containers for little treasures such as a jade bead, a pearl, or a tiny fish. *Spondylus* containers are not scraped out; instead, the interior is usually heavily coated with red cinnabar. *Spondylus* valves and freshwater shells were entirely absent from Tikal stela caches, and freshwater shells were all but absent from structure caches.

One of the most interesting aspects of the occurrence of shells and shell artifacts in caches is their relatively restricted time span. One Late Preclassic structure cache produced a *Spondylus* shell bead paired with one of jade, a situation recalling the matched stone and shell beads of the Burial 121 necklace. Shell beads, pendants, and earflares occur now and then in the much more numerous caches of the Early Classic period. The most conspicuous innovation of the Early Classic period was the frequent deposition of quantities of unworked shells, as well as other invertebrate marine material such as coral, bryozoa, sponges, and gorgonian. Such marine caches were also characteristic of the Middle Classic period (Ik ceramic complex) and then disappeared during the Late Classic.

Shells and the Ancestors

Although either a sociotechnic or an ideotechnic function may be attributed to a given shell or shell artifact on the basis of its archaeological context, some artifacts and objects were specially deposited in both caches and burials. During the Early and Middle Classic periods, higher-status sociotechnic artifacts such as beads, earflares, and scarcely-altered *Spondylus* valves were sometimes placed in structure caches, and artifacts and objects usually associated with structure caches, such as unworked marine shells, coral, bryozoa, gorgonian, and anthromorphic cutouts, occur sporadically in tombs and other elite burials.

This apparent interchangeability of context (also seen in other materials such as obsidian, jade, and sting ray spines) could be taken as support of the hypothesis of a "royal cult," advanced by Adams (1977a:263, 310, 328; 1977b:98) and others. Adams suggests that by Classic times, ancestor worship had generated a "royal cult," wherein the elite of the society were regarded as semidivine and capable of influencing worldly matters even after death. The archaeologically recognizable components of the Classic period royal cult form a three-part functional assemblage comprising the grave, the temple erected over it, and the associated monument or monuments in front of it. The offerings placed in the grave or

with the associated temple and monument also belong to this assemblage.

From present evidence, it would seem that the "royal cult" was incipient toward the end of the Preclassic period, the time of the Cauac ceramic complex, when tomb burials, temples, and structure caches were all present (W. R. Coe 1965a, 1965b). The cult became much more important during the Early Classic, and the character of the offerings changed. In the Late Preclassic the offerings seem to have been objects of value used in daily life, but in Early Classic times many offerings, especially cached offerings, appear never to have been used for anything. Besides the quantities of unworked marine shell and other invertebrate marine material already mentioned, one thinks here of *Spondylus* fragments (usually deposited with fragments of jade) and anthropomorphic cutouts as well as artifacts of other materials, such as quantities of flint and obsidian debitage, eccentric flints and obsidians, specialized ceramic cache vessels, and so on. The increasingly symbolic nature of the associated offerings as well as their increased quantity indicates development of the royal cult and, by implication, of the political position of the ruler and of the elite class. Further political development seems to have taken place during the Late Classic period when some kinds of tomb offerings become more numerous, stela caches become quite standardized, and structure caches are greatly reduced. Tomb offerings seem to have been emphasized at the expense of cached offerings.

Shells had symbolic connotations for the ancient Maya. Among the several mentioned by Andrews (1969:48–53) and Thompson (1950), of special concern here are those of the Underworld and of death.

Conch shells and *Spondylus* valves are often depicted on Classic period funerary ceramics (examples in M. D. Coe 1973, 1975, 1978). Sometimes these shells are held or worn by humans (W. R. Coe 1967:102), but more often they are associated with deities. The aged Underworld deity, the Mam or God N, wearing or emerging from a conch is a frequent motif. Thorny oyster shells are worn over the ears of the Underworld deity, God G1 (M. D. Coe 1973, no. 45; 1975, no. 5), and sometimes of God B, identified with the Rain God, Chac (Trik 1963, figs. 6, 7).

Conches and *Spondylus* occasionally appear in effigy in ceramic. Burial 10 at Tikal produced a spouted, stuccoed vessel in the form of a bird with the body of a conch-shell trumpet (fig. 10.9). A tripod plate in the form of a conch shell split lengthwise was placed with Burial 116 (fig. 10.10; also Trik 1963:9). The approximately contemporary tomb, Burial 5, at Piedras Negras included eight scarcely-altered *Spondylus* valves, including a "head" shell, five of which were real shells and three accurate representations in pottery, complete with suspension holes (W. R. Coe 1959:124, 125, figs. 58b, c, d, and 64).

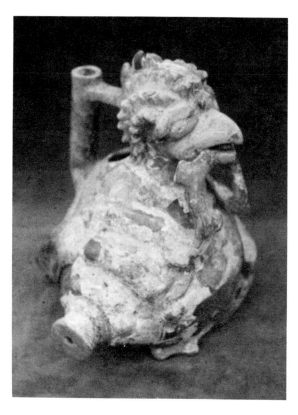

Figure 10.9. A spouted jar in the form of a bird with the body of a conch shell trumpet, as indicated by the added mouthpiece. What may be a speech-scroll emerges from either side of the bird's beak. The entire vessel bears a post-firing decoration of polychrome painted stucco. From Burial 10, Late Manik ceramic complex. Height, 21.5 cm. Photograph by Hans-Ruedi Hug.

It is not surprising that shells would form common burial offerings and, if one accepts the royal cult hypothesis, that shells and other marine materials would also be considered suitable cache offerings. In the Central Lowlands, at least, Andrews's "cult of the sea" (Andrews 1969:53) may have been an integral part of the royal cult.

Extensive social and ceremonial use of shells and shell artifacts was widespread and characteristic of the Classic Lowland Maya, extending to intersite identities in the kinds of shells and types of artifacts used. Besides indicating a possible exchange network in finished products, this widespread and uniformly patterned use of shell implies close social interaction among various sites, as suggested by Ball (1977:122–123) and Marcus (1976), among others. It also implies a commonly held belief system, such as the hypothesized royal cult.

Summary

Present evidence for ancient social and ceremonial use of marine and freshwater shell at Tikal supports hypotheses derived from other data about social structure, social stratification, craft specialization, and the presence of a royal cult.

The social use of shells in artifactual form was the most long-lived, from the later Middle Preclassic into the Terminal Classic period, almost the entire duration of occupation of the site. The distribution of such artifacts in burials and in occupation debris indicates that each type had its special status connotations.

The ceremonial use of shells and artifacts was fairly well restricted to caches of the Early, Middle, and early Late Classic periods, a practice perhaps entirely abandoned by the middle of the ninth century.

At the uppermost level of the social structure, the distinction between sociotechnic and ideotechnic function seems to have been overridden by the royal cult, which integrated both.

Present evidence also suggests that the social and ceremonial use of shell at Tikal was typical of the entire Central Lowland area, at least during the Classic period.

Figure 10.10. A tripod plate in the form of a conch shell split lengthwise. Decorated with white slip with a glyph-like device in black, perforated by a neatly drilled kill-hole. From Burial 116, Imix ceramic complex. Greatest diameter, 27.7 cm. Photograph by Hans-Ruedi Hug.

Tables 10.1–10.3.
Definitions and Comments

Counts

Counts should be considered preliminary since research on Tikal artifacts is still underway. No major changes are anticipated, however.

The figures on the tables include fragments as well as complete items. Separate tabulations will be presented in the final Tikal artifact report (Tikal report no. 27). In general, preservation of shell outside of special deposits was poor. Most finds were incomplete, especially larger objects such as scarcely-altered and unworked shells, flat broad rings, and cut conch artifacts. Preservation of freshwater mussel and other nacreous shell was poor everywhere.

Material

Dull, compact shell was always assumed to be of marine origin. Reddish shell was assumed to be *Spondylus* spp., and whitish shell was assumed to be of other marine species, although conceivably some small items such as beads could be of the white inner lining of *Spondylus* shells.

Because pearly shell can be of freshwater or marine origin, small items were grouped together as unidentified nacreous shell.

Freshwater mussels included both thick-walled and thin-walled species. The former are characteristic of rivers and the latter of lakes. Neither is found in the immediate vicinity of the site today.

Freshwater snails were overwhelmingly of the species *Pomacea flagellata* (Say), which lives in a variety of habitats including the local Tikal waterholes (Moholy-Nagy 1978). About 16 snails from archaeological context were of the genus *Pachychilus*, found in both lakes and rivers.

Land snails found in excavations at Tikal seem to be the same forms as those found on the site today. Unfortunately, in most cases, they were not expertly identified. Therefore, I hesitate to attribute their presence to human or natural causes.

The pearls all appear to be of marine origin. Besides free pearls, the Maya utilized shell or blister pearls. These were cut free of the oyster shell and glued or pegged together around a core of now white, stucco-like material to form composite pendants.

Stone-and-shell mosaic assemblages were often placed in special deposits during the Early Classic period. Although *Spondylus*, white marine, and nacreous shell were all used for mosaic elements, as well as for the somewhat larger, loose, cut pieces of uncertain use termed simple forms, it seemed pointless to list each kind of shell separately. The counts have been combined.

Some incompletely catalogued shells were no longer available for examination. These are listed in the combined counts and no data column.

Context

Most of the categories used here have fairly well established meanings. In tabulating Tikal shells I found it useful to define some additional contexts, such as "other elite" and "lower-class" burials, and burial-like and cache-like problematical deposits. These should be regarded as tentative.

For the purposes of this chapter, I have defined the archaeological contexts given on the tables as follows.

A tomb burial was placed in a specially constructed or excavated chamber that provided considerably more space than that required by the body or the principal body. This definition is approximately the same as that published in Moholy-Nagy (1963:74).

All other kinds of graves found associated with Civic-Ceremonial, Range-Structure, or Intermediate Structure Groups have been classified here as "other elite" burials.

Lower-class burials are all those associated with Smaller Structure Groups. Only one exception was made here: the Late Preclassic burial, Burial 128, containing pottery of the Cauac ceramic complex, although associated with Smaller Structure Group 6E-1, was classified as an elite burial because of the strong artifactual resemblances it showed to the coeval tomb burial, Burial 85, on the North Acropolis.

A stela cache is a cache placed with a stela. Caches have not been found with altars at Tikal.

A structure cache was placed with a structure defined on other grounds as a temple or, more rarely, as a range structure (palace).

"Problematical deposit" is a working term that was formulated to designate specially deposited or incidentally constituted collections of material that depart from what researchers have come to regard as expectable. Precisely because it is a working term, the entire problematical deposit category should be regarded as subject to redefinition.

"Problematical deposits: burial-like" contained enough human bone or artifacts usually associated with more typical burials as to suggest that one or more individuals had actually been interred. Other problematical deposits lacking burial-associated artifacts or including few or no human remains have been classified as cache-like. They have been found in various situations but never with monuments.

General excavations implies incidental deposition and includes finds from the surface, middens, construction fill, chultuns, quarries, and so on, and any combination of these.

References

Adams, R. E. W.
1977a   *Prehistoric Mesoamerica.* Little, Brown, Boston.
1977b   "Rio Bec Archaeology and the Rise of Maya Civilization." In *The Origins of Maya Civilization*, edited by R. E. W. Adams. University of New Mexico Press, Albuquerque, pp. 77–99.

Andrews, E. W. IV
1969   *The Archaeological Use and Distribution of Mollusca in the Maya Lowlands.* Tulane University, Middle American Research Institute publication 34.

Ball, J. W.
1977   "The Rise of the Northern Maya Chiefdoms: A Socioprocessual Analysis." In *The Origins of Maya Civilization*, edited by R. E. W. Adams. University of New Mexico Press, Albuquerque, pp. 101–132.

Binford, L. R.
1962   "Archaeology as Anthropology," *American Antiquity* 28.2:217–225.

Coe, M. D.
1973   *The Maya Scribe and His World.* Grolier Club, New York.
1975   *Classic Maya Pottery at Dumbarton Oaks.* Dumbarton Oaks, Trustees for Harvard University, Washington.
1978   *Lords of the Underworld: Masterpieces of Classic Maya Ceramics.* The Art Museum, Princeton University.

Coe, W. R.
1959   *Piedras Negras Archaeology: Artifacts, Caches, and Burials.* Museum Monographs, University Museum, Philadelphia.
1965a   "Tikal, Guatemala, and Emergent Maya Civilization," *Science* 147.3664:1401–19.
1965b   "Tikal: Ten Years of Study of a Maya Ruin in the Lowlands of Guatemala," *Expedition* 8.1:5–56.
1967   *Tikal: A Handbook of the Ancient Maya Ruins.* University Museum, Philadelphia.

Culbert, T. P.
1977   "Early Maya Development at Tikal, Guatemala." In *The Origins of Maya Civilization*, edited by R. E. W. Adams. University of New Mexico Press, Albuquerque, pp. 27–43.

Keene, A. M.
1971   *Sea Shells of Tropical West America.* 2nd ed. Stanford University Press.

Kidder, A. V.
1947   *The Artifacts of Uaxactun, Guatemala.* Carnegie Institution of Washington 576.

Longyear, J. M., III
1952   *Copan Ceramics: A Study of Southwestern Maya Pottery.* Carnegie Institution of Washington 597.

Marcus, J.
1976   *Emblem and State in the Classic Maya Lowlands: An Epigraphic Approach to Territorial Organization.* Dumbarton Oaks, Trustees for Harvard University, Washington.

Merwin, R. E., and G. C. Vaillant
1932   *The Ruins of Holmul, Guatemala.* Peabody Museum Memoirs, vol. 3, no. 2, Harvard University.

Moholy-Nagy, H.
1963   "Shells and Other Marine Material from Tikal," *Estudios de Cultura Maya* 3:63–83. México.
1966   "Mosaic Figurines from Tikal," *Archaeology* 19.2:84–89.
1976   "Spatial Distribution of Flint and Obsidian Artifacts at Tikal, Guatemala." In *Maya Lithic Studies: Papers from the 1976 Belize Field Symposium*, edited by T. R. Hester and N. Hammond. Special Report no. 4, Center for Archaeological Research, University of Texas at San Antonio, pp. 91–108.
1978   "The Utilization of *Pomacea* Snails at Tikal, Guatemala," *American Antiquity* 43.1:65–73.

Pendergast D. M.
1969   *Altun Ha, British Honduras (Belize): The Sun God's Tomb.* Royal Ontario Museum, Art and Archaeology, Occasional Paper 19, Toronto.
1971   "Evidence of Early Teotihuacan-Lowland Maya Contact at Altun Ha," *American Antiquity* 36.4:455–460.

Smith, A. L.
1950   *Uaxactun, Guatemala: Excavations of 1931–1937.* Carnegie Institution of Washington 588.
1972   *Excavations at Altar de Sacrificios: Architecture, Settlement, Burials, and Caches.* Peabody Museum Papers, vol. 62, no. 2, Harvard University.

Thompson, J. E. S.
1950   *Maya Hieroglyphic Writing.* Carnegie Institution of Washington 589.

Trik, A. S.
1963   "The Splendid Tomb of Temple I at Tikal, Guatemala," *Expedition* 6.1:2–18.

Chapter 11

The Role of Marine Resources in the Maya Economy:
A Case Study from Cozumel, Mexico

Nancy L. Hamblin

It has been suggested in recent years that the Maya made extensive use of marine resources. Lange (1971) asserts that the prehistoric population of a large portion of the Yucatán was dependent upon marine products as a primary protein source, particularly in the Classic and Late Postclassic periods. Some studies of settlement pattern data have tended to refute this hypothesis, however, at least as far as the specific time periods are concerned (Ball and Eaton 1972). Still, the existence of a diverse resource exploitation pattern including marine fauna, in contrast to the old concept involving nearly complete dependence on maize, is no longer doubted. What has been needed is evidence to support this idea. Analysis of fauna recovered from Cancun (Wing 1974), Lubaantun (Wing 1975), and Cerros (chap. 8) are among the rare studies revealing the importance of marine fauna in the Maya economy. Analysis of data from eight sites on Cozumel lends substantial support to this view.

Nancy L. Hamblin is zooarchaeologist, University of Nebraska State Museum, Lincoln.

Elizabeth Wing guided me in using the comparative fish collection at the Florida State Museum, Gainesville. Stephen Hale helped me identify sharks using his method of taking measurements of vertebra height, width, and internal angle and correlating the measurements with comparative specimens. The crabs were identified using the Florida State Museum collection as well as with the aid of John B. Sparling's blue crab (*Callinectes sapidus*) specimens. Donald A. Thomson (University of Arizona, Department of Ecology and Evolutionary Biology) supplied information on the ecology, habits, and procurement techniques of reef fishes.

Funding for the research for this chapter was provided by the National Geographic Society and Sigma Xi, the Scientific Research Society.

I would like to thank the Peabody Museum for permitting figure 11.1 to be reprinted from *Changing Pre-Columbian Commercial Systems: The 1972–1973 Seasons at Cozumel, Mexico*, by Jeremy A. Sabloff and William L. Rathje, Peabody Museum Monographs, no. 3. Copyright 1975 by the President and Fellows of Harvard College.

Finally, it should be noted that an expanded version of this chapter appears in *Animal Use by the Cozumel Maya*, by Nancy L. Hamblin. Copyright 1984 by the University of Arizona Press, Tucson.

Bone Recovery and Frequency Calculations

Our sample contains the fauna that occurred in areas excavated on Cozumel (fig. 11.1). During the 1973 field season excavators screened all dirt with 1/4 inch mesh. During the previous 1972 season, screening was not done routinely but was started whenever large concentrations of artifacts or bone material began to appear from a specific provenience. The 1972 season included only a small proportion of the total excavations on the island, because the greatest effort was concentrated on survey. Our belief that recovery was thorough is supported by the fact that the total faunal sample includes 377 bird bones, nearly 300 amphibian bones, more than 8,500 fish bones, approximately 3,500 reptiles, 2 very fragile bat skulls, and several thousand other mammal bones.

Minimum numbers of individuals (MNIs) were calculated using neither the minimum nor the maximum-distinction methods (see Grayson 1973) but a compromise between the two. Within each site, MNIs were calculated separately by pit and trench (the primary excavation units used here), but the levels within these, whether cultural or arbitrary, were ignored. In addition, the fauna in pits or trenches adjacent to one another were grouped together, since these were considered parts of the same cultural unit (e.g., two pits close together inside a temple structure). Using the method described by Bökönyi (1970), the bones of each species were then subdivided and matched up, not only on the basis of how many lefts and rights of each element were present, but taking into account age groups (immature versus adult) and sizes of individual animals (small, medium, and large).

Results and Discussion

Fishes, crabs, and sea turtles represent numerically the most significant of all the Cozumel fauna. With 8,674 specimens comprising 42.0 percent of the total sample, marine fauna surpass even mammals (7,499 bones, or

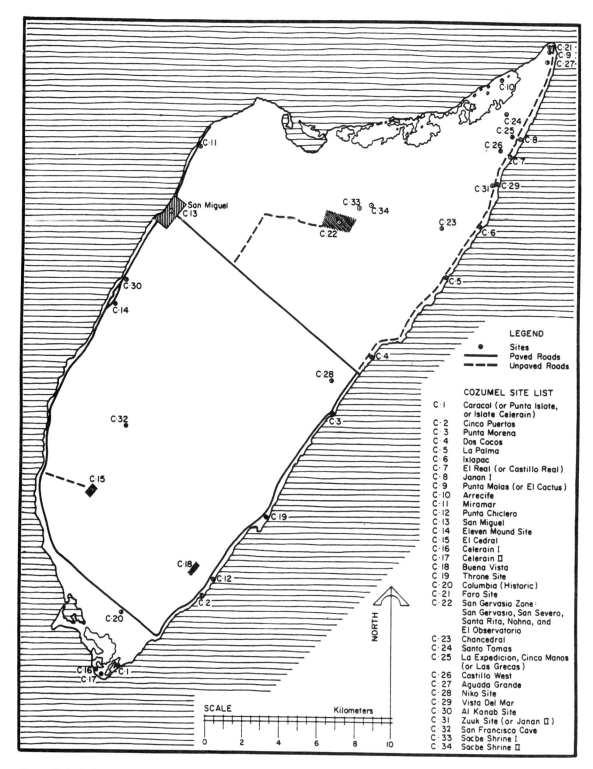

*Figure 11.1. Archaeological sites on
Cozumel. From Sabloff and Rathje
1975.*

LEGEND

• Sites
—— Paved Roads
---- Unpaved Roads

COZUMEL SITE LIST

C·1   Caracol (or Punta Islote,
      or Islote Celerain)
C·2   Cinco Puertos
C·3   Punta Morena
C·4   Dos Cocos
C·5   La Palma
C·6   Ixlapac
C·7   El Real (or Castillo Real)
C·8   Janan I
C·9   Punta Molas (or El Cactus)
C·10 Arrecife
C·11 Miramar
C·12 Punta Chiclero
C·13 San Miguel
C·14 Eleven Mound Site
C·15 El Cedral
C·16 Celerain I
C·17 Celerain II
C·18 Buena Vista
C·19 Throne Site
C·20 Columbia (Historic)
C·21 Faro Site
C·22 San Gervasio Zone:
      San Gervasio, San Severo,
      Santa Rita, Nohna, and
      El Observatorio
C·23 Chancedral
C·24 Santo Tomas
C·25 La Expedicion, Cinco Manos
      (or Las Grecas)
C·26 Castillo West
C·27 Aguada Grande
C·28 Niko Site
C·29 Vista Del Mar
C·30 Al Kanab Site
C·31 Zuuk Site (or Janan II)
C·32 San Francisco Cave
C·33 Sacbe Shrine I
C·34 Sacbe Shrine II

NORTH

SCALE   Kilometers

0   2   4   6   8   10

36.32 percent of all remains). If MNIs are used as the basis of comparison, the contrast is more striking; marine fauna account for 40.86 percent (965) of all excavated animals, and mammals comprise only 29.81 percent (704) of the sample.

The marine fauna exhibit a high degree of diversity. There are at least 24 species of crabs, sharks, stingrays, sea turtles, and coral reef fishes present in the faunal sample (table 11.1). Most of these remains come from contexts dated to the Late Postclassic period (table 11.2); less than 4 percent of the bones were recovered from earlier time periods. (Even the mixed and undated fauna are suspected to date mainly from the Late Postclassic.)

As table 11.3 shows, reef fishes comprise the majority of all marine fauna. These fishes represent more than 96 percent of the bones or nearly 83 percent of the minimum number of MNIs. Crabs are next in importance, with approximately 2 percent of the remains or more than 9 percent of the MNIs. Sharks, stingrays, and sea turtles made relatively minor contributions to the total marine resources of Cozumel.

A breakdown of the percentages of identified reef fishes by family (table 11.4) reveals that the top five are groupers, triggerfishes, grunts, parrotfishes, and surgeonfishes. Together these comprise approximately 89 percent of the MNIs. The remaining 11 percent is made up of moray eels, barracudas, snappers, wrasses, and porcupinefish.

There are several significant categories of information that can be obtained from a study of marine faunal remains. Exploitation of microenvironmental zones, prehistoric subsistence, food preparation practices, cultural selection factors, fishing technology, implications for long-distance trade, and ceremonial and religious practices are examined here.

Environmental Habitats

The salient characteristic of all these marine species is that they are typical inhabitants of the coral reef environment. None can be considered pelagic, that is, deep-water or oceanic species. Instead, they all (including the sharks and sea turtles) either live in or spend a fair amount of time in shallow inshore waters.

Coral reefs provide the setting for the most diverse fish communities. They are among the most biologically productive of all natural communities (Lowe-McConnell 1977; Johannes 1976). More ecological niches exist here than in almost any other biotope. Corals can grow only where the mean annual temperature is at least 20° C (or 68° F), and preferably 23° C (73.4° F). Coral reef communities often provide a stable environment for the resident fishes over long periods of time. This stability probably explains the complex interrelationships that have developed between species inhabiting the reefs (Lowe-McConnell 1977). Some reef fishes habitually feed on algae and corals. Other species consume invertebrates, while still others are large or small fish feeders (see fig. 11.2). The Cozumel fishermen did not concentrate on any one category of fish, but made widespread use of species from every part of this food web.

Ideal habitat for the blue crab is provided by the lagoons on Cozumel; Landa mentions an abundance of crabs in the lagoons of Yucatán (Tozzer 1941; Collier 1964:138). The fact that most of these bodies of water are located in the northern part of the island probably accounts for the predominance of these crustaceans in the northern sites and their total absence in the other sites. Both the blue and the stone crab would have been easily obtained in the shallow waters close to Cozumel's coastline.

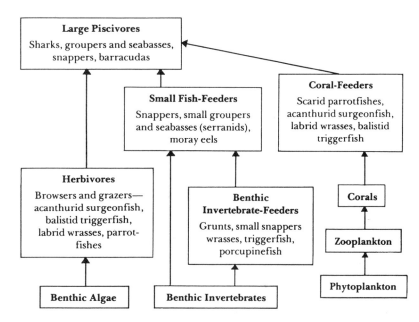

Figure 11.2. Simplified food web showing trophic relationships among coral reef fishes. From Hamblin 1984; adapted from Lowe-McConnell 1977, p. 35 with additional information from Randall 1968.

Table 11.1. Summary of Cozumel marine fauna.

Taxon	No. of bones	% of bones	MNI	% of MNI
Brachyura (true crabs)	37	0.43	17	1.76
Callinectes sapidus (blue crab)	84	0.97	39	4.04
Menippe mercenaria (stone crab)	62	0.71	36	3.73
Squaliformes (sharks)	6	0.07	6	0.62
Ginglymostoma cirratum (nurse shark)	10	0.12	6	0.62
Galeocerdo cuvier (tiger shark)	3	0.03	3	0.31
? *Carcharhinus* sp. (requiem sharks)	1	0.01	–	–
Carcharhinus sp. (requiem sharks)	25	0.29	18	1.87
Carcharhinus maculipinnis (large black-tipped shark)	1	0.01	1	0.10
Sphyrna sp. (hammerhead sharks)	26	0.30	16	1.66
Sphyrna cf. *S. mokarran* (great hammerhead shark)	2	0.02	2	0.21
Sphyrna cf. *S. zygaena* (common or smooth hammerhead shark)	1	0.01	1	0.10
Dasyatidae (stingrays)	17	0.20	7	0.73
Dasyatis americana (southern stingray)	9	0.10	3	0.31
Osteichthyes (bony fishes)	6,713	77.39	–	–
Muraenidae (moray eels)	18	0.21	7	0.73
Muraena miliaris (goldentail moray)	7	0.08	5	0.52
Enchelycore nigricans (viper moray)	6	0.07	6	0.62
Sphyraena sp. (barracudas)	54	0.62	14	1.45
Sphyraena barracuda (great barracuda)	21	0.24	16	1.66
Serranidae (groupers, sea basses)	95	1.10	30	3.11
Epinephelus sp.	258	2.97	91	9.43
Mycteroperca sp. (groupers)	54	0.62	29	3.01
Lutjanus sp. (snappers)	33	0.38	21	2.18
Haemulon sp. (grunts)	282	3.25	94	9.74
Labridae (wrasses)	7	0.08	4	0.41

Table 11.1 (continued).

Taxon	No. of bones	% of bones	MNI	% of MNI
Bodianus sp. (hogfishes)	1	0.01	1	0.10
Bodianus rufus (Spanish hogfish)	1	0.01	1	0.10
Halichoeres sp.	7	0.08	6	0.62
? Scaridae (parrotfishes)	2	0.02	–	–
Scaridae (parrotfishes)	2	0.02	2	0.21
Sparisoma sp.	220	2.54	104	10.78
Sparisoma cf. *S. viride* (stoplight parrotfish)	1	0.01	1	0.10
Scarus sp.	26	0.30	20	2.07
Acanthurus sp. (surgeonfishes)	167	1.93	167	17.31
Balistidae (triggerfishes)	131	1.51	74	7.67
Balistes sp.	146	1.68	83	8.60
Balistes cf. *B. vetula* (queen triggerfish)	7	0.08	5	0.52
Melichthys niger (black durgon)	12	0.14	11	1.14
Diodon hystrix (porcupinefish)	100	1.15	7	0.73
Cheloniidae (sea turtles)	16	0.18	11	1.14
? Cheloniidae (sea turtles)	3	0.03	–	–
TOTAL	8,674	99.97	965	100.01

Table 11.2. Distribution of Cozumel marine fauna through time.

Time period	No. of bones	% of bones	MNI	% of MNI
Late Postclassic/historic	5,862	67.58	551	57.10
Postclassic	336	3.87	60	6.22
Pre-Late Postclassic	73	0.84	20	2.07
Pre-Postclassic	2	0.02	1	0.10
Pure Florescent	192	2.21	35	3.63
Mixed Preclassic, Classic, and Terminal Classic	59	0.68	18	1.87
Mixed and no date	2,150	24.79	280	29.02
TOTAL	8,674	99.99	965	100.01

Table 11.3. Cozumel marine fauna by subdivision.

Subdivision	No. of bones	% of bones	MNI	% of MNI
Crabs	183	2.11	92	9.53
Sharks	75	0.86	53	5.49
Sting rays	26	0.30	10	1.04
Reef fishes	8,371	96.51	799	82.80
Sea turtles	19	0.22	11	1.14
TOTAL	8,674	100.00	965	100.00

Table 11.4. Relative importance of Cozumel reef fishes by family.

Taxon	No. of bones	% of bones	MNI	% of MNI
Osteichthyes (bony fishes)	6,713	80.19	–	–
Muraenidae (moray eels)	31	0.37	18	2.25
Sphyraenidae (barracudas)	75	0.89	30	3.75
Serranidae (groupers, sea basses)	407	4.86	150	18.77
Lutjanidae (snappers)	33	0.39	21	2.62
Pomadasyidae (grunts)	282	3.36	94	11.76
Labridae (wrasses)	16	0.19	12	1.50
Scaridae (parrotfishes)	251	2.99	127	15.89
Acanthuridae (surgeonfishes)	167	1.99	167	20.90
Balistidae (triggerfishes)	296	3.53	173	21.65
Diodontidae (porcupinefishes and burrfishes)	100	1.19	7	0.87
TOTAL	8,371	99.95	799	99.96

The sea turtles may have been harvested from along the southeastern coast of Cozumel. This area is known to be a habitual breeding and grazing ground for the green turtle (*Chelonia mydas*), since it provides a rich bank of the marine grasses and algae upon which this turtle is known to feed extensively (Pritchard 1967; Pope 1964). The sea turtles in the sample could not be identified beyond the family level, although it is probable that these remains belong to the green turtle. Nevertheless, two other species present in the general area cannot be ruled out: the loggerhead (*Caretta caretta*) and the hawksbill (*Eretmochelys imbricata*).

Nutritional Implications

Both of the crabs utilized on Cozumel are considered highly desirable today, making sizable contributions to the fishing industry in areas such as Florida and Chesapeake Bay, Virginia (Schmitt 1965; Street 1966). In particular, the large, heavy claw of the stone crab is commonly eaten. The fishermen in Sarasota Bay, Florida, have developed a practice of breaking off this claw and throwing the crab back to grow another one for next year's market (Schmitt 1965). The Cozumel Maya might also have employed the same practice.

This fact might explain the lack of a single carapace fragment in the faunal sample, although the comparatively fragile nature of these elements might also have precluded their preservation.

Sharks in the present study were probably fished primarily for use as food, since this is well documented historically in Yucatán (Borhegyi 1961; Thompson 1932; Stephens 1841). Since less than 22 percent of the Cozumel shark remains are artifacts or unmodified shark's teeth, most undoubtedly represent food refuse. According to E. H. Thompson (1932), sharks were fished to obtain their livers. He describes the boiling of livers in earthen pots to obtain the oil. A nineteenth-century traveler to Central America, John Lloyd Stephens, stated (1841:462) that in Campeche shark meat was sold "regularly in the market and eaten by all classes."

Shark liver is significant for its nutritive value, its iodine, and its high fat-soluble vitamin content (Borhegyi 1961). Nutritionist Scrimshaw informed Borhegyi that "consumption of shark liver would be a very rich source of vitamin D in the diet and would also make a significant contribution to the protein and B-complex content of a diet which otherwise consists primarily of corn and beans. Indeed, such a practice could well make the difference between good nutrition and poor nutrition for a population group, even if it were only a bi-weekly occurrence." (Borhegyi 1961:281) Borhegyi (1961) believes that the consumption of shark meat and oil-rich shark liver in pre-Columbian times may have helped prevent many nutritional diseases and protein deficiencies, such as pellagra, rickets, and anemia.

The stingrays found in the Cozumel sites were probably not captured for food. There is evidence to support the idea that the tail spine of these animals was utilized for ceremonial purposes, as will be discussed below.

The sea turtles undoubtedly provided an addition to the prehistoric diet; Landa (Tozzer 1941:192) mentions sea turtles with shells "larger than large shields" and refers to them as having plenty of flesh and being good to eat. Unfortunately, his description does not allow one to distinguish the species. The seventeenth-century Dominican friar Thomas Gage wrote that the Maya ate many water and land tortoises (Thompson 1958). The green turtle is the one presently preferred for soup; its flesh is renowned for its flavor (Pope 1964). For some years a turtle meat packing plant was in operation on Cozumel (Wright 1970). Turtle eggs are also a staple item in some parts of Latin America, and it has been reported that the shell forms the basis for a soup (Gans 1975). It seems surprising that so few marine turtles appear in the Cozumel sites given the accessibility of green turtles off the southeastern coast and the cultural acceptance of these animals as food items. Perhaps the less dense and poorly con-

structed marine turtle shells (Pope 1964) did not survive the native cooking practices. Alternatively, the eggs of the green turtle may have been preferred by the island's inhabitants, a consumption pattern that would leave few archaeological traces.

Of all the marine resources utilized on Cozumel, reef fishes made the greatest contribution to the diet. Regardless of species, fish is a nutritious food. Relatively small amounts of marine resources per person would have provided the necessary protein balance in a diet dominated by plant products such as corn, root crops, and beans, which had been grown on thin and perhaps nearly exhausted soils (Lange 1971). Fish are an excellent source of protein, which not only includes the quantity of this basic nutrient consumed but also supplements the quality of dietary protein. A diet consisting of a moderate amount of regular protein can be transformed into one with an adequate amount of high quality protein if only small amounts of fish are consumed (Mayer 1962). The protein content of edible fish portions has been noted as 15–20 percent when water is included (one researcher says the average is 19 percent, Stansby 1962). By dry weight, however, protein is usually over 50 percent and occasionally as high as 90 percent (Driver 1961:63). Curing by drying, salting, or smoking has relatively little effect on the overall nutritive value of fish, especially protein, although the loss of some vitamins can occur as a result of the processing and storage (Cutting 1962).

In addition to protein, fish are sources of unsaturated fats (compared to meats), calcium, potassium, phosphorus, iron, B-vitamins, Vitamin A, iodine, and many essential trace elements such as copper, manganese, zinc, cobalt, fluorine, vanadium, molybdenum, chromium, and selenium (Driver 1961; Guha 1962; Kuhnau 1962; Sever 1975). The role of these trace elements in the human body is only recently beginning to be understood. Many of them act as catalysts for normal metabolic processes and maintenance of general health (such as copper, manganese, zinc, cobalt, and fluorine); others are needed for fixing iron into blood hemoglobin for bone formation and action of hormones (manganese), protein metabolism (cobalt), integrity of the teeth (fluorine), regulation of the thyroid (iodine), protection of the liver (selenium), and others. (See Kuhnau 1962 for a discussion of these trace elements.) Recent studies have shown that zinc is an especially vital element, deficiencies resulting in markedly retarded growth and sexual development as well as possible congenital malformations of the central nervous system (Sever 1975). Fish is a particularly valuable source of these elements, since isotope studies have shown they are concentrated in the muscle and viscera of fish up to 100–10,000 times their original level in sea water (Kuhnau 1962).

Besides the fish species discussed here, other nutritious marine resources would have been available to the inhabitants of Cozumel: squid, shrimp, octopus, and shellfish. The first three invertebrates would have left no osteological traces and the numerous shellfish recovered from these sites have been analyzed elsewhere (Vokes 1978).

Food Preparation Practices

Techniques of cooking the various groups of marine fauna differed. For example, a high percentage of the crabs and sea turtles seem to have been roasted directly over a fire, while none of the sharks and very few of the reef fishes were treated in this fashion.

Nearly 75 percent of the crab claws (137 fragments) are heat-affected. Most of them (120) are either burnt or heat-darkened, and the remainder (17) are merely heat-calcined. The occurrence of similar calcined fragments in an early Guatemalan coastal site in the Ocos region led Coe and Flannery (1967) to theorize that some of the crabs had been boiled in soup pots. This practice occurs in the area today and does result in a calcined appearance. In addition, they found one crab pincer still adhering to the interior of a potsherd. The burnt claws in their sample were believed to have been roasted (Coe and Flannery 1967). The evidence from Cozumel indicated that crabs were both roasted directly over coals or fire and boiled, with an emphasis on the former cooking method. The 46 claw fragments that do not exhibit any effects of heat may have been broken open, and the meat was either consumed raw or extracted for cooking later.

None of the shark elements are burnt, but it would have been a simple matter to cut large chunks of shark meat away from the vertebral column in order to cook it. Many of the sharks caught by Cozumel fishermen were probably butchered on the beaches so that the few elements found in these sites represent only a small percentage of the total shark consumption. Even if shark elements other than teeth, calcified vertebrae, or perhaps dermal ossicles were transported to some sites, their cartilaginous nature would not permit archaeological preservation.

More than 63 percent of the sea turtle elements (12) are burnt, suggesting that these reptiles were often roasted in their shells directly over a fire before they were eaten. In her study of five Maya sites, Pohl (1976:272) mentions that the carapaces of some turtles were often discolored and burnt and that roasting of turtles is still practiced in Petén today.

Very few burnt bones were discovered among the reef fishes, less than 1 percent. Fish were either filleted before cooking or boiled in soups and stews; only occasionally were they roasted over a fire. The burnt bones seem to cover a normal cross section of

several major fish families (groupers, parrotfishes, grunts, and triggerfishes).

Cultural Selection Factors

There is circumstantial evidence that the inhabitants of Cozumel avoided fishes that can cause poisoning in man. Ecological requirements may also have had an influence on absence of certain species, and cultural preference may explain the relatively high or low percentages of others.

Ciguatera poisoning can result in weakness, diarrhea, and a host of other physical symptoms sometimes terminating in coma or death (Randall 1968). Thus it appears significant that several fishes that can cause this potentially serious illness either occur in very low quantities or are missing entirely from the Cozumel sample. These include the large members of the moray eel family (Muraenidae), large individuals of the great barracuda species (*Sphyraena barracuda*), some of the large members of the grouper family (especially *Mycteroperca* sp.), and the large species of snapper (Lutjanidae).

The wrasses (Labridae) occur in extremely low quantity here (16 bones, or less than 1 percent of all fish bone). This fact is difficult to understand since some of the species in this family are among the most numerous on coral reefs (Randall 1968; Hoese and Moore 1977), and they are easily obtained in shallow water with the use of hooks and lines, spears or traps (Donald Thomson, personal communication, 1979). The Cozumel fishermen evidently preferred other species. The triggerfishes (Balistidae) fall into this latter category, comprising approximately 18 percent of MNIs for all fishes and crabs. One member of this family, the black durgon (*Melichthys niger*), would have presented more of a challenge to obtain; it most commonly occurs in the clear waters of outer reef at depths of 50 feet or more (Randall 1968). Its distinctive spine may have been attractive to the Maya for ceremonial uses.

Despite the lengthy list of fishes excavated from Cozumel, the most noteworthy thing about it is what is missing. A list derived from the sixteenth-century Spanish chroniclers Oviedo and Landa reports mullets (*Mugil* spp.), freshwater mullet (*Agonostomus* sp.), mojarras (*Gerres* spp.), snook (*Centropomus* spp.), jacks (*Caranx* spp.), soles (*Achirus* spp.), and sardines (*Sardinella* spp.) as pre-conquest items of food and commerce for the Yucatán Maya (Collier 1964:139; Tozzer 1941). Not one of these species mentioned appears in the Cozumel sites; the only one on the original list that does occur here is the stingray (*Dasyatis*). Collier also mentions two other families of probable importance to the aboriginal economy: snappers (Lutjanidae) and anchovies (Engraulidae). The latter do not appear in the Cozumel sample and, although the snappers do, they seem to be of minor importance (representing less than 1 percent of the fish bones). As mentioned, this low frequency may reflect the fact that the large species of snapper are known to produce ciguatera poisoning, if fished from toxic areas of reefs. At other Maya sites where fish remains have been reported at least some of these species observed by the Spaniards were utilized. For example, snook were found at Lubaantun (Wing 1975); jacks occurred at Dzibilchaltun, Lubaantun, and Cancun (Wing and Steadman 1980; Wing 1975; Wing 1974), and a mojarra was reported from Mayapan (Pollock and Ray 1957).

Some indication as to why these species were not being utilized on Cozumel may come from the ecological requirements of the animals. Mullets, for instance, are more characteristic of brackish water than sea water of full salinity, particularly the adults of the species. The freshwater mullet, naturally, could not exist at all on Cozumel. Of the snooks, only one species is mentioned as "occasionally seen in reef areas near mangroves" (Randall 1968:89), which implies that the animal was not available in any quantity. Jacks are not considered residents of reefs, even though they may briefly pass through the reef community when feeding on the resident fishes. Similarly, soles do not inhabit the reefs, since they are usually confined to turbid water (Randall 1968). The three genera of herring that are apt to be encountered in the clear shallow water of reefs do not include the one (sardines) mentioned as a food item by Collier (1964); even if these three genera were used on Cozumel, their small and delicate bones might not have been preserved. This is probably the case, since Bean (1890:206) reported two members of one of these genera in his survey. The mojarras are usually found on sand or mud bottoms in shallow water, and only three species are reported by Randall (1968) as possibly occurring on or near Caribbean coral reefs. Several different species of mojarra (*Gerres* spp.) were collected by Bean in his 1888 work on the island (Bean 1890:203). Apparently the inhabitants of Cozumel did not like mojarra, or these fish were comparatively scarce on the reef. Finally, there is only one species of anchovy likely to occur inshore over reefs (Randall 1968), and even if this tiny fish were utilized prehistorically, its soft bones would not be preserved archaeologically (especially if this fish was eaten whole, as is done today).

Other fishes known to occur on the island (Bean 1890) that do not appear in the present sample include: trunkfishes (Ostraciontidae), angelfishes (Pomacanthidae), gobies (Gobiidae), and damselfishes (Pomacentridae). None of these is mentioned as a food item by Bean, although he does discuss others that were so utilized on the island in 1888 (Bean 1890:194). Randall (1968:273) refers to only one of these four families, the trunkfishes, as being consumed as food. Nevertheless, he also mentions that these fish secrete a toxic substance that can kill other fishes and that human consumption can result in illness. If the Cozumel fishermen avoided trunkfishes for this reason, they would have been following the same pattern observed above for other species known to cause poisoning.

Fishing Techniques

The nature of the marine fauna recovered from the Cozumel sites suggests that the fishing technology required would not have been complex. Since none of the species present here is primarily pelagic, the majority of them could have been captured easily in relatively shallow inshore waters.

The crabs could have been procured with the use of baited traps, hand lines, dip nets, or spears (Schmitt 1965; Sparling, personal communication, 1976). The sluggish stone crab can even be captured by hand from the holes and crevices in rocks where it often burrows (Schmitt 1965).

Shark fishing would have required only a canoe and some simple equipment, if modern ethnographic reports are any indication. For example, E. H. Thompson (1932) relates the story of a shark fishing expedition in northwestern Yucatán in which he participated some years after his arrival in 1885. In a small dugout canoe, he accompanied two Maya fishermen who managed to capture seven sharks in one night with rudimentary equipment (a lance, two wooden mallets, some large hooks, chains, and long coiled ropes). The mallets and lance were used to dispatch each shark after it had swallowed a hook embedded in bait and after it had been allowed to wear itself out struggling. Borhegyi (1961:280) states that this account was more than just an isolated instance. The fact that two fishermen, armed with primitive fishing gear and wooden mallets, were able to catch seven sharks longer than their own canoe in only a few hours "suggests a well-integrated and probably age-old tradition of shark fishing."

The Maya apparently had two methods for obtaining sea turtles. Wing (1974:187) cites Oviedo's description of the use of dragnets as well as the more common practice of capturing the turtles on the beach when they left the sea to lay their eggs.

Several of the reef fishes found on Cozumel could have been procured either with the use of a hook and line or a spear; these include the moray eels, barracuda, groupers, snappers, and wrasses. Species that do not readily take a hook and would have been more easily caught by spearing, trapping, or the use of nets include the parrotfishes, surgeonfishes, triggerfishes, and the porcupinefish (Randall 1968; Hoese and Moore 1977; Thomson, personal communication, 1979).

The Maya had considerable boat-building expertise; Díaz refers to canoes on the northeast coast of Yucatán capable of holding 40 men (Roys 1943:50; Lange 1971; J. E. S. Thompson 1932). Borhegyi (1961:276) cites an early sixteenth-century description by Peter Martyr of a Maya fishing expedition near Cozumel: "Off the coast of Yucatán and well on the way from the island of Cozumel, the Spaniards encountered a canoe filled with golden hooks." A mural from the Temple of the Warriors at Chichen Itza illustrates boats and fishing activities, as do some scenes on incised bone found in a tomb below Temple I at Tikal (Wing and Hammond 1974). A creel for fish is shown on one of these incised bones, although the nature of the fishing gear is not apparent. Landa refers to the use of trammel nets, sack nets, hooks, harpoons, and bows and arrows (Tozzer 1941:156, 190, 191).

Wing and Hammond (1974) have suggested that the quantities of notched pottery "netsinkers" found at many classic sites (including Lubaantun) imply the use of seine nets. Pohl (1976:273) also refers to Preclassic and Postclassic artifacts identified as netsinkers from the site of Topoxte and Postclassic "fishline weights" found at both Macanche and Barton Ramie, although she acknowledges that the function of these is still a matter of debate. These notched potsherds were also found at the site of Tancah on the east coast of the Yucatán, and they may have been used "with henequen nets to entrap large parrotfish, which congregate near the mouths of the many underwater limestone caves from which fresh water pours into the sea." (Miller 1977:100–101) Shoals of fish come to the mouths of these caves to feed on plant life and are eaten by larger carnivorous fish. Miller (1977) often witnessed the east coast Maya fishermen walking out into the shallow water to the tops of these caves and throwing out a net with sinkers attached to trap the fish. Netsinkers are also found at Xcaret, to the south of Cancun on the east coast, and grooved potsherds matching the description of netsinkers are abundant in other east coast sites dated to the Late Postclassic period (Wing 1974). According to D. Rice, netsinkers occur at Yaxha in the Postclassic (personal communication to Pohl, 1980). Three worked sherds which are probably sinkers appear in the Mayapan artifacts, and at Dzibilchaltun netsinkers are one of the most common artifacts present (Wing 1974).

Netsinkers (*mariposas*) also occurred in great numbers on Cozumel; they represent the most numerous artifact at these sites (see Phillips 1979:246). The Cozumel fishermen probably used some nets in combination with hooks, lines, spears, and possibly fish traps. Many of the reef fishes previously discussed were supposedly obtainable by hook and line or by spearing. Nevertheless, Bean's collecting expedition of 1888 proved that for most of the species he captured on Cozumel, "hook fishing was essentially a failure." (Bean 1890:193) He reported that some species, for example, the queen triggerfish (*Balistes vetula*) and a trunkfish, were caught by angling, and a few by gill nets (two parrotfishes, *Scarus* spp.). His greatest success was obtained using a seine net 25 fathoms (150 ft.) in length. This may be what the island's prehistoric fishermen had already discovered centuries earlier. The overall picture is a fishing strategy on Cozumel characterized by the use of canoes or small boats and the probable deployment of several different fishing methods, depending on the habits of the target species.

Implications for Long-Distance Trade

The exploitation of marine resources may have been undertaken at least partially for the sake of long-distance trade. Roys noted (1943:41) that "fish have always been good and abundant in Yucatán waters, and the people of the coast devoted most of their energy to fishing, both for consumption and for sale to the inhabitants of the interior." Because maize did not grow well there, the chief occupations along the coast were said to be fishing, salt gathering, and commerce (Roys 1943:52–53; Scholes and Roys 1948:170–171). Landa mentions that fishing was a prominent industry in aboriginal Yucatán and he reports that the catch was salted, dried in the sun, or roasted, depending on the kind of fish, and traded over considerable distances (Tozzer 1941:190). Pollock and Ray (1957:650) feel that this may explain the great quantity of saltwater fish bones present at Mayapan, a site located far inland from the sea. Similarly, the great numbers of netsinkers found at Tancah on the east coast of the Yucatán led Miller (1977:101) to infer that the local people were fishing for export, as well as for their own needs.

Cozumel may have been involved in the trade of marine resources, although the evidence is not conclusive. The Postclassic was a period dominated by waterborne trade (Sabloff 1977:71). The Maya made use of the sea's "readily available protein and lanes of easy transport for quantities of bulky and heavy trade goods over long distances." (Miller 1977:97) The Cozumel Archaeological Project has demonstrated the involvement of this island and the coast of Yucatán in the Postclassic maritime trade (Sabloff 1977; Miller 1977). The great number of netsinkers in the Cozumel sites may be indicative of fish trading with the mainland. The abundance of fish and crab remains, however, may only reflect exploitation of the available sea resources for local consumption. The fact that there is no indication of fish drying or preservation activities (since skull elements appear in adequate percentages) tends to cast some doubt on this hypothesis. On the other hand, fish caught for export would not necessarily leave any archaeological evidence if the heads were removed on the beach and discarded in the Caribbean Sea. The remaining body parts would also be absent, since the preserved flesh would have been traded elsewhere. Perhaps some of the marine fish excavated at Mayapan were originally caught on Cozumel.

Ceremonial and Religious Significance of Marine Fauna

Several marine species may have been used for ceremonial or other nonsubsistence purposes. A little more than 14 percent of all shark elements exhibited some kind of cultural modification. Of these, one is a drilled shark's tooth, and the remaining ten are vertebrae with holes drilled through their centers as if for stringing on a necklace or bracelet (see Olsen 1971:4). A similarly drilled fossil shark tooth listed as a "pendant" was reported from a cache at Zacaleu, Guatemala (Woodbury and Trik 1953). An additional five shark's teeth appear in the Cozumel sample. Although these are unmodified, they may be significant, since Landa refers to "very sharp teeth of fishes" being used for arrowheads (Tozzer 1941:121). Presumably, shark's teeth could have served this purpose (Pollock and Ray 1957:652).

Borhegyi (1961) reports that Maya sites are mostly characterized by nonperforated teeth, found either as burial offerings or in offering vases and caches. He believes that their common association with other marine objects, such as sea shells, coral, echinoderms, and stingray spines, suggests ceremonial significance. Further, shark's teeth were used sparingly as ceremonial offerings in the Mexican and Maya area throughout all time periods. They are found as early as the Preclassic at La Venta, all the way up through the late Postclassic at Mayapan (Borhegyi 1961).

The drilled Cozumel shark vertebrae and teeth occur in a variety of contexts. Only three of the elements appear in burials (two unmodified shark's teeth and one drilled vertebra); a total of six drilled vertebrae occur in household midden or rubble fill contexts; the remaining seven were associated with ceremonial and administrative structures (three drilled vertebrae, one drilled tooth, and three unmodified teeth). Use of these items was not necessarily restricted to any one aspect of Cozumel life; they may have played a role in personal adornment as well as in ceremonial or other functions. All the datable proveniences were assigned to the Late Postclassic.

Stingrays were probably not captured for food but were utilized in ceremonial scarifications and bloodletting: to pierce the tongue, nose, ears, and to mutilate the penis (Kidder, Jennings, and Shook 1946:156; Coe 1959:64–66; Thompson 1966:218; Tozzer 1941:190–191; Borhegyi 1961; Lange 1971; Moholy-Nagy 1963; Olsen 1971). As previously mentioned, shark's teeth and stingray spines commonly occur together in caches, burials, or offerings (Borhegyi 1961; Wing and Steadman 1980; Olsen 1972). Borhegyi suggests that the unperforated shark's teeth in Maya sites may also have been used for bloodletting and penitential purposes.

On Cozumel the majority of stingray elements are found in burial contexts (20 out of 26, or 76.9 percent). All but one of the tailspines (88.8 percent) and 12 out of the 17 vertebrae (70.58 percent) occur in burials. In two-thirds of the proveniences where stingray spines occur they are associated with unperforated shark's teeth. Thus the Cozumel stingrays and shark's teeth follow the pattern established for other Maya sites. Nevertheless, the suggestion (Borhegyi 1961:283), that these fish may have been caught by accident, their spines imbedded in shark jaws, does not hold true. If this were so, one would not expect to find stingray vertebrae, especially not in the numbers exhibited by the Cozumel sites.

A pattern emerges if the stingray elements are analyzed by site. Of the eight sites containing fish and crab remains, only two produced stingrays. Most (80.76 percent) come from San Gervasio (C-22), a site comprised primarily of elite residences, administrative complexes, and ceremonial precincts. The remaining tailspines are all from one elite burial at El Cedral (C-15). The other large sites with ceremonial contexts and burials may have contained such elements at one time but may have since been looted, a documented occurrence at some sites. Or perhaps it was only by chance that the burials at other sites with stingrays in them were not excavated. Otherwise, it is difficult to understand why stingrays appear at only two sites.

One feature of the reef fishes is the high proportion (43.4 percent of the MNIs) represented by species possessing distinctive dorsal, caudal, or body spines: the surgeonfish, triggerfishes, and porcupinefish. One wonders whether species other than stingrays were attractive to the Maya for similar reasons. Since these fish are edible, there was probably a dual purpose involved in their selection. That the spines comprise the majority of all elements present for these species certainly is cause for suspicion. The only skeletal element identified from these sites as acanthurid (surgeonfish) is the retractable caudal spine. Other factors contributing to this pattern might be differential preservation (triggerfishes in particular have very heavy, durable spines) and the fact that other skeletal elements are comparatively undiagnostic.

Besides their use as ceremonial objects, fish apparently played a symbolic role in the counting system and in Maya religion. Thompson (1944) discusses the appearance of fish and fish heads in Maya glyphs (in the Dresden Codex, sculpture, ceramics, and elsewhere) and concludes that the animal was used as a symbol for counting. Linguistic evidence lends support to this hypothesis. The Maya word for counting is *xoc* (or *xooc*), but in Yucatec the word also appears to stand for an ill-defined group of large fish (especially sharks) or whales (Roys 1933). Thompson (1944:3–4) notes that some of the glyphs display the prominent serrated teeth and elongated snouts characteristic of sharks. Since the traits of these fish glyphs are variable, he states that *xoc* probably does not represent any one species (or group) of fish but was more likely "a large mythological creature with no immutable characteristics, and with a tendency to become anthropomorphized." (Thompson 1944:17)

Landa refers to the religious significance of fish, and he describes a number of deities and rituals related to this group of animals (Tozzer 1941:155–156). Landa writes of fishermen anointing their implements prior to a fishing expedition, and he refers to sacrifices and offerings made by fishermen at a shrine before putting out to sea. Roys (1943) mentions temples near the seashore frequented by hunters and fishermen. Of interest here is his reference to fishing shrines on Cozumel as well as on the east coast of Yucatán (Roys 1943:19). Lange (1971:633) feels that the positioning of another temple on Cozumel purportedly in honor of the rain god suggests that there was a much closer relationship between Maya water deities and maritime concerns than previously thought. The water these deities symbolized and cared for may not just have been rain but the sea as well.

The moon goddess Ixchel also shared a central position on Cozumel with Chac and the fishing deities. She was a prominent deity (especially for the east coast Maya) and was associated with the moon, childbirth, procreation, weaving, medicine, shells, and water in general (Miller 1977; Lange 1971), all these associations having to do with the concept of renewal. Since the moon rises in the east and appears to be born out of the sea, it is logical that this astronomical association of the moon goddess should be most important on the east coast of Yucatán. Pregnant women consulted the Ixchel idol on Cozumel where there was a major shrine to the moon goddess. According to Miller (1977:107), "When a child is born, it emerges from an interior world of its mother. Perhaps the association of a newborn child and the moon seemingly reborn out of the belly of the earth in the eastern sky was a part of the metaphorical Maya belief in the association of the new moon with birth." Since the Maya devoted considerable effort to tracking the cycles of the moon and were accomplished in the field of astronomy, they were probably familiar with the moon's tidal effects, a crucial factor in fishing and seafaring. Thus at least part of the moon deity's significance to the Maya may have derived from maritime associations (Lange 1971:633).

Summary

The large and diverse sample of reef fishes, sharks, stingrays, sea turtles, and crabs excavated from Cozumel lends weight to the hypothesis that the Maya relied on marine resources in the Late Postclassic. The nutritional impact of these fauna, particularly the sharks and reef fishes, was significant to the Cozumel Maya. The technology required to procure these typical reef-dwelling species was not complex; the fishermen probably depended mainly on nets or hooks and lines. Large numbers of netsinkers found in these sites support this assumption and may also imply the involvement of fish in Cozumel's long-distance trade network. Cultural preferences, the avoidance of species that can cause poisoning, and the ceremonial use of some elements all appear to have influenced the selection of marine resources.

References

Ball, Joseph W., and Jack D. Eaton
   1972   "Marine Resources and the Prehistoric
           Lowland Maya: A Comment," *American
           Anthropologist* 74.3:772–776.

Bean, Tarleton H.
   1890   "Notes on Fishes Collected at Cozumel,
           Yucatan, by the U.S. Fish Commission,
           with descriptions of New Species," *Bulletin
           of the U.S. Fish Commission* vol. 8 for
           1888, no. 4:193–206.

Bökönyi, S.
   1970   "A New Method for the Determination of
           the Number of Individuals in Animal Bone
           Material," *American Journal of Ar-
           chaeology* 74:291–292.

Borhegyi, Stephan F. De
   1961   "Shark Teeth, Stingray Spines, and Shark
           Fishing in Ancient Mexico and Central
           America," *Southwestern Journal of An-
           thropology* 17.3:273–296.

Coe, Michael, and Kent V. Flannery
   1967   *Early Cultures and Human Ecology in
           South Coastal Guatemala.* Smithsonian
           Contribution to Anthropology 3. Smith-
           sonian Press, Washington, D.C.

Coe, William R.
   1959   *Piedras Negras Archaeology: Artifacts,
           Caches, and Burials.* Museum Monographs,
           The University Museum, Philadelphia.

Collier, Albert
   1964   "The American Mediterranean." In *Hand-
           book of Middle American Indians*, edited
           by Robert Wauchope. University of Texas
           Press, Austin, I, 122–142.

Cutting, C. L.
   1962   "The Influence of Drying, Salting, and
           Smoking on the Nutritive Value of Fish."
           In *Fish in Nutrition*, edited by Eirik Heen
           and Rudolf Kreuzer. Food and Agriculture
           Organization of the United Nations,
           Technology Branch, Fisheries Division.
           Fishing News (Books), London, pp. 161–
           179.

Driver, H.
   1961   *Indians of North America.* University of
           Chicago Press.

Gans, Carl
   1975   *Reptiles of the World.* Ridge Press (Bantam
           Books), New York.

Grayson, Donald K.
   1973   "On the Methodology of Faunal Analysis,"
           American Antiquity 39.4:432–439.

Guha, B. C.
   1962   "The Role of Fish in Human Nutrition." In
           Fish in Nutrition, edited by Eirik Heen and
           Rudolf Kreuzer. Food and Agriculture
           Organization of the United Nations,
           Technology Branch, Fisheries Division.
           Fishing News (Books) London, pp. 39–42.

Hale, H. Stephen
   1977   "Quarterly Report on the Development of a
           Key for the Identification of Shark Species
           on the Basis of Variation in Vertebrate
           Morphology." Manuscript on file at the
           Florida State Museum, Gainesville.

Hamblin, N.
   1984   *Animal Use by the Cozumel Maya.* Univer-
           sity of Arizona Press, Tucson.

Hoese, H. Dickson, and Richard H. Moore
   1977   *Fishes of the Gulf of Mexico, Texas,
           Louisiana, and Adjacent Waters.* Texas
           A&M University Press, College Station.

Johannes, Robert E.
   1976   "Life and Death of the Reef," *Review*
           (December 1976). Reprinted from *Audubon*
           1976.

Kidder, Alfred V., Jesse D. Jennings, and
Edwin H. Shook
   1946   *Excavations at Kaminaljuyu, Guatemala.*
           Carnegie Institution of Washington 561.

Kuhnau, Joachim
   1962   "Importance of Minor Elements in Food,
           Especially in Fish." In *Fish in Nutrition*,
           edited by Eirik Heen and Rudolf Kreuzer.
           Food and Agriculture Organization of the
           United Nations, Technology Branch,
           Fisheries Division. Fishing News (Books),
           London, pp. 298–300.

Lange, Frederick W.
   1971   "Marine Resources: A Viable Subsistence
           Alternative for the Prehistoric Lowland
           Maya," *American Anthropologist*
           73.3:619–639.

Lowe-McConnell, R. H.
   1977   *Ecology of Fishes in Tropical Waters.* The
           Institute of Biology's Studies in Biology 76.
           Edward Arnold, London.

Mayer, Jean
   1962   "Fish Proteins in Nutrition and Their Im-
           portance in the Prevention of Protein
           Malnutrition." In *Fish in Nutrition*, edited
           by Eirik Heen and Rudolf Kreuzer. Food
           and Agriculture Organization of the United
           Nations, Technology Branch, Fisheries
           Division. Fishing News (Books), London,
           pp. 248–256.

Miller, Arthur G.
1977   "The Maya and the Sea: Trade and Cult at Tancah and Tulum, Quintana Roo, Mexico." In *The Sea in the Pre-Columbian World*, edited by Elizabeth P. Benson. Dumbarton Oaks, Trustees for Harvard University, Washington, pp. 97–138.

Moholy-Nagy, Hattula
1963   "Shells and Other Marine Material from Tikal," *Estudios de Cultura Maya* 3:65–85.

Olsen, Stanley J.
1971   *Zooarchaeology: Animal Bones in Archaeology and their Interpretation.* Addison-Wesley, Reading, Mass.

1972   "Animal Remains from Altar de Sacrificios." In *The Artifacts of Altar de Sacrificios*, by Gordon R. Willey. Peabody Museum Papers, vol. 64, no. 1, Harvard University, pp. 243–246.

Phillips, David A.
1979   "Material Culture and Trade of the Postclassic Maya." Ph.D. dissertation, University of Arizona, Tucson.

Pohl, Mary E. D.
1976   "Ethnozoology of the Maya: An Analysis of Fauna from Five Sites in the Peten, Guatemala." Ph.D. dissertation, Harvard University.

Pollock, H. E. D., and Clayton E. Ray
1957   *Notes on Vertebrate Animal Remains from Mayapan.* Carnegie Institution of Washington Report 41, Washington, D.C., pp. 633–656.

Pope, Clifford H.
1964   *The Reptile World.* Alfred A. Knopf, New York.

Pritchard, Peter C. H.
1967   *Living Turtles of the World.* TFH Publications, Neptune City, N.J.

Randall, John E.
1968   *Caribbean Reef Fishes.* TFH Publications, Hong Kong.

Roys, R. L.
1933   *The Book of Chilam Balam of Chumayel.* Carnegie Institution of Washington 438.

1943   *The Indian Background of Colonial Yucatan.* Carnegie Institution of Washington 548.

Sabloff, Jeremy A.
1977   "Old Myths, New Myths: The Role of Sea Traders in the Development of Ancient Maya Civilization." In *The Sea in the Pre-Columbian World*, edited by Elizabeth P. Benson. Dumbarton Oaks, Trustees for Harvard University, Washington, D.C., pp. 67–88.

Schmitt, Waldo L.
1965   *Crustaceans.* University of Michigan Press, Ann Arbor.

Scholes, F. V., and R. L. Roys
1948   *The Maya Chontal Indians of Acalan-Tixchel.* Carnegie Institution of Washington 560.

Sever, Lowell E.
1975   "Zinc and Human Development: A Review," *Human Ecology*, 3.1:43–57.

Stansby, Maurice E.
1962   "Proximate Composition of Fish." In *Fish in Nutrition*, edited by Eirik Heen and Rudolf Kreuzer. Food and Agriculture Organization of the United Nations Technology Branch, Fisheries Division. Fishing News (Books), London, pp. 55–60.

Stephens, John Lloyd
1841   *Incidents of Travel in Central America, Chiapas, and Yucatan.* Vol. 2. Harper and Brothers, New York.

Street, Philip
1966   *The Crab and Its Relatives.* Faber and Faber, London.

Thompson, Edward H.
1932   *People of the Serpent: Life and Adventure Among the Mayas.* Houghton Mifflin, Boston.

Thompson, J. Eric S.
1932   *The Civilization of the Mayas.* Field Museum of Natural History, Chicago.

1944   *The Fish as a Maya Symbol for Counting and Further Discussion of Directional Glyphs.* Carnegie Institution of Washington, Division of Historical Research, Cambridge, Mass.

1958   *Thomas Gage's Travels in the New World.* University of Oklahoma Press, Norman.

1966   *The Rise and Fall of Maya Civilization.* Rev. ed. University of Oklahoma Press, Norman.

Tozzer, Alfred M.
1941   *Landa's Relación de las Cosas de Yucatán.* Peabody Museum Papers, vol. 18, Harvard University.

Vokes, Arthur W.
1978   "They Don't Make Them Like They Used To." Paper presented to the 43rd annual meeting of the Society for American Archaeology, Tucson.

Wing, Elizabeth S.
1974   "Vertebrate Faunal Remains." In *Excavation of an Early Shell Midden on Isla Cancun, Quintana Roo, Mexico*, by E. Wyllys Andrews IV et al. Tulane University, Middle American Research Institute 31. pp. 186–188.

1975 "Animal Remains from Lubaantun." In *Lubaantun: A Classic Maya Realm*, by Norman Hammond. Peabody Museum Monograph, no. 2, Harvard University, pp. 379–383.

Wing, Elizabeth S., and Norman Hammond
1974 "Fish Remains in Archaeology: A Comment on Casteel," *American Antiquity* 39.1:133–134.

Wing, Elizabeth S., and D. Steadman
1980 "Vertebrate Faunal Remains from Dzibilchaltun," In *Excavations at Dzibilchaltun, Yucatan, Mexico. E. W. Andrews IV and E. W. Andrews V. Tulane University, Middle American Research Institute 48.*

Woodbury, Richard B., and Aubrey S. Trik
1953 *The Ruins of Zacaleu, Guatemala*. Vols. I and II. United Fruit Co., William Byrd Press, Richmond, Va.

Wright, N. Pelham
1970 *A Guide to Mexican Mammals and Reptiles*. Minutiae Mexicana Series, Mexico City.

Chapter 12

Isla Cozumel Archaeological Avifauna

Nancy L. Hamblin and Amadeo M. Rea

Ethnohistoric accounts dating to the time of the Spanish conquest describe Cozumel as a port on a long-distance trade network and record that pilgrims traveled to the famous Ixchel shrine located on the island. Excavations conducted by Sabloff and Rathje in 1972 and 1973 have greatly enhanced our knowledge of this Late Postclassic florescence with its distinctive commercial orientation and have demonstrated that Cozumel's ritual and merchantile role began much earlier. The faunal remains provide evidence for far-flung contacts as well as for the status of wealthy traders.

Amadeo M. Rea is curator of birds and mammals, San Diego Natural History Museum, California. See chapter 11 for Nancy L. Hamblin's affiliation.

The research for this paper was funded by two grants. One from the National Geographic Society provided support for the computer analysis and travel funds from Tucson, Arizona, to Cozumel, Mexico, for field research. A grant-in-aid-of-research from Sigma Xi, the Scientific Research Society of North America, contributed travel funds so that comparative work with other ornithology collections could be done.

Thanks are due to William L. Rathje and Jeremy A. Sabloff, whose excavations on Cozumel made the present work possible. Stanley J. Olsen provided many helpful suggestions throughout the course of this research. Interpretation of the soil sample results was aided by Ted McCreary, head of the University of Arizona Soils, Water, and Plant Tissue Testing Laboratory (College of Agriculture, Department of Soils, Water, and Engineering).

We identified the avian remains with the use of comparative material from the National Park Service collection (Western Archaeological Center, Tucson, Arizona) the University of Arizona Department of Ecology and Evolutionary Biology, Tucson and the U.S. National Museum, Washington, D.C., as well as the collections of Pierce Brodkorb (Gainesville, Florida), Lyndon L. Hargrave (Prescott, Arizona), and Amadeo M. Rea (University of Arizona, Tucson, at the time identifications were made).

Discussion

Six different sites on the island are represented by the bird bone material (table 12.2). As is true of all the Cozumel sites, each has an elite residential and administrative complex (Rathje and Sabloff 1975b:137). There are formal plaza groups at five of these sites: one at La Expedición, one at Zuuk, one at Buena Vista, three at El Cedral, and seven at San Gervasio. These usually contain masonry architecture palaces, temples and shrines. As is typical of the Lowland Maya at other sites, the data suggest that they were used exclusively for elite residential and civil-administrative functions (Freidel and Leventhal 1975:70). All but one of these six sites (San Miguel) contain stone foundations or perishable features tentatively identified as dwellings (Freidel and Leventhal 1975:67). It is notable, however, that nearly all the bird bone in our sample comes from elite contexts, either residential or ceremonial.

The outstanding feature of this assemblage is the variety of birds present in these six sites. Thirty-eight different taxa are represented by the avian remains, 30 of which are determinations to at least the generic level, and only 13 bones out of the total 377 (or 3.4 percent) are totally unidentified (table 12.1). A survey of the literature reveals that no other Lowland Maya archaeological site has anywhere near the variety represented in its avifauna and generally not the volume of bird bone encountered here (Olsen 1972; Olsen 1978; Wing 1974; Wing and Steadman 1980; Wing 1975; Woodbury and Trik 1953; Pohl 1976). Even in a site such as Mayapan, which produced a very large avian collection (more than 1,100 identified bird bones), only eight different taxa are represented (Pollock and Ray 1957). This diversity holds true when the total faunal collection is examined. Cozumel contained 20,649 specimens representing at least 77 different species, while the fewer than 7,000 bones from Mayapan comprised some 53 species (Pollock and Ray 1957). The Cozumel sites are characterized by a relatively high dependence on fishes and crabs (over 40 percent of the minimum number of individuals, MNIs), very few deer (less than 1 percent), and a comparatively high utilization of reptiles (nearly 25 percent). Thus it appears one cannot make generaliza-

Table 12.1. Total MNIs and bone counts of Cozumel birds.

Taxon	No. of bones	% of bones	MNI	% of MNI
Sula leucogaster (brown booby)	1	0.3	1	1.2
cf. *Fregata magnificens* (magnificent frigatebird)	1	0.3	–	–
Ardea cf. *herodias* (great blue heron)	2	0.5	1	1.2
Ardea (Hydranassa) tricolor (Louisiana heron)	2	0.5	1	1.2
Dichromanassa rufescens (reddish egret)	10	2.7	1	1.2
Nycticorax (Nyctanassa) violaceus (yellow-crowned night heron)	1	0.3	1	1.2
Mycteria americana (wood stork)	5	1.3	1	1.2
cf. *Mycteria americana* (wood stork)	1	0.3	–	–
Accipiter bicolor (bicolored hawk)	1	0.3	1	1.2
Buteo cf. *magnirostris* (roadside hawk)	2	0.5	1	1.2
Galliformes	3	0.8	–	–
Large Galliformes	88	23.3	–	–
cf. Large Galliformes	7	1.9	–	–
Cracidae	2	0.5	–	–
cf. Cracidae	2	0.5	–	–
Crax rubra (great curassow)	28	7.4	14	17.2
Crax sp.	4	1.1	2	2.5
cf. *Crax* sp.	2	0.5	–	–
cf. *Dactylortyx thoracicus* (singing quail)	1	0.3	–	–
Gallus gallus (domestic chicken)	3	0.8	3	3.7
cf. *Gallus gallus* (domestic chicken)	1	0.3	–	–
Meleagridinae	14	3.7	–	–
cf. Meleagridinae	2	0.5	–	–
Meleagris gallopavo (domestic turkey)	46	12.2	12	14.8

Table 12.1 (continued).

Taxon	No. of bones	% of bones	MNI	% of MNI
cf. *Meleagris gallopavo* (domestic turkey)	8	2.1	-	-
Meleagris (Agriocharis) ocellata (ocellated turkey)	54	14.3	15	18.5
cf. *M. (Agriocharis) ocellata* (ocellated turkey)	10	2.7	-	-
Porphyrula martinica (purple gallinule)	1	0.3	1	1.2
Fulica americana (American coot)	1	0.3	1	1.2
Charadriiformes	1	0.3	-	-
Tringa cf. *melanoleuca* (greater yellowlegs)	1	0.3	1	1.2
Columbiformes	5	1.3	-	-
cf. Columbiformes	9	2.4	-	-
Columbidae	1	0.3	-	-
Columba leucocephala (white-crowned pigeon)	1	0.3	1	1.2
cf. *Columba leucocephala* (white-crowned pigeon)	2	0.5	-	-
Columba sp.	5	1.3	4	5.0
cf. *Columba* sp.	1	0.3	-	-
cf. Psittaciformes	1	0.3	-	-
Ara cf. *militaris* (green or military macaw)	1	0.3	1	1.2
Ara macao (scarlet macaw)	12	3.2	4	5.0
Ara sp. (macaw)	1	0.3	1	1.2
Aratinga sp. (parakeet)	1	0.3	1	1.2
Amazona xantholora (yellow-lored parrot)	4	1.1	2	2.5
Amazona cf. *xantholora* (yellow-lored parrot)	1	0.3	1	1.2
cf. *Amazona xantholora* (yellow-lored parrot)	3	0.8	-	-
Tyto alba (barn owl)	1	0.3	1	1.2
Celeus cf. *castaneus* (chestnut-colored woodpecker)	1	0.3	1	1.2

Table 12.1 (continued).

Taxon	No. of bones	% of bones	MNI	% of MNI
Scaphidura (Psomocolax) oryzivora (giant cowbird)	2	0.5	2	2.5
Quiscalus (Cassidix) mexicanus (great-tailed grackle)	5	1.3	4	5.0
cf. *Quiscalus (Cass.) mexicanus* (great-tailed grackle)	1	0.3	–	–
Quiscalus (Cassidix) sp. (grackle)	1	0.3	1	1.2
Marine bird	1	0.3	–	–
Large non-galliform bird	2	0.5	–	–
Large bird	3	0.8	–	–
Medium-large bird	2	0.5	–	–
Medium-small bird	2	0.5	–	–
Small bird	3	0.8	–	–
TOTAL	377	100.5	81	99.5

tions about Maya economy on the basis of the few sites whose fauna have been studied so far.

Second, the Cozumel sites appear to be the first to produce the common turkey, *Meleagris gallopavo*, in archaeological context in the Maya Lowlands. Until now, only the ocellated turkey, *Meleagris (Agriocharis) ocellata*, had been identified from Maya sites in the region (Schorger 1966:8; Steadman 1980). On Cozumel common turkeys are present at four sites, and perhaps at a fifth (one bone = cf. *Meleagris gallopavo*), always accompanying ocellated turkeys in the same contexts. The northern species (*M. gallopavo*) is represented by 46 bones, indicating at least 12 distinct individuals in many different proveniences, too many to be due to chance or intrusion. The identification of these bones was accomplished with the aid of Lyndon L. Hargrave's excellent collection in Prescott, Arizona, from which approximately a dozen individual skeletons of both turkey species were used for comparative purposes.

The third major result of this study has been to confirm the presence of a long-distance trade network between Cozumel and other parts of Mexico and Central America. The presence of the common turkey (*M. gallopavo*) would indicate contact with central Mexico, if only indirectly, since the original range of the bird did not extend beyond the Isthmus of Tehuantepec (Schorger 1966), and some sources indicate no farther

south than Michoacan in western Mexico and central Veracruz on the east (Leopold 1959). (See Aldrich's and Duvall's 1955 specimen maps.)

Three species of macaw are present in these sites, none of which is native to the island. The scarlet macaw (*Ara macao*) is a rain forest species of southern Mexico, not even found on the Yucatán Peninsula (Paynter 1955), and thus unquestionably a trade item on Cozumel. It is represented by 12 bones from at least four individuals. There is one bone that is probably a military macaw (*Ara* cf. *militaris*), a wide-ranging northern Mexican species, presumably a trade item, since it is "absent from humid forests of the Caribbean lowlands" (Forshaw 1973). The element presently designated as *Ara* sp. is osteologically distinct from either the military or scarlet macaws; it may be *Ara ambigua* (a Central American species) and thus a trade item, although it is possibly also an extinct or previously undescribed non-Yucatecan species. In addition, there is one parakeet bone (*Aratinga* sp.), which is not the species common on the Yucatán Peninsula (*Aratinga astec*) nor *A. holochlora*, a larger species of the Caribbean and Pacific lowlands. It too represents either a trade item or an extinct species.

Besides the three findings already discussed, the Cozumel avifauna can be used to examine several other specific areas of interest. It is possible to compare the exploitation of avifauna by the several sites in terms of differing utilization of ecological zones and to examine the relative significance of various birds in the Cozumel diet. The use of certain avian species for ceremonial and religious and other nonfood purposes, the distribution of skeletal elements, and the time periods in which they occur are also discussed.

Utilization of Ecological Zones

An examination of the species found at each site (tables 12.2, 12.3) shows that they have two things in common. One is the presence at all six sites of species that characteristically inhabit old rain forest. The great curassow (*Crax rubra*), which occurs in five of the sites, requires old rain forest, secluded portions of dense, undisturbed, humid tropical forest (Edwards 1972; Blake 1953; Peterson and Chalif 1973). These conditions are not present on the island now, and the endemic Cozumel race of the species (*Crax rubra griscomi*) is considered "on the very brink of extinction" if not already gone (Paynter 1955; Delacour and Amadon 1973). Maya agricultural practices over a long period of time have resulted in a gradual habitat modification. Further support for this habitat change comes from San Miguel (C-13), the only site without the curassow. Here two other rain forest species appear, the bicolored hawk (*Accipiter bicolor*) and the chestnut-colored woodpecker (*Celeus* cf. *castaneus*[1]); neither of these occurs on the island today.

The other factor common to all the sites is the presence, and usually the predominance, of turkeys. At all but two sites, Zuuk (C-31) and Buena Vista (C-18), both common and ocellated turkeys occur together. The lack of *M. gallopavo* at these two sites may be only an artifact of the small sample size — 11 bones from Buena Vista, and only 5 from Zuuk. Neither of the two turkeys appears to be native to the island; as previously mentioned, *M. gallopavo* must have been imported originally from the pine-oak uplands of central Mexico (Leopold 1959). The ocellated turkey, however, occurs on the Yucatán Peninsula and inhabits open deciduous forest, savannas, *milpas*, and other clearings, as well as the edges (but not the interior) of dense rain forest (Paynter 1955). Once brought to the island from the mainland, this species would have flourished, since these are the environmental conditions that obtain on Cozumel (now and apparently in the Late Postclassic as well) (Sabloff and Rathje 1975).

If we examine each site in detail (table 12.2), we find that four of them appear to contain birds from only half of the available habitats on the island, disregarding the nonnative species such as the turkeys.

San Miguel (C-13) exhibits two rain forest birds (the hawk and the woodpecker) and an unidentified marine species. El Cedral (C-15) yields one old rain forest species (the curassow) and possibly one from the woods and fields ecotone (one bone is questionably a parrot, cf. Psittaciformes). Buena Vista (C-18) contains the curassow (old rain forest species), and two birds that require woods and fields ecotone — a pigeon (Columbidae) and the roadside hawk (*Buteo* cf. *magnirostris*). Zuuk (C-31) also exhibits the curassow and a pigeon (Columbiformes, woods and fields ecotone).

The other two sites yield birds that cover the entire spectrum of habitats on the island. From San Gervasio (C-22) come four birds inhabiting beach and stream areas (*Tringa* cf. *melanoleuca*, a sandpiper; *Porphyrula martinica*, purple gallinule; *Fulica americana*, American coot; and *Ardea tricolor*, Louisiana heron); five species requiring the woods and fields ecotone (cf. *Dactylortyx thoracicus*, singing quail; *Columba leucocephala*, white-crowned pigeon; *Amazona xantholora*, yellow lored parrot; *Tyto alba*, barn owl; and *Quiscalus mexicanus*, great-tailed grackle); one old rain forest bird, the curassow (*C. rubra*); and one marine species, the magnificent frigatebird (cf. *Fregata magnificens*). Similarly, the site of La Expedición (C-25) also yields four species from the beach and stream habitat (*Ardea* cf. *herodias*, great blue heron; *Dichromanassa rufescens*, reddish egret; *Mycteria americana*, wood stork; and *Nycticorax violaceus*, yellow-crowned night heron); four birds inhabiting the woods and fields ecotone (*Columba* sp., a pigeon; *Amazona xantholora*, yellow-lored parrot; *Scaphidura oryzivora*, Giant Cowbird; and *Quiscalus* sp., a grackle); the curassow (*C. rubra*) requiring old rain forest; and one marine species (*Sula leucogaster*, brown booby).

The extraordinary variety in terms of the number of different habitats utilized and the number of species involved is a radical departure from the situation at the other four sites. The variety cannot be explained in terms of differential access to environmental zones, since La Expedición is a northeast coastal site on the island, whereas San Gervasio is a north-central interior site, away from the coast. The other four sites are similarly varied: two are coastal, and two are interior. Besides, the island is small, a minimum of 24 mi. long by 8 mi. wide. Inhabitants of all the sites would easily have been able to obtain birds from all habitats. Sample size cannot totally account for this variety either, since El Cedral, which has the largest bird bone sample (133 bones), is the site where only two habitat zones were being utilized.

The explanation must be cultural. This conclusion is supported by the fact that the two sites with the largest variety of bird species, San Gervasio and La Expedición, are two of the largest and most culturally

---

1. Where the scientific name is referred to genus or species (*Celeus* cf. *castaneus*, etc.), the English name should also be understood to be referred.

Table 12.2. Distribution of Cozumel birds by site.

Taxon	No. of bones	MNI
SITE C-13		
Gallus gallus	1	1
cf. *Gallus gallus*	1	–
Meleagris (Agriocharis) ocellata	23	1
cf. *Meleagris (Agriocharis) ocellata*	1	–
Accipiter bicolor	1	1
Celeus castaneus	1	1
Meleagridinae	1	–
cf. *Meleagris gallopavo*	1	–
Indeterminate marine bird	1	–
Indeterminate large bird	1	–
SUBTOTAL	32	4
SITE C-15		
Large Galliformes	75	–
Meleagridinae	1	–
Meleagris gallopavo	30	4
Meleagris (Agriocharis) ocellata	6	3
cf. *Meleagris (Agriocharis) ocellata*	3	–
Crax rubra	12	3
Crax sp.	3	1
cf. Psittaciformes	1	–
Indeterminate medium–small bird	2	–
SUBTOTAL	133	11
SITE C-18		
Large Galliformes	1	–
Meleagridinae	1	–
Meleagris (Agriocharis) ocellata	1	1
cf. *Meleagris (Agriocharis) ocellata*	1	–
Crax rubra	3	2
Columbidae	1	–
Buteo cf. *magnirostris*	2	1

Table 12.2 (continued).

Taxon	No. of bones	MNI
Indeterminate large bird	1	–
SUBTOTAL	11	4
SITE C-22		
Tyto alba	1	1
Tringa cf. *melanoleuca*	1	1
Porphyrula martinica	1	1
Fulica americana	1	1
cf. *Fregata magnificens*	1	–
Ardea tricolor	2	1
Amazona xantholora	1	1
Amazona cf. *xantholora*	1	1
Aratinga sp.	1	1
Cassidix mexicanus	5	4
cf. *Cassidix mexicanus*	1	–
Columbiformes	3	–
cf. Columbiformes	8	–
Columba sp.	4	3
cf. *Columba* sp.	1	–
Columba leucocephala	1	1
cf. *Columba leucocephala*	2	–
Charadriiformes	1	–
Large Galliformes	3	–
Galliformes	1	–
cf. large Galliformes	7	–
Crax rubra	7	6
Crax sp.	1	1
Cracidae	2	–
cf. *Crax* sp.	1	–
cf. *Dactylortyx thoracicus*	1	–
Meleagrididae	8	–
cf. Meleagridinae	1	–

Table 12.2 (continued)

Taxon	No. of bones	MNI
Meleagris gallopavo	11	6
cf. *Meleagris gallopavo*	6	–
Meleagris (Agriocharis) ocellata	15	4
cf. *Meleagris (Agriocharis) ocellata*	2	–
Gallus gallus	2	2
Indeterminate small bird	3	–
Indeterminate medium-large bird	2	–
Indeterminate non-galliform bird	1	–
Indeterminate large bird	1	–
SUBTOTAL	111	35
SITE C-25		
Sula leucogaster	1	1
Ardea cf. *herodias*	2	1
Dichromanassa rufescens	10	1
Mycteria americana	5	1
cf. *Mycteria americana*	1	–
Ara cf. *militaris*	1	1
Ara macao	12	4
Ara sp.	1	1
Amazona xantholora	3	1
cf. *Amazona xantholora*	3	–
Nycticorax sp.	1	1
Scaphidura oryzivora	2	2
Cassidix sp.	1	1
Columbiformes	1	–
Columba sp.	1	1
Large Galliformes	9	–
Galliformes	2	–
Meleagridinae	3	–
cf. Meleagrididae	1	–
Meleagris gallopavo	5	2

Table 12.2 (continued).

Taxon	No. of bones	MNI
cf. *Meleagris gallopavo*	1	–
Meleagris (Agriocharis) ocellata	9	6
cf. *Meleagris (Agriocharis) ocellata*	2	–
Crax rubra	6	3
cf. *Crax* sp.	1	–
Indeterminate large non-galliform bird	1	–
SUBTOTAL	85	27
SITE C-31		
Columbiformes	1	–
cf. Columbiformes	1	–
cf. *Meleagris (Agriocharis) ocellata*	1	–
cf. Cracidae	2	–
SUBTOTAL	5	–
TOTAL	377	81

important sites on the island. San Gervasio was the major interior settlement throughout the history of Cozumel serving as the island's capital. It was an administrative center, a cult center for the oracle, and in the Late Postclassic, a residential and commercial district (Freidel 1976:339).

La Expedición was the dominant religious center on the northeastern coast. The quantity and design of its community temples reflects a concern for religious ritual. This site appears to have been a true ceremonial center, designed for festivals participated in by local people or by the transient foreign pilgrims. Its formal plaza group complements San Gervasio's administrative center (Freidel 1976:275). Festivals may have been a medium for the transmission of political and economic policy; those at La Expedición could have provided an effective mechanism for disseminating information from the capital of San Gervasio to the northeast coast communities as well as a means of solidifying bonds between this subregion of the island and the capital (Freidel 1976:275). Thus these two sites appear to have been linked together and probably represent the two most significant sites on the island in terms of elite ceremonial and civil administrative functions. It seems that the avifauna reflects this interpretation.

Relative Dietary Importance of Various Avian Species

The determination of which fauna at an archaeological site represent food species is always difficult. Only one bone (an ocellated turkey) in the entire avian collection showed butchering marks so this approach is of limited utility in confirming or rejecting possible food species. What we have done here is to select those birds for which there are some ethnographic data to support their use as food and to include those that have a fair amount of usable meat. Those that were probably or possibly used mainly for ceremonial and religious or other cultural purposes were eliminated. Since we may be excluding some birds that were consumed (in addition to their primary uses in clothing decoration, ritual), this list should be considered conservative. The birds we regard as probable food species on Cozumel are: the curassow (*C. rubra*), the singing quail (cf. *D. thoracicus*), the domestic chicken (*Gallus gallus*, which is probably a modern intrusion), the common turkey (*M. gallopavo*), the ocellated turkey (*M. ocellata*), the white-crowned pigeon (*C. leucocephala*), other pigeons (*Columba* sp.) and the blackbirds (*S. oryzivora*, giant cowbird; *Q. mexicanus*, great-tailed grackle; and *Quiscalus* sp.).

Table 12.3. Habitats of Cozumel birds.

Taxon	Marine	Beach and stream	Woods/ fields ecotone	Old rain- forest	Domestic or trade	Intrusive
Sula leucogaster (brown booby)	X					
cf. *Fregata magnificens* (magnificent frigatebird)	X	X				
Ardea cf. *herodias* (great blue heron)		X				
Ardea (Hydranassa) tricolor (Louisiana heron)		X				
Dichromanassa rufescens (reddish egret)		X				
Nycticorax (Nyctanassa) violaceus (yellow-crowned night heron)		X				
Mycteria americana (wood stork)		X				
Accipiter bicolor (bicolored hawk)[a]				X		
Buteo cf. *magnirostris* (roadside hawk)			X			
Crax rubra (great curassow)[b]				X		
cf. *Dactylortyx thoracicus* (singing quail)[a,b]			X	X	?	
Gallus gallus (domestic chicken)[b]						X
Meleagris gallopavo (domestic turkey)[b]					X	
Meleagris (Agriocharis) ocellata (ocellated turkey)[b]					X	
Porphyrula martinica (purple gallinule)		X				
Fulica americana (American coot)		X				
Tringa cf. *melanoleuca* (greater yellowlegs)		X				

Table 12.3 (continued).

Taxon	Marine	Beach and stream	Woods/ fields ecotone	Old rain- forest	Domestic or trade	Intrusive
Columba leucocephala (white-crowned pigeon)[b]			X			
Columba sp. (pigeons)[b]			X			
Ara sp. (macaws)					X	
Ara cf. *militaris* (green or military macaw)					X	
Ara macao (scarlet macaw)					X	
Aratinga sp. (parakeet)					X	
Amazona xantholora (yellow-lored parrot)			X			
Tyto alba (barn owl)[a]			X			
Celeus castaneus (chestnut-colored woodpecker)[a]				X		
Scaphidura oryzivora (giant cowbird)[a]			X			
Quiscalus (Cassidix) mexicanus (great-tailed grackle)[b]			X			
Quiscalus (Cassidix) sp. (grackle)[b]			X			

a. Apparently not part of modern avifauna (Paynter 1955).

b. Probable food species.

An examination of each site reveals that these food species represent 51–100 percent of all the bird bones present, with an overall average of 82 percent (table 12.4). Thus most of the avian remains on the island seem to represent exploitation of these animals for food. Galliform birds are the most important avian food items at every site. The galliform group includes both species of turkeys, the curassow, the chicken, and the quail. These species represent 60–100 percent of all the avian food bone, for an average of 84.6 percent overall. Within this group, turkeys are the most abundant (averaging 45.7 percent overall), followed by the curassow, which averages 23.3 percent in the five sites where it occurs. Quail apparently was not a significant food item. Only one quail bone (cf. *D. thoracicus*) appears (at San Gervasio).

The four chicken bones (from two different sites) are too few to represent a real food source, but their presence in itself is noteworthy. Carter (1971) suggested, primarily on the basis of linguistic similarities and comparative diffusion rates, that one or more races of chicken were present in Central and South America before the time of European contact. Serious doubt is cast on this theory by the fact that chicken remains rarely appear in archaeological sites. The four bones that occur in the Cozumel material are the only ones, to our knowledge, excavated from prehistoric Maya sites. If chickens were as common and widespread in pre-Hispanic Latin America as Carter believes, one would expect larger quantities of such material to appear or that this species be at least represented in many more sites. Furthermore, the

Table 12.4. Distribution of food species by site.

Site	% of avian bones represented by food species	% of avian bones represented by Galliformes[a]	% of avian food bones represented by turkeys[b]	% of avian food bones represented by curassows	% of avian food bones represented by Columbiformes (pigeons)	% of avian food bones represented by Icterids[c]
San Miguel (C-13)	87.5	99.6	92.6	0	0	0
El Cedral (C-15)	97.5	99.9	30.7	11.5	0	0
Buena Vista (C-18)	72.2	87.5	37.5	37.5	12.5	0
San Gervasio (C-22)	84.6	72.4	46.0	11.6	20.2	6.3
La Expedición (C-25)	51.1	88.1	47.4	15.8	4.4	6.7
Zuuk (C-31)	100.0	60.0	20.0	40.0	40.0	0
AVERAGE	82.15	84.58	45.7	23.28[d]	19.28[d]	6.5[d]

a. Galliformes include curassows, singing quail, domestic chickens, common turkeys, and ocellated turkeys.

b. Turkeys include both the ocellated and common species.

c. Icterids include both giant cowbirds and great-tailed grackles.

d. These averages exclude sites with values of zero.

Cozumel chickens are from the top levels of pits in sites where modern contamination is a distinct possibility. The two bones from San Miguel (C-13) have been dated Late Postclassic-historic, meaning that European items were present in this level as well as Maya artifacts. This strongly suggests that these remains are post-Hispanic. The two chicken bones from San Gervasio (C-22) came from the top levels of a pit dated Late Postclassic. There is a ranch on the site today, and sightseers often come to look at the ruins — ample opportunity for someone to drop the remains of his Kentucky Fried Chicken lunch into the site. Chickens are also raised at the ranch. Still another possibility is that these may represent Spanish chickens, despite the absence of Spanish artifacts in this particular pit, which would lend support to this idea. In sum, we feel that all of the Cozumel chickens are intrusive, but whether they are modern or early Spanish chickens cannot be determined at this time.

After Galliformes, the next most important group of bird in the Cozumel diet is Columbiformes (pigeons or doves). These are not present in all the sites, but in the four where they do occur, they account for an average of 19.3 percent of the avian food bone. Grackles are the least important of the food species, since they appear in only two of the sites and represent an average of merely 6.5 percent. (We are assuming that grackles were food items because they are large-bodied birds, readily obtainable at clearings and not likely to be collected for feathers [dark brown or black].)

Since turkeys are the most significant avian food item on the island and since both of the species had to have been imported, these birds might have been raised on Cozumel either as domestic animals or as tame captives. The common turkey, *M. gallopavo*, was domesticated and widely distributed in Mexico before the conquest (Leopold 1959:275). Schorger (1966) cites Oviedo to the effect that the Indians on Cozumel presented turkeys to the Grijalva expedition of 1518. The Cortes expedition of 1519 revealed that the turkey was commonly kept as a domestic bird in the Maya Lowlands at that time. Forty of the animals were taken from the Indians' homes when the expedition landed on Cozumel (Schorger 1966:6). One problem has been that many of the Spanish terms in the ethnographic literature confuse the ocellated with the common turkey. The ocellated turkey (*M. ocellata*) has never been domesticated, however, since its offspring do not do well in captivity (Schorger 1966), possibly because of its superior flight capabilities in contrast to the northern turkey (Leopold 1959). Therefore the common turkey (*M. gallopavo*) was probably being raised on Cozumel.

Though not domesticated, the ocellated turkey was also being periodically captured and tamed for use as food. The presence of at least six immature individuals (36 bones) from four different sites on the

Table 12.5. Results of tests on soil samples from Buena Vista stone circles.

Sample	Soluble salts (ppm)[a]	Soluble nitrates (N) (ppm)[a]	Kjeldahl (organic N_2 and NH_4) (ppm)[b]	Ortho-phosphates (ppm)[c]
Circle #4	1,673	27.0	17,000	18.5
Control #4[d]	1,519	15.0	20,400	23.5
Circle #6	1,519	41.25	18,310	9.5
Control #6[d]	1,379	35.5	23,800	11.75

a. Both salts and nitrates are components of animal urine and manure. Note high values for these two elements inside the stone circles.

b. Lower organic nitrogen and ammonia values inside the circles indicate less microbial decomposition (probably of vegetation) taking place there.

c. This indicates the amount of phosphorus in the soil available to plants. Note the lower values inside the circles.

d. Control samples were taken from the soil just outside each of the stone circles tested.

island supports this hypothesis. Two of these individuals were so immature (one was approximately five days old, and the other was between one and five months of age) that the species could not be determined. But the remaining four individuals were all ocellated turkeys, suggesting, if not hatching in captivity, at least capture of the animals at a young age. Landa says (Tozzer 1941:202) that the Indians stole eggs of certain large birds and raised them tame after they were hatched.

The presence of stone circles in some of the sites may point to captivity. These enclosures range in diameter from 5 to 15 m and have walls of dry-laid masonry up to a maximum preserved height of 1.5 m (Freidel and Leventhal 1975:69). Soil samples were obtained from two of these stone circles at Buena Vista and were tested at the University of Arizona Soils, Water, and Plant Tissue Testing Laboratory (College of Agriculture, Department of Soils, Water, and Engineering) with some interesting results. (See table 12.5). The total ppm (parts per million) of soluble salts and soluble nitrates were both higher inside the circles than in the control samples taken just outside each of them, according to Ted McCreary, head of the Soils Laboratory (personal communication, 1978). Both salts and nitrates are common components of animal waste products (urine and manure), so that high values for these elements may indicate that animals were kept in these enclosures. Lower kjeldahl values (organic nitrogen and ammonia) inside the circles indicate that less microbial decomposition (probably of vegetation) was taking place there compared to outside the circles. The orthophosphates are also lower inside the circles, which means the phosphorus available to plants was not as great as outside the circles. The presence of animals in these enclosures could account for these facts, although it is not possible to say that this proves our hypothesis.

The ethnohistoric data support the idea that the prehistoric circles may have been used as pens. Landa (Tozzer 1941:127) says that women raised fowl for food and for sale, and there is mention of cooked turkeys being available in the markets of Yucatán (Schorger 1966:12). Not all these birds were necessarily turkeys, since Schorger (1966:8, 13) cites various historic references to the capturing and raising of curassows and chachalacas. Only the former species appears in the Cozumel sites. Landa mentions the rearing of doves and white mallard ducks (Tozzer 1941:201). We find doves in our sample, but not a single duck appears in any of the sites.

Ceremonial and other Nonfood Uses of Birds

Thirty different birds have been identified to at least the generic level from Cozumel, and only about a third of these have been designated as probable food species. Quite a few species are unaccounted for. Many, if not all, of these were probably utilized for cerermonial or other nonfood purposes. Landa refers repeatedly to the sacrificial offering of birds, their blood, their hearts, and their feathers (Tozzer 1941:23, 109, 114, 163, 165). Some animals that were offered as ritual sacrifices were "presented whole, some living and some dead, some raw and some cooked" (Tozzer 1941:114), and this presumably included birds.

Many birds may have had dual functions. A common ritual was the decapitation of a turkey as a sacrifice to the gods (Tozzer 1941:141, 145, 147; Tozzer and Allen 1910:325, 326, 327). Offering a turkey's head as a sacrifice would not preclude the rest of the animal being consumed as food. The only two bird skulls found were both common turkeys (*M. gallopavo*), and these were in an elite burial context at El Cedral. Tozzer and Allen (1910:325) refer to the frigatebird, pictured in the Maya Codices, as an offering, and this bird was also considered useful for medicinal purposes (Tozzer 1941:203).

Brightly colored bird feathers were utilized in male puberty rites (Tozzer 1941:106), to decorate clothing (Tozzer 1941:89, 127), in headdresses (Tozzer and Allen 1910:324, 328, 338, 345 specifically mention turkeys and the military macaw for this purpose), for banners, helmets, shields, and a certain "bird with rich plumes" served as money (Tozzer 1941:89). The Cozumel archaeological remains include five brightly colored members of the parrot family, all but one of

Table 12.6. Proveniences of Cozumel birds.

Provenience	No. of bones	% of bones	MNI	% of MNI
Burials and ceremonial/ administrative contexts	247	65.52	50	61.73
Housemounds	12	3.18	5	6.17
Indeterminate	118	31.30	26	32.10
TOTAL	377	100.0	81	100.0

which must have been imported to the island. The feathers of these species (which include the green and scarlet macaws, a parakeet, and the yellow-lored parrot) may well have been used for decorative purposes. Many other species found in the Cozumel sites were also probably used for their feathers. Such species include the great blue heron, the Louisiana heron, the yellow-crowned night heron, the reddish egret, the wood stork, the bicolored and roadside hawks, and the owl. Owl feathers were used in headdresses (Tozzer and Allen 1910:324, 338).

The owl is cited as an animal of mythologic significance (Schellhas 1904:45), and possibly this bird was utilized in ritual as well as for decoration. Pygmy owls are common in caches, for example in the Río Bec region (Waide, personal correspondence to Pohl, 1979) and at Copan (Pohl 1983).

Examination of burnt bone from the Cozumel sites provides more information on ritual uses of avifauna. Only 9.8 percent of all the bird bone was burned or heat-darkened. It would be easy to assume that this pattern reflects cooking practices, especially since most of the bones involved are curassows, turkeys, and pigeons, species considered food animals. But eight of the burnt bones were parrots and macaws. (At least five individuals are represented.) These too must have been food species, or they were sacrificially burned. Excavations conducted by the Instituto de Antropología e Historia de Guatemala in Group G at Tikal produced a number of burnt bones probably dating to Terminal Late Classic times (Pohl 1979). In contrast to all other faunal remains, Pohl mentions (1976:272) that mealy parrot (*Amazona farinosa*) bones were heavily charred. An owl bone was also observed to have been heat-darkened. The mealy parrot was one of the few high forest residents represented in the faunal assemblage, and these birds may have been imported to Tikal because the other animals were mostly open country forms. Parrots, macaws, and owls might have been eaten, but the ancient Maya may have been most concerned with ritual use of these birds.

If the proveniences are examined (table 12.6), it is apparent that the majority of bird bones were excavated from burials and ceremonial or administrative contexts (more than 65 percent of the bones or nearly 62 percent of the MNIs). Only about 3 percent of the material or approximately 6 percent of the MNIs were found in housemounds. (The remainder are from indeterminate contexts, but these would not be sufficient to affect the general pattern.) Nevertheless, this does not necessarily imply nonfood uses for over 65 percent of the Cozumel birds. It may only mean that birds were utilized for some purpose by the people inhabiting elite precincts and hence were deposited there. Still, a proportion of them, particularly the species discussed above, were undoubtedly used as ritual offerings.

Additional Considerations: Skeletal Elements and Time Periods

A study of the skeletal elements present in the avian sample (table 12.7) shows that most (over 48 percent) are major limb bones. Since these are the meat-bearing portions of the body, there might have been a concentration on birds as food sources. These are also the largest, most durable, and most diagnostic parts of a bird skeleton, factors that may be inflating these results. It may be significant that so few skull elements appear in the sample (less than 5 percent). Preservation factors may be involved, since bird skulls are usually paper-thin and fragile. Many birds may have been decapitated in the field as they were captured, before being brought back to the sites. All of the other skeletal elements are present in sufficient quantities to suggest that whole bird carcasses were used and then discarded within a relatively small area. Since most of the bird bone is not burnt or heat-darkened (90.2 percent), preparation for food purposes probably involved stewing most of the time.

A tabulation of the time periods in which birds occur (table 12.8) reveals that nearly 42 percent of the bones (or almost 57 percent of the MNIs) were excavated from proveniences dated to the Postclassic, Late Postclassic, or historic periods. Only a small proportion (less than 3 percent of the bones, or fewer than 8 percent of the MNIs) came from contexts dated to earlier time periods. Material from undated proveniences might modify this picture to some extent. In general, however, it appears that the cultural patterns observed here are primarily Late Postclassic.

Conclusions

A number of findings have resulted from the study of the Isla Cozumel bird bone. These six sites represent the greatest diversity of avifaunal exploitation by any Lowland Maya group reported so far, with 30 genera identified from the island. The bird bones, the majority of which date to Postclassic or historic times, relate specifically to elite contexts and provide data on status differentiation. For the first time, the northern species of turkey (*M. gallopavo*) has been identified in a Lowland Maya archaeological context. The presence of this species on Cozumel, in contrast to Mayapan, underscores the trading function of the island.

The operation of a long-distance trade network has been confirmed by the presence of several members of the parrot family not native to Cozumel. The birds include three different macaws and one parakeet as well as the northern turkey.

An analysis by ecological zone shows that most of the sites were making use of birds from only two of the habitats on the island. The two sites most prominent ceremonially and politically exhibit birds from all

Table 12.7. Distribution of skeletal elements of Cozumel birds.

Skeletal element	No. of bones	% of bones
Skull elements[a]	17	4.51
Major limb bones[b]	182	48.27
Vertebrae[c]	59	15.65
Phalanges, carpals, claws	34	9.02
Miscellaneous[d]	76	20.16
Indeterminate	9	2.39
TOTAL	377	100.0

a. Includes mandibles, premaxillae, skulls, frontals, quadrates, palatines, and nasals.

b. Includes carpometacarpi, humeri, radii, ulnae, femora, fibulae, tibiotarsi, and tarsometatarsi.

c. Includes axes, cervicals, thoracics, fused thoracic column, synsacra, and coccygeals.

d. Includes sterna, furcula, ribs, scapulae, and coracoids.

Table 12.8. Time periods of Cozumel birds.

Time period	No. of bones	% of bones	MNI	% of MNI
Late Postclassic and historic	155	41.11	45	55.56
Postclassic	3	0.80	1	1.23
Pre-Postclassic	1	0.26	1	1.23
Pure Florescent	4	1.06	2	2.47
Terminal Classic	4	1.06	2	2.47
Early Period (Classic)	1	0.26	1	1.23
No date	209	55.44	29	35.80
TOTAL	377		81	

four major habitats available and a generally much higher diversity of species.

The distribution of skeletal elements indicates a concentration on birds primarily as food sources. When the percentages of the probable food species are examined, the two turkeys, *M. gallopavo* and *M. ocellata*, emerge as the "birds of choice" of the ancient inhabitants of Cozumel. The probability that one or both turkeys were being raised on the island was discussed. Soil analysis suggests that large stone circles may have functioned as animal pens. Ethnographic sources indicate that the nonfood avian species were utilized for ceremonial and decorative purposes.

References

Aldrich, J. W., and A. J. Duvall
  1955 *Distribution of American Gallinaceous Game Birds*. Fish and Wildlife Service, U.S. Department of Interior Circular 34.

Blake, Emmet R.
  1953 *Birds of Mexico: Guide for Field Identification*. University of Chicago Press.

Davidson, William V.
  1975 "The Geographical Setting." In *Changing Pre-Columbian Commercial Systems*, edited by Jeremy A. Sabloff and William L. Rathje. Peabody Museum Monographs, no. 3, Harvard University, pp. 47–59.

Delacour, Jean T., and Dean Amadon
  1973 *Curassows and Related Birds*. American Museum of Natural History, New York.

Edwards, Ernest P.
  1972 *A Field Guide to the Birds of Mexico*. Ernest Edwards, Sweetbriar, Va.

Forshaw, Joseph M.
  1973 *Parrots of the World*. Landsdowne Press, Melbourne, Australia.

Freidel, David A.
  1976 "Late Postclassic Settlement Patterns on Cozumel Island, Quintana Roo, Mexico." Ph.D. dissertation, Harvard University.

Freidel, David A., and Richard M. Leventhal
  1975 "The Settlement Survey." In *Changing Pre-Columbian Commercial Systems*, edited by J. A. Sabloff and W. L. Rathje. Peabody Museum Monographs, no. 3, Harvard University, pp. 60–76.

Leopold, A. Starker
  1959 *Wildlife of Mexico*. University of California Press, Berkeley.

Olsen, Stanley J.
  1972 "Animal Remains from Altar de Sacrificios." In *The Artifacts of Altar de Sacrificios,* by Gordon R. Willey. Peabody Museum Papers, vol. 64, no. 1, Harvard University, pp. 243–246.
  1978 "Vertebrate Faunal Remains." In *Excavations at Seibal*, edited by Gordon R. Willey. Peabody Museum Memoirs, vol. 14, nos. 1, 2, 3, Harvard University, pp. 172–176.

Paynter, Raymond A., Jr.
  1955 *The Ornithogeography of the Yucatan Peninsula*. Peabody Museum of Natural History, Yale University. Bulletin 9.

Peterson, Roger T., and Edward L. Chalif
  1973 *A Field Guide to Mexican Birds*. Houghton Mifflin, Boston.

Pohl, Mary E. D.
  1976 "Ethnozoology of the Maya: An Analysis of Fauna from Five Sites in Peten, Guatemala." Ph.D. dissertation, Harvard University.
  1979 "The Last Days at Tikal." Manuscript, Florida State University, Tallahassee.
  1983 "Maya Ritual Faunas: Vertebrate Remains from Burials, Caches, Caves, and Cenotes in the Maya Lowlands." In *Civilization in the Ancient Americas*, edited by R. Leventhal and A. Kolata. Peabody Museum and University of New Mexico Press, Albuquerque.

Pollock, H. E. D., and Clayton E. Ray
  1957 "Notes on Vertebrate Animal Remains from Mayapan." *Current Reports* 41, Carnegie Institution of Washington.

Rathje, William L., and Jeremy A. Sabloff
  1975a "Theoretical Background: General Models and Questions." In *Changing Pre-Columbian Commercial Systems*, edited by J. A. Sabloff and W. L. Rathje. Peabody Museum Monographs, vol. 3, Harvard University, pp. 6–20.
  1975b Summary, pp. 136–138, in 1975a.

Sabloff, J. A., and W. L. Rathje
  1975 "Cozumel's Place in Yucatecan Culture History." In *Changing Pre-Columbian Commercial Systems*, edited by Sabloff and Rathje, pp. 21–28.

Schellhas, Paul
  1904 *Representations of Deities of the Maya Manuscripts*. Peabody Museum Papers, vol. 14, no. 1, Harvard University.

Schorger, A. W.
  1966 *The Wild Turkey*. University of Oklahoma Press, Norman.

Steadman, D. W.
  1980 A Review of the Osteology and Paleontology of Turkeys (Aves: Meleagridinae). *Contributions in Science, Natural History Museum of Los Angeles County* 330:131–207.

Tozzer, Alfred M.
  1941 *Landa's Relación de las Cosas de Yucatán*. Peabody Museum Papers, vol. 18, Harvard University.

Tozzer, Alfred M., and Glover M. Allen
  1910 *Animal Figures in the Maya Codices*. Peabody Museum Papers, vol. 4, no. 3, Harvard University.

Vokes, A. W.
  1978 "They Don't Make Them Like They Used To." Paper presented at the 43rd annual

meeting of the Society for American
Archaeology, Tucson.

Wing, Elizabeth S.
1974   "Vertebrate Faunal Remains." In *Excavation of an Early Shell Midden on Isla Cancun, Quintana Roo, Mexico* by E. Wyllys Andrews IV and others. Tulane University, Middle American Research Institute Publication 31, pp. 186–188.
1975   "Animal Remains from Lubaantun. In *Lubaantun: A Classic Maya Realm*, by Norman Hammond. Peabody Museum Monograph, no. 2, Harvard University, pp. 379–383.

Wing, Elizabeth S., and D. Steadman
1980   "Vertebrate Faunal Remains from Dzibilchaltun." In *Excavations at Dzibilchaltun, Yucatan, Mexico*, by E. W. Andrews IV and E. W. Andrews V. Tulane University, Middle American Research Institute Publication 48.

Woodbury, Richard B., and Aubrey S. Trik
1953   *The Ruins of Zacaleu, Guatemala*, vols. 1 and 2. William Byrd Press, Richmond, Va.

Conclusion

Chapter 13
Issues Related to Subsistence and Environment among the Ancient Maya

B. L. Turner II

The "man-land" theme has a tradition in Maya studies as attested by the interdisciplinary research of the various Carnegie Institution of Washington projects in the first half of this century (Turner 1980). Nevertheless, it is fair to conclude that an emphasis on "cultural ecological" research dealing with the prehistoric Maya and their homelands did not take root until the mid-1960s (e.g., Puleston 1971) as various disciplines that deal with prehistory began to combine research themes, objectives, and data with those of the archaeologists.[1] The emergence of this research focus was undoubtedly related to the development of cultural ecology in American archaeology and the influence of its proponents, such as Sanders (1956) and Palerm and Wolf (1957), on Mesoamerican studies in general, the development of research on settlement pattern-sustaining area among Mayanists, instigated by Willey (1965) and others (Bullard 1960; Haviland 1970; Kurjack 1974; Rice 1978), and the works of several paleoecologists, particularly Deevey and his colleagues (Tsukada and Deevey 1967), who formulated a research interest in the Maya Lowlands.

Initial studies demonstrated the complexities and interrelatedness of the various data sets, indicating that integrated, interdisciplinary projects were needed to address adequately cultural ecological questions. Following Deevey and his colleagues (chap. 6), several basic themes have emerged from such efforts: that evidence from a highly altered landscape in prehistory is difficult to interpret in regard to "primal" causes of the modifications; that cultural ecological issues should be addressed by deriving a "best fit" explanation from numerous lines of evidence; and that the evidence can be improved and expanded by continued field work and by the use of various research specializations that have been sparsely employed in Maya studies to date. The contributions to this book demonstrate these themes.

It is beyond the scope of this discussion to entertain the variety of studies in the Maya area that fit loosely into a cultural ecological framework. Indeed, a large amount of field work in recent years, regardless of the specific topic or locale, has emphasized some aspects of livelihood-environment relationships. Here I briefly allude to several issues of these themes.

Environments and Their Changes

The nature of environmental zones in the lowlands and the changes in them through time are most difficult topics of Maya prehistory to address and are the subject of considerable controversy.[2] At issue are questions of environmental composition and diversity, both in absolute terms and relative to other biotic zones in Mesoamerica, and of interpretations of their conditions in the past, including the sources of the changes that have been identified. These issues are complex and will undoubtedly remain the center of debate for some time. Deevey and his colleagues (chap. 6) have discussed most of these issues, and only brief comments are warranted here.

Discrepancies exist in the quantity and quality of information on the variables needed to describe environments in the lowlands. Vegetation patterns and complexes are best understood, with a history of study stemming from the first half of this century (Lundell 1937; Standley 1930; Wright et al. 1959; Miranda 1959; Pennington and Sarukhan 1968). More recently, considerable work has been devoted to the study of soils in the lowlands (Simmons, Tarano, and Pinto 1958; Olson 1977; Darch 1983; Turner et al. in press). Nevertheless, systematic studies of fauna are sparse, and the number of micro-level investigations of environments, however defined, are few (Wright et al.

B. L. Turner II is director, Graduate School of Geography, Clark University, Worcester, Massachusetts.

1. Outside North America long-standing traditions in multidisciplinary approaches to prehistory exist. In many of these traditions archaeology is recognized as only one of several disciplines of prehistory.

2. Originally I had asked Alan Covich to join me in producing a broader synthesis of environmental issues raised in this book. Unfortunately, time constraints interfered with the production of a larger synthesis, and the subsequent chapter by Deevey, Vaughan, and Garrett-Jones illuminated much of what we intended to say. As a result, I have presented only a few comments in regard to environmental issues independent of agriculture.

1959; Kellman 1975). Because of these and other problems, descriptions of biotic or physiographic zones of the lowlands tend to be overly simplified (Turner 1978a). Nevertheless, one contribution of this research to the Maya prehistorian is the recognition that environmental diversity exists, both on a macro- and micro-level. The comparative diversity of lowland habitats to that of other areas, such as the highlands, and the meaning of it remain controversial (Wiseman 1978; Sanders 1979).

Interpretations of past environmental conditions in the lowlands, as noted by Deevey and colleagues (chap. 6), are hampered by inadequate understanding of the contemporary conditions, relationships, and processes. Several examples demonstrate the point. The interpretations of molluscan remains retrieved from prehistoric contexts have been hindered by the level of understanding of the conditions that support a particular species or set of species. For instance, remains of *Neocyclotus* are found in a variety of archaeological contexts in the area, but the environmental meaning of the finds is not clear (Covich 1983). Also, it is recognized that sea level changes took place during Maya occupation of the lowlands (High 1975), but the impacts of such changes on Maya land use in near-coastal habitats are not known, largely because of the complexity of local hydrologies and our insufficient understanding of them. A recent example demonstrating such impact is the evidence of possible natural deposition over the Preclassic fields adjacent to the Río Hondo on Albion Island, northern Belize (Bloom et al. 1983). This deposition is attributed in part to the fluvial impact of sea level changes.

Finally, and this point cannot be overemphasized, the causes of the broad environmental changes that can be detected in the Maya Lowlands are difficult to assess because of the degree of environmental alterations established by the Maya. Hence, an environmental change during Maya prehistory could be the result of natural change (climatic or sea level changes), Maya landscape alterations, or some synergistic relationship between the two. This problem is not unique to the Maya Lowlands but is apparent anywhere large populations and the associated scale of landscape modification existed in prehistory.

These caveats aside, we do know that the prehistoric Maya Lowlands were composed of a number of distinct environments, that the ancient Maya utilized most of them for various activities, and that in numerous instances significant modifications of those habitats took place. For instance, much of the lowland forest was destroyed or altered in composition, soil loss occurred, and drainage systems were modified. We are beginning to understand where and when some of these types of change were intentional. The interpretations of the long-term impact of such changes, intentional or not, remain to be clarified and require the cooperation of the various experts.

Agriculture and Related Issues

The ancient means of food, fuel, and fiber production have been the core of much of the work on the prehistoric cultural ecology of the lowland Maya. The reasons for this emphasis have been dealt with elsewhere (Turner 1978b, 1980, 1983b) and need not be reiterated here. The number of studies is large, and each cannot be treated adequately in this commentary. Here I deal with some of the themes emerging from this book, particularly those related to the data and issues of wetland cultivation.

Determining Agricultural Types

Several approaches have been employed to suggest and establish the types of agriculture pursued by the ancient Maya. These approaches can be described as environmental possibility, enthnographic analogy, and direct evidence (see Turner and Miksicek 1984). Typically, these approaches are combined to produce an argument for the past existence of an agricultural type.

Environmental possibility searches the modern environments of the lowlands, or similar habitats elsewhere, for cultivars or other food, fiber, and fuel products that the Maya could have utilized. Cultivars (or other economic species) in themselves do not identify a type of agriculture, but in some instances such identification allows reasonable speculation as to the manner of cultivation. The number of "possibilities" for the ancient Maya are enormous. Nevertheless, the environmental possibility approach tends to emphasize those economic species and practices thought to be the most efficient in terms of ecological or energetic criteria. Parts of the *ramón* (*Brosimum alicastrum*), root crop, and artificial forest theses, as detailed in the text, are products of this approach. Environmental possibility is useful as a means of developing "hypotheses" of Maya agricultural types, but a danger exists that the possibility may merge into probability or assumed fact, even though the direct evidence is sparse. Agriculture is not merely the product of environmental expediency, a fact that many agricultural development schemes have learned the hard way. The possibility must be tested against the evidence, such as Wiseman's (1978) efforts to establish the validity of the artificial forest thesis.

Ethnographic analogy postulates agricultural types by comparison to historic or contemporary systems in the area or in broadly similar environs. The swidden thesis was based largely on this approach (Turner 1978b). As is the case with environmental possibility, ethnographic analogy is a useful means of establishing possibilities but can be subject to errors of transferability. First, use of early Spanish accounts to determine agricultural types at contact suffers from the problem of insufficient or unclear descriptions

(Miksicek et al. 1981a; Reina and Hill 1983). Rarely are techniques, practices, and so forth described. Information is largely limited to crops or passing references to canals, ditches, or burning, such that it can be used to support a variety of arguments. For example, Landa's (Tozzer 1941) descriptions of post contact agriculture in northern Yucatán could apply to any number of agricultural systems. Likewise, it is erroneous to infer that the Spaniards' use of the term *milpa* (cornfield) implies a slash-and-burn technology or a maize-bean-squash dominance (Hellmuth 1977).

Perhaps a more critical problem of the ethnographic analogy, compared to those mentioned, is the danger of selecting an analogy on environmental criteria alone. Types of agriculture are products of the interplay between environmental and socioeconomic variables. For the Maya during Classic times an analogy should include a densely settled and highly stratified society in a lowland, wet-dry tropical zone (ideally karst). Although I do not necessarily agree with every aspect of his analogy, Sanders (1977, 1981) has provided examples that attempt to find analogies that fit both environmental and socioeconomic variables thought to have existed at the height of the Classic Maya civilization.

Direct evidence of types of agriculture pursued by the ancient Maya is provided by references in art and remains of economic species, tools, and, most important, technologies, such as irrigation, raised fields, and terrace networks. Combined, these data provide knowledge of relationships among tools, crops, and landscape manipulation and of the areal scale of various land uses. They do not provide precise knowledge of cropping procedures, frequency of cultivation, or levels of output, except by analogy to similar systems. Herein is a key point for the selection of analogies. Maya terraces are stone structures representing considerable effort for construction (Turner 1983a; 1983b), such that extant, nonstone terracing data may not be appropriate in regard to the economics of the Maya counterpart. The same can be said for the various wetland systems as well.

Agricultural Identifications and Functions

Of the various agrotechnologies identified in the Maya Lowlands, the existence and function of fields and canals in wetlands have been the focus of study and controversy of late. Initially this controversy involved the interpretation of the ground patterns found in the depressions of northern Belize and southern Quintana Roo (Siemens 1978; Turner 1974; Harrison 1977). Puleston (1978) entertained the possibility that only those patterns in riverine environments were Maya fields and canals and that those in depressions were gilgai or ground swells created by expansible clays. At the time of Puleston's writing the only ground confirmation of Maya wetland fields and canals were those

produced by Siemens and himself (1972; Puleston 1977; Siemens 1977, 1983) along the Río Candelaria in Campeche and at Albion Island, Belize. Subsequent work identified fields and canals at Barber Creek, near Lamanai (Lambert, personal communication, 1980), at Cerros (Freidel and Scarborough 1982), along the Belize River (Kirke 1980), at Pulltrouser Swamp (Turner and Harrison 1981, 1983), and now at Bajo Morocoy (Gliessman et al. 1983). Radar imagery suggests that fields and canals may be found throughout much of the central Maya area (Adams, Brown, and Culbert 1981). Pedological and geomorphological work at Albion Island (Antoine, Skarie, and Bloom 1982) and at Pulltrouser Swamp indicates conclusively that gilgai or other large natural ground patterns do not form in those environs. Indeed, the lowland habitats most suited for gilgai formation, seasonally inundated savannas that tend to desiccate appreciably during the dry season, do not display ground patterns of any kind that can be detected by ordinary photography and aerial observation.

A subsequent issue involves the construction of the fields and canals. Puleston (1977) had suggested that at Albion Island a two phase construction was evident: a lower or initial phase with canaling but only minimal field raising and an upper or secondary phase with major raising by use of marl (unconsolidated limestone). More recent work (Antoine, Skarie, and Bloom 1982) led to the interpretation that the canals had been dug into underlying peat and that the subsequent deliberate raising of the fields as postulated by Puleston never occurred. In short, the fields in question may only be channelized, not raised in a major way (Bloom et al. 1983). Work by Pohl, Bloom, and Stein at Albion Island should allow clarification of this issue (chap. 2). Nevertheless, it is becoming clear that many wetland fields, especially in certain riverine and edge-of-depression contexts, were principally channelized features. That channelization implies mere drainage functions is questionable. Many channels on Albion Island still retain water throughout the dry season despite their increased elevation above the river due to sedimentation.

Recent work at Pulltrouser Swamp in northern Belize has led us to conclude that major field raising was involved away from the edge of the depression (Turner and Harrison 1981, 1983). Several lines of evidence were used to reach this assessment, mostly involving the character of a gray zone with white "mottling" that ranges from about 30 cm to 150 cm below the surface. This "fill" zone differed visually and analytically from the soil above and the unconsolidated limestone below and occurred only in the fields within the depression (not on the edge of the depression and not in any of the segments of the swamp or savanna with no visual signs of fields and canals that were tested [Darch 1983]). Samples from a number of the "fill" zones in the fields of the depression were found to maintain considerable variations in particle size distributions, while the material above and below it shows much less variability (Darch 1983). This result suggested that the "fill" zone throughout the depression did not have a common origin as expected if it were the product of natural deposition. The white, speckled material in this zone (referred to as mottle-like) occurred in no other features within the depression. The material was identified both as calcium carbonate casts containing sand grains and as pieces of limestone because of reaction to acid tests. The fill zone also contained larger rocks, ceramics, lithics, and botanical remains of upland and wetland species, including maize (Turner and Harrison 1983). These remains stopped abruptly at the juncture of that zone with the carbonates below. Furthermore, the ceramics were vertically mixed, commonly with Late Preclassic sherds near the top (30 cm in depth) and Late Classic sherds near the bottom (150 cm in depth) of the same fill zone. Lithics included several bifaces (or fragments of bifaces) with striations indicative of cutting into a soft but abrasive material, such as the soils or underlying carbonates of the depression (Shafer 1983). One intact biface was found on the juncture of the zone and the material below.

Under the fill zone was found a white, calcium carbonate material that contained large crystals of gypsum, not unlike the material comprising the channelized fields at the swamp edge. But toward the interior, about one field away from the edge of the depression, a black, gastropod-rich material was found between the fill zone and the lower carbonate material. The black zone was probably the original swamp topsoil. Subsequent work, still in analysis, has revealed the presence of this soil throughout many of the interior fields at Pulltrouser. Finally, the profiles of the fields and canals showed that the canals did not contain the gray zone or the buried soil but had been cut about 1 m into the white, carbonate material.

Utilizing these lines of evidence, our "best fit" interpretation was that the gray zone was an artificial fill or Maya-made platform of a raised field. This fill was obtained by the use of the material taken from the excavation of the canals with additions of upland or dryland materials. Some material, other than that from the canals, was thought to have been used because there may not have been sufficient, excavated canal material to build the platforms and because of the presence of upland materials (maize pollen, limestone fragments, rocks) found in the fill only. It seemed unlikely that the absence of these materials and the ceramics and lithics at the juncture of the fill and buried soil or carbonate zone was mere coincidence.

Independent work by Pohl and Bloom has indicated that the fill zone has high levels of gypsum and higher clay content than was originally reported. They suggest that this information may require reinterpretation of the fill zone, a matter that the 1981 Pulltrouser Project and they are pursuing. For the moment, however, we remain with the fill interpretation for those reasons given — the location of the fill, the artifactual materials in but not below it, the absence of the mottle-like features anywhere but in the fill zone (not in the canals), and the buried soil. Also, we must consider that the most logical place for the Maya to put the meter or more of material taken from the canals was on the adjacent fields. Finally, the origins of the gypsum levels in the fill zone can be attributed to a number of sources, including its inclusion as part of the fill material from the canals or as a product whose formation was facilitated by the construction of the fields.

The studies at Pulltrouser Swamp and at Albion Island have each produced evidence that appears inconsistent with the interpretations of field morphology. At Pulltrouser we have postulated the creation of a raised cropping platform. Bloom and colleagues (chap. 2) have suggested that, based on soil analysis alone, the material in the platform could be interpreted as natural. This material does not occur throughout the swamp, however, and the vertical mixing of ceramics within it is difficult to explain as a result of natural processes alone. Another inconsistent element is the minor amount of economic plant remains found in the material. One would expect to find such remains in reasonable numbers in an old planting bed.

At Albion Island fields are postulated to have been created principally by cutting canals into peat. The latter material and the clay-peat unit above it have agricultural indicators. The problem here, as noted by the researchers (chap. 2), is that two of these postulated agricultural units (VII and VIII) display banding, as if deposited naturally and not tilled for cultivation. To circumvent this problem the researchers suggest that the use of dibble sticks and cutting weeds would have not disturbed the banding. This reasoning is suspicious because of the ancient Mesoamerican practice of mounding maize, particularly in poorly aerated clays, such as Unit VII.

The other interpretation involving inconsistent data postulates that the materials creating the mounds adjacent to the canals at Albion Island are undisturbed, natural deposits (chap. 2). The problems here are several. First, why would hundreds of years of deposition create mounds, rather than a level surface? Second, the material in Units IV and V (shelly marl) apparently occurs only over some of the fields and not in the canals. This find seems strange given the interpretation that the material is naturally deposited after agriculture ceased. The explanation that the distribution of this shelly marl relates to differences in water depth needs clarification. If only natural processes were at work, why would the canals not have been filled with sediments such that the shelly marl would extend across field and canals? Finally, the vertical mixing of ceramics in the upper, nonagricultural zones (II) of the fields cannot be explained away as easily as it has been (chap. 2). The depth of the mixing is not reported, but Zone II is about 100 cm in depth. The issue then becomes how do Late Classic ceramics find their way through massive clays to depths 60 cm or more below Preclassic or Early Classic ceramics, if the material is naturally deposited and unaltered?

These issues cannot be resolved at this time. I raise them to demonstrate that none of the interpretations is without problems, perhaps major ones.

The various works dealing with channelized and raised fields have led to a number of interpretations of their function, either as drainage features or *chinampa*-like constructions. Siemens (1983) correctly notes that most traditional technologies in wetlands tend to involve drainage (removal of water) only to a limited extent and that subtle control of, or adaptation to, fluctuations in water levels tend to be more common strategies. Nevertheless, he contends that many fields in the Maya area should be more appropriately described as drained fields or drainage systems. I have deliberately avoided a functional term for the features in question and have employed constructional terms: channelized for fields created mainly by canaling and raised for fields created by canaling and major raising.

I maintain that methods of construction and form of the fields and canals impute little about function. To determine function, the field-canal network must be assessed in regard to its presumed dimensions and the past environmental circumstances in which it occurred. In this regard, a tendency exists for field raising and canaling in depressions, as opposed to riverine environs, in Mesoamerica (Palerm 1973) or elsewhere (Denevan and Turner 1974), not to be associated with drainage in terms of total or substantial removal of water. Rather, the attempt is typically to make use of water in place by regulating it to "deep" canals and by raising a planting surface above that of the water table. Such a system seems feasible throughout many depressions in the Maya lowlands, particularly at low elevations, because of the minimal slope for drainage. Drainage may have been accomplished on levees or along the edges of depressions, but within many depressions a large amount of water was present throughout most years. Initial gastropod data from Pulltrouser suggest that permanent water was a characteristic of the system. In contrast, at Bajo Morocoy, a seasonally inundated depression in Quintana Roo, water may have been restricted to canals during the wet season but slowly lost during the dry season (Gliessman et al. 1983).

But how do water levels pertain to agricultural interpretation? Siemens (1982, 1983) suggests that some wetland fields were dry season sources of cultivation, indicating that too much water was present during the wet season for cropping. Drainage would have extended the beginning and end of the dry season conditions on the fields, providing a second crop in addition to that obtained on upland fields. This interpretation is also given by Bloom and colleagues (1983). Gliessman and associates (1983) suggest that wet season cultivation took place on the fields and a dry season crop in the canals at Bajo Morocoy. These interpretations may never be resolved. At Pulltrouser, however, the planting surface of the fields may have been above water all year or inundated only for brief periods. One reason for this assessment is the presumed cost-benefit assumptions concerning construction of the system (Turner 1983a; Turner and Harrison 1983). Obviously, this subject requires considerable study.

Agricultural Sequence

Various schemes of agricultural change have been applied to the Maya, with the evidence of wetland cultivation acting as a catalyst. The most developed schemes are those applied by Sanders (1973; Sanders, Parsons, and Santley 1979) and others (Rice 1978; Turner and Harrison 1978), which are synthesized here as scheme A. This view assumes that Mesoamerican farmers exhibited basic responses to changes in demand for production as do traditional farmers in general (Boserup 1965; Brookfield 1972; Chayanov 1966). These responses are tendencies to utilize certain classes of environment in an orderly pattern based on cost-risk relationships. Environments are distinguished according to their suitability for various classes of cultivation. Where possible, low cost-risk cultivation is pursued in the most "optimal" environments. Changes in this pattern occur as demands rise with a tendency toward the employment of increasingly higher cost, if not higher risk, agriculture and the use of other, "less optimal" habitats. In some cases, a technological threshhold may occur, such as the development of hydraulic agriculture, that may have the effect of offsetting the diminishing returns to high input cultivation or to the use of a certain environment. A significant drop in demand for production is thought to reverse scheme A, given a lag time.

Scheme A suggests that incipient cultivation in the Maya Lowlands took place in a land extensive circumstance where demands for production were low. An extensive, low cost-risk cultivation could have supplied needs, and the most suitable zones were the agriculturally fertile, well-drained mollisols of the uplands. In these, drainage problems were insignificant, wet season precipitation was probably more than adequate for a variety of crops, including maize, soil fertility was good, and erosion minimal if sufficient fallow were employed (Turner 1978a, 1979; Sanders 1977). Perhaps the only zone of higher native fertility were riverbanks in which a marceño-type of cultivation could have been pursued during the dry season. These zones are rare in the Maya area.

As demands on production increased, various agricultural responses occurred, predicated largely on local conditions and choice of cultigens. Nevertheless, a broad pattern is expected in which farmers expanded along the mollisols and vertisols of the uplands where swidden cultivation could have been utilized. Eventually demands necessitated the use of other, less suitable habitats and high input cultivation. Input intensification took place in the more feasible habitats and was commonly necessitated in marginal zones in order that the land be made suitable for cultivation. The primary zones in the central Maya Lowlands invaded during this second stage of change were wetlands — riverine zones and depressions.

Initial inputs to reform these zones for cultivation would have been high in comparison to the drylands, but potential rewards were also high. Shallow inundation may have only required the use of drainage networks. Canals and field raising were necessitated in deep inundation. Once the initial labor inputs were incurred, the wetlands systems may have become more efficient than their intensive dryland counterparts. The reason for such a shift in efficiency was the ability to produce at least two harvests during the year in the wetlands. The second or dry season crop was possible because drainage was not complete; water was retained in canals. The effect of wetland cultivation, once developed, may have been to alleviate the pressures on dryland. Scheme A, then, suggests that the overall pattern of agricultural land use in the central Maya Lowlands would have been from extensive, swidden-type of cultivation on drylands, through intensification on drylands and experimentation with wetland edges, to intensive use of wetlands and drylands, with perhaps a slight disintensification of dryland cultivation where wetland systems were abundant.

A variety of data supports the basic propositions of scheme A. Cuello, the earliest dated Maya site, has revealed botanical evidence indicating that upland species were first used there (Hammond and Miksicek 1981). The earliest settlements around Lagunas Yaxha and Sacnab in Petén appear to have been on the higher slopes of the lake basins as reported by Rice and colleagues (chap. 7), suggesting an upland agricultural emphasis. The pollen data from throughout the Maya Lowlands (chaps. 5, 6) indicate early tampering with the upland forests, presumably for agriculture. Furthermore, the dating of the wetland systems at Pulltrouser Swamp and at Bajo Morocoy indicate a late development, possibly Late Preclassic but probably Classic in time (Turner and Harrison 1981, 1983; Gliessman et al. 1983).

Challenges have been made to scheme A. One view suggests that intensive house gardens may have preceded extensive, swidden systems (Hammond 1978). The issue cannot be resolved at this time, although house gardens are common to most all extensive agricultural systems, and their use in this context is not incompatible with scheme A. If they were the primary source of staples, then scheme A would require re-evaluation.

Another view suggests that Maya cultivation was always multi-dimensional with a number of practices operating at once (Wiseman 1978, 1983a). This point is undeniable but may not reflect broader tendencies. That is, while many systems of cultivation are multi-dimensional, broad input risk patterns are discernible as levels of demand change within local constraints, resulting in patterns of land use. These broader patterns are the focus of scheme A.

The more serious challenge to scheme A is the argument of an early or initial emphasis on wetland agriculture. Several authors (chaps. 2 and 4; Puleston and Puleston 1971; Bloom et al. 1983) note the possible antiquity of wetland cultivation in the Maya area, suggesting its early use in the Preclassic period. The thrust of this argument, as proposed by Siemens (1982, 1983), emphasizes a levee usage because of the ease or ability to obtain a dry season crop (see Wilk, chap. 4). If permanent or dry season levee cultivation could have been obtained with minimal inputs, then costs would have been comparable to those of swidden, and the principles on which scheme A is based would hold. Furthermore, as noted elsewhere (Turner and Harrison 1978), several possibilities that do not violate the thrust of scheme A can explain an early date for wetland use. For example, the antiquity of all cultivation in the Maya area may be much earlier than is accepted, such that demands for production were high by Preclassic times in some areas, or specialty crop production may have necessitated early wetland use. Indeed, the need for a security or dry season crop would suggest either a considerable demand for output or an environmental change such that upland, wet season cultivation was less productive than is suspected.

The principles of scheme A were challenged by the Pulestons (1971) and discussed by Hammond (1978). The former suggested that the Maya may have entered the central lowlands via river routes while practicing intensive raised or drained field agriculture. Later, the Maya spread inland practicing swidden and other forms of cultivation, with a special emphasis on the collection of ramón. This scheme (B) contradicts scheme A by asserting that the Maya opted for high input agriculture at a time when, presumably, efficient dryland systems were available that could have supported production needs and that the general trend in agriculture was from intensive wetland to extensive dryland cultivation (as measured in terms of inputs) as demands for production grew. The intensity of wetland cultivation was not defined and ramón collection was postulated to have been an efficient, intensive output form of food procurement. (The evidence to support the ramón argument is discussed later.)

Scheme B relied primarily on a radiocarbon date of 1110 ± 230 B.C. (1400 B.C., corrected) for a post found below a canal at Albion Island. Subsequent dating of maize stem charcoal from below that canal supports the view that the Preclassic Maya were utilizing riverine edges for some form of activity (chap. 2; Bloom et al. 1983). This activity was apparently not associated with major field raising (Bloom et al. 1983). In contrast, the depression fields at Pulltrouser and Morocoy date later than those at Albion Island. The Pulltrouser fields displayed vertically mixed ceramics of Late Preclassic through Late Classic origins; a radiocarbon date from a channelized field there is A.D. 150 ± 150 (uncorrected), suggesting that the edge of the depression may have been used before the interior. Also, the canals and small fields at Cerros, Belize, are thought to be no earlier than Late Preclassic in origin (Scarborough 1980:249). Examination of photographs of surface ceramics at Bajo Morocoy indicate a Late Classic presence on the fields there (Fry, personal communication, 1981), although early material may be found below.

Obviously more data are required for clarification of the sequence of agricultural change in the Maya Lowlands, particularly in regard to the wetland systems. A merger of various aspects of schemes A and B may be appropriate. While the behavioral assumptions of scheme A are probably correct, the locational complexity of the variables and the parameters of the costs and risks of various Maya agricultural activities may require a synthesis of several opinions. The sum of the data does not support a general shift through time from wetland cultivation to upland agriculture and tree cropping. The paleoecological data uniformly demonstrate upland forest disturbance in Preclassic times, suggesting upland emphasis through much, if not most, of the Maya area. In some instances, however, water's edge agriculture may have also developed where low inputs or costs were involved. Even where channelized fields may date to Preclassic times, such as at Albion Island, the pollen record suggests that the uplands had been cleared (Bloom et al. 1983).

Field raising in depressions was probably a later phenomenon, as attested by the evidence at Pulltrouser and Morocoy. The pollen record from Pulltrouser shows a probable eradication of much of the upland forests in the area previous to swamp use (Wiseman 1983b). These systems may be Late Preclassic but are more probably Late Classic in date, particularly for full development. The use of these depressions undoubtedly coincided with demand-cost factors but might also be linked to sea level changes,

which made such use more feasible. The key point is that extensive manipulation of wetlands probably took place after intensification was well underway on uplands but was perhaps previous to or concomitant with the use of some of the intensive upland terrace systems. The latter agriculture apparently dates to the Classic period, especially the Late Classic (Turner 1974, 1979, 1983b; Healy, van Waarden, and Anderson 1980).

Finally, the shifts to intensive upland-wetland agriculture were undoubtedly related to increasing demands for production or to subtle decreases in yields brought on by hundreds of years of cultivation. Even if wetland cultivation were precipitated by a need for dry season production, such a need is indicative of a demand for production (unless major environmental degradation occurred in the uplands) (Turner and Denevan, in press). Demand for production resulted from several sources, including trade, taxes, and population. Of these, population cannot be overemphasized because it is the only demand variable for which direct evidence exists and because the evidence indicates that Maya population was large. Conservative estimates of Maya population uniformly indicate population sizes by Late Preclassic and undoubtedly Late Classic times sufficient to have necessitated shifts to intensive types of cultivation (see Ashmore 1981). To deny the fundamental role of this variable to agricultural change in the lowlands seems illogical.

Finally, several comments on Wilk's (chap. 4) conclusions about population pressure models and the Maya are warranted. His assertion that pressure or demand models have in the past been oversimplified is correct. Indeed, I plead guilty to the charge. Nevertheless, such simplification should be seen as the first stage in the maturation process of an intellectually appealing argument proposed by Ester Boserup (1965). As noted above, the models have been expanded to account for nonpopulation demand variables, and input or output definitions of intensification have superseded that of fallow cycles. Wilk may have oversimplified his own reaction. There is a logical and demonstratable reason why an increasing need for more output per unit area and time will ultimately lead to a decrease in the fallow cycle of an extensive form of cultivation. Furthermore, most demand models of which I am aware do not assume a "strict maximizing behavior."

Cultivars and Other Foods

Although the Maya undoubtedly cultivated a large number of crops (Lundell 1933), recovery in fossil context has been limited (Hammond and Miksicek 1981; Turner and Miksicek 1984). In large measure, sparse recovery is attributable to problems of pollen preservation and identification in the area but is also related to the lack of emphasis on pollen retrieval from direct archaeological context and failure to develop alternative botanical recovery techniques. The traditional Maya crop complex of maize and squash is supported by the botanical evidence; evidence of beans is scarce. Remains of *Gossypium*-type pollen (possibly cotton), *Agave*, and *Amaranthus* have also been found. Although we know that the Maya cultivated cotton, the domesticated species cannot be detected by grain morphology alone. Work on the microscopic structure of maize (Banerjee and Barghorn 1972) and chenopod and amaranth pollen allows for greater confidence in distinguishing cultivated from wild varieties.

Specific cultivars associated with wetland agriculture in the Maya area, particularly in northern Belize, has been the subject of controversy for several reasons. A wetland emphasis on a specialty crop, such as cacao (*Theobroma* sp.), might explain the use of wetlands in Preclassic times before production pressures associated with local populations were thought to have been sufficient to warrant the inputs required to transform wetlands in a major way. Emphasis on cacao, which needs moist but noninundated soils, would be one means of explaining "culturally induced" production pressures (Turner and Harrison 1978). Furthermore, Hammond (1974) and Dahlin (1979) produced arguments involving symbiotic relationships of cacao, midges, and fish that would have made the wetland systems productive to the Maya in several ways. In this scheme, midges living in the canal-field interface would pollinate the cacao and would in turn be eaten by canal fish, such that both vegetable and aquatic resources would be produced. The cacao thesis is enhanced by records that northern Belize was a prime cacao production zone at contact times.

Unfortunately, no direct evidence has been produced indicating that cacao was grown on raised or channelized fields (Turner and Miksicek 1984). The Pulltrouser Project floated a large number of soil samples for recovery of plant remains from raised fields and from the neighboring settlement of Kokeal. Analysis of the materials revealed one cacao fragment, and it was from the fill materials of an earth mound (Miksicek 1983). Hammond (personal communication, 1981) has noted that cacao remains, especially husks, make an excellent fertilizer and that this circumstance may explain the few remains of the species at Kokeal and its absence from the fields at Pulltrouser. Nevertheless, no parts of the cacao, such as stems and roots, were found at Pulltrouser either, although numerous finds were made of other potentially economic and noneconomic species (Miksicek 1983; Turner and Miksicek 1984).

My position is not to reject the cacao thesis, particularly given the early stages of research on the question, but to emphasize the direct data. The studies at

Albion Island and Pulltrouser both produced maize pollen in field contexts (Bloom et al. 1983; Wiseman 1983b). Furthermore, a carbonized maize stem fragment was found in one field at Pulltrouser. In addition to maize, the Albion Island study suggested the possible presence of pollen of *Amaranthus* and *Gossypium* (Puleston 1977). Similar pollen was found in the Pulltrouser fields, but Wiseman (1983b) warns that *Gossypium*-type pollen may well be some malavaceous type and not cotton and that *Amaranthus* pollen could result from weedy species that would have pervaded wetlands, especially along canal edges. The strongest evidence of a cultivar associated with wetland fields is maize, although further work on cotton identification may provide support for its presence too. Bloom (personal communication, 1981; see chap. 2) notes that levels of soluble salts are presently too high in many wetland fields to support good maize growth. The maize issue will require further study.

The dependence of the Maya of the central lowlands on ramón is another controversial issue. Puleston (1971), in a clever bit of reasoning, explained the abilities of the densely settled Maya of the northern Petén zone to subsist by collecting and perhaps preserving the ramón. His evidence was indirect, based on the prevalence of the species in the area, particularly around ruins, and experiments with storing the ramón in the doubled-chambered chultuns at Tikal. Several arguments have been raised against the ramón thesis (Sanders 1973; Turner and Harrison 1978). Wiseman (chap. 5) suggests that stands of ramón maintained by the Maya in Petén would not be detectable in the fossil pollen record. The thesis must be addressed either indirectly or through the use of plant remains or some other analysis that has not been used extensively so far in Maya studies.

The distribution of ramón in the Maya area may reflect edaphic factors (Turner and Harrison 1978; Turner and Miksicek 1984). Work by Lambert and Arnason (1978; 1982) in Belize and by Charles Peters (ecologist, personal communication, 1980) in Tabasco and Vera Cruz support the edaphic distribution theme. In addition, evidence against the ramón thesis has recently been uncovered in archival records and in analysis of remains from chultuns. Reina and Hill (1980) describe accounts of chultun usage in Alta Vera Paz, Guatemala, for maize storage, but only after the grain had been cured to harden the kernels, a procedure not employed in Puleston's experiments. Direct evidence for plants used by the ancient Maya has been produced by the Cuello Project (Miksicek et al. 1981b). Analysis of macrofossils from a chultun at the site revealed maize and other species but not ramón. In sum, maize storage in chultuns has now been established for the northern, southern, and eastern peripheries of the Petén zone. As Reina and Hill (1980) conclude, it does not seem reasonable to assume an atypical function for Petén chultuns.

The botanical evidence suggests the use of a variety of cultivated and wild fruits and nuts, maize, cotton, squash, and other possible food, fiber, and fuel species (Hammond and Miksicek 1981; Turner and Miksicek 1984). Undoubtedly, the list of identified species from botanical remains will increase as the techniques of retrieval are expanded.

Animal Protein

The production of animal protein by the Maya, other than by hunting, has received minimal attention in comparison to the amount of work on agriculture in the lowlands (D. Harris 1978). The possibilities of pisiculture in canals in wetlands (Thompson 1974; Dahlin 1979) and the rearing of semi-domesticated animals (Harris 1978; Turner and Harrison 1978) have been advanced. Now, however, studies of remains and related works are increasing and providing more details on protein captured by hunting and other means (see Carr, chap. 8).

The work of Hamblin (chap. 11) and Hamblin and Rea (chap. 12) demonstrates the importance of marine resources and avifauna, particularly the domesticated and ocellated turkeys (*Meleagris gallopavo* and *M. ocellata*), to the Postclassic inhabitants of Cozumel. The association of the two turkeys in the fossil record hint that the wild species may have been semidomesticated or that incipient manipulation of the ocellated turkey was on-going. Hamblin may be correct in asserting that the ocellated turkey was, at least, tamed by the Maya.

I am intrigued by the suggestion that stone circle enclosures found at Cozumel were used as animal pens; analysis of the enclosure soils revealed high levels of soluble salts and nitrates as would have been left by animal wastes. Containment of animals, if used at Cozumel, was most assuredly done on the mainland as well where various assortments of stone walls also occur. Whether such practices are strictly Postclassic in origin and related only to avifauna, presumably turkey, are not known. It seems inconceivable that the Classic Maya did not have "controlled" sources of animal protein, including the domesticated turkey, but the evidence to date does not indicate an abundance of fossil bones of the species in middens or other parts of Maya sites. Deer (probably *Odocoileus virginianus*) may have been kept in enclosures. Landa (Tozzer 1941) reported that deer were herded from the village to feed in the forest in sixteenth-century Yucatán. Even today it is not uncommon for Maya to keep tame deer. Unfortunately, the evidence suggests relatively few deer on Cozumel. Deer keeping may well explain the number of remains of white-tail species found by Pohl (chap. 9) at Seibal, however.

A final comment is warranted on the role of fish in Maya diet. I find it hard to believe that the Classic Maya would not have intensively utilized aquatic resources, particularly fish, although cultural preferences (Simoons 1961) or not so obvious functional relationships (M. Harris 1966) can result in unusual food avoidances. Some evidence suggests that fishing was significant (Puleston 1977; Hammond 1981). Nevertheless, faunal remains of freshwater fish in archaeological contexts are not abundant for most Classic Maya sites, although remains of inland and marine molluscs are abundant (see chap. 10). To date, only coastal or Postclassic sites have revealed large numbers of fish remains, as in the case of Cerros (chap. 8). What happened to the freshwater fish remains that should occur at noncoastal sites previous to the Postclassic, particularly those along rivers and lakes or adjacent to suspected pisiculture areas? It is difficult to argue for preservation problems because remains of other fauna are found, often in large numbers. The answer may be inadequate sampling procedures, emphasis on food other than fish by Classic Maya, or perhaps special uses of fish remains.

Agricultural Degradation and Collapse

The role of agricultural failures or environmental catastrophes in the collapse of the Classic Maya in the central lowlands is a time honored thesis (Cooke 1931). Variations arise as the data change and as assessments become more sophisticated (Harrison 1977). Maya agriculture did collapse. At issue is the relationship between the agricultural and cultural collapses. Did an extended agricultural failure lead to a cultural collapse? Did a cultural collapse lead to abandonment and hence collapse of agriculture? Or did sociopolitical and agricultural forces interact in a synergistic fashion to create a cultural collapse and regional abandonment?

The data on agriculture indicate that the Maya were on a par with any New World cultivators and that environmental conditions for agriculture throughout much of the lowlands were favorable. Barring some major climatic disruption or the introduction of some exogenous pathogen, for which there is no evidence, little reason exists either ecologically or agronomically to suspect that an agricultural disaster precipitated the cultural collapse. We have no direct evidence that the Maya reached levels of agricultural demand for which they could not provide in terms of techniques or environmental conditions. Furthermore, no relationship has been demonstrated between the spatial and temporal characteristics of the cultural collapse and the environmental conditions or agrotechnologies of various lowland zones. Any agriculture can be disrupted by sociopolitical forces, which in turn affect its infrastructure, however. Once the infrastructure of the system is disrupted, agriculture may decay, and degradation takes place as land manipulation devices, such as terraces, canals, and so forth, are allowed to degenerate. Hence, evidence for agriculturally related degradation in the lowlands need not imply an agriculturally induced cultural collapse of the Maya. It may well reflect a cultural collapse and abandonment and the resulting ramifications for the agricultural landscape. Agricultural collapses are not used to explain the decline of highland Mesoamerican cultures, such as Teotihuacan, a circumstance suggesting the possibility of perceptual biases toward lowland tropical environments.

The various chapters in this volume wisely maintain a cautious view of the agricultural-environmental collapse issue, although certain lines of evidence suggesting some environmental problems cannot be dismissed. The data on colluviation and nutrient sequestering at Lakes Yaxha, Sacnab, and Quexil provide the most dramatic case of environmental degradation of the type that could have affected agriculture. Nevertheless, the deliveries of phosphorus to the lakes seem to correspond neatly with population growth in the lake basins, such that environmental degradation in terms of soil nutrients alone is not necessarily an issue. That is, if phosphorus deliveries are proportional to the population size, then phosphorus decreases in those soils cultivated are not necessarily demonstrated.

The colluviation process need not indicate serious soil erosion in the lake basins brought on by agriculture. The "urbanization" around the lakes, particularly at Yaxha, hints that immediate lacustrine slopes may not have been utilized for extensive agricultural activities and that erosion was stimulated largely by construction. The time of largest occupation in the central Maya lowlands, the Late Classic, is associated with lower carbonate and silicate influx rates found there (chap. 7), suggesting that sedimentation in the lakes may have been related principally to forest clearance and construction, and that Late Classic occupants may have been regulating erosion in a better fashion than the former occupants.

Another possibility for the explanation of influx rates into the central Petén lakes is the use of wetland fields and canals along their low-lying shores, particularly to the south. Intensive cultivation on such fields and their ultimate abandonment might explain much of the erosion and captured nutrients in the lakes, particularly if the fields were fertilized with nightsoils or other phosphorus-rich materials.

In summary, the Petén work provides evidence of environmental degradation open to various interpretations, and the cautious approach used by the project is most welcomed. Perhaps comparative data on the agricultural or occupational effects of influx characteristics at other tropical lakes will provide insight into the degree of "degradation" implied by the Maya data. Similar sedimentation and nutrient se-

questering may have occurred over extended periods at any heavily occupied or cultivated lakeshore without significant effect on the local production systems.

Wiseman (chap. 5) raised another argument for agricultural degradation in the central Petén lake zone. His statistical work demonstrates the existence of a maize "pulse" in the fossil pollen for Lake Petenxil, as does Tsukada's profile (1966). Wiseman interprets this pulse as a sudden and short-term increase in maize production around the lake during the latter stages of the Late Classic or Terminal Classic. If the evidence is valid and the chronology is accepted, then what could account for the pulse? The local populace may have been producing more maize for some reason. Speculation abounds as to why. It seems inconsistent to pin the cause on environmental problems or inadequate cultivation procedures elsewhere in the lowlands. Rather, it may reflect an adjustment in local agriculture to exogenous influences, such as the cutoff of the lake region from trade foods, refusal of outlying zones to provide produce, loss of land by local chiefdoms or city-states, to name a few. The pulse thesis fits well with recent work suggesting a cultural collapse from the peripheries of the central Maya Lowlands inward (Hamblin and Pitcher 1980), such that an interior zone that was relying on "outside" produce, once cut off, had to produce more themselves for a period of time before they too succumbed to the same forces as did those in the periphery.

Environmental and Agricultural Relationships

Interdisciplinary research demonstrates that environmental influences on human activity, such as subsistence or other production, are rarely simplistic or deterministic. Livelihoods are not determined by physical conditions alone, but are a product of interaction between socioeconomic and environmental factors. In farming, for example, the level of output desired by the farming unit is, beyond biological needs, largely determined by socioeconomic factors. The economic feasibility of obtaining that level of output and the manner in which it is achieved are influenced by environmental circumstances. Farmers (or some other cultural component) decide whether the inputs required to increase outputs merit the effort. Environmental conditions usually act as a constraint, not a limit, on farmers' decisions. When a farmer tells us that he cannot cultivate a particular soil or increase output in a particular field, he usually means that he is unwilling to accept the economic consequences of manipulating that habitat. But as economic conditions change, so may the acceptability of the consequences. Traditional farmers have been known to go to great lengths to manipulate the most marginal environment for cultivation, such as carrying soil to a barren coral reef to create garden beds (Brookfield 1972).

The lesson here is that physical conditions determined Maya activity only within the socioeconomic context of the people. Initially, dryland farming was dominant in the central lowlands not because the Maya were incapable of cultivating wetlands but because dryland agriculture offered the most acceptable levels of efficiency, given output demands. Numerous Maya farmers ultimately adopted or developed a variety of technologies and procedures to manipulate their wetlands.

The preceding argument has been labeled ecologically naive in that it assumes that prehistoric farmers could handle virtually any environmental circumstance. Short of "big bang" disasters, such as crop infections and severe and prolonged droughts, traditional (and Neolithic) farmers have demonstrated an ability to manipulate landscapes in the manner described. I doubt that the Maya were exceptions. The impact of sea level changes in Preclassic times, such as that discussed for Albion Island (Bloom et al. 1983), may be viewed as a "big bang" environmental change, and yet it is not associated with the collapse of the Maya in that area or the lowlands in general. The view taken here does not imply that environmental degradation did not take place in lowland cultivation or that some Maya schemes were not ecological or economic failures. It does suggest, however, that in most instances Maya farmers recognized the environmental effects of their methods, if only in decreased crop production, as subtle environmental changes took place. Their decision to counter or not to counter the degradation and declining yields was primarily a socioeconomic one. It has not been demonstrated that any indigenous or contemporary "Neolithic" farming unit has been limited by purely environmental circumstances from using the landscapes available to them or that their activities alone have led to ecological disaster. Indeed, agricultural or ecological disruptions are invariably associated with major sociopolitical disruptions of the farming units, be it in the Sahel (Franke and Chasin 1980) or in the prehistoric Maya zone.

References

Adams, R. E. W., W. E. Brown, Jr., and
T. P. Culbert
   1981   "Radar Mapping, Archaeology and Ancient Maya Land Use," *Science* 213:1457–63.

Antoine, P. P., R. L. Skarie, and P. R. Bloom
   1982   "The Origin of Raised Fields Near San Antonio, Belize: An Alternative Hypothesis." In *Maya Subsistence: Studies in Memory of Dennis E. Puleston,* edited by K. Flannery. Academic Press, New York.

Ashmore, Wendy, editor
   1981   *Lowland Maya Settlement Patterns.* University of New Mexico Press, Albuquerque.

Banerjee, U. C., and E. S. Barghorn
   1972   "Fine Structure of Pollen Grain Extexine of Maize, Teosinte and Tripsacum," *30th Annual Proceedings: Electron Microscopy Society of America*, pp. 226–227.

Bloom, Paul R., Mary Pohl, Cynthia Buttleman, Frederick Wiseman, Alan Covich, Charles Miksicek, Joseph Ball, and Julie Stein
   1983   "Prehistoric Maya Wetland Agriculture and the Alluvial Soils Near San Antonio Río Hondo, Belize," *Nature* 301:417–419.

Boserup, Ester
   1965   *The Conditions of Agricultural Growth.* Aldine, Chicago.

Brookfield, Harold C.
   1972   "Intensification and Disintensification in Pacific Agriculture: A Theoretical Approach," *Pacific Viewpoint* 13:30–48.

Bullard, William R., Jr.
   1960   "Maya Settlement Pattern in Northeastern Peten, Guatemala," *American Antiquity* 25:355–72.

Chayanov, A. V.
   1966   "Peasant Farm Organization." In *A. V. Chayanov in the Theory of Peasant Economy*, edited by D. Thorner, B. Kerblay, and R. E. F. Smith. R. D. Irwin, Homewood, Ill.

Cooke, C. W.
   1931   "Why the Mayan Cities in the Peten District Were Abandoned," *Journal of the Washington Academy of Science* 21:283–87.

Covich, Alan P.
   1983   "Mollusca: A Contrast in Species Diversity from Aquatic and Terrestrial Habitats." In *Pulltrouser Swamp: Ancient Maya Habitat, Agriculture, and Settlement in Northern Belize*, edited by B. L. Turner II and P. D. Harrison. University of Texas Press, Austin.

Dahlin, Bruce H.
1979   "Cropping Cash in the Protoclassic: A Cultural Impact Statement." In *Maya Archaeology and Ethnology*, edited by N. Hammond and G. R. Willey. University of Texas Press, Austin.

Darch, Janice P.
1983   "The Soils of Pulltrouser Swamp: Classification and Characteristics." In *Pulltrouser Swamp: Ancient Maya Habitat, Agriculture, and Settlement in Northern Belize*, edited by B. L. Turner II and P. D. Harrison. University of Texas Press, Austin.

Denevan, William M., and B. L. Turner II
1974   "Forms, Functions and Associations of Raised-Field Agriculture in the Old World Topics," *Journal of Tropical Geography* 39:24–33.

Franke, R., and B. Chasin
1980   *Seeds of Famine: Ecological Destruction and the Development Dilemma in the West African Sahel*. Osmun, Universe Books, New York.

Freidel, David A., and Vernon Scarborough
1982   "Subsistence, Trade and Development of the Coastal Maya." In *Maya Subsistence: Studies in Memory of Dennis E. Puleston*, edited by K. Flannery. Academic Press, New York.

Gliessman, S. R., B. L. Turner II, F. J. Rosado May, and M. F. Amador
1983   "Ancient Raised-Field Agriculture in the Maya Lowlands of Southeastern Mexico." In *Drained Field Agriculture in Central and South America*, edited by J. P. Darch. British Archaeological Reports International Series 189, Oxford.

Hamblin, Robert L., and Brian L. Pitcher
1980   "The Classic Maya Collapse: Testing Class Conflict Hypotheses," *American Antiquity* 46:93–112.

Hammond, Norman
1974   "Preclassic to Postclassic in Northern Belize," *Antiquity* 48:177–189.
1978   "The Myth of the Milpa: Agricultural Expansion in the Maya Lowlands." In *Pre-Hispanic Maya Agriculture*, edited by P. D. Harrison and B. L. Turner II. University of New Mexico Press, Albuquerque.
1981   "Classic Maya Canoes," *International Journal of Nautical Archaeology and Underwater Exploration* 10:173–185.

Hammond, Norman, and Charles H. Miksicek
1981   "Ecology and Economy of a Formative Maya Site at Cuello, Belize," *Journal of Field Archaeology* 8:259–269.

Harris, David R.
1978   "The Agricultural Foundations of Lowland Maya Civilization: A Critique." In *Pre-Hispanic Maya Agriculture*, edited by P. D. Harrison and B. L. Turner II. University of New Mexico Press, Albuquerque.

Harris, Marvin
1966   "The Cultural Ecology of India's Sacred Cattle," *Current Anthropology* 7:51–66.

Harrison, Peter D.
1977   "The Rise of the *Bajos* and the Fall of the Maya." In *Social Process in Maya Prehistory: Studies in Memory of Sir Eric Thompson*, edited by N. Hammond. Academic Press, London.

Haviland, William A.
1970   "Tikal, Guatemala, and Mesoamerican Urbanism," *World Archaeology* 2:186–197.

Healy, P. F., C. van Waarden, and T. J. Anderson
1980   "Nueva Evidencia de Antiguas Terrazas Mayas en Belice," *América Indígena* 40:773–796.

Hellmuth, Nicholas
1977   "Cholti-Lacandon (Chiapas) and Petén-Ytzá Agriculture, Settlement Pattern, and Population." In *Social Process in Maya Prehistory, Studies in Memory of Sir Eric Thompson*, edited by N. Hammond. Academic Press, New York.

High, L. R., Jr.
1975   "Geomorphology and Sedimentology of Holocene Coastal Deposits, Belize." In *Belize Shelf-Carbonate Sediments, Clastic Sediments, and Ecology*, edited by K. F. Wantland and W. T. Pusey, III. American Association of Petroleum Geologists, Studies in Ecology 2.

Kellman, Martin
1975   "Evidence for Late Glacial Age in a Tropical Montane Savanna," *Journal of Biogeography* 2:57–63.

Kirke, C. M. St. G.
1980   "Prehistoric Agriculture in the Belize River Valley," *World Archaeology* 2:281–287.

Kurjack, Edward B.
1974   *Prehistoric Lowland Maya Community and Social Organization*. Tulane University, Middle American Research Institute 31.

Lambert, John D. H., and Thor Arnason
1978   "Distribution of Vegetation on Maya Ruins and Its Relationship to Ancient Land-Use at Lamanai, Belize," *Turrialba* 28:33–41.

1982   "*Ramón* and Maya Ruins: An Ecological, Not an Economic, Relation," *Science* 216:298-299.

Lundell, Cyrus L.
1933   "The Agriculture of the Maya," *Southwest Review* 19:65-77.
1937   *The Vegetation of Peten.* Carnegie Institution of Washington 418.

Miksicek, Charles H.
1983   "Macrofloral Remains of the Pulltrouser Swamp Area; Settlements and Fields." In *Pulltrouser Swamp: Ancient Maya Habitat, Agriculture, and Settlement in Northern Belize,* edited by B. L. Turner II and P. D. Harrison. University of Texas Press, Austin.

Miksicek, Charles H., K. J. Gliesser, I. A. Wuebber, K. O. Bruhns, and N. Hammond
1981a   "Rethinking Ramón: A Comment on Reina and Hill's Lowland Maya Subsistence," *American Antiquity* 46:916-919.

Miksicek, Charles H., R. Mck. Bird, B. Pickersgill, S. Donaghey, J. Cartwright, and N. Hammond
1981b   "Preclassic Lowland Maize from Cuello, Belize," *Nature* 289:56-59.

Miranda, F.
1959   "Estudios Acerca de la Vegetación." In *Los Recursos Naturales del Sureste y su Aprovechamiento.* Vol. I, edited by E. Beltran. Instituto Mexicano Recursos Naturales Renobles, Mexico, D.F.

Olson, Gerald W.
1977   "Significance of Physical and Chemical Characteristics of Soils at the San Antonio Archaeological Site on the Río Hondo in Northern Belize," *Journal of Belizean Affairs* 5:22-35.

Palerm, Angel
1973   *Obras Hidraúlicas Prehispánicas en el Sisterna Lacustre del Valle de México.* Instituto Nacional de Antropología e Historia, México, D.F.

Palerm, Angel, and Eric R. Wolf
1957   *Ecological Potential and Cultural Development in Mesoamerica.* Pan American Union, Social Science Monograph, Epoca 2, vol. I. Panamerican Union, Washington, D.C.

Pennington, T. D., and Jose Sarukhan
1968   *Manual para la Identificación de Campo de los Principales Arbolas Tropicales de México.* Instituto Nacional de Investigaciones Forestales, Secretaría de Agricultura y Granadería, México, D.F.

Puleston, Dennis E.
1971   "An Experimental Approach to the Function of Maya Chultuns," *American Antiquity* 36:322-335.
1977   "The Art and Archaeology of Hydraulic Agriculture in the Maya Lowlands." In *Social Process in Maya Prehistory: Studies in Memory of Sir Eric Thompson,* edited by N. Hammond. Academic Press, London.
1978   "Terracing, Raised Fields, and Tree Cropping in the Maya Lowlands: A New Perspective in the Geography of Power." In *Pre-Hispanic Maya Agriculture,* edited by P. D. Harrison and B. L. Turner II. University of New Mexico Press, Albuquerque.

Puleston, Dennis E., and Olga S. Puleston
1971   "An Ecological Approach to the Origins of Maya Civilization," *Archaeology* 24:330-337.

Reina, Rubin E., and Robert M. Hill II
1980   "Lowland Maya Subsistence: Notes from Ethnohistory and Ethnography," *American Antiquity* 45:74-79.
1983   "Response to Miksicek, Elsesser, Wuebber, Bruhns, and Hammond," *American Antiquity* 48:128-131.

Rice, Don S.
1978   "Population Growth and Subsistence Alternatives in a Tropical Lacustrine Environment." In *Pre-Hispanic Maya Agriculture,* edited by P. D. Harrison and B. L. Turner II. University of New Mexico Press, Albuquerque.

Sanders, William T.
1956   "The Central Mexican Symbiotic Region." In *Prehistoric Settlement Patterns in the New World,* edited by G. R. Willey. Viking Fund Publication in Anthropology, 23. Wenner-Green Foundation for Anthropological Research, New York.
1973   "The Cultural Ecology of the Lowland Maya: A Re-evaluation." In *The Classic Maya Collapse,* edited by T. P. Culbert. University of New Mexico Press, Albuquerque.
1977   "Environmental Heterogeneity and the Evolution of Lowland Maya Civilization." In *Origins of Maya Civilization,* edited by R. E. W. Adams. University of New Mexico Press, Albuquerque.
1979   "The Jolly Green Giant in Tenth Century Yucatan, or Fact and Fancy in Classic Maya Agriculture," *Reviews on Anthropology* 6:493-506.

1981   "Classic Maya Settlement Patterns and Ethnographic Analogy." In *Lowland Maya Settlement Patterns*, edited by W. Ashmore. University of New Mexico Press, Albuquerque.

Sanders, William T., J. R. Parsons, and R. S. Stanley
1979   *The Basin of Mexico: Ecological Processes in the Evolution of a Civilization*. Academic Press, New York.

Scarborough, Vernon C.
1980   "The Settlement System in a Late Preclassic Maya Community: Cerros, Northern Belize." Ph.D. dissertation, Southern Methodist University.

Shafer, Harry J.
1983   "The Lithic Artifacts of the Pulltrouser Area: Settlement and Fields." In *Pulltrouser Swamp: Ancient Maya Habitat, Agriculture and Settlement in Northern Belize*, edited by B. L. Turner II and P. D. Harrison. University of Texas Press, Austin.

Siemens, Alfred H.
1978   "Karst and the Pre-Hispanic Maya in the Southern Lowlands." In *Pre-Hispanic Maya Agriculture*, edited by P. D. Harrison and B. L. Turner II. University of New Mexico Press, Albuquerque.
1982   "Prehispanic Agricultural Use of the Wetlands of Northern Belize." In *Maya Subsistence*, edited by K. V. Flannery. Academic Press, New York, pp. 205–225.
1983   "Oriented Raised Fields in Central Vera Cruz," *American Antiquity* 48:85–102.

Siemens, Alfred H., editor
1977   *Journal of Belizean Affairs* no. 5. Special issue: *The Río Hondo Project. An Investigation of the Maya of Northern Belize*. St. John's College, Belize City, Belize.

Siemens, Alfred H., and Dennis E. Puleston
1972   "Ridged Fields and Associated Features in Southern Campeche: New Perspectives on the Lowland Maya," *American Antiquity* 37:228–239.

Simmons, C. S., J. M. Tarano, and J. H. Pinto
1958   *Clasificación de Reconocimiento de los Suelos de la Republica de Guatemala*. Editorial del Ministerio de Educación Publica, Guatemala.

Simoons, Frederick J.
1961   *Eat Not This Flesh: Food Avoidances in the Old World*. University of Wisconsin Press, Madison.

Standley, Paul C.
1950   *Flora of Yucatan*. Field Museum of Natural History, Publication 279. Botanical Series 3.3. Chicago.

Thompson, J. Eric S.
1974   "'Canals' of the Rio Candelaria Basin, Campeche, Mexico." In *Mesoamerican Archaeology: New Approaches*, edited by N. Hammond. Duckworth, London.

Tozzer, Alfred M., editor
1941   *Landa's Relación de las Cosas de Yucatán*. Peabody Museum Papers, vol. 18, Harvard University.

Tsukada, Matsuo
1966   "The Pollen Sequence." In *The History of Laguna de Petenxil* by U. M. Cowgill and G. E. Hutchinson. Memoirs of the Connecticut Academy of Arts and Sciences 17, pp. 63–66.

Tsukada, Matsuo, and Edward S. Deevey, Jr.
1967   "Pollen Analyses from Four Lakes in the Southern Maya Area of Guatemala and El Salvador." In *Quaternary Paleoecology*, edited by E. J. Cushing and H. E. Wright, Jr. Yale University Press, New Haven.

Turner, B. L., II
1974   "Prehistoric Intensive Agriculture in the Maya Lowlands," *Science* 185:118–124.
1978a   "Ancient Agricultural Land Use in the Central Maya Lowlands." In *Pre-Hispanic Maya Agriculture*, edited by P. D. Harrison and B. L. Turner II. University of New Mexico Press, Albuquerque.
1978b   "The Development and Demise of the Swidden Thesis of Maya Agriculture." In *Pre-Hispanic Maya Agriculture*, edited by P. D. Harrison and B. L. Turner II. University of New Mexico Press, Albuquerque.
1979   "Prehispanic Terracing in the Central Maya Lowlands: Problems of Agricultural Intensification." In *Maya Archaeology and Ethnohistory*, edited by N. Hammond and G. R. Willey. University of Texas Press, Austin.
1980   "Geography and Prehistory in Southern Mesoamerica," Historical Geography of Latin America. Papers in Honor of Robert L. West, edited by A. V. Davidson and J. J. Parsons. *Geoscience and Man* 21:9–15.
1983a   "Constructional Inputs for Major Agrosystems of the Ancient Maya." In *Drained Field Agriculture in Central and South America*, edited by J. P. Darch.

British Archaeological Reports International Series, Oxford.

1983b *Once Beneath the Forest: Prehistoric Terracing in the Rio Bec Region of the Maya Lowlands.* Dellplain Series in Geography. Westview Press, Boulder.

Turner, B. L., II, and William M. Denevan
In press "Prehistoric Manipulation of Wetlands in the Americas: A Raised-Field Perspective." In *Prehistoric Intensive Agriculture in the Tropics*, edited by I. Farrington. British Archaeological Reports International Series, Oxford.

Turner, B. L., II, and Peter D. Harrison
1978 "Implications from Agriculture for Maya Prehistory." In *Pre-Hispanic Maya Agriculture*, edited by P. D. Harrison and B. L. Turner II. University of New Mexico Press, Albuquerque.
1981 "Prehistoric Raised Field Agriculture in the Maya Lowlands," *Science* 213:399–405.

Turner, B. L., II, and Peter D. Harrison, editors
1983 *Pulltrouser Swamp: Ancient Maya Habitat, Agriculture, and Settlement in Northern Belize.* University of Texas Press, Austin.

Turner, B. L., II, W. C. Johnson, G. Mahood, F. M. Wiseman, B. L. Turner, and J. Poole
In press "Habitat y Agricultura en la Región de Copan," *Introducción a la Arqueología de Copan.* Vol. I, chap. 1. Edited by C. Baudez. Costa Rica.

Turner, B. L., II, and Charles H. Miksicek
1984 "Economic Species Associated with Prehistoric Agriculture in the Maya Lowlands," *Economic Botany* 38:179–193.

Willey, G. R., W. R. Bullard, Jr., J. B. Glass, and James C. Gifford
1965 *Prehistoric Maya Settlements in the Belize Valley.* Peabody Museum Papers, vol. 54, Harvard University.

Wiseman, Frederick M.
1978 "Agricultural and Historical Ecology of the Maya Lowlands." In *Pre-Hispanic Maya Agriculture*, edited by P. D. Harrison and B. L. Turner II. University of New Mexico Press, Albuquerque.
1983a "Subsistence and Complex Societies: The Case of the Maya," *Advances in Archaeological Method and Theory* 6:143–189.
1983b "Analysis of Pollen from the Fields at Pulltrouser Swamp." In *Pulltrouser Swamp: Ancient Maya Habitat, Agriculture, and Settlement in Northern Belize*, edited by B. L. Turner II and P. D. Harrison. University of Texas Press, Austin.

Wright, A. C. S., D. H. Romney, R. H. Arbuckle, and V. E. Vial
1959 *Land Use in British Honduras.* Her Majesty's Stationery Office, London.